D1478513

Boulevard Theater and Revolution in Eighteenth-Century Paris

Theater and Dramatic Studies, No. 22

Bernard Beckerman, Series Editor

Brander Matthews Professor of Dramatic Literature
Columbia University in the City of New York

Other Titles in This Series

No. 14	*Stanislavski's Encounter with Shakespeare: The Evolution of a Method*	Joyce Vining Morgan
No. 15	*The Art of the Actor-Manager: Wilson Barrett and the Victorian Theatre*	James Thomas
No. 16	*Male-Female Comedy Teams in American Vaudeville, 1865–1932*	Shirley Staples
No. 17	*Distance in the Theatre: The Aesthetics of Audience Response*	Daphna Ben Chaim
No. 18	*French Theatre Experiment Since 1968*	Lenora Champagne
No. 19	*Evreinov: The Theatre of Paradox and Transformation*	Spencer Golub
No. 20	*William Poel's Hamlets: The Director as Critic*	Rinda F. Lundstrom
No. 21	*Gertrude Stein's Theatre of the Absolute*	Betsy Alayne Ryan
No. 23	*A Critical Examination of Theatrical Designs of Charles Ricketts*	Eric Binnie
No. 24	*Theatre in Revolt: Revolutionary Aesthetics in the American Theatre*	Ira A. Levine

Boulevard Theater and Revolution in Eighteenth-Century Paris

by
Michèle Root-Bernstein

UMI RESEARCH PRESS
Ann Arbor, Michigan

Produced and distributed by
UMI Research Press
an imprint of
University Microfilms International
A Xerox Information Resources Company
Ann Arbor, Michigan 48106

Library of Congress Cataloging in Publication Data

Root-Bernstein, Michèle.
Boulevard theater and revolution in eighteenth-century Paris.

(Theater and dramatic studies ; no. 22)
Revision of thesis–Princeton University, 1981.
Bibliography: p.
Includes index.
1. Theater–France–Paris–History–18th century.
2. France–History–Revolution, 1789-1799–Literature and the revolution. 3. Theater and society–France–Paris.
4. Theater–Political aspects. 5. French drama–18th century–History and criticism. 6. Paris (France)–Popular culture. I. Title. II. Series.
PN2633.R6 1984 792'.0944'361 84-2545
ISBN 0-8357-1551-5

Plate 1. A *parade* or outdoor skit on the boulevard, 1760. Canvas by Gabriel-Jacques de Saint-Aubin. Reproduced by courtesy of the Trustees, the National Gallery, London.

Contents

List of Plates

List of Tables and Figures

Tables

Figures

Acknowledgments

Many persons and institutions have generously contributed to my research needs. I would like to acknowledge among them the librarians and archivists of the Bibliothèque nationale, the Bibliothèque de l'Arsenal, the Bibliothèque de la Comédie-Française, the Archives nationales, the Archives de la Seine, the Archives de la Préfecture de police, and the Archives de l'Assistance publique, all in Paris. In the U.S., I am particularly grateful to Princeton University Library and the Center for Research Libraries for purchasing microfilm copies of many of the plays used in my study of popular theater. The University of California, San Diego Library has graciously allowed me inter-library loan privileges as an independent scholar.

Professors at Princeton University, chief among them Robert Darnton and Natalie Davis, criticized my earliest ideas and drafts. Emmet Kennedy of George Washington University commented extensively and invaluably on the dissertation version of this book. To these colleagues I extend sincere appreciation. Above all, I wish to thank my husband and family for their encouragement, their support and their willingness to shoulder other of my responsibilities while I worked on the little theaters of the boulevard. Very special thanks to my second mother, Maurine Bernstein.

Introduction: Theater and Culture in Eighteenth Century France

Theater in the Old Regime World

In 1838 an obscure Parisian playwright and chronicler of the French stage declared that "the history of theaters is perhaps the most curious, the most amusing of all, because it embraces not only the history of literature, but, even more, that of politics and manners."[1] Considering the country of his birth, as well as his own times and the century and more that preceded them, Nicolas Brazier spoke truly. The profound political and cultural importance of theater in the France of yesteryear can hardly be exaggerated. Nor can it be compared to the limited role of the twentieth century stage. For throughout the seventeenth and eighteenth centuries the very best of intellectual and practical minds that the French could muster turned towards the organization and evaluation of dramatic art.

In the political realm, prime ministers and even kings concerned themselves personally with theatrical affairs. By law in 1641 Cardinal Richelieu, minister to Louis XIII, sought to regulate the behavior of actors and troupes. Louis XIV, with the help of Colbert, organized French players into three great companies or monopolies of dramatic art. The Sun King's successors periodically interfered in the internal affairs of the Opéra, the Comédie-Française, and the Comédie-Italienne by means of royal decree, while day to day government of these great theaters fell to the Gentlemen of the Bedchamber and other ministers of the King's Household. Even minor dramatic spectacles ostracized to the fairgrounds of Paris, and after 1750 permitted on the boulevard du Temple, fell under the jurisdiction of prominent officials such as the minister of Paris and the lieutenant-general of police.

Men of the cloth and men of letters, for their part, quarreled almost continuously for two centuries over the artistic and moral worth of the stage. The Gallican Church stubbornly maintained the immorality and license of public theater and condemned the professional actor and actress to excommunication. Critics tried to counter religious arguments with long disquisitions upon the social benefits and aesthetic influences of the stage. By mid-eighteenth century the greatest of the salon intellectuals and *philosophes* had joined the controversy. Voltaire, considered one of the masters of tragedy by his contemporaries, fulminated against religious prejudice for actor and play. Diderot involved himself in the aesthetic development of a moral and moralizing dramatic genre. D'Alembert suggested liberal attitudes towards the cause and cure of moral irregularities on and back stage.

Enlightened, secular opinion gained ground, despite Rousseau's famous attack upon the psychological and moral deception of the actor and theater. Indeed, in the years following his *Letter to M. d'Alembert on Theaters* of 1757, Rousseau drew no serious direct or indirect response—perhaps because his contemporaries believed him, as author of several operas and comedies, to be indulging perversely in intentional paradox. By the middle decade of the century the controversy seemed to have reached a stalemate of sorts. Dramatic art had become acceptably orthodox, at least where the three great theaters of Paris were concerned. The king's actors and actresses had breached the doors to salon society; titles of incorporation for all three companies had been fully recognized by law; the Church in practice had grown quiescent in its antagonism. Yet in the coming decades the slow, steady growth of minor spectacles and theaters in the fairgrounds of Paris and along the boulevard du Temple rekindled the quarrel in new and different guise. Theater per se was not at issue in this subsequent debate; theater for the people, for the middle and lower classes of the Third Estate was.

Brazier, author of the first history of the little theaters of Paris, would without doubt have argued that the history of the popular, boulevard stage—and not that of the three great companies of Paris—proved to be the "most curious" and "most amusing." Certainly the growth and development of the boulevard's dramatic industry revealed an important focus of cultural stress during the declining years of the old regime. The boulevard posed for the eighteenth century questions of literary, economic, social and cultural politics. The king's ministers grappled with the problems of licensing an entire industry in violation of the acknowledged principles of privilege and monopoly. The police of Paris authorized the presentation of plays that purposefully eschewed dramatic orthodoxy and competed with classical genres and repertory for public interest. Government officials, critics and pamphleteers worried about the broad appeal of boulevard theater and the dissolution of class distinction in audiences mixed in rank and occupation. In their concern for popular manners, contemporaries debated the effect of low comedy upon the popular mind and discoursed upon the cultural distances that were meant to obtain between the great and the popular stage.

Given the stress the boulevard placed upon the politics and manners of the age, it cannot be surprising that more conservative contemporaries should have descried "revolution" on the boulevard long before 1789. The royal actors of the Comédie-Française used that very word to describe what they saw as a subversion in the theatrical order dating from the early 1760s. In those years popular fair theaters first gained protection and place on the boulevard. Revolution or change in the Parisian hierarchy of theaters comprised not only the economic infringement of privileged monopolies, but that of cultural hegemonies as well. By the mid-1780s most of the boulevard "spectacles" were calling themselves "theaters"—a semantic distinction the three great companies of Paris found presumptuous and abusive. On the boulevard the nature of classicism and economic privilege, and the aristocratic culture to which they were tied, were thrown into relief all the more clearly for their juxtaposition to a literature, an economy and a marginal culture non-aristocratic and non-classical in inspiration and intent. When the Revolution as we understand it today rocked the whole of French society, the boulevard stage was picked out again as the source of revolutionary perversion:

> ... our manner of thinking has undergone a revolution like our manner of speaking.... One of the principal sources of these new opinions is the fairgrounds, the boulevards and other similar places; it is there that lessons have been drawn for the past twenty years, there that has been schooled a generation that will dominate in its turn ...[2]

The study that follows is an attempt to seek out these revolutions on the boulevard and to understand their shape and influence. The actors, playwrights, entrepreneurs, even the plays of the eighteenth century boulevard have disappeared from the conscious repertory of remembered theater, yet they hardly need justification to draw our attention today. The bustling world of popular theater serves as a microcosm, not just of the stage, but of the political and cultural forces that gave direction to experimentation, reform, and eventually revolution in the last decades of the eighteenth century.

The Historiographical Debate

Eighteenth century perceptions of boulevard "revolutions" have made it imperative to consider and address two modern interpretations of cultural structure and cultural change in old regime France. The first, introduced more than a decade ago by the French historian Robert Mandrou in *On Popular Culture of the 17th and 18th Centuries, The Bibliothèque bleue of Troyes* (Paris, 1964), argues that the cultural body of old regime France was split in two. "Elite" and "popular" arts and mentalities, distinguishable one from the other, were in fact discrete traditions separated by a yawning cultural gap. The second interpretation, advanced in 1971 by Robert Darnton in "The High Enlightenment and the Low-Life of Literature in Pre-revolutionary France" (*Past and Present,* 1971), suggests that social barriers between high and low arts in the republic of letters may have had a direct effect on the radical upheaval of cultural institutions and traditions in the years 1789-1794.

For Mandrou it is a commonplace that intellectual and artistic traditions fragmented along the socio-economic barriers of society: "... cultural levels ... coincide with social stratifications ... ideological structures and social cadres are inseparable ... "[3] In his pioneering study of the Bibliothèque bleue, unbound chapbooks hawked throughout the French countryside in the seventeenth and eighteenth centuries, Mandrou explicitly embraces what he has more recently called an ethnological definition of socio-cultural structures. This ethnology grants any socially homogeneous group within society a cultural unity; by implication, any cultural unity belongs to a socially homogeneous group. Yet Mandrou has at the same time insisted that contact and exchange between "popular" and "elite" cultures be studied.[4] In his own work this is incompletely achieved, the result of an uneasy balance between the ethnological or structural approach to cultural artifacts and a sociological or literary approach that seeks to locate those same artifacts in a network of inter-social relationships.[5] In *The Bibliothèque bleue of Troyes* Mandrou explores the intellectual flow between "elite" and "popular" literatures, but he is unwilling to track the *social* interaction between the two because he believes, ethnologically, that cultural participation is socially determined.[6]

Like all historians drawn to the problems of cultural history, I owe an intellectual debt to the questions raised by Mandrou's original efforts in this field. But there are objections to the methodological resolution of his work. If cultural traditions are, fundamentally, socially discrete, then how does one explain intellectual and artistic exchange? Further, how does one study the historical process of contacts[7] between cultural traditions, which Mandrou himself has urged is necessary, without exploring their social interaction? The historian Peter Burke has already argued for replacing the notion of an elite-popular gap in eighteenth century culture with a model of socially asymmetrical traditions.[8] What he calls the "great" or learned tradition was accessible only to that minority who gained entry to institutions of formal schooling; the "little" or residual tradition was transmitted informally in church, tavern or marketplace, and excluded none. Burke, too, describes a cultural gap along social boundaries, but importantly, access is blocked in only one direction.

The appeal of Burke's model lies primarily in its terminology. It allows us to discard the value-laden meanings of "elite" and "popular," both tied to notions of exclusive social consumption. In their place it offers "great" and "little," both of which suggest that the cultural shape or status of an artistic tradition may be determined independently of its social purview. In his own work Burke essentially redefines the word "popular" as synonymous with "little," so that popular culture, culture of the widest common denominator, can be understood and appreciated by members of many ranks and occupations. "Great," "little" and "popular," moreover, were terms that eighteenth century contemporaries used and understood in reference to theaters and dramatic art. For this reason, distinctions will be made in the following study between "great" and "little" or "popular" culture. The practice is meant to imply not only contemporary perception, but a sociological approach to the interaction of men, institutions, genres and ideas belonging to apparently discrete cultural traditions. The social and institutional matrix for popular dramatic culture can largely be recovered and, once reconstructed, can offer us answers to questions of inter-cultural relationship and exchange. Were cultural traditions of the old regime socially exclusive or in fact socially porous? What were the extent of social relations, whether the formal interactions of institutions or the informal contacts of individual men, between "great" and "little" traditions? And in what manner did such social interaction inform the quality and quantity of conceptual and artistic exchange?

Contemporary perceptions of the boulevard's role in the Revolution of 1789-1794 also urge comparisons of the world of little theater with Darnton's depiction of the literary low-life. Darnton finds in general that the Parisian world of letters in the last twenty-five years of the old regime was split by an "unusual gulf."[9] He speaks of a gap that was cultural in kind; the "domesticated" Enlightenment of an elite stood at an "ideological distance" from a more radical Rousseauistic Enlightenment of the common people. It is Darnton's major contribution to address this gap during a period of stress and rapid change as a phenomenon of social organization and mobility. Juxtaposed to the corporate structures and social circles of established literary culture, but cut off from that world, Darnton poses an informally organized "Grub Street," or intellectual underworld; in opposition to successful and accomplished *philosophes* he places a literary proletariat, bitter and frustrated in its intellectual and social ambitions by a bottleneck between the street and the salon.

Darnton further suggests that these social and institutional barriers which cut across the Parisian world of letters effected in large measure the radical upheaval of cultural institutions and intellectual traditions in the years 1789-1794. The exclusive circles of the literary elite had long since forced the revolutionary spirit of the Enlightenment underground; bitter "Grub Street" hacks, he argues, turned their pens against the established world and radicalized the literary culture of the "little people" well before the outbreak of revolution. "Once the Revolution came, the opposition between the high and low life of literature had to be resolved. Grub Street rose, overthrew *le monde* and requisitioned the positions of power and prestige. It was a cultural revolution," Darnton writes, "... the Revolution turned the cultural world upside down.... Perhaps the genres of Grub Street... gained ground as the Parisian populace gained power."[10]

Darnton's thesis of radicalized "popular" genres and cultural overthrow after 1789 strongly depends on his assumption of a large cultural gap on the eve of the Revolution. If one questions and explores the nature of this gap, therefore, one must question and explore the nature and extent of cultural upheaval as well. Did the boulevard experience similar strains between exclusive circles of great theater and frustrated hacks of the popular stage? Did the boulevard rise en masse in the revolutionary years? And did popular theater oust fine drama from its position of cultural dominance? Not only the nature of the cultural gap between learned and common traditions under the old regime will be studied in these pages, but so too, the nature of its resolution in the years 1789-1794.

Theater Histories

By and large the questions raised above have so far gone unanswered in the field of theater history. To a great extent this reflects the paucity of recent interest in the fair and boulevard theaters of eighteenth century Paris or in their relationship with the great companies of the king. The basic histories of the minor Parisian theaters were all written in the late 1800s or first decade of the twentieth century. E.D. de Manne in collaboration with C. Ménétrier, Jules Bonnassiès, and Emile Campardon, the first pioneers in the study of the popular stage, all wrote within the eleven-year period 1869-1877. In *Historical Gallery of Nicolet's Troupe of Actors* (1869) de Manne and Ménétrier compiled brief biographies of entrepreneurs and actors on the boulevard that remain standard references even today for these obscure men and women. Jules Bonnassiès recovered information on the minor theaters and their competitive relationship with the privileged dramatic companies of Paris as he worked on the archives of the Comédie-Française. With these records he sketched the first scholarly history of the boulevard theaters in *The Fair Theaters and the Comédie-Française* (1875). Two years later Emile Campardon presented a two-volume compilation of original documents that he had assiduously discovered in the French National Archives and other primary sources. For any student of popular theater, especially those unable to travel to France, *Spectacles of the Fair* (two volumes, 1877) endures as a fantastic source of archival material on the artists, entrepreneurs and theaters of the eighteenth-century fairs and boulevard. After a hiatus of twenty-five years or so another cluster of books on the minor theaters of the boulevard made their appearance—most of them derivative of earlier scholarship. One must include in this category Georges Cain's *Old Theaters of Paris, The Boulevard Theaters* (1906) and M. Beaulieu's *The Theaters of the Boulevard of Crime* (1905). Maurice Albert stood head and shoulders above the rest with his two companion texts, *The Theaters of the Fair (1660-1789)* (1900), and *The Theaters of the Boulevards (1789-1848)* (1902). Although he also depended heavily on Bonnassiès in particular, Albert fleshed out with much independent research the most comprehensive history of the minor theaters known at the time.

As a group, these dated studies of boulevard theater in the late-eighteenth century present the modern student of the subject with significant problems. De Manne, Bonnassiès and Albert disagree over the facts. Scholarly standards different from our own mean a lack of documentation in their work. Mistakes that run throughout the texts weaken credibility in their interpretation of short- and long-term events. Nor can we rely on these studies to approach the boulevard stage with our own historical sympathies and concerns. There is little room in these institutional histories for literary or cultural analysis of the popular dramatic idiom, for economic analysis of entrepreneurial endeavor, for social analysis of the minor acting profession. De Manne found no use for the expense accounts of an important boulevard theater; Bonnassiès did not conceal his hostility for the popular stage. A quarter of a century later, Albert had shed the prejudices of Bonnassiès but had not yet acquired the more modern interests in the economic and socio-cultural life of the boulevard, or in the relationship of a popular tradition to the theatrical forums of great theater and great culture.

This relationship between great and little dramatic art does form the focus of very recent literature concerning the fair and boulevard theaters. In *Theater and Revolution, the Culture of the French Stage* (1980), Frederick Brown devotes an early chapter to the ideological divide drawn by classical taste between the language and practice of official theater and the vulgar idiom of popular, fairground entertainment. Sapped of nearly all energy by overrefinement, great theater of the eighteenth century, he argues, stood in sorry contrast to the vitality and innovation of the ostracized fair theater, a point made somewhat differently by Oscar G. Brockett in 1965.[11] Brown does draw us one step nearer historical contacts between dramatic traditions by noting at some length aristocratic society's tremendous fascination with attending fairground entertainments and boulevard theater. Brown's own interests clearly lie, however, with the influence of popular dramatic idioms and forms upon great theater, from the years of the Revolution through the twentieth century. As it concerns the boulevard theaters of the late 1700s, Brown's essay is impressionistic and, at times, marred by the errors of the earlier, secondary literature upon which he depends.[12]

The overriding need to return to the primary sources ploughed so long ago by de Manne and Ménétrier, Bonnassiès, Campardon, and Albert has met with initial redress in the work of historian Robert Isherwood. In "Entertainment in the Parisian Fairs of the Eighteenth Century," the first fruit of his labors on the original materials concerning the fairs of the late 1600s and 1700s, Isherwood has recreated with veracity and attention to detail a whole world of popular entertainment—acrobatics, fireworks, marionettes, animal shows, magic lanterns, automatons—which he, like Brown, sees in subversive relation to official, or great, culture. Moreover, Isherwood explicitly posits the question, what might be the relation between this popular culture and the Revolution of

1789? Leaning heavily on Bakhtin for his interpretation of the seventeenth and early eighteenth century fair theater, Isherwood assumes that an earthy celebration of bodily function and its implicit critique of great culture characterized the fair and boulevard stage on the eve of Revolution and may have "rattled the foundations of a society vulnerable to criticism and upheaval."[13] Isherwood's tentative answers, however, are flawed by inadequate knowledge of the profound transformation in popular theater from the first to the second half of the eighteenth century. What contemporaries called the obscenities of the fairground farce had been largely shed from boulevard theater by the 1770s and '80s in favor of love intrigues and sentimental dramas imitative of great theater and supportive of dominant cultural values. Isherwood indeed seems to realize, rhetorically at least, that the expansion of popular theater and its protection by the police in fact pointed to a different relationship between the boulevard stage and society of the old regime. But the evidence for this will be found in my own study.

A necessary supplement to studies of the popular theaters under the old regime are the more general histories of revolutionary theater. In large part, the historiography of revolutionary theater has advanced very little from studies written in the later nineteenth and early twentieth centuries. The earliest efforts are those of Victor Hallays-Dabot, *History of Theatrical Censorship in France* (1862); E. Jauffret, *The Revolutionary Theater* (1869); and Henri Welschinger, *The Theater of the Revolution 1789-1799* (1880). Scholarship remains indebted to Hallays-Dabot in particular for his numerous transcriptions of documents subsequently destroyed by the Parisian fires of 1870. Since Welschinger followed Hallays-Dabot without question, the analyses by both men of censorship, of governmental programs and governmental control—all of tremendous importance to the minor theaters of the boulevard as well as the more prestigious stages—are riddled with Hallays-Dabot's original errors in dating and interpretation. These flaws were largely discovered and corrected by M.J. Guillaume in his *Minutes of the Committee of Public Instruction* (seven volumes, 1891-1957), but they have been insufficiently rectified in subsequent histories of revolutionary theater.

A second group of revolutionary theater studies appeared between 1909 and 1922, including Ernest Lunel's *The Theater and the Revolution* (1909), Paul d'Estrée's *The Theater under the Terror (1793-1794)* (1913), and Jacques Hérissay's *The World of Theaters during the Revolution* (1922). Except for d'Estrée these histories were biased towards the trials and tribulations of the most prestigious theaters of revolutionary Paris. Very little original research was expended on the boulevard theaters, whose incomplete histories were often appropriated from earlier secondary sources. D'Estrée distinguished himself by innovative attention to the biographies of scores of actors, actor-authors and playwrights, big and small, who participated in revolutionary theater. It was not his purpose, however, to study the sociological or cultural fortunes of boulevard artists or the boulevard idiom. The best efforts of all these French historians inform the most recent of revolutionary theater histories, that of Marvin Carlson. In the *Theatre of the French Revolution* (1966) Carlson consciously attempts to focus attention not only on the Comédie-Française, but on the " 'thousand and one' theaters that sprang up . . . to challenge the old monopoly . . . "[14] But with virtually no archival work of his own into the affairs of these minor theaters, Carlson depended for his information on previous studies of the boulevard and its revolutionary experience. Carlson's history, with respect at least to the popular theaters of revolutionary Paris, is sadly derivative and thus faulty.

Given the uneven quality of previous scholarship on the boulevard, I have relied largely on archival evidence and contemporary observation for my study of the minor theaters before and during the Revolution. Although the institutional histories of these little theaters will never be as complete as those of the great stages, new approaches to the boulevard in manuscript and printed records of the past have been fruitful. I have consequently tried to broaden our knowledge of Parisian popular theater in three new ways. First, a sampling of theater advertisements in the *Annonces, affiches et avis divers,* popularly called the *Petites Affiches,* for the years 1785-1794 allowed me to determine with a great deal of precision the enduring repertory of the little theaters before and during the Revolution and the nature of cultural upheaval in dramatic traditions after 1789. By supplementing the sampling of titles with an extensive reading of plays, I have hoped to reconstruct something of the intellectual and artistic vision of the boulevard stage and its revolutionary change. Secondly, records of the police, of the revolutionary justice of the peace, and of revolutionary government have permitted me to study in detail unknown facets of the social and economic life of actors, authors and entrepreneurs on the boulevard. Thirdly, I have sought to understand what role the boulevard milieu and its theater may have had in the breakdown of the old regime and in the turmoil of the Revolution. Truly, we are more fortunate than Brazier imagined, for the history of boulevard theater may instruct as well as amuse and delight us.

Part I

Formality and Practice in the Parisian Hierarchy of Theater

Prelude: Theater Placards and Protocol

> "An understanding of the dramatic hierarchy truly used to be a science difficult to acquire..."
>
> —Millin de Grandmaison
> *On the Liberty of Theater,* 1790

In 1769 a minor fair spectacle located on the boulevard du Temple posted its announcement of recess in the manner of a royal theater. This breach of protocol did not pass unnoticed by the fashionable and official world disclosed in the *Secret Memoirs* of Louis Petit de Bachaumont:

> The theaters closed for recess today, *in accordance with the king's orders.* That is the customary formula; but it was taken badly that Mr. Nicolet, master of marionettes, who ought to put in accordance with the orders of the Lieutenant general of police, ranked himself with the great theaters, with the theaters pensioned by His Majesty. The case is all the more grave as that Mountebank has already been reprimanded for similar audacity. Without doubt the comic powers that be will demand this time that he be sent to Bicêtre for the repetition of his insolence...[1]

Whether or not the said Nicolet spent a night in jail for a mouthful of words is unknown. What is known is that the three great companies of Paris, the Opéra, the Comédie-Française and the Comédie-Italienne, claimed a rank and distinction superior to those of upstart theaters on the boulevard and in the fairs. Even more, royal actors, government officials and social chroniclers proved sensitive to the expression of that precedence. Their concerns were met in the exacting supervision of bill-posters charged with the distribution of theater bills.

In eighteenth century Paris the daily posting of theater announcements claimed the attentions of three out of the forty bill-posters in the city. These three men were commonly provided with exhaustive lists of each wall and door to receive a theater bill.[2] Placards for the great theaters were not to be confused in display with those of minor theaters performing at the fairs or along the boulevard. The lieutenant general of police prohibited the posting on certain street corners of any bills but those of the Opéra, the Comédie-Française and the Comédie-Italienne. Where fair and boulevard theater placards did appear with those of the royal companies, the bill-posters arranged them with a care sanctioned by decades of accepted custom. Louis-Sebastien Mercier, the astute observer of Parisian life and mores, claimed as much in the 1780s:

> The theater bills are applied to the walls without fail first thing in the morning; they observe among themselves a certain rank: that of the Opéra dominates the others; the fair spectacles are placed to the side out of respect for the great theaters. The arrangement of the mounting is as well observed as in a circle of fashionable society. The bill-poster is a master of ceremonies . . . [3]

The ceremonial distinctions drawn by the bill-poster through the 1760s and 1770s were duplicated thereafter in the pages of the *Journal de Paris* and the *Petites Affiches.* Beginning in the late 1770s both of these competitive Parisian newspapers announced theatrical performances daily. For the first five years or so, the journals carried only the bills of the three great theaters. Not until the early 1780s did they announce performances at minor theaters as well. Like the placards on the wall, the announcements spaced on the journal page gave precedence to the Opéra, the Comédie-Française and the Comédie-Italienne, each separated from the other by a fine line or space. A longer, heavier bar in the *Petites Affiches* or a bold-faced heading such as "Saint Germain Fair" or "Boulevards" in the *Journal de Paris* divided the great theaters from the three most prominent spectacles of the boulevard: the Grands-Danseurs du Roi, the Ambigu-Comique and the Variétés-Amusantes. (See Figure 1.)

For Mercier, postered wall and printed page represented a visual abstraction of the chasm that divided the theatrical world into great and small, distinguished and disdained. It was highly significant, then, when the traditional form of display abruptly changed in the mid-1780s. On the 20th of April, 1785, the layout of theatrical announcements in the *Petites Affiches* altered significantly and permanently. One of the boulevard theaters, the Variétés-Amusantes, was removed from the rank of the subordinate spectacles and placed directly below the great theaters. At the end of June the pages of the *Journal de Paris* followed suit. Instead of a bipartite division of theater bills on the page, there were now three tiers of theater bills, each separated from the other by lines.

In the following years the French actors of the Comédie-Française supposedly claimed that the alteration on the pages of the *Petites Affiches* had been the result of venal instincts on the part of that journal's editor, the abbé Aubert:

> [Dorfeuille, director of the Variétés-Amusantes] gave the abbé Aubert four free tickets, for placing a black line between the [Variétés] and [the spectacles] of the Boulevard.[4]

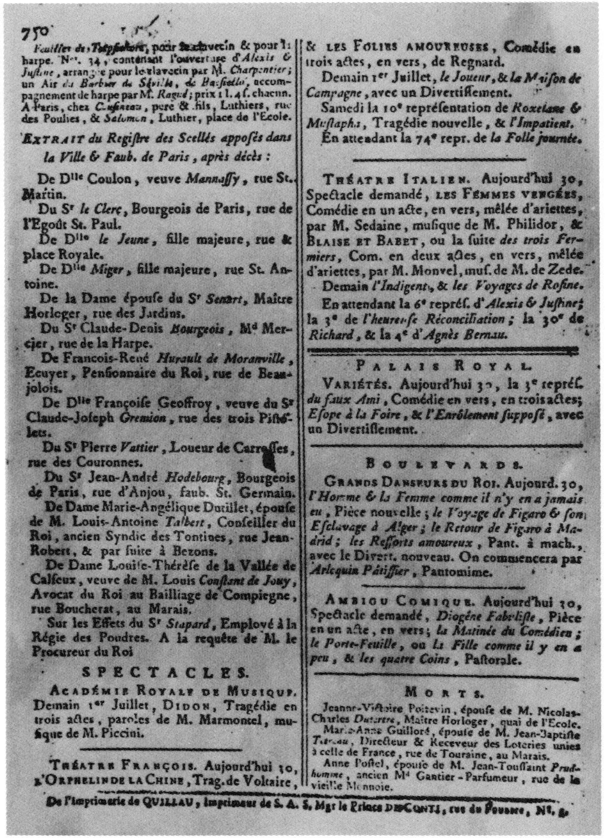

750

Feuilles de Terpsichore, pour le clavecin & pour la harpe. No. 34, contenant l'ouverture d'*Alexis & Justine*, arrangée pour le clavecin par M. *Charpentier*; un Air du *Barbier de Séville*, de *Basfiello*, accompagnement de harpe par M. *Ragué*; prix 1 l. 4 s. chacun. A Paris, chez *Cousineau*, pere & fils, Luthiers, rue des Poulies, & *Salomon*, Luthier, place de l'École.

EXTRAIT du Registre des Scellés apposés dans la Ville & Faub. de Paris, après décès :

De Dlle Coulon, veuve *Mannassy*, rue St. Martin.

Du Sr *le Clerc*, Bourgeois de Paris, rue de l'Egoût St. Paul.

De Dlle *le Jeune*, fille majeure, rue & place Royale.

De Dlle *Miger*, fille majeure, rue St. Antoine.

De la Dame épouse du Sr *Senart*, Maître Horloger, rue des Jardins.

Du Sr Claude-Denis *Bourgeois*, Md Mercier, rue de la Harpe.

De Francois-René *Hurault de Moranville*, Ecuyer, Pensionnaire du Roi, rue de Beaujolois.

De Dlle Françoise Geoffroy, veuve du Sr Claude-Joseph *Gremion*, rue des trois Pistolets.

Du Sr Pierre *Vattier*, Loueur de Carrosses, rue des Couronnes.

Du Sr Jean-André *Hodebourg*, Bourgeois de Paris, rue d'Anjou, faub. St. Germain.

De Dame Marie-Angélique Dutillet, épouse de M. Louis-Antoine *Talbert*, Conseiller du Roi, ancien Syndic des Tontines, rue Jean-Robert, & par suite à Bezons.

De Dame Louise-Thérèse de la Vallée de Calfeux, veuve de M. Louis *Constant de Jouy*, Avocat du Roi au Bailliage de Compiegne, rue Boucherat, au Marais.

Sur les Effets du Sr *Stapard*, Employé à la Régie des Poudres. A la requête de M. le Procureur du Roi.

SPECTACLES.

ACADÉMIE ROYALE DE MUSIQUE. Demain 1er Juillet, DIDON, Tragédie en trois actes, paroles de M. Marmontel, musique de M. Piccini.

THÉATRE FRANÇOIS. Aujourd'hui 30, L'ORPHELIN DE LA CHINE, Trag. de Voltaire, & LES FOLIES AMOUREUSES, Comédie en trois actes, en vers, de Regnard.

Demain 1er Juillet, *le Joueur*, & *la Maison de Campagne*, avec un Divertissement.

Samedi la 10e représentation de *Roxelane & Mustapha*, Tragédie nouvelle, & *l'Impatient*.

En attendant la 74e repr. de *la Folle journée*.

THÉATRE ITALIEN. Aujourd'hui 30, Spectacle demandé, LES FEMMES VENGÉES, Comédie en un acte, en vers, mêlée d'ariettes, par M. Sedaine, musique de M. Philidor, & BLAISE ET BABET, ou la suite *des trois Fermiers*, Com. en deux actes, en vers, mêlée d'ariettes, par M. Monvel, mus. de M. de Zede.

Demain *l'Indigent*, & *les Voyages de Rosine*.

En attendant la 6e représ. d'*Alexis & Justine*; la 3e de *l'heureuse Réconciliation*; la 30e de *Richard*, & la 4e d'*Agnès Bernau*.

PALAIS ROYAL.

VARIÉTÉS. Aujourd'hui 30, la 3e représ. *du faux Ami*, Comédie en vers, en trois actes; *Esope à la Foire*, & *l'Enrôlement supposé*, avec un Divertissement.

BOULEVARDS.

GRANDS DANSEURS DU ROI. Aujourd. 30, *l'Homme & la Femme comme il n'y en a jamais eu*, Pièce nouvelle; *le Voyage de Figaro & son Esclavage à Alger*; *le Retour de Figaro à Madrid*; *les Ressorts amoureux*, Pant. à mach., avec le Divert. nouveau. On commencera par *Arlequin Pâtissier*, Pantomime.

AMBIGU COMIQUE. Aujourd'hui 30, Spectacle demandé, *Diogène Fabuliste*, Pièce en un acte, en vers; *la Matinée du Comédien*; *le Porte-Feuille*, ou *la Fille comme il y en a peu*, & *les quatre Coins*, Pastorale.

MORTS.

Jeanne-Victoire Poitevin, épouse de M. Nicolas-Charles *Dutertre*, Maître Horloger, quai de l'Ecole.

Marie-Anne Guilloré, épouse de M. Jean-Baptiste *Tireau*, Directeur & Receveur des Loteries unies à celle de France, rue de Touraine, au Marais.

Anne Postel, épouse de M. Jean-Toussaint *Prud-homme*, ancien Md Gantier-Parfumeur, rue de la vieille Monnoie.

De l'Imprimerie de QUILLAU, Imprimeur de S. A. S. Mgr le Prince DE CONTI, rue du Fouarre, No. 3.

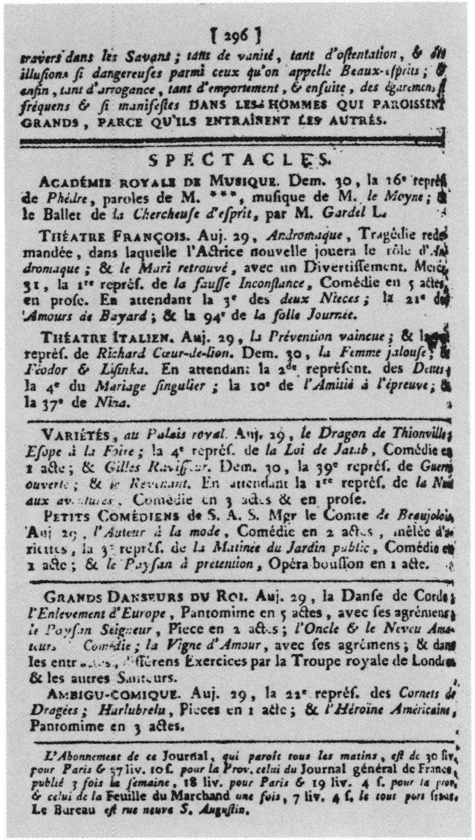

[296]

travers dans les Savans; tant de vanité, tant d'ostentation, & des illusions si dangereuses parmi ceux qu'on appelle Beaux-esprits; & enfin, tant d'arrogance, tant d'emportement, & ensuite, des égaremens si fréquens & si manifestes DANS LES HOMMES QUI PAROISSENT GRANDS, PARCE QU'ILS ENTRAÎNENT LES AUTRES.

SPECTACLES.

ACADÉMIE ROYALE DE MUSIQUE. Dem. 30, la 16e représ. de *Phèdre*, paroles de M. ***, musique de M. *le Moyne*; & le Ballet de *la Chercheuse d'esprit*, par M. *Gardel* L.

THÉATRE FRANÇOIS. Auj. 29, *Andromaque*, Tragédie redemandée, dans laquelle l'Actrice nouvelle jouera le rôle d'*Andromaque*; & *le Mari retrouvé*, avec un Divertissement. Merc. 31, la 1re représ. de *la fausse Inconstance*, Comédie en 5 actes, en prose. En attendant la 3e des *deux Nieces*; la 21e des *Amours de Bayard*; & la 94e de *la folle Journée*.

THÉATRE ITALIEN. Auj. 29, *la Prévention vaincue*; & la représ. de *Richard Cœur-de-lion*. Dem. 30, *la Femme jalouse*; & *Feodor & Lisinka*. En attendant la 2de représent. des *Deux*; la 4e du *Mariage singulier*; la 10e de *l'Amitié à l'épreuve*; & la 37e de *Nina*.

VARIÉTÉS, *au Palais royal*. Auj. 29, *le Dragon de Thionville*; *Esope à la Foire*; la 4e représ. de *la Loi de Jacob*, Comédie en 1 acte; & *Gilles Ravisseur*. Dem. 30, la 39e représ. de *Guerre ouverte*; & *le Revenant*. En attendant la 1re représ. de *la Nuit aux aventures*, Comédie en 3 actes & en prose.

PETITS COMÉDIENS de S. A. S. Mgr le Comte *de Beaujolois*. Auj. 29, *l'Auteur à la mode*, Comédie en 2 actes, mêlée d'ariettes, la 3e représ. de *la Matinée du Jardin public*, Comédie en 1 acte; & *le Paysan à prétention*, Opéra bouffon en 1 acte.

GRANDS DANSEURS DU ROI. Auj. 29, la Danse de Corde; *l'Enlevement d'Europe*, Pantomime en 5 actes, avec ses agrémens; *le Paysan Seigneur*, Piece en 2 actes; *l'Oncle & le Neveu Amateurs*, Comédie; *la Vigne d'Amour*, avec ses agrémens; & dans les entr'actes, différens Exercices par la Troupe royale de Londres & les autres Sauteurs.

AMBIGU-COMIQUE. Auj. 29, la 22e représ. des *Cornets de Dragées*; *Hurlubrelu*, Pieces en 1 acte; & *l'Héroïne Américaine*, Pantomime en 3 actes.

L'Abonnement de ce Journal, qui paroît tous les matins, est de 30 liv. pour Paris & 37 liv. 10 s. pour la Prov. celui du Journal général de France, *publié 3 fois la semaine, 18 liv. pour Paris & 19 liv. 4 s. pour la prov. & celui de la* Feuille du Marchand *une fois, 7 liv. 4 s. le tout port franc.* Le Bureau *est rue neuve S. Augustin.*

Plate 2. Pages from the *Journal de Paris* (30 June 1785), on the left, and the *Petites Affiches* (29 January 1787), on the right, reflect institutional status in the Parisian hierarchy of theaters from 1785-1789. Note that in this issue of the *Petites Affiches* there is no bipartite division of theaters (see Figure 1).

But as the *Journal de Paris* made clear, the shift in the layout of the page reflected the transfer of the Variétés-Amusantes away from the boulevard to the Palais-Royal in the center of Paris, recently renovated by the Duc d'Orleans to house shops, cafés and theaters. The new three-tiered division did reflect as well, however, more subtle changes in the hierarchy of Parisian theaters. In the same year, 1785, the French actors complained bitterly in a public memoir that a "revolution" had upset the customary prominence of the major theaters.[5] As they had done in 1769, so they protested in 1785 that at least some of the minor theaters had been allowed to approach too closely the rank and esteem traditionally granted the three great theaters alone. There could be little doubt that what remained of the old protocol amongst theaters was severely threatened, or so it was mischievously claimed on the actors' behalf in a spurious list of grievances:

> . . . and since men allow themselves to be guided by words and by what they see, the black line of the abbé Aubert persuaded many Parisians that the Spectacles of the Palais Royal were as good as the great Spectacles. . . . Let us fear, Gentlemen, that if Dorfeuille should give yet another four tickets to the abbé Aubert, he will remove the line that separates the Variétés from the great Spectacles, to place it on the same level with us.[6]

With amazing rapidity the thorough leveling that the actors were said to fear did come to pass. In November of 1789 the *Petites Affiches* dropped all lines between theater listings. By implication all theaters now shared the same formal rank. Paris, of course, had been caught in the throes of a political revolution that would stretch from 1788-89 to 1794 and beyond. Was there a related upheaval in the traditional world of theater? ". . . Our way of thinking," wrote the minor littérateur and professor Nicolas-Joseph Sélis in his consideration of Parisian theater in 1789, "has undergone a revolution . . . "[7]

What do the ceremonial distinctions caught upon the printed page reveal about the theatrical world of late eighteenth century Paris? These formalities of rank were meant to maintain the conceptual boundaries between the great and the minor theaters that had mapped the cultural body of France for decades. Of what substance were these boundaries? What caused their abrupt adjustment in 1785 and again in 1789? In search of answers, the formal shape and pragmatic outlines of a complex theatrical culture shall be explored.

1

The Formal Rank of the Boulevard in Parisian Theater

The Classical Order of Cultural Privilege and Civil License

The postered walls and newspaper pages of eighteenth-century Paris reflected a theatrical order of great complexity. Ranked at the head of all spectacles in the city were the royal companies, supported by government pensions in lavish style and supervised by administrators within the Royal Household.[1] By all and sundry the Opéra, the Comédie-Française and the Comédie-Italienne were considered privileged bodies, for all three exercised privilege, that "Power accorded to a Person or a Commonalty to do or enjoy something to some advantage to the exclusion of others."[2] Together these three theaters possessed monopolistic rights to the performance of all genres recognized within the great dramatic tradition. The Opéra exploited all art forms in music, song and dance and alone produced opera and ballet; the Comédie-Française claimed as its domain the performance of tragic drama and comedy in the French manner; the Comédie-Italienne held rights to comic plays reminiscent of the *commedia dell'arte,* a traditional, improvised theater of Italy, and to comic opera.

The legal foundation of these exclusive rights differed importantly for each of these theaters. The Opéra, at the head of the great theaters, possessed a formal privilege to song and dance registered in Parlement in 1669 and 1769 by letters patent—the highest of legal acts conceding exclusive rights to an industry or exploitation. Through the late seventeenth century and the first half of the eighteenth, neither the Comédie-Française nor the Comédie-Italienne could boast this formal privilege, but by reason of long association with king and government and by the favorable interpretation of their lesser titles in the judicial courts, both were supported in exclusive monopolies of tragedy and/or comedy. In 1761 the French actors finally obtained secure legal footing like the Opéra. According to Des Essarts, lawyer in Parlement and historian of Parisian theater, before Parlement registered letters patent for the actors in that year,

> they only existed by virtue of the King's order and special agreements; now their existence is based upon the titles that the laws require in order to give a guild or a commonalty a legal status.[3]

In principle, exclusive rights to the genres of dramatic art amounted to an industrial monopoly of all theatrical enterprise by the three great theaters. In fact, a host of minor theaters, small booths and itinerant shows in the streets of Paris posed an industrial competition noxious to the privileged theaters. Throughout the eighteenth century the king and his courts were frequently pressed by the royal theaters to enforce the great dramatic monopolies and suppress this theatrical trade. The government and the courts, however, resisted the full sway of dramatic privilege and supported in semi-legal fashion the minor theatrical industry. Licensed by the police with simple permits, like all petty commerce in the markets and public squares, this minor trade in irregular dramatic forms was tolerated on the seasonal fairgrounds of Paris and along the boulevard du Temple on the northeastern outskirts of the city. In the early 1780s the two or three theaters whose announcements were posted to the side, or separated by a forbidding line from those of the great theaters, did not belong to the privileged world of theater but were marginal to it.

The legal and industrial gap between great and little theaters in eighteenth century Paris had its foundation in the "grand century" of arts and letters. It was in the late 1600s that the Sun King first granted the privileges that buttressed the dominant positions of the Opéra, the Comédie-Française and the Comédie-Italienne; it was also in these years that the first minor theaters, properly so called, were segregated in the fairs. However, this organization of Parisian theater reflected the policies of a mature king. In his minority and early reign Louis XIV had presided without discrimination over a motley range of theatrical entertainment. Although the theatrical world to which he had fallen heir in 1643 had had at its core the industrial monopoly of the Confrèrie de la Passion, the theatrical rights of that religious corporation had severely lapsed since their origin in the early fifteenth century.[4] By the mid-1600s three French stages—the Hôtel de Bourgogne, the Théâtre du Marais and the Troupe de Molière—competed for the custom of court and city. So, too, did companies of Italian and Spanish players, and the puppets and acrobats at the seasonal fairgrounds of Saint Germain and Saint Laurent.[5] Royal favor and patronage were bestowed upon the many: from the Hôtel de Bourgogne, the "royal troupe" that specialized in the tragedies of Corneille and Racine, to the fairground marionette show of Brioché called to entertain the court on more than one occasion and protected by the king.[6]

In time, Louis and his minister Colbert were to rationalize and centralize the world of theater as they did the realms of commerce, finance and administration. While Colbert stimulated the disciplined production of the Beaux Arts, Louis turned his hand to the organization of the stage. It is

Plate 3. View of the Saint-Ovide Fair, detailing the small theater halls of Mister Gaudon and Mister Nicolet, as late as 1770. Paris, Musée Carnavalet. Photo: Giraudon/Art Resource, Inc.

significant that he granted privileged rights to those forms of theatrical entertainment that were later to be known as minor, as well as to those later understood as great. In 1669 the young king accorded the abbé Perrin, by letters patent, legal privilege "for an academy of opera or representations in music, in the French tongue..."[7] Henri Guichard received in 1674 letters patent for an Academy of Spectacles that authorized the construction of "circuses and amphitheaters for carousels, tournaments, races, jousts, battles, animal combats, illuminations and fireworks..."[8] In 1675 letters patent granted Dominique de Normandin the legal privilege to exploit a new kind of marionette capable of imitating human dance in a Royal Troupe of Pygmies.[9] By royal order in 1680 Louis ordered the French actors, reduced to two troupes after the death of Molière, to unite into a single company, the Comédie-Française.[10]

It soon became apparent, however, that not all these monopolies were to be of equal value or industrial weight. Although Louis had continued to grant royal privilege to wide-ranging forms of theatrical entertainment in the decade after 1669, he proved in fact unwilling that his prized Academy of Music suffer competition or eclipse. In 1672 Jean-Baptiste Lully, the superintendent of music at court who had succeeded to Perrin's privilege the year before, was granted by royal edict exclusive rights over all the theatrical productions of a musical nature throughout France; to the dismay of many at court Lully claimed sole right to the composition as well as the production of operas, thereby securing a full monopoly of dramatic music.[11] Nearly all of the privileges granted by Louis XIV thereafter faltered before the exclusive monopoly of Lully's Opéra. In an attempt to override the prohibition of music in his projected Academy of Spectacles, Guichard became involved with Lully in litigation before Parlement; his suit failed, and in 1676 he was denied the right to register the letters patent granted two years before.[12] In 1677 the Théâtre des Bamboches, the enterprise granted as the Royal Troupe of Pygmies, was also suppressed at the behest of the Opéra.[13]

As shaped over the decade 1669-1680, Louis' politics in matters of the stage tended towards the minimization of competition and the unification of theatrical industry according to dramatic type. In 1673 and 1675 the king hindered the French actors from using music or song in their performances on the grounds that this harmed the "success" of Lully's Opéra. This curtailment of competitive productions contributed greatly to the development of theater-types, dedicated to the perfection of exclusive genres within the dramatic arts. When Louis united the rival French theaters into one company in 1680, it was with the express desire that one stage alone perform and perfect the dramatic repertory hitherto produced by competitive troupes:

> ...and in order to give them means to perfect themselves more and more, His Majesty wishes that only the said troupe may represent comedies in Paris, forbidding all other French

actors to establish themselves in the said city and environs, without express order of His Majesty . . .[14]

By the latter half of Louis' reign, royal patronage of a theatrical industry characterized by a wide range of genres and forms and overlapping liberties had been restricted to a few privileged stages—the Opéra, the Comédie-Française and the Comédie-Italienne[15]—in the service of the king and French splendor. Louis' theatrical politics had entailed the exclusion of all but the royal stages from legally-recognized rights. In consequence, entertainments outside royal favor and privilege banded together on the fairgrounds of Paris, areas traditionally immune from corporate monopolies. When in 1697 the Italian actors were banished for political ridicule of Louis' morganatic consort, the vacuum created by their departure was quickly filled by several impromptu theaters in the fairs performing the dramatic genres of the proscribed actors; none of these minor stages received privilege or favor from an aging king. Louis bequeathed his heirs a range of theater legally and economically split asunder: on the one hand, an official theatrical order of corporate bodies granted state patronage and privileged monopolies; on the other, a marginal world of privately-tendered enterprise dependent upon the precarious license of the police and the immunity of the fairs.

Since the economic privileges granted by Louis XIV had been defined in terms of artistic exploitation, the legal and economic gap between great and little theaters reflected as well an aesthetic disposition of the stage. In art as in law the three great companies stood apart from the minor theaters of the fairs and boulevard in eighteenth-century Paris. The royal theaters alone were held to unite in the first degree all the genres of dramatic art.[16] The minor theaters had no part within this artistic order. The reign of Louis XIV had realized not only a doctrine of economic order but one of neo-classical expression. It was a tenet of this doctrine that different dramatic forms reflected different stations of life. The abbé d'Aubignac, one of the more important critics of the mid-seventeenth century, argued further that each of the several genres, depicting as they did the characteristics of distinct social groups, appealed in theory almost exclusively to spectators of similar condition. Different states of birth, training and habit radically distinguished aristocratic society from that of the "people," and distinguished, too, the dramatic genres to which they were sensitive:

It is for this very reason that we see in the French Court Tragedies more warmly received than Comedies, and that amongst the little People Comedies, and even the Farces and sordid buffooneries of our theaters, are held to be more diverting than Tragedies. In this Kingdom persons of birth, or those raised among the Great, foster among themselves only generous sentiments and indulge only in worthy aims either from the movements of virtue or from the transports of ambition; it follows that their lives have much in common with the representations of tragic theater. But the Populace, born in the mire, and raised upon dishonest sentiments and speech, finds itself well disposed to consider good the paltry

> buffooneries of our farces and always takes pleasure in seeing the images of that which it is accustomed to say and do.[17]

This social theory of dramatic forms, as expressed by d'Aubignac, was part and parcel of a nascent cultural politics. Despite the fact that, as Richelieu's superintendent of theaters, he himself had drawn plans for a theater that housed "persons of condition" as well as the "little people," d'Aubignac later argued that the classical stage should appeal to the educated elite alone.[18] Indeed, according to the scholar Réné Bray, classical letters had never, at any time, with any author, been a popular art.[19] The generation of d'Aubignac, drawn within the ideological orbit of Richelieu and his king, had elaborated the rules and doctrine of a learned art. Their critical successor Nicolas Boileau-Despréaux carved a wide social gap between that classical art and much of the rich literature current since the beginning of the seventeenth century.[20] In his *The Art of Poetry,* written in 1674, Boileau stigmatized literary genres considered without rule or method—the novel, the tragi-comedy, the pastorale, the burlesque and the farce—as popular forms unfit for the social elite.[21] Bawdy prologues and farce had accompanied tragedy and comedy at the Bourgogne and the Marais in the early seventeenth century; now Boileau objected strongly to any mixture of forms on the French stage, including the farcical comedies of the master Molière.[22] Farce and buffoonery no longer had their place on the stage of the royal theaters. They belonged, rather, on the open-air planks of Pont-Neuf[23] before a plebian audience:

> I prefer an obliging author for the stage,
> Who, without making a fool of himself in the public eye,
> Pleases with reason alone and never offends against it.
> But as for the would-be Wag of coarse quibbles,
> Who, for my diversion has nothing but obscenities;
> Let him go mount a trestle stage, if he would,
> Amuse the Pont-Neuf with his tasteless twaddle,
> And for the lackeys assembled there, perform his masquerades.[24]

The seventeenth-century clarification of artistic and social boundaries within the dramatic arts had triggered the withdrawal[25] of classical theater from the realm of common culture.

Boileau's distinctions between art and common form, between a rational and a popular appeal, between the classical stage and open-air planks, gave expression to the intellectual and artistic consciousness of an aristocratic society. In the seventeenth century, these cultural politics were as yet very much a prescriptive conception; by the eighteenth century they had greatly matured as a normative perception. Despite a certain impatience with the authority of the ancients and their seventeenth century imitators,[26] the eighteenth century remained heir to the intellectual legacy of the classicists. In the eighteenth century, as in the seventeenth, art was universally understood as the rational manufacture of a thing according to certain rules, and in this sense it was opposed to an unembellished nature.[27] By this token, it was argued in the *Encyclopédie* (1st edition, 1751-1772), dramatic spectacle was of two kinds: curiosities, or spectacles that required bodily strength or agility and almost no "art"; and theater, or "spectacles of art" that demonstrated the actions of the mind and soul, and thus required an "infinite art." The first, simply reflecting nature or reality, had at one time appealed to entire nations; now "most civilized peoples enjoy only those spectacles [of art] that relate to the soul: operas, comedies, tragedies and pantomimes..."[28] Farce and the *parade,* originally a sketch performed on outdoor balconies in order to lure passersby inside, had long since been dropped from this lexicon of theatrical art. The very manner in which these genres were defined indicated their strong association with the proscribed tastes of the people and with the "curiosities" of the fair.[29] In 1777 Des Essarts could proclaim with truth that the great dramatic tradition was at present utterly removed from the common genres and the common man:

> Our theatrical plays today are no longer gross and obscene farces, nor our Actors Buffoons meant to amuse the populace. We have relegated that class of contemptible men to the wooden planks along the Capital's Boulevards and in public squares...[30]

Ideal conceptions of art and aesthetic doctrine alone, however, did not carve the gap in theatrical culture. It was, rather, the dramatic monopolies of the royal theaters that provided the mechanism, and their very real economic interests the practical stimulus. In the first several decades of the eighteenth century all the royal theaters but one attempted to enforce an absolute monopoly of theatrical industry within the city of Paris. Throughout the years 1699-1711, during which time the Comédie-Italienne was expelled from France, the French actors energetically persecuted their only other competitors, the small spectacles of the fair.[31] The actors' protests in 1690 and again in 1699 before the lieutenant-general of police had resulted in police sentences prohibiting the performance of comedy and, significantly enough, of farce on the minor fair stages of Bertrand, Maurice von der Beck, Alard and others. These directors appealed to the Parisian Parlement, which initially judged in 1703 in favor of the French actors. The men of the fair, however, would not be defeated. There followed a furious round of police sentences, appeals to the Parlement, petitions to the Provost of Town Hall and decrees of the Grand Council of State. Not until March 1710, after a decade of clever defense,[32] did the fair theaters finally lose their battle for a theatrical industry in the decision of the Council of State:

> ...that prohibition is set for them and all others, of whatever quality and condition they may be, against performing, either in the enclosure of the fairs of St. Laurent and St. Germain or in the city of Paris, any comedy, dialogued farce and other divertissements that resemble comedy, under the pretext of privilege and sanction of the fairs...[33]

The purpose of the French actors had been to suppress the dramatic competition of the fairs altogether. The attempts of the fair spectacles to disguise their theatrical industry with innovative forms such as the monologue, in which only one actor spoke on stage—and then rarely—or the pantomime were unacceptable compromises. Nor did the actors' final victory in 1710, the suppression of all speech on the popular stage, satisfy their visions of a global monopoly. As early as 1708 several fair theaters had obtained tacit permission from the Opéra to the multiple scenery changes, the singers, dancers, and sung couplets of comic opera.[34] In this new genre, beyond the jurisdiction of the Comédie-Française, the fair theaters had guardedly introduced spoken monologue or dialogue with song and ballet to be performed after the regular fare of tight-rope dancing and acrobatics. The actors' petition that the fair theaters be deprived even of these pantomimes and short scenes of comic opera, deprived indeed of their right to perform anything other than tight-rope dancing, was rejected by the Council of State in 1711. Despite a decree of this same court in 1709 that had forbidden the Opéra to rent out permission to song and music, the Opéra's practices were tacitly overlooked in the years 1711, 1712, 1713, until in 1714 the Royal Academy was permitted by law to sell these dramatic rights to the fair theaters. It was this venal extension of the Opéra's privilege that blunted and finally thwarted the efforts of the Comédie-Française to achieve a full monopoly of theatrical industry at the expense of the popular spectacles of the fair.

The police sentences and governmental decrees restricting the popular spectacles of the fairgrounds to tight-rope dancing, marionettes, pantomimes, and in later years to simple farces and parades were intended to protect the artistic, if not the commercial, monopolies of the royal companies. Under the old regime, however, the formal repetition of ordinances all too often replaced effectual execution of the law. Throughout the first half of the century the royal theaters had at their disposal no practical mechanism for the restraint or repression of minor dramatic activity other than formal protest to the lieutenant-general of police or legal prosecution. These procedures were heavy-handed and uncertain in execution. In concert with the newly-returned Comédie-Italienne (1716), the Comédie-Française had managed a complete suppression of the fair theaters in 1718-19; but the royal companies were unable to prevent a vigorous resurgence of these spectacles in the coming year. Tacit permission to perform comic opera was given by the Opéra to Lahauze and Restier frères; by 1721 a society of fairground entrepreneurs exploited this genre at the Saint Laurent Fair and in the same year a certain Francisque established a second fair theater of comic opera. Once again the French actors managed the crude suppression of both fair spectacles, this time through 1724. From 1724 to 1727 Honoré and Picard managed to resurrect the fairground permission to comic opera and it was their enterprise that first took the name of

Opéra-Comique. Under many different entrepreneurs the Opéra-Comique continued without interruption until 1745. The great success of this fair theater and the comic operas of Favart in particular prompted the Comédie-Française to vigorous objections that were honored with a six-year hiatus for the Opéra-Comique between 1745 and 1751. By 1752 the Opéra-Comique had reopened—it did not close until its union with the Comédie-Italienne in 1762.[35]

The "Réunion," as it was called, of 1762 left a vacuum in the fairs that was quickly filled by a number of petty amusements and minor theaters, the very ones that migrated about this time to the boulevard du Temple in between fairground sessions. By 1769 a direct and delicate mechanism for their artistic repression had replaced the clumsy, wholesale suppression or co-optation hitherto practiced by the great stages. The French and Italian actors were invested with powers of preliminary review and censorship over all dramatic pieces to be performed on the minor stages of Paris. Prior to this, plays destined for the minor stages of Paris had simply been submitted to the royal censor, who reviewed all dramatic pieces to be represented in the city, and to the lieutenant-general of police for approval and license to perform. Virtually nothing is known about the purposes and policies of this original surveillance. In February of 1769 Papillon de la Ferté, intendent of Petty Entertainments (Menus plaisirs) in the Royal Household, named two royal actors to review all plays destined for the fairs and boulevard and to return them, along with a statement of approval or of grievance, to the royal censor and the lieutenant-general of police.[36] These officials, and not the actors, were empowered to take action appropriate to the interests of the royal stage. Nevertheless, it was the latter whom contemporaries subsequently blamed for a brutal censorship of the popular stage.[37] The royal companies, it would seem, used their right of review to disfigure systematically any dramatic merit on the boulevard and in the fairs.[38]

A censorship register kept by the Comédie-Française for the years 1784-1789 reveals more precisely the criteria with which the actors fulfilled the task of review and censure granted them in 1769.[39] Their evaluation and censorship of boulevard plays were based upon privileged conceptions of theatrical property and classical notions of dramatic art. The first and most obvious of their interests was the protection of their own theatrical property. Once performed on their stage, a play formed part of a jealously guarded repertory. Thus the royal actors argued in 1785 that *Present Times,* a comedy in one act and prose by Legrand first performed on their stage in 1725, "belongs to the Comédie-Française... and forms part of the Plays in its Repertory" and must therefore be forbidden to the boulevard. The protection of dramatic property also entailed the suppression of parodies and plagiarisms of the classical fare. *The Marriage of Tristando or the Tiresome Day,* a parody of Beaumarchais' *The Marriage of Figaro,* was suppressed on these grounds. So, too, *The Widow as Rare as They Come,* charged by the actors with "the same outline, the same composition, the same comic intention" as *The Unforeseen Obstacle,* performed by the royal company. Significantly enough, the actors guarded as well the characters created on their stage. In the wake of Beaumarchais' highly successful Figaro a spate of plays written for the boulevard sported this character and his supporting players. The actors argued that the original names must be dropped from these plays "because the names specify new characters that belong to the French Theater... and consequently they should not be either denatured or weakened..."[40]

For the French actors of the eighteenth century the conception of dramatic property was significantly broader than that allowed by modern notions of copyright, in which the playwright retains ownership of the play. By custom, a play once performed by the royal company belonged not to the playwright but to the French actors. An ordinance of Louis XIV in 1674 had allowed theatrical companies exclusive rights to the performance of their program before its publication. Since that time the French actors had assumed, by virtue of their monopoly, that they alone possessed the right to all plays in the classical genres of comedy and tragedy, whether or not they had already been published. By the eighteenth century it had become a recognized privilege of the actors to command any such play for the royal stage and forbid its performance to all other theaters. It was, in fact, with this prerogative that the actors suppresed or appropriated many plays originally written for the boulevard. In 1785 the actors asked the police to forbid the performance of *It is He, or the Benevolent Financier* on any stage other than their own and protested the performance of *Servants Aping Masters,* an imitation of Garrick's *High Life Below Stairs:*

> ...the dignity of the French Theater cannot suffer the dispersion and mutilation of the works of a man who has honored the stage so greatly... [Moreover,] by the terms of the agreed upon Demarcations, it is not allowed to the fair theaters to appropriate as they choose published plays that may be suitable for the French Theater.[41]

By the word "Demarcations" the royal actors referred to the artistic boundaries that distinguished their theatrical exploitation from that of the minor spectacles of the fairs and boulevard. In this sense, the notion of property was conflated with the notion of art. Indeed a great deal of the actors' censorship concerned the evaluation of the "genre of the plays." On no account were the boulevard theaters to be permitted "a complete Spectacle," as it was judged by the aesthetics of classicism. Most classical plays comprised five acts; the boulevard was reduced to no more than three. Verse was considered the highest form of dramatic art and was consistently protested when it appeared in boulevard plays—"the Lieutenant-general of Police promised to forbid the fair Spectacles any play in verse." The social rank of personages as well as the quality of subject and action offered as many occasions for formal remonstrance. In the case of one popular play the actors complained about the use of "a councillor in Parlement, a Baron, a Countess, a Marquise" who had no place in a play "destined to a Theater made for amusing that portion of Society which has no intimate Communication with the Class that is above it." The boulevard was also to be denied serious or political subjects—"Several Maxims of Government are treated therein, and a Play destined to the subordinate Theaters cannot be the setting for such lessons ... "—and heroic deeds such as those of Bayard, a national hero of the early sixteenth century:

> The name and person of Bayard must not be used by the Theaters of the Boulevards. If the character is as noble as he should be, these theaters will manifestly overstep the bounds that it has seemed just to prescribe for them. If Bayard is made to act and speak as it becomes these Spectacles, one of our most famous heroes is in some part degraded and the veneration he ought inspire is weakened.[42]

In the minds of the royal actors, and no doubt in those of many contemporaries, the censorship of the minor theaters had effected important distinctions between serious dramatic art and non-serious "curiosity" or spectacle. Contemporaries indulged in a general scorn for the minor dramatic tradition, in an opprobrium shaped by the aesthetic criteria of a classical art. Whether by friend or by foe, boulevard fare was considered bawdy, gross, trivial, empty, an unwholesome mix of "obscene and detestable plays ... [with] the most cringing buffooneries."[43] In 1756 the popular tradition was judged to be "equally opposed to good sense, to good humor, to morals and to decency."[44] So it was judged some thirty years later:

> Imagine would-be comedies without the unities, without interest; for piquancy explicit obscenities or what used in former days to be called gibes [*quolibets*] and what are now called puns [*calembours*]. Think of dances devoid of character and executed by feeble children, dances that are surpassingly like monstrous pantomimes, mixtures of buffoonery and the heroic.[45]

The critical distinctions were aesthetic; they were by implication cultural as well, since "these imitations, which charm the vile populace, are not to the taste of respectable persons."[46] So powerful was the hold of classical doctrine on the world of theater that some believed the aesthetic itself directly responsible for the social segmentation of theatrical culture. Mercier, a life-long opponent of classicism, wrote in 1773 that

> We do not have in France Spectacle properly so-called, but particular assemblies, where several men, reunited after having formed a delicate taste that is composed but artificial, have given an exorbitant value to works which, although beautiful, have in their structure and in their idiom something strange and inaccessible to the rest of the nation ...[47]

The Opéra and the two Comédies were theaters of the king and his elite and the rest, "placed on the Boulevard ... are regarded as the theaters of the people."[48] It is this cultural gap between great and little theaters and their dramatic traditions that the hierarchical arrangements and heavy bar on the pages of the *Petites Affiches* most vividly expressed.

The Classical Order Compromised, 1784-1785

In 1785 the representation of the theatrical order to be found on the pages of the *Petites Affiches* or the *Journal de Paris* altered significantly from a two-tiered to a three-tiered hierarchy. A momentous change in governmental policies implemented the year before had strained severely the customary bipolar distinctions between the great and the little theaters.[49] On the 18th of July 1784 Louis XVI in council granted an indebted Opéra the right to an economic exploitation of all minor theaters in the city of Paris. By this decree the Royal Academy was accorded the privilege or usufruct of all fair stages "which until now could not be established without the authorization of the lieutenant-general of police."[50] In effect, boulevard and fair entrepreneurs were bereft of all civil or police license to theatrical industry. The right to such industry had now to be petitioned from the Opéra and paid for dearly in weekly or monthly sums. According to the terms of the royal decree the Opéra was not bound to treat with entrepreneurs who currently owned theatrical enterprises on the boulevards or at the fairs, for little distinction was made between the privilege to exploit a certain theater and ownership of the property—the hall, the props or the costumes—which made up that theater. When the Opéra decided in September of 1784 to confer the privilege for the Variétés-Amusantes and the Ambigu-Comique on Gaillard and Dorfeuille, two entrepreneurs without previous holdings in Paris, the original owners and directors of those boulevard theaters found themselves dispossessed of their theatrical license and their theatrical property as well.[51]

François Duval Malter, disenfranchised director of the Variétés-Amusantes, brought suit before the Council of State in the course of 1785 against the appropriation of his theatrical enterprise by Gaillard and Dorfeuille. It was Malter's plea that on the grounds of proprietary right, "a sacred right that no one might infringe ...,"[52] he continue to hold title to both his theatrical license and his theatrical possessions. Malter's lawyers argued that, as emanations of the same authority, royal privilege and police permit were of equal juridical weight; whether the recipient of one or the other, the cessionary might regard himself as a proprietor of theatrical industry. Indeed, the long tenure of many theaters on the boulevard in the last decade had blurred distinctions between the police permit and royal monopolies. Given the official underwriting of his nine-year lease, Malter claimed that the sanction of government lay behind the continuation of his permit or "privilege," as he purposely called it, for at least that length of time.

In fact, the legal rights of the boulevard theaters were much more fragile. Before the same court Gaillard and Dorfeuille successfully deflated the proprietary claims of the boulevard entrepreneur. It was argued in their favor that despite the apparent longevity of boulevard theatrical industry, the arbitrary conventions of civil license distinguished it radically from the permanent exploitations of privileged enterprise. The boulevard stage was in fact only an annual possession:

> The necessity to renew this permit every year, and even many times during the year, the prohibition against making contracts with actors that exceeded a year's duration, the rule against beginning these contracts before the week that preceded the Easter reopening, all combined to take from Malter and other fair directors the conceit of a permanent possession, such as that which could result from a privilege...[53]

Moreover, Gaillard and Dorfeuille claimed to have lawfully purchased the theater halls and materials of the Variétés-Amusantes from Malter's clamoring creditors.[54] As the case was resolved by a special commission, Malter was granted only a modest sum for the dispossession of his moveable property.[55] Privilege had prevailed over property. This was not so for Nicolas Médard Audinot, former director of the Ambigu-Comique, who had also filed suit before the Council of State—but one opposite in intention from Malter's. Instead of pleading for the return of his exploitation, Audinot attempted to force Gaillard and Dorfeuille to indemnify him fully for theatrical property rendered useless by the usurpation of his theatrical license. Rather than contest Audinot's claims in court, Gaillard and Dorfeuille voluntarily relinquished the exploitation of the Ambigu-Comique, which had, in any case, become burdensome to them. By the end of 1785 Audinot regained both his property and his license, though by no act of the court.[56]

The government's decree in favor of the Opéra and the court's support of this privilege at the expense of licensed property had smashed with one blow the legal pinions of the fair and boulevard trade, such as they had been for nearly a century. But ironically, rather than cripple the minor theatrical industry, the government and court rulings had in fact replaced its bulwarks with much stronger stuff. The privilege with which Gaillard and Dorfeuille had roughly seized the Variétés-Amusantes—and even, temporarily, the Ambigu-Comique—was accorded as well in smaller dosage to Jean-Baptiste Nicolet, the wily director of the Grands-Danseurs du Roi who had come to terms with the Opéra on his own. Nicolet signed a contract with the Royal Academy which specified that "a portion of the privilege accorded by decree of the Council... to the said Royal Academy of Music for all Spectacles in the city of Paris is necessary to the said Mister Nicolet in order to continue the operation of his theater . . . "[57] Instead of the precarious police permits renewed annually, all boulevard and fair spectacles were, like Nicolet's Grands Danseurs, henceforth granted leases—usually of fifteen years—to privileged and often exclusive exploitations. The contract by which a certain Melan, for example, rented the "exclusive privilege" to open the Vauxhall d'Eté, a dance-hall of sorts at the Saint Laurent Fair, specifically prohibited the Opéra from granting a duplicate license to any other spectacle. At least three more theaters and as many cabarets, wax museums and puppet shows signed similar contracts in these same years. For the first time in their history, fairground theaters and amusements were allowed a regular legal existence in the economic order of France.

This legal integration of boulevard theater into the theatrical order of Paris greatly alarmed the Comédie-Française. Although the French actors' censorship of boulevard plays would indicate a tacit acquiescence in that theatrical trade, the royal company had not ceased in its hostility to minor industrial competition. Legal action undertaken by the actors against the fair theaters in 1778, however, had languished in the courts.[58] The economic reorganization of the boulevard in 1784-85 galvanized the actors anew and in May of 1785 the royal company brought suit once more against the minor theaters of Paris. It was the company's contention, developed in the *Memoir and Consultation on the Case Pending in the Great Chamber of Parlement between the French Actors . . . and the . . . Entrepreneurs of Fair Theaters* (1785) that the extension of privilege to the fair theaters violated the "wise politics" of Louis XIV—not only by regularizing the fair but by supporting the theatrical pretensions of the Variétés-Amusantes under the direction of Gaillard and Dorfeuille.

From the start, the new directors of the Variétés-Amusantes had made use of their unprecedented lease of privilege to elevate their theater to a median position between the fair and the royal stage. Taking advantage of their broadly-worded contract, Gaillard and Dorfeuille closed their halls on the fairgrounds less than two months after their direction had begun in October 1784 and moved their boulevard enterprise to a hastily built theater in the Palais-Royal. For the French actors this was a clear sign that the Variétés-Amusantes, now fixed and permanent, aspired to the status of the great theaters: "Messrs. Dorfeuille and Gaillard erect the Théâtre des Variétés-Amusantes as a true rival of the Comédie-Française."[59] Indeed, Gaillard and Dorfeuille openly confessed their desire to make of the Variétés-Amusantes the second theater of France,[60] producing fare equal in excellence to that of the Comédie-Française. In the event, the institutional rivalry of the Variétés-Amusantes was great enough, the actors argued in their *Memoir* of 1785, to damage the artistic monopoly vital to the dramatic perfection of the Comédie-Française. Louis XIV had justly perceived that competition within the beaux-arts threatened the concentration of exceptional talents and thus hindered the achievement of artistic excellence on any stage. To admit a rival of the Comédie-Française necessarily meant the dissipation of talent—both of authors and actors—and a consequent decline in the standards of dramatic art.

The French actors' professed concern for artistic standards masked more compelling interests in the maintenance of the traditional theatrical order. With characteristic sarcasm, Friedrich Melchior Grimm belittled the "grave" and "moral" *Memoir* of the royal company,

> in which, with much dignity, they made the most of the old titles that were accorded them by Louis XIV and by his successor; entirely forgetting personal interest, they only occupied themselves with the cause of morals and good taste...[61]

The actors feared, in fact, that their monopoly of the classical and elite theater of France had come to an end. Indeed Gaillard and Dorfeuille published a memoir of their own attacking with a success borne out by events the royal company's claims to exclusive privilege.[62] The directors criticized the industrial and artistic monopoly of the Comédie-Française on two grounds. The ordinance of 1680, by virtue of which the actors claimed exclusive right to the performance of drama in Paris, had been worded in such a way, Gaillard and Dorfeuille claimed, that the king and government reserved the right to enforce or relax the actors' monopoly at will.[63] Moreover, despite the actors' claims that competition ruined dramatic art, it was evident that competition excited emulation, thereby contributing to the "progress of art." Gaillard and Dorfeuille had both circumstance and public opinion on their side. Royal authorization had sanctioned the theatrical industry of the Variétés-Amusantes; men of letters and a general public of "amateurs" lobbied vociferously for a second troupe competitive with the French actors in the interests of theatrical progress.[64] All contemporaries did not reason, as did the French actors, that an economic adjustment of the theatrical hiearchy meant a consequent breakdown in the classical order of dramatic art and culture. That adjustment did require, however, the adaptation of new artistic elements into the classical order. Just as the boulevard theaters had been legally assimilated into the theatrical establishment of Paris, popular genres were haltingly accorded some partial value and place in the hierarchy of dramatic art.

As early as 1769 Pierre Jean Baptiste Nougaret, a minor playwright and literary hack, had written a treatise in defense of the comic opera, a minor genre fully developed by the Opéra-Comique and performed by the Comédie-Italienne after 1762. In his *On the Art of Theater* (1769) Nougaret argued within the classical framework that, just as comedy was destined for the rich and distinguished, fairground genres belonged to the "little people":

> D'Aubignac should have seen that the theater, which seems to be dedicated to one kind of Poem, nevertheless accommodates many, among which one may remark some diversity.... Either d'Aubignac expressed himself poorly, or his reasoning is false... If he

> pretends that there are only three sorts of characters in theater, he is wrong again. The Stage does not pass in one bound from Princes to simple Bourgeois and these latter ought not all be placed in the same class.... Each estate should have a Spectacle within its ken, and proper to its morals.[65]

For those who would defend the minor genres in the coming decades, the worth of a popular theater was, even more importantly, bound to its utility. The short dramas, sketches, pantomimes, and dialogued pantomimes meant for the lower orders of society might be harnessed to the moral education of the masses.[66] Mercier suggested at numerous points in his *Tableau of Paris* that the frivolous fare on the boulevard be replaced with a repertory of moral and instructive plays:

> ...the theaters [of the Boulevards] are those which would most merit the attention of the Magistrate, and the plays ought to be agreeable and moral compositions...[67]

Nougaret argued as much in his *Fairground Almanac,* a manual dedicated to the fair theaters in the years 1773-1788, perversely adding that "geniuses" of the first order and none other should be encouraged to write for the minor stage. A century of prejudice forbade this, however, and champions of the boulevard rather surmounted the aesthetic limitations of the popular stage by emphasizing the moral function of the minor genres: "What do theatrical rules matter provided that [the people] are presented with wholesome morals?"[68] The *Great Vocabulary,* a French dictionary of the mid-century, had allowed as early as 1768 that art broadly-conceived included the useful, simple arts as well as the tasteful beaux-arts.[69] It was no doubt this perception that led Nougaret and others to realize that a moral utility would elevate the dramatic forms of the boulevard to the ranks of art: "The people need to be roused to useful actions: that is the way to make the establishment of fair theaters necessary."[70] To the extent that a moral utility could be recognized, the popular stage gained a position of value in the dramatic order of Parisian theater.

Some contemporaries believed that boulevard theater moved perceptibly towards a moral utility in the 1770s and 1780s. As early as 1771 the authors of the *Secret Memoirs* had suggested that one fair theater, the Ambigu-Comique, might serve as a "school for virtue"; in 1785 they broadened that observation to include the entire range of minor theaters when they wrote that "the Boulevard has just about become the school of good moral character..."[71] Much of the "moralization" of boulevard fare was achieved by a tremendous development of new forms; the smutty sketches and farces had been increasingly supplemented by sentimental dramas and "moral pantomimes."[72] Contemporaries were well aware of this change in the style and tone of popular theater:

> The plays that [the fair theaters] used to represent were worth less for good morals than those of today... at the boulevards the public is often concerned, touched, softened in seeing the heroic courage of *Joan of Arc,* the virtue of *Marie Millet,* the heroism and beneficence of *Henri IV* and the victorious innocence of *Sophie de Brabant.*[73]

Those who had hailed the Variétés-Amusantes as an "intermediate spectacle" between the royal theaters and the petty enterprises of the boulevard expected on this stage especially a refinement of the popular repertory once it had moved to the Palais-Royal:

> The Theater of the Variétés is going, without doubt, to purge itself of the farces that have been much applauded [on its stage]. It must assume a tone suited to the place it [now] occupies and made for the amusement of the well-to-do public that will attend it [there].[74]

Gaillard and Dorfeuille, too, wanted to bridge the artistic gap between the minor and the great theaters, and at their request in early 1786 the government granted the Variétés-Amusantes formal dispensation from the preliminary censorship of the French and Italian actors.[75] In return for this loss of preliminary review the royal actors were permitted the right of daily entry to the Variétés-Amusantes and of grievance against plays in production. Nevertheless the artistic "demarcations" or boundaries between the dramatic art of the great theaters and that of the Variétés-Amusantes had been redrawn. The royal ruling of March 25, 1786 maintained the property rights of the Comédie-Française and Comédie-Italienne and recognized gross distinction in genre. Gaillard and Dorfeuille were forbidden to plagiarize or perform the privileged repertory and, furthermore, "the Theater of the Variétés will not be allowed to represent any tragedies or even comic plays in five or four acts."[76] But the willful discrimination practiced by the actors between a classical and a popular dramatic art had been removed. Repeated comment in the *Petites Affiches* indicated in the coming months the appearance of high-ranking personages, of verse and proper comedies on the stage of Gaillard and Dorfeuille.[77] The Variétés-Amusantes, wrote J.A. Dulaure in his *New Description of the Curiosities of Paris* for 1787, had distinguished itself in artistic matters from all other minor theaters in the city—"it has shaken the tyrannical yoke of the French actors."[78]

Though the legal and aesthetic gap between a great and a minor stage had been bridged after 1784 by the Variétés-Amusantes, Parisian theaters remained clustered in "circles" or social sets that recalled seventeenth century, classical distinctions between dramatic cultures. Dulaure's Parisian guide observed that "Paris encloses Spectacles for all tastes and for all classes of citizens . . . "[79] In the layout of theatrical announcements theaters were now clustered in three groups: the royal companies, the theaters of the Palais-Royal, and those of the boulevard. Contemporaries recognized at least three broad theatrical publics: persons of high estate, the middle bourgeoisie, and the people. Each of these three publics was supposed to frequent a separate tier in the hierarchy of theaters. The upper class was to attend the royal theaters, the middle class the Variétés-Amusantes and other small stages of the Palais-Royal and the people the little theaters of the boulevards and fairs.[80] The simple division of theatrical culture into a classical elite order, on the one hand, and a marginal, popular order on the other, it would seem, had been rendered obsolete. In fact, the formation of an integrated legal and aesthetic order, the development of an intermediate stage between the great and little theaters, had done little to dispel the traditional notion of an elite-popular gap in Parisian theatrical culture. It had merely obscured that notion. The more conservative *Journal de Paris* still separated the great theaters from the Palais-Royal as well as from the boulevard by a heavy line; in the *Petites Affiches* demarcation was made between the royal companies and the theaters of the Palais-Royal as one group and the popular halls of the boulevard as another. Compared one with the other, the *Journal de Paris* and the *Petites Affiches* reflect a muddiness of perception and lack of consensus amongst contemporaries concerning the recognition and status of Parisian theaters and theatrical traditions in the years following 1784. Despite tremendous adjustments in the economic and artistic structures of Parisian theater, the conceptual divide between a great and a popular dramatic culture had not been forgotten.

The Classical Order Undone, 1789-1791

Within seven years of the reorganization of theater in 1784-85 the format of theatrical announcements changed once more. In November of 1789 the ceremonial boundary drawn between great and little theaters, as well as those lines between one tier and another, disappeared entirely from the *Petites Affiches* and in the next two years from other journals and almanacs of theater. A change more profound than that of 1784-85 swept through the Parisian theatrical order. Indeed, the whole of French society was shaken by a tremendous political revolution. The Estates General, an archaic political body hastily convened in May 1789 to raise taxes for a bankrupt state, instead transformed itself and an absolute kingship into the National Assembly and constitutional monarchy of the French people. The members of this Assembly embarked upon a political and economic renovation of the old regime, of its privileges and antiquated institutions condemned by themselves in the Decrees of August 4th and the Declaration of the Rights of Man and Citizen of August 27th, 1789. In the wake of these proclamations of reform the *Petites Affiches* and other papers had but raised the banner of a new and revolutionary organization of Parisian theater. By 1792 even the *Spectacles of Paris and all of*

France, an almanac devoted since 1751 to the great stages of Paris, opened its covers to great and little theaters alike:

> Now, finally, all line of demarcation being effaced, we must reserve a place for all domains great and small in the theatrical republic.[81]

For many contemporaries a tremendous leveling of a once imposing hierarchy of theaters took place in the years after 1789, culminating in the reform of theatrical industry and dramatic culture by law in January 1791. Article 1 of the 13-19 January 1791 law declared all theatrical industry free and equal:

> Any citizen will be able to open a public theater... by making, prior to the establishment of his theater, a declaration to the municipality...[82]

Implicit in this decree, and indeed explicit in the accompanying discourse, was the belief that theatrical enterprise was akin to the mechanical arts and like those trades must flourish in an open and competitive market. The legal victory of this doctrine of economic laissez-faire in the January law of 1791 had been presaged by a stillborn attempt on the part of the Commune, the self-appointed government of Paris, to exploit Parisian theaters for municipal profit.[83] Deputies in the National Assembly argued successfully, however, that "a theater cannot be the object of communal monopoly... it is a kind of industry, the exercise of an individual talent... [which] cannot be alienated..."[84] The tenacity of belief in a privileged and restrained economy of theater had at last been vanquished by an enlightened liberalism.

The longstanding dissension in French political life that opposed a privileged to a propertied organization of theatrical industry, a restrained to a free market of theaters,[85] was intimately tied to questions of dramatic culture. It had long been axiomatic that the economic organization of the stage affected the quality and the form of its art. Louis XIV's grants of theatrical privileges to the Comédie-Française or the Royal Academy of Music had had for their purpose the perfection of French drama and opera.[86] In the coming century this aesthetic justification continued for a while to bolster the monopolies of the royal theaters, but by the 1780s the proposition that privilege and perfection went hand in hand was no longer accepted without debate. Grimm challenged the French actors' claim in 1785 that their artistic perfection depended upon exclusive rights.[87] Others argued more aptly that under the security of privilege the art of the royal actors had grown complacent and their talent indolent.[88] It had been in the hopes of revitalizing a stagnant stage by means of competitive emulation that men of letters and amateurs of theater in the 1770s and 1780s loudly proclaimed the necessity for a second theater of

France and supported the elevation of the Variétés-Amusantes. For those who supported the liberation of all theatrical industry in 1789-1791, it was as obvious that a thoroughly untrammelled market would produce art's greatest flowering.

Well before the outbreak of revolution and the January law of 1791, however, conservative opinion had denounced the deleterious effect of a competitive market on the quality of the stage. Examples abounded within the very midst of the privileged world of theater, it was argued, for the minor theaters of the boulevard, barely constrained in numbers, strove harshly against one another for theatrical custom:

> All these theaters are bad in principle, because they have been instituted by a multitude of greedy entrepreneurs aided by playwrights equally necessitous and hardly delicate.[89]

The need to cater to and please the public—and the "people" at that—in order to survive commercially lowered dramatic standards and popularized taste. Many feared that the economic liberation of theaters would mean the disappearance of the great dramatic tradition and the proliferation of a commercial, hence popular, stage such as that known on the boulevard.[90] Proponents of an unrestricted liberty of theatrical industry were forced to defend economic freedom with an extended refutation of these conservative apprehensions. While generations of classicists had linked the popular stage to a commercial arena, men such as the antiquarian and littérateur Millin de Grandmaison argued that the privileged order itself had created and determined the popular tradition by the arbitrary censorship of the minor stage. Millin did not deny the coarse nature of the popular dramatic tradition developed under the old regime, but he believed that, granted full artistic as well as an economic liberty, the minor stages would spontaneously shed all trace of moral license and aesthetic degeneration and rise to the standards of great art.

It can be no surprise, then, that in the act of destroying the traditional economic order of theater in January 1791 the National Assembly undermined as well traditional restraints upon the performance of genre and the production of plays. The censorship of the minor theaters by the royal actors had been quietly discontinued in the course of 1789[91] and the popular stage, at least, was no longer held to repressive bounds. In 1791 this new-found freedom was generalized by law. Article 1 of the January law stipulated not only a freedom of industry but a freedom of artistic exploitation: "Any citizen will be able to open a public theater and to have performed there plays in all genres..."[92] Theatrical companies could no longer claim exclusive rights to any genre, nor were they themselves to be excluded from the performance of any and all dramatic forms. Moreover, by virtue of articles 2 and 3 of the January law, ownership of dramatic pieces was transferred from the performing theater to the playwright, and five years after his death to the public domain. This meant, in effect, that the classical repertory, long harbored by the great theaters of Paris, was "a public property and can, notwithstanding all old privileges which are abolished, be represented on all theaters indiscriminately."[93] The dramatic hierarchy of theaters traditionally typed by genre was undone—neither the major genres nor the classical repertories were subject to monopoly by one or several great stages. By this legal act the National Assembly eradicated the institutional mechanisms with which dramatic arts had been organized under the old regime.

Like the notion of an open marketplace of theaters, the prospect of a breakdown in theater-types stimulated controversy in the years 1789-91. More than just a custom of the past, the institutional control of genres had been used to manipulate the form and extent of dramatic cultures. The Commune's consideration of theatrical organization had unleashed dozens of proposals, including their own, that specified for similar reasons the number of theaters and genres that ought to be allowed in the new order.[94] Very few contemporaries seem to have been consciously aware, however, that their debate over theater-types masked more profound, yet vaguely articulated, concerns of a sociological nature. The more conservative defenders of a hierarchy of theater-types recognized that the breakdown of this order severely threatened the social and cultural segmentation of French society. In classical theory each dramatic genre expressed the tastes and values of a single social group. The freedom to mix genres on any and all stages indiscriminately, conservatives argued, necessarily implied the confounding of social estates within one broad public. In *Letter to a Family Man on the Little Spectacles of Paris,* one of the most outspoken of conservative tracts, the boulevard theaters once again were used to illustrate the moral and cultural decadence attendant upon the breakdown of rank and distance between social groups:

> The well-to-do crowd has learned the way to the covered Meadow at the Abbey [the Saint Germain Fair], to the Saint Laurent neighborhood and to the rue de Richelieu [the Palais-Royal]. At first, it kept incognito [but] little by little the very license of these amusements accustomed the well-to-do to place itself above the constraint of propriety, the last safeguard of good manners. All the Estates mixed together have been more bold in braving the shame of it.[95]

Those men of letters and Commune commissioners who had wished in early 1790 to temper the privileged monopoly of the Comédie-Française with a limited competition had also argued to maintain theaters typed by dramatic genre and by socially-discrete publics. In a world without socio-cultural restraint both they and more intransigent conservatives feared that the lowest denominator of theatrical art would not fail to infect all theaters and all classes of society commonly—and "... a nation where everything becomes plebian is to be pitied."[96]

Such proclamations of socio-cultural decadence on the part of conservatives and moderates alike seem to have been pointedly ignored by those liberals inspired by the principles of 1789. For men such as Millin, the abolition of artistic privilege guaranteed equal access to the great theatrical culture for all Frenchmen, since in a market free from despotic fetters all theaters were expected to fulfill naturally the enlightened goals of public instruction. Rather than founder on popular ignorance and immorality, the new society would upgrade all its ranks through the power of education to fashion man and citizen anew. Millin ignored the question of socio-cultural decadence because in his optimism he did not believe it possible. For Millin the popular dramatic idiom had been a repressive byproduct of the despotic regime. It could have no lifeblood under the reign of liberty.

Not all liberals shared Millin's belief that the popular stage would spontaneously disappear. Some, indeed, welcomed a civil parity of the old dramatic arts in the new state. But they did not necessarily mean by this generosity to confound one with the other in the natural order of things. The Declaration of the Rights of Man and Citizen, from which the liberals had drawn sustenance, had purposefully distinguished between the civil equality of men before the law and the natural, useful inequalities of men in society. Those who framed this document and those who honored it were in no sense social or cultural "levelers."[97] In its vigorous condemnation of the privileged and restricted organization of theater under the old regime, the anonymous *Figaro to Parisians... Amateurs of Theater and of Liberty* (1790) had proposed in its place the liberation of theaters. Significantly enough, however, neither social rank nor cultural order would be threatened in the new regime, since each theater would devote itself naturally in the open market to the tastes and traditions of a single class:

> Each class of citizen must find in the marketplace its own genre of amusement; rather than diminish [theaters in number] they must be increased, so that they may be varied in their tastes, their practices and their financial capacities.[98]

"Figaro's" liberal organization of free and equal dramatic arts resembled closely traditional hierarchies of theater-types and publics.

The January law, however, did not honor the socio-cultural reservations implicitly subsumed within the liberal argument. Ideology required that in language and in perception "the old routine" be broken. Now, according to the *General Almanac for all the Theaters of Paris* (1791), talent and zeal in the arts and not arbitrary privilege should determine the quality and prestige of Parisian theaters:

> [now] that all theaters are subject to the immediate inspection of the municipality, they are all equal in the social order...[99]

The foundations of Parisian theater established by Louis XIV over one hundred years before were severely undermined: gone were the restraints of industry, the inequalities of license and the monopolies of trade; gone the privileged hoarding of certain genres and of a classical repertory; and gone, too, the institutional mechanisms of a cultural segmentation between the great and the popular stage at the heart of French theater. In theory at least, a formal and imposing organization of theatrical culture had been brought to the ground and trampled underfoot.

2

The Pragmatic Place of the Boulevard in Parisian Theater

The Popular Pose of Little Theaters on the Boulevard, 1760-1769

We turn from the economic, cultural and social organization of the eighteenth century Parisian world of theater to consider the pragmatic behavior of men and institutions within that same world. There existed a lived relationship between the little and the great stage, as well as formal one; a relationship to be found in the activities and decisions of boulevard entrepreneurs, government officials, hospital administrators, royal actors and the men and women of the theatrical public. The interactions of these persons determined a practical set of cultural boundaries between the boulevard theaters and the great stage, boundaries neither so hard nor fast as the decorous lines drawn between great and little theatrical cultures.

The reasons for these less distinct boundaries lay in the nature of interaction between the boulevard theaters and the privileged powers of eighteenth century French society.[1] The conflicting interests of government officials, hospital administrators and royal actors, all of whom possessed title to coercive authority, mediated the fundamental hostility of a privileged and classical order towards the popular stage. Entrepreneurs and directors on the boulevard took skillful advantage of the uneven and changeable balance of powerful interests to improvise the institutions and forms of a popular dramatic tradition. In the thirty years after 1759 the complex process of give and take between the little theaters and coercive institutions slowly broke down the barriers that had separated the marginal economic and cultural activity along the boulevard from the privileged theatrical world of Paris.

According to one well-known guidebook of Paris from the 1780s, the boulevards that encircled the city had received their name from a game of bowls played there on the grass in the early eighteenth century.[2] After 1760 the boulevard du Temple on the northeastern outskirts of Paris on the right bank of the Seine became the scene of many more pasttimes, a "perpetual fair."[3] Minor amusements confined to the seasonal grounds of the Saint Germain or the Saint Ovide Fairs in the first half of the century now settled with impunity on the boulevard in between fair seasons. By the 1770s and '80s cafés, taverns, and restaurants had followed suit, as had, indeed, "all those pleasures that wit can produce to divert the idle and refresh the busy..."[4] One admiring contemporary among dozens of others found much to marvel at on the boulevard du Temple:

> An infinite crowd of people, an amazing quantity of carriages, street merchants darting in and out amongst... the horses with all sorts of merchandise, chairs set upon the sidewalks for those who want to watch—and for those who want to be watched—, cafés fitted up with an orchestra and French and Italian singers, pastry-cooks, restaurant-keepers,... marionettes, acrobats,... giants, dwarfs, ferocious beasts, sea monsters, wax figures, automatons, ventriloquists, [and] the surprising and enjoyable sideshow of the wise physicist and mathematician Comus.[5]

Like the fairs of the early eighteenth century, the late-blooming boulevard fell heir to the minor dramatic forms and popular idiom banished from the stages of the royal companies and elite recognition. A certain gaiety, or carnival spirit, characterized the theater halls, the mountebanks, animal trainers and itinerant street performers that crowded the avenue: "one can laugh, play and relax there day and night..."[6] Yet the boulevard had not sprung full grown from the grass-lined borders of Paris, nor was it a simple outgrowth of the longstanding Parisian fairs. "Our fathers saw it start from nothing," wrote one near contemporary in 1838; they saw it grow and prosper as well.[7]

It is uncertain at what date the boulevards in general, and the boulevard du Temple in particular, began to attract minor games and shows in the interim periods of the Parisian fairs. Police records indicate that at least a few fair spectacles stationed themselves intermittently on the boulevard throughout the 1750s.[8] A certain François-Paul Nicolet, puppeteer and mime, held a spectacle at the fairs and on the boulevard in 1757. Nicolas Bienfait II and Pierre-Toussaint Martin probably opened their marionette show on the rue Saintonge near the boulevard sometime after 1751. A sieur Gaudon directed a spectacle of tight-rope dancers on the boulevard as well as in the Saint Ovide Fair in 1761, if not before. Many more pedlars of artifice and distraction, now unknown, no doubt joined these few small stages in these years.[9] It was, however, yet another entrepreneur and another minor spectacle whose presence proved most responsible for the subsequent development of the theatrical district along the boulevard.

In 1759 Jean-Baptiste Nicolet, elder brother of the puppeteer François-Paul, moved to the boulevard a small theater of real actors that had already gained success at the Saint Germain Fair. As legend had it, Jean-Baptiste Nicolet alone paved over the mud and lighted the dark nights of a still barren and undeveloped boulevard.[10] By the same token it was believed that the appearance of his small stage on the boulevard marked the beginnings of a "revolution" in the theatrical order of Paris.[11] The Théâtre de Nicolet rather than any of the other small spectacles grouped on the boulevard in the early 1760s was singled out by contemporaries in later years largely because of their hindsight of twenty years or more. Nicolet directed the most prosperous theater on the boulevard for some thirty years without interruption, whereas Gaudon, Bienfait, Nicolet frère and their small stages retreated to the fairs or dropped from sight within a decade's time.[12] Nicolet, Gaudon and others had all challenged anew the monopolies of theatrical art and industry held by the Comédie-Française and the Comédie-Italienne; unlike some of his predecessors of the early eighteenth century, or even his original fellows on the boulevard, Nicolet met with unexpected success.

Jean-Baptiste Nicolet had been born in 1728 to a family of petty entertainers.[13] His parents directed a successful theater of marionettes at the Saint Laurent and Saint Germain Fairs, which they ceded, probably in the early 1760s, to their younger son François-Paul. Well before this retirement, in 1753 or earlier, the elder Jean-Baptiste had opened his own puppet booth at the Saint Germain Fair.[14] But he did not confine himself long to the trade learned from his father. Within several years Nicolet had acquired actors, himself included, a repertory of plays and parades, and a growing ambition. His early success at the fair must have encouraged him to try his luck the year round, for in 1759 he located his show in an empty hall on the boulevard while the fairs were not in session. Once on the boulevard the Théâtre de Nicolet continued to expand. Sometime before 1762 Nicolet picked up a license for tight-rope dancing and acrobatics.[15] Within these same years he added musicians and dancers as well to his growing troop. The fledgling company performed the *commedia dell'arte* of old Italian theater and the discarded comic operas of the Opéra-Comique, in addition to pantomimes, parades, comedies and farces written at Nicolet's behest.[16]

The French actors were not pleased. For the first half of the eighteenth century the privileged companies of Paris had triumphantly withheld from the spectacles of the fair the use of speech and regular art forms. The only exception to this suppressive policy had been the Théâtre de la Foire, or Opéra-Comique, whose contract with the Opéra for the song and dance necessary to comic operas had sheltered it from prosecution by either the Comédie-Française or the Comédie-Italienne. It was no doubt with surprise, then, that the French actors heard the Parisian minister's response to their initial protest against the use of speech on the minor stages of the boulevard—"There must be amusements for the people," he said, "Louis XIV's system is to be changed..."[17] Saint-Florentin's words signaled a momentous shift in the balance of powerful interest between the police and the privileged companies of Paris. The ease with which the royal theaters had quashed minor competitors in the years after 1680 now met new and powerful resistance.

Plate 4. The boulevard, with a view of the Théâtre de Nicolet, as it appeared in the 1760s. Photo: Bibl. nat. Paris.

The reforming hand of Choiseul's ministry had begun to shake Colbert's corporate order in the spheres of commerce and manufacture.[18] In the case of theater, such economic liberalism suited well the new-found concerns of the government and the police for the public tranquility of Paris. The laboring classes, having grown tremendously throughout the century, now numbered more than half of the Parisian population as a whole.[19] Urban misery and popular revolt, such as that which had menaced both Paris and Versailles in 1750, were harsh realities.[20] Rather than practice the brutal roundups and repressions of a former police, however, the new government sought to appease the rude tempers of the popular classes, to feed them amusement as well as bread. Ranking officials of the ministry and the police cautiously extended their protection of popular spectacles beyond the traditional confines of the fair and licensed additional theatrical enterprise along the boulevard du Temple.

By the early 1760s the privileged companies of Paris had readied themselves to attack the theatrical ventures of Nicolet, as well as Gaudon "and others." The union of the Opéra-Comique with the Comédie-Italienne in 1762 stripped these other, petty spectacles of the fair and boulevard of a regularized or acceptable existence. In June of that year, then, the Italian actors requested that the lieutenant-general of police, Sartines, prohibit the use of song or speech on the minor stages of Nicolet and his fellows:

> You have always given [the Italian actors] such tokens of goodwill that they hope to obtain directly from you, Monsieur, the justice that is their due, such that, given the right that belongs to them alone to perform comic operas and new plays intermixed with song, you will want to use your authority to forbid the said Gaudon, Nicolet and others to have spoken or sung on their stages any play whatsoever, and will oblige them to restrain themselves to pantomime, the only thing it should be permitted them to perform.[21]

Papillon de la Ferté, Intendent of Petty Amusements and for that reason minister in charge of the royal actors, also went to plead their case before Sartines. He found that "all I could understand from his response was that he very much protects the spectacles of the boulevard."[22] Indeed, Sartines turned a deaf ear both to the Intendent and to the Italian actors.

By early 1764, however, the combined petition of the French and Italian actors and their support by the Maréchal de Richelieu, Gentleman of the Bedchamber, could no longer be ignored by the lieutenant-general of police.[23] Sartines forbade the use of speech by the minor theaters of Paris, probably sometime after the close of the Saint Germain Fair in April. The bulk of their dramatic activities rudely suppressed, Nicolet, Gaudon and others were permitted to perform only pantomimes and tight-rope dancing acts.[24] Still, the French actors were no longer as successful in the proscription of dramatic forms from the minor theaters as they had been in the early 1700s, for within the same year, 1764, Nicolet, at least, had been allowed to restore comic scenes and farces to his boulevard stage.[25] This vacillating repression of the boulevard stage, in 1764 and indeed for the next several years, reflected a conflict of interest within the royal government, a power struggle of sorts between the forces of the old order and the forces of reform. The balance of powerful interest had begun to shift demonstrably away from privileged dramatic industry in favor of a social dispersion of theater. Public and private voices of opinion articulated a new support for the minor stage and a compromise of the privileged theatrical order. All eyes were focused on the fate of one boulevard theater amongst all others—the Théâtre de Nicolet.

In April of 1764, in anticipation of the royal actors' move against the minor spectacles on the boulevard, a manuscript memoir probably originating within the offices of the police had presented a considered argument for the minor theaters on the grounds of civic order and tranquility.[26] A growing population amongst the lower classes could not be deprived of the "sorry farces of the fair" to which they were accustomed, it was argued within *Minor Spectacles,* without serious repercussion within the social body: "[The people], above all in France, also want some fun... gay spirit that does not lead to brutal pleasure is one of the police's most useful buffers."[27] The government's reckoning with the lower classes of Paris would have to be at the expense of the industrial monopolies of theater. It was not, however, to be at the expense of cultural privilege, understood as the domination of high art. The "so-called comedies" of the popular stage did not rival the classical theater, the memoir suggested, but ensured its continued prestige. The ascendant position of the royal theaters over the popular spectacles lay not in distinctions in kind of dramatic activity but in distinctions in kind of public. The minor spectacles that did draw crowds were supposed to hold little attraction for the habitual audience of the royal theaters. Similarly, those who went to Nicolet's for four or eight sous[28] had no taste for the *Misanthrope* or *Britannicus,* performed by the great stages:

> If one closes the door to Nicolet's [by suppressing speech on the minor stage, the people] would without hesitation prefer that of the tavern to that of the Comédie-Française, where everything would be too refined for their taste and too expensive for their pocketbooks.[29]

If the boulevard theater was bereft of its farces, it would lose its popular appeal. The lower-class worker had no taste for pantomime and would quit the boulevard. The silent stage, however, did hold attraction for more sophisticated clientele: "that really would be capable of attracting a better public."[30] The proscription of farces and comedies from the minor theaters of Paris, it was concluded, would suppress the necessary amusement of the people, and fragment that of the upper classes.

Protest against the suppression of speech on the boulevard and in the fairs rose from yet another quarter, in the form of a tongue-in-cheek "petition" by a "very humble and very obedient servant Nicolet."[31] It is likely that the *Petition to the Ladies,* so called because women seated in the loges were addressed as arbiters of dramatic taste and propriety, represented one of the first of protests by men of letters against the property rights and artistic monopoly of the Comédie-Française.[32] The *Petition to the Ladies* also addressed issues pertinent to the position of a minor stage within the theatrical order of Paris. The fictitious Nicolet of this illegal brochure disregarded the distinctions in publics so carefully drawn by the author of the memoirs *Minor Spectacles,* in order to champion a more egalitarian truth. His troupe was "made for the amusement of the great and the little, the clerk and the officer, the lawyer's wife and the Counsellor's, in a word, the whole city . . . without distinctions of rank or office."[33]

According to the *Petition* the true purpose of the minor stage, however, was not the amusement of a general public but the schooling of the rough-mannered lower classes. The suppression of speech and hence of the minor forms of comedy crippled the essential "service" of the popular theater:

> The people, who are in my opinion the most substantial part of the State, have been deprived of the only means they have to learn their native tongue, to cure themselves of their vices, to purify their morals in attending to me, to draw from the force and eloquence of my actors the examples of virtue that I know how to invest in each play, each act, each scene.[34]

There can be no doubt that these words were meant, in part, to ridicule the theatrical pretensions of Nicolet as well as to criticize the elite monopoly of the Comédie-Française. The *Petition to the Ladies* left none unscathed.[35] Yet these words were also, in part, intended to embrace the minor stage within certain novel conceptions of theater as a school of virtue,[36] capable, even in its most popular forms, of sensitizing and educating the public.

As an expression of public opinion the defense of the minor theaters was of considerable influence, whether in a memoir circulating amongst government officials or in a pamphlet circulating under clandestine covers. Malesherbes, director of the book trade in the 1750s and later a secretary of state, apparently argued before the Académie-Française that the public voice in general had become an independent tribunal, a "power" to be reckoned amongst the vested interests and sanctions of society.[37] Indeed, some comment by Grimm on the affair of 1764 indicates that the general sympathies of an enlightened and fashionable public lay with the minor theaters:

> I am quite put out that some clever wit has not laid hold of Mister Nicolet's cause; he could have made out of it an excellent jest of exclusive privileges.[38]

Yet this same tribunal judged the *Petition of the Ladies* to be too radical an attack upon the theatrical establishment of Paris. The pamphlet's rejection of a social gulf between the great and little theaters, as well as more specific attacks upon the privileged monopoly, were doubtless too bold for "the Public [which] itself seems to favor more the royal actor."[39] Grimm scornfully dismissed the *Petition,* which he believed had been written by Nicolet. It seems unlikely, however, that the boulevard director should have jeopardized his enterprise even further by antagonizing the royal actors with such a protest. In fact, unknown to Grimm, Nicolet had denounced the *Petition to the Ladies* before a commissioner of police a full month before Grimm gave it notice.[40]

Nicolet did assume a position in the public arena, but his voice more nearly echoed the conservative appeal of the police. In July of 1764, several months after the *Minor Spetacles* had been penned and weeks before the appearance of the *Petition to the Ladies,* the boulevard entrepreneur addressed a personal petition to the French actors in assembly. In every line the *Humble Memoir of Mister Nicolet*[41] emphasized the economic, social and cultural distance that must obtain between the royal, privileged stage and an obscure, popular amusement:

> Messieurs, the nature of your privileges and the extent of your rights subordinate to you all who carry a resemblance to actors outside His Majesty's theater, you will not then find it ill that Nicolet comes to ask of you protection and favor.... Committed by trade to the populace, trained in its tastes and seeking only its satisfaction, he has offered it alone those performances which the critic's eye has always scorned to note...[42]

The cobblers, carpenters, menders and soldiers, who had populated the Théâtre de Nicolet before the suppression of comedies and farces, the boulevard director artfully suggested, had in effect confined his stage to a plebian audience; and this in turn prohibited any real competition with the royal theaters. But the recent suppression of his habitual repertory had raised the quality of his stage and, perforce, his audience:

> I submitted to your wishes; I produced quite expensive pantomimes. I took on jumpers and other acrobatic exercises. A Respectable public came all the more willingly to my stage; but the plebian and servant class just about abandoned me. My theater has become more decent but I feel each day how impossible it is for me to live with high society.[43]

Nicolet's discomfort, if it was more than a rhetorical pose, certainly had to do with reasons other than he would allow in his *Humble Memoir.* He had yet to win broad protection for his small enterprise or the royal actors' consent to his theatrical industry. Like the *Minor Spectacles,* the *Humble Memoir* clothed the boulevard's compromise of the theatrical order in conservative dress. Such were the claims that Nicolet's boulevard stage infringed upon neither the industrial nor the artistic monopoly of the Comédie-Française, that social participation utterly removed this minor spectacle, intended for the people, from the realm of privileged art and theater. Nicolet had posed his stage as a popular amusement for the popular classes, nothing more and nothing less.

No doubt it was Sartines who in September of 1764 allowed Nicolet to perform once more "small detached scenes, without intricacies, without intrigue, without denouement..,"[44] convinced as he must have been that the compromise of privilege had been publicly accepted as a political and social necessity. The royal actors and their protector, the Maréchal de Richelieu, did not agree. Obviously, they dismissed the policies of the police as they had dismissed the *Humble Memoir* of Nicolet—"the Comédie can grant nothing!"[45] In the next four years there followed a farcical round of repression and permission of theatrical activity on the boulevard, as Sartines now resisted, now succumbed to the political influence of the Maréchal. As Grimm would later complain, the actors of Nicolet's stage "sometimes... could not speak, sometimes they could not sing."[46] In August 1766 Sartines again acceded to the pressures of the Maréchal by informing him that "he had forbidden Mister Nicolet, under pain of punishment, to offer upon his stage any play, either in the French or Italian manner."[47] Yet clearly the police did little or nothing to enforce the prohibition of spoken plays on the boulevard. By the following year Nicolet had quietly returned to his old ways. It was not until 1767 that a third party stepped into this struggle between the royal actors and the police. Saint Florentin, that same minister who had initially protected the right to speech on the boulevard, now warned Sartines that the artistic privileges of the royal companies must be respected:

> The King's intention is that the actors' privileges be conserved in their entirety and that Nicolet, Audinot[48] and others be allowed to offer in their huts only Tight-Rope dancing, Pantomimes, Marionettes and the short Sketches that they perform outside their Amusement Halls.[49]

Still the police refrained from repressive action. In January 1768 Nicolet presented *The Kiss Given and the Kiss Returned,* a two-act comic opera that enjoyed a tremendous run of many months. It was, Bachaumont observed, worthy of the royal actors' jealousy, for "it has action, intrigue and above all, high spirits."[50] This and other unprecedented successes on the boulevard that year forced the hands of the police. An ordinance dated 14 April 1768 sharply curtailed the dramatic activity of the fair theaters:

> ...despite the constant attention we have brought to bear in order that Jumpers and Mountebanks be constrained within the limits prescribed to them, it has been seen that for some years now they have overstepped those limits and have encroached upon the regulated Theaters of this city...
>
> We, acting upon the indictment of the King's Procurator, forbid to all Jumpers, Mountebanks and Tight-Rope Dancers, etc. to represent on their theaters, either at the

> Saint-Germain, Saint-Laurent or Saint-Ovide Fairs, on the Boulevards, or in any other place that might be, any Plays belonging to the Italian and French Actors . . . or even any scenes taken from the said Plays; forbid them likewise to perform in their theaters any other Plays but buffooneries or parades, and those only after having received our express permission . . .[51]

Not until late 1768 or early 1769, however, were this and other repressive measures belatedly enforced. The ordinance of police had forbidden the performance of comedies on the minor stages but not the performance of comic operas such as *The Kiss Given*. It was for this reason that, in December of 1768, the Maréchal de Richelieu brought pressure to bear upon the Opéra to close down the Théâtre de Nicolet.[52] The Opéra did not act to suppress the Théâtre de Nicolet, but it did withdraw permission to use song from the minor stage.[53] So too, at least temporarily, did the police or government ministry withdraw Nicolet's permission to use speech.[54] Then in February 1769 the Comédie-Française and Comédie-Italienne were granted a censorship of the fair theaters, in which they were enjoined "to let no play pass that might resemble a comedy . . ."[55] The minor stage, it was evident, might speak once more, but would no longer do so without a preliminary review and mutilation of all dramatic material by the royal actors. By these measures the government secured dramatic activity on the fair stage without serious challenge to the artistic prerogatives of the great theaters.

For all intents and purposes the privileged theaters had been forced to accept an economic compromise—of sorts—of the classical order. Contrary to the ordinance of 1680 concentrating theatrical industry on the stage of the Comédie-Française, there were now several more theaters producing a competitive drama akin to comedy. From the first, of course, these theaters had been tolerated "in order to procure the people relaxation from their labors."[56] The ordinance of 1768 had carefully implied that this popular amusement was to be restricted to social groups beyond the habitual public of the royal companies. It was the belief of government officials that this might be accomplished, in part, by restraints upon the economic growth and development of the fair theaters. Thus in 1767 Saint Florentin had ruled that no fair spectacle might have more than six violins or ten dancers.[57] The ordinance of 1768 simply stipulated that the cost of seats at the minor theaters be reduced from prices competitive with those of the royal stages. Nicolet's first seats had originally cost six livres, comparable to the more expensive places of the Comédie-Française; now they fell to half that amount, it being forbidden the fair theaters "to charge more than three livres for the First Places, 24 sous for the Second, and 12 sous for the Last . . ."[58]

This preliminary reduction in prices, however, proved inadequate to the social constraint of the minor theatrical industry. Papillon de la Ferté remarked in January 1769 that a more drastic cut in prices had been necessary:

> Monsieur le comte de Saint-Florentin, upon the urgent solicitations of Monsieur le Maréchal [de Richelieu], just ended the matter of the fair spectacles by reducing the seats to 24 sous, 12 sous and six sous for the last seats. It is hoped by this expedient to chase out the well-to-do public.[59]

Yet even these prices, now significantly lower than the cheapest seats at the Comédie-Française, did not restrict the boulevard spectators to the lower classes. Fashionable partisans of the boulevard amusements such as Grimm sneered at the assumption that lower prices might distill the social elite from a common public:

> They flatter themselves that, by confounding in this way persons of high society with the populace, the well-to-do will leave [the boulevard] and will be compelled, willy-nilly, to bore themselves at the Comédie-Française and the Opéra.[60]

But the restraint of the fair theaters had another very real effect. If the royal actors were concerned that the boulevard stage did not strain the popular understanding, the government had also made certain it did not strain their pockets. The people would not starve for gaiety, for a theatrical culture of their own.

Powerful Protection and Boulevard Aspirations, 1769-1789

By 1769, seven years after the Opéra-Comique had been absorbed within great theater, royal companies and governmental bureaus finally agreed—or so it would seem—on a severe restraint of the small theaters that remained on the fairgrounds and the boulevard du Temple. These petty enterprises were to be economically constrained to a small number of performers, artistically constrained to non-classical genres, socially constrained to the lower classes. Yet, despite the formal gap that such policy imposed between these spectacles and the companies of the king, numerous points of contact and exchange between the little and great theaters appeared in the decades that followed 1769.

That this was so was due primarily to the tremendous growth of popular amusements and the boulevard economy—a growth that soon violated the spirit of the law and eventually impinged upon the cultural order of privileged theater. This growth on the boulevard had several measures. Though the small stages held by Gaudon, Bienfait and others had quietly failed in the stormy decade of the 1760s, as many others joined the tenacious Théâtre de Nicolet in the ten years after 1769. Nicolas-Médard Audinot, a former fair actor and playwright, moved his fairground marionettes next door to Nicolet in 1769 and soon replaced them with a troupe of young children. The buffoon Nicolas Vienne and his partner Louis-Gabrielle Sallé, a practiced Arlequin, established the Théâtre des Associés in 1774. Fleury de l'Ecluze, fair actor-dentist-author versed in the *genre poissard* or billingsgate, opened the Variétés-Amusantes in 1778 at the Saint Laurent Fair and moved quickly to permanent quarters on the boulevard. A former Opéra dancer, Abraham, and the provincial actor Tessier founded the Spectacle des Elèves pour la danse de l'Opéra in 1779.

At the same time that theaters and competition increased along the boulevard, the wealth and success of a few fortunate directors grew by leaps and bounds. Chief among these was Nicolet, to whom ten years of relative isolation and a demanding market had given a tremendous advantage. In 1769 Bachaumont estimated Nicolet's assets for the last several years to have reached 100,000 écus or 300,000 livres; by the late 1770s his fortune was believed to rival that of a "financier of second rank." Mercier estimated the director's yearly income in 1783 at 50,000 livres.[61]

Growing economic productivity on the boulevard had yet another gauge. After 1769 the minor theaters along that avenue sustained with little ill-effect a large amount of taxation and economic control, much of which is documented in the registers of the Hôtel-Dieu, the second largest hospital in Paris.[62] Sometime in 1773 the lieutenant-general of police ordered that the poor tax, levied by the General Hospital on the privileged stages of Paris since 1699, would fall on the boulevard theaters as well.[63] By right, Parisian hospitals were entitled to a quarter of the gross receipts at theater doors. In practice, the royal companies negotiated much less burdensome levies. The French actors, for instance, did not pay the hospitals more than 12 percent of their annual receipts.[64]

Unfortunately, there is no way to verify the actual percentage any one boulevard theater was forced to relinquish in the 1770s. Records for the Grands-Danseurs du Roi, as the Théâtre de Nicolet was called in later years, indicate that in the 1780s Nicolet paid anywhere from 21 to 24 percent of his gross income.[65] Recurrent squabbles between the minor theaters and the hospitals do suggest, however, that beginning in the early 1770s, the boulevard spectacles tried to resist the full imposition of the quarter tax. When in 1776 hospital clerks attempted to collect a quarter of the proceeds on performances at the Saint Ovide Fair as well as on the boulevard, Nicolet, Audinot and their peers raised a hue and cry before the lieutenant-general of police:

> Absolute authority ordered in 1773 and 1774 that the Quarter Tax for the Poor be levied on the Boulevard; it was said then that it would not be levied at the Saint Ovide Fair.... Your Lordship knows that these taxes can, in one month's time, destroy the Spectacles ...[66]

Protests of economic hardship notwithstanding, the hospitals extended the tax of boulevard theaters to the fairground sessions. The hospitals proved more lenient, however, with later requests by boulevard entrepreneurs for temporary respite from the poor tax. The register of the Hôtel-Dieu is in fact riddled with notations that specify the nominal payments agreed to with Audinot, Nicolet

Plate 5. View of the Ambigu-Comique, one of the many small theaters which joined the Théâtre de Nicolet along the boulevard in the decade after 1769. Photo: Bibl. nat. Paris.

and others in lieu of a percentage of their receipts for several weeks or several months at a time. Initially at the prodding of Lenoir, lieutenant-general of police, the hospitals were in fact acting to indemnify the minor theaters in some measure for the economic expansion forced upon them by the police of Paris.

Since the mid-1770s Lenoir had been bent on stimulating the flagging or defunct economies of the Parisian fairs. The theater halls of Nicolet and Audinot at the Saint Germain Fair attracted much custom and Lenoir encouraged the entrepreneurs to establish themselves at the Saint Ovide Fair as well. It was he who negotiated with the hospitals a dispensation of 4,000 livres for Audinot from the quarter tax levied at that fair in 1776, on the grounds that Audinot had been inadequately compensated for his great expense in the construction and decoration of a new hall. This first experiment in theatrical expansion came to an abrupt end the following year, however, when the Saint Ovide Fair was completely destroyed by fire. Undiscouraged, Lenoir determined by 1779-1780 that all the minor spectacles of the boulevard would be required to attend the Saint Laurent Fair, reopened for a two-month session each August and September. Nicolet, Audinot and Malter, the new director of the Variétés-Amusantes, were expected to build yet another set of theater halls, since none had previously frequented the Saint Laurent fairgrounds, run down after 1750. Lenoir requested in their behalf that the hospitals exempt these entrepreneurs from the quarter tax for the next three or four years. The hospitals had been asked, in effect, to finance the growth of the minor theatrical industry. Overlooking numerous objections to the curtailment of their own privilege, hospital administrators yielded—at least in part—to the suasions of the police. They agreed for the fair season of 1779 only that the minor theaters relocating to the fairground would be levied a modest sum of 300 to 400 livres.

In due time the commercial concerns of Lenoir became the hospitals' own. In order to evaluate the claims for recompense of the little theaters hospital administrators painstakingly reconstructed the costs incurred by the boulevard entrepreneurs. When Audinot and Malter complained in 1780 that they had not yet recouped their losses at the Saint Laurent Fair, administrators determined that the extraordinary expenses of erecting new halls had in fact not yet been covered. The two directors were consequently granted total relief from the poor tax for fifteen days. The administrators dealt leniently with Nicolet as well, although his stubborn refusal to build a hall at the Saint Laurent Fair in the summer of 1779 had cost them aggravation and income.

Lenoir had forbidden the obstinate director day performances on the boulevard during the Saint Laurent Fair, since these gave him an unfair advantage over those entrepreneurs who obeyed the lieutenant-general's request to appear at the fair. Nicolet opened his boulevard hall at night, however, even though night performances along that avenue had only been authorized by Lenoir as compensation for the construction of fairground halls. Not to be shortchanged, the hospitals levied the poor tax on Nicolet's nightly boulevard performances. By the following year, these various and sundry pressures had convinced Nicolet to build the required hall at the Saint Laurent Fair for the 1780 season. In the form of investment compensation, the hospitals remitted to Nicolet in 1780 the tax they had levied on his night performances in August and September of 1779. The director was to ask no further indemnity for his construction costs. But when Nicolet complained in August 1780 that the haste with which he contracted for land and building materials had raised his expenses to 90,000 livres, almost twice the amount incurred by Audinot or Malter, the hospitals quietly disregarded their own ultimatum. In lieu of a percentage tax Nicolet was allowed a nominal subscription of 300 livres, and in the following year he wheedled some fifteen days additional reprieve from the burdensome levy.[67]

The hospitals' leniency in these matters cannot be hard to understand. Since the fiscal year April 1777-April 1778, taxes from the little theaters on the boulevard alone had already surpassed the individual payments of the three privileged companies of Paris. In the fiscal year ending in April 1780 the combined income from the fairs and the boulevard netted the Hôtel-Dieu approximately 56,773 livres, or 89 percent of the total deposits of all three privileged theaters.[68] Given the yield of this proportional levy, it is clear that the hospitals' interests lay not simply in the maintenance but in the continued and growing prosperity of the minor theaters. The clement treatment of Audinot, Malter and Nicolet, all forced to locate to the Saint Laurent Fair in the years 1778-1780, quickly paid off. By April 1781 the additional levy at that fair helped increase the tax contribution of the little theaters to a full match with the combined payments of the three great stages of Paris.

Crippling as it may have been to the gross profits of the minor theaters, the poor tax in fact helped stabilize the boulevard economy. Lenoir's concern for an economic growth that did not compromise healthy competition relied heavily on the hospitals' willingness to underwrite the expansion of the minor theatrical industry by reducing its tax. Strong incentives for the commercial prosperity of the minor theaters along the boulevard and in the fairs in turn heightened the hospitals' sensitivity to the wages of petty competition and to the dividends of entrepreneurial investment. Despite the despotic powers of the police and the hospitals, boulevard theaters such as the Grands-Danseurs, the Ambigu-Comique and the Variétés-Amusantes expanded their range of business and increased their revenues in a regulated environment protective of their enterprise.

The pretensions of the boulevard theaters grew in tandem with their expansion and their economic success. Within a decade Nicolet, Audinot and other entrepreneurs who joined them on the boulevard had violated the social and artistic confines set for the popular stage in the late 1760s. Contemporaries were apt to believe that the minor stage had improved in quality since the days of Nicolet's solitary tenure on the boulevard and they attributed its enhanced appeal to the effects of competition.[69] Close-pitched rivalry amongst three and four theaters after 1769 honed the commercial skills of the boulevard entrepreneurs. At the larger theaters such as the Grands-Danseurs, the Ambigu-Comique and the Variétés-Amusantes the fare announced on theater bills was altered daily. A single performance at Nicolet's theater, for instance, offered a spectacular mix of farce, comedy, pantomime and tight-rope dancing, such as that advertised in a handbill of 1779:

> The troupe of the Great-Dancers of the King will present today, Thursday the 4th of February 1779, different excercises by the Jumpers, the Masked Ball, and a ballet called the One-Eyed, Cripple Lover, followed by the Rose and the Button, spectacular pantomime mixed with dialogue and concluded with a dance by "Little Devil."[70]

Year round imitation between one theater and another forced the best of boulevard entrepreneurs to be innovative in their repertory, to improve and extend their companies of actors and artists, and to enhance the design and extravagance of their costumes and props. Almost from its inception the Ambigu-Comique had become a spectacle "à la mode."[71] When Nicolet's public flagged in favor of that stage around 1775, he countered by importing Catalan rope-dancers from Spain.[72] Some years later Audinot diverted the competitive blow of the Variétés-Amusantes by turning almost exclusively from bawdy comedy to sentimental pantomime. Boulevard entrepreneurs generally hired more and better actors and actresses and surreptitiously increased the numbers of their musicians and dancers, officially curtailed by decree in 1767. Between 1773 and 1778 Audinot's troupe fluctuated from 29 to 40 actors and actresses, many of whom had grown by the end of that decade from children into young adults. By 1774 Nicolet could boast of not just six but eight violins and not ten but twenty-six dancers, though in following years the latter decreased to about fifteen.[73]

At times the little theaters rivaled even the great stages of Paris. Nicolet's lavish production of the "heroic and burlesque Pantomime of the Abduction of Europe" in 1773 prompted the *Secret Memoirs* to compare this minor stage with the Opéra:

> It is inconceivable how far hard work and industry have brought this buffoon, whose theater is now the rival of the Théâtre lyrique, and surpasses it in its very well coordinated and very precise stage machinery, by the magnificence of the sets, the good taste in costumes, the spectacular pomp, the number of actors, and, finally, by an admirable perfection in execution.[74]

The same *Memoirs* highly praised a spectacular pantomime entitled *The Four Sons of Aymon* at the Ambigu-Comique in 1779:

> The size of the theater and its advantageous form made it possible to stage the play in all its beauty, and it must be admitted that the great number of military and picturesque tableaux struck in the course of the pantomime could not be presented with more vivacity, precision or truth . . .[75]

Nicolet and Audinot, if not others along the boulevard, had considerably enlarged upon the limited resources and "simple Buffooneries and *parades*" allowed the popular stage in 1769.

It is significant that the boulevard's artistic expansion in the early 1770s was largely at the expense of the Opéra. The censorship practiced by the Comédie-Française and the Comédie-Italienne since 1769 effectively stifled any competitive experimentation in farce or comedy. In response the minor stage channeled its energies into spectacular forms of pantomime, accompanied by music and dance, over which the royal actors had no artistic jurisdiction. Yet it was not long before the development of musical entertainment on the boulevard did raise the suspicion and ire of the third great spectacle of Paris, the Royal Academy of Music. The Opéra first took serious offense with boulevard theater over Nicolet's production of *The Abduction of Europe* in 1773. The Royal Academy's demand that the pantomime be suppressed was, however, resisted by the police. Lenoir blocked all penalties against the minor theater "the more so because [Nicolet] has gone to great expense, for which it is natural he compensate himself."[76] The police apparently understood that the Opéra would not require the same assurances of artistic monopoly enjoyed by the royal Comédies. And they were right. The Academy of Music had preferred a more lucrative treatment of those who poached on their artistic preserves at the beginning of the eighteenth century. In keeping with that tradition, the Opéra simply arranged that the boulevard theaters pay for the advantages of music and dance.

The earliest known contract between the Opéra and a boulevard stage dates from about 1771 or 1772. According to the historian Bonnassiès the Opéra had attempted to curtail the use of music and dance at the Ambigu-Comique sometime in 1771. Concerted resistance—possibly within the ministry of police[77]—forced the Opéra to withdraw its penalties and settle with Audinot for an exorbitant fee of 12,000 livres paid annually. Nicolet's spectacular production of *The Abduction of Europe* in the following year probably served as pretext for a similar lease between the Opéra and that boulevard entrepreneur in 1773. It is more than likely, however, that the Opéra's practice of leasing music and dance to the boulevard theaters was, initially, neither wholly accepted by the minor entrepreneurs nor regularly and efficiently collected. A summons delivered to Nicolet in 1779 demanded on the part of the Opéra the payment of some 2,800 livres by reason of 24 livres per day performance and 12 livres per night performance stipulated in a contract passed the year before.[78] Rated in this manner, Nicolet would have paid in a

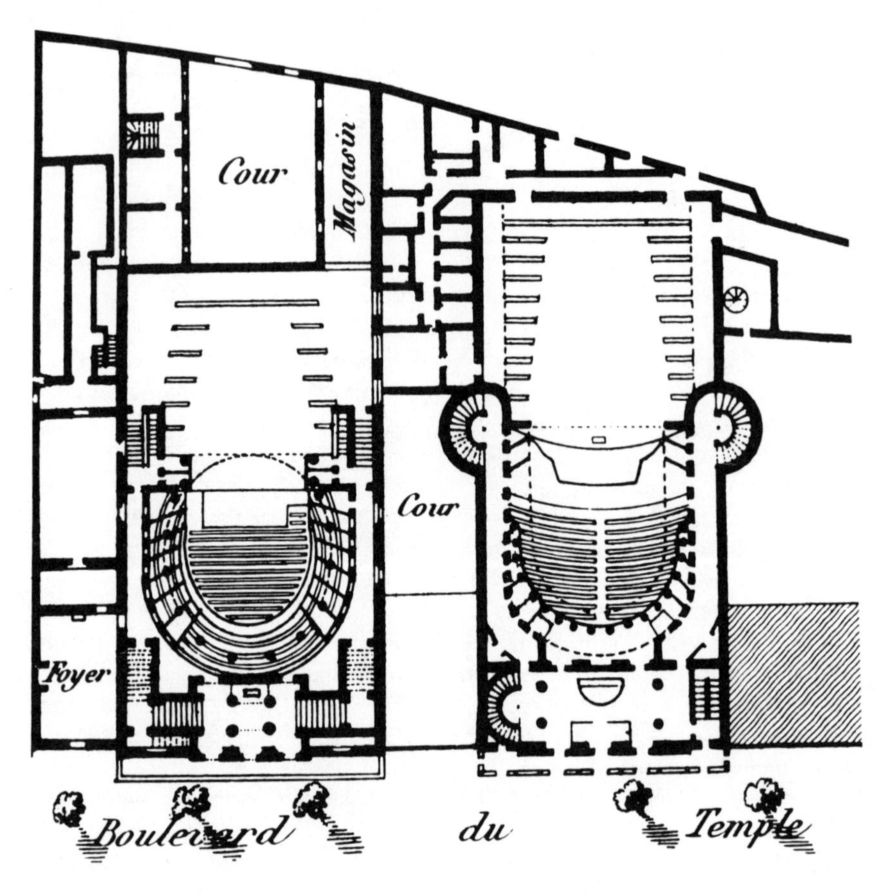

Plate 6. Ground plans of the Grands-Danseurs (right) and the Ambigu-Comique (left), drawn in the nineteenth century. From Alexis Donnet, et. al., *Architectonographie des théâtres* (Paris, 1837-1840).

year's time close to the 12,000 livres charged Audinot in 1772. In fact Nicolet seems to have ignored all payment to the Opéra from January or at least May of 1779. Moreover, his refusal to pay up was sustained by circumstance.

The Opéra's administration was in total disarray. Though in principle the Academy fell under the jurisdiction of the Royal Household, the expense and complexity of running the Opéra had forced the government more than once to shift the burden to the city of Paris. Between 1777 and 1780 this municipal exploitation had proved disastrous; Vismes de Valgay, the private entrepreneur to whom the city had ceded its rights, had plunged the Opéra into enormous debt. Nicolet no doubt sensed the impending failure of de Valgay's direction and took advantage of the Opéra's confusion and impotence to resist the weighty tax on his performances. Nicolet's relative freedom and that of other boulevard theaters was, nonetheless, short-lived. A decree of March 1780 abruptly withdrew the Opéra concession from the municipality and placed the administration once more under royal supervision.[79]

The king's ministers had managed to balance the Opéra's books in early 1777; they resolved to do so again. It came to their attention that the Opéra had hitherto eked no more than an irregular tribute from the minor theaters using music and dance. Papillon de la Ferté, the king's commissioner for the Academy of Music, and Amelot, minister of Paris, determined that this income should be routinely ordered and collected. To this end, Amelot wrote to Papillon, "I just recommended to Monsieur le Berton [the new director of the Opéra] that he occupy himself with the Boulevard Spectacles."[80] Berton, Amelot and Papillon worked quickly, for within four months Nicolet, Audinot, Malter and Parisau, directors of the four largest spectacles on the boulevard, were complaining to the hospitals of Paris that the right to continue their theatrical enterprise now depended on daily payments to the Opéra.[81]

Only one contract signed at this time between the Opéra and the boulevard entrepreneurs is known in its entirety. By agreement passed in May of 1780 Nicolet assented to pay 12 livres per day performance and 6 livres per night performance to the Academy of Music. In exchange for a more efficient and regularized collection, the Opéra had lowered Nicolet's tax from earlier years by half. The contract is less interesting for these monetary arrangements, however, than it is for the terms agreed upon for theatrical exploitation of music and dance on the boulevard:

> I consent as well not to have performed by my orchestra or in my theater any ballet airs or others taken from works received and executed within the last ten years at the Opéra, or at the Comédie-Italienne, with the exception of those used up until now in Pantomimes in order to indicate the meaning or sense of action and having no relation to dance, binding myself in this latter regard to use only that music which I commission expressly for my theater.... [The Royal Academy of Music consents on its part] to grant me the operation of my Spectacle and enterprise, in its present state, without any innovation, and with the same number of musicians who compose my orchestra.[82]

Although couched in negative terms—Nicolet formally recognized certain specific restrictions upon his theatrical productions—the lease conceded to the boulevard entrepreneur much of his artistic presumption and growth since 1769. The Opéra insisted that in all future dances and pantomimes the Grands-Danseurs limit itself to musical airs that had become obsolete at the Academy of Music or the Comédie-Italienne. It was understood, in turn, that Nicolet's audacious use of current operatic or dance music up to 1780 would be overlooked in his pantomimes, though not in his ballet. The Opéra agreed, moreover, to give sanction to the status quo. Nicolet was permitted no further expansion in art or company, nor was he required to retract the gains he had made in pomp and personnel over the last decade.

Despite the Opéra's express purpose to halt dramatic innovation on the minor stage, boulevard entrepreneurs apparently construed their contracts for music and dance as artistic cartes blanches. Daily payoffs for musical airs once performed on the premier stage of Paris tended to obscure the line between operatic art and boulevard fare. The minor theaters improved upon their musical spectacle and one in particular dared upon privileged art itself. In early September 1780 the Opéra's administrative committee, composed of the director and principal artists, learned of a pantomime soon to be performed at the Ambigu-Comique:

> The Committee has just read the Program for a Ballet mixed with dialogue and bits of music, having for a title *The Curiosity of Young Girls*...
>
> This Ballet is nothing other than the subject of *Cupid and Psyche*...[83]

The "burlesque title" of Audinot's pantomime-ballet did not conceal from the committee that the entrepreneur had abandoned "the lowest subjects" proper to the boulevard for a grand theme from classical mythology, by customary right the property of the Academy. Like the French and Italian actors, the artists of the Opéra laid claim to the subject—both actual and potential—of their art as well as its form. The committee seized upon Audinot's transgression to condemn similar violations all along the boulevard:

> The minister is asked to give prompt orders to arrest the progress of these spectacles which violate at one and the same time the agreements made between them and the committee and the original character of their theaters, which does not allow them representations such as those which take place daily and which are so detrimental to the Royal spectacles.[84]

At the committee's behest, Amelot acted quickly to suppress the offending pantomime-ballet.[85] He responded as well to its strident warning that without effective restraint the boulevard theaters would appropriate for their own the very best art of the privileged stages: "the most Precious selections from our operas, the most outstanding scenes from our Ballets,... the masterpieces of Corneille, Racine, Molière and Quinault."[86] Amelot arranged with the Baron de Breteuil, also with the Royal Household, and no doubt with Papillon to talk over the artistic constraint of the boulevard theaters with Lenoir, lieutenant-general of police. Unfortunately, the initimate discussions of these authorities are unknown; no police regulations or ministerial orders in the course of 1780-1781 announced their resolutions.

Indeed, no direct action seems to have been taken to shore the crumbling wall between the privileged and the popular stage. Perhaps Lenoir resisted artistic restrictions that would have jeopardized the theatrical economy along the boulevard and in the fairs. Perhaps he insisted upon the financial benefits available to the Opéra if boulevard theaters were allowed to prosper and grow. It is known that in lieu of restraint, the Academy opted for increased indemnification. The administrative committee obtained its request to break the contracts recently signed with the minor theaters. In renegotiating terms, it imposed greater fines on the boulevard entrepreneurs. According to the original lease for 1780 Nicolet was to have paid approximately 6,000 livres for the year; by 1782 he relinquished to the Opéra 16,128 livres, a sum that increased again by a fifth in 1784 to 19,208 livres.[87] Artistic growth for the popular stage, like commercial expansion, had its price as well as its reward.

Both aspects of the Opéra's economic parasitism had their keenest effect on the boulevard in 1784 and following years. Despite its reorganization in 1780 and an annual pension accorded by the king, the Opéra continued to accumulate staggering debts. More drastic financial measures were called for. In an effort to boost the Academy's revenues from the boulevard, the government reaffirmed in a decree of 13 March 1784 the Opéra's exclusive monopoly of plays in music or song, of concerts, ballets, pantomimes and balls. The annual perquisites to which the Opéra was entitled from the boulevard were augmented to 100,000 livres.[88] The Ambigu-Comique now paid 11,808 livres, the Variétés-Amusantes 11,376 livres. Two other fair spectacles which the Opéra taxed—the Wauxhall at the Saint Germain Fair and the Redoute Chinoise, both a kind of dance pavillon-pleasure ground—together paid 2,064 livres. Including the Grands-Danseurs, whose tax jumped in that same year from 16,320 to 19,208 livres, these spectacles netted the Opéra 41,568 livres.[89] To reach the goal of 100,000 livres or more annually, the government had to strengthen the Opéra's exploitation of petty theatrical industry.

Another decree of July 1784 supplemented the Opéra's monopoly of musical genres with the privilege to the boulevard theatrical industry, lock, stock and barrel. Indeed, the Opéra now owned the right to exploit all theatrical resources of minor rank in the city of Paris. The purpose, of course, was to provide the ailing Academy with sufficient and growing means of economic support:

> ...the King in council has accorded and accords to the Royal Academy of Music the privilege to all public spectacles now existing or that may exist in the future in the city,

> suburbs and ramparts of Paris as fair theaters.... His Majesty permits the Royal Academy of Music to exercise, have exercised or concede said privilege to whomever, and at whatever costs, clauses and conditions that may be agreed upon...[90]

Quite in keeping with its new-found right and with government intention, the Opéra leased exploitation of the various boulevard halls to the highest bidders. Malter and, initially, Audinot were outbid for the Variétés-Amusantes and the Ambigu-Comique. A certain Gaillard and Dorfeuille agreed to pay 40,000 and 30,000 livres respectively for the exploitation of those theaters. Nicolet held onto the Grands-Danseurs for 24,000 livres a year.

In exchange for these more onerous taxes, the minor theaters of Paris received the powerful protection of the Opéra and the royal ministers in charge of its administration. Even before the Opéra's economic interest in the boulevard and the fairs had been sanctioned by privilege, its pecuniary needs had probably shielded Nicolet and Audinot from the legal prosecutions of the French actors begun in the Great Chamber in 1778.[91] The actors seem to have renewed their suit against the boulevard theaters sometime in 1784 in an effort to forestall their legitimate concession by the Opéra. This time ministers within the Royal Household openly lobbied in support of the minor theatrical industry. In a memorandum to the Opéra's administrative committee, Papillon de la Ferté urged the terms of this defense:

> It should be in the wise administration, in the reasoned economy of its revenues, that the Opéra ought find all the resources that the splendor of its spectacle requires. The Opéra had need of outside aid, it depended upon royal authority [...] to procure that aid. The Entrepreneurs of the small theaters, stripped of the consideration and protection which they perhaps merit, can only moan of their impotence and submit. But in demanding of them oppressive payments, ought not the Opéra take it upon itself to become their protector?... It is in maintaining and in protecting these little theaters, it is in assuring their success, that the Opéra can count upon the constancy of the payments which it requires of them. It cannot, therefore, neglect to place them under its wings. Its interests demand that it protect them vigorously against the renewed pestering to which the Royal actors will subject them.[92]

The pressing financial needs of the Opéra effected a profound change in the ministry's attitudes towards the cultural organization of Parisian theater. Papillon de la Ferté, who as Intendent of Petty Amusements had cared for the interests of the Comédie-Française throughout the 1760s and '70s, argued in the mid-'80s for a dissolution of its industrial and artistic monopoly. The rigid separation of publics and dramatic arts between the great and the little theaters had made sense in the late 1760s, Papillon argued, when the stagnant receipts and modest shares of the French actors were susceptible to competition of any kind. Since 1774, however, the royal actors' incomes had doubled and even tripled. There was no longer need to restrain the minor theatrical industry; it was, indeed, because of that industry that the actors had prospered:

> ... it is easy to prove that it is to the little theaters that [the actors] owe the extension of theatrical taste in all the orders of the state.... The income of the Actors, since the permanent establishment of the Fair Spectacles, has more than doubled, and that which seemed certain to hasten their ruin [according to the actors] has, on the contrary, augmented their fortune.... The establishment of these Fair Spectacles, where the Bourgeoisie has been attracted by a good bargain, has inspired [that class] with a general, yet strong, taste for all theaters. Tiring of plays with little interest, [the bourgeoisie] is now excited by the desire to see good works.[93]

The boulevard theaters no longer pilfered the most important, aristocratic portion of the public from the great stages. They had, rather, stimulated the tremendous growth of a non-aristocratic audience in Paris: "The population of Paris is big enough to fill all theaters every day."[94]

The privileged monopoly of all recognized art forms had consequently lost its justification. The growth of the public beyond the capacities of the great companies of Paris must be met, Papillon reasoned, by other theaters suited in genre and style to the middle as well as the lower classes:

> ... it is known as well that these honest Citizens complain daily that there are no seats for them at the great theaters, due to the ill-judged annual subscription of the small boxes.... Because of this there ought to be other theaters where they can, after all, go enjoy the pleasure that is refused them in the great theaters.[95]

If the "good bourgeois" was to find entertainment proper to his position in society, however, the severe censorship of boulevard plays by the actors must come to an end. Indeed, the bawdy, immoral tone and lack of taste in the boulevard idiom were in fact of the royal actors' making:

> With regard to good taste, the Actors, in announcing its loss as a consequence of the establishment of the little theaters, contradict themselves, since without cease they have sought to excise from the plays of the Fair Spectacles—which are admittedly sent to them—all that smacks of a good scene, even though it may be drowned, as it usually is, by a great number of very mediocre ones...[96]

The formal boundary which Papillon himself had helped draw in the 1760s between the privileged art of the social elite and the dramatic corruptions of the people was to be traced anew according to a simple hierarchy of genres and publics. Under the direction of Papillon and others in the ministry, the government determined to reduce privileged monopolies of genre, in practice, to monopolies of repertory and no more. To the lieutenant-general of police remained the delicate task of enforcing the cultural proprieties:

> The Magistrate is too interested in the success and glory of the national theaters for them to believe that he will not take great care to keep the Fair Spectacles from flying too high, which might harm the great Theaters...[97]

The reform in government attitude towards the organization of Parisian theater entailed an important shift in perception of the socio-cultural order. To a large extent Papillon simply admitted what had long been true—that great and popular dramatic cultures were in fact not discrete but overlapped one another along a common border. It was, of course, the economic bonds and artistic treaties between the boulevard and the privileged world of theater of which government officials were most aware, since they themselves had permitted and organized the Opéra's parasitic dependency on the minor theatrical industry throughout the 1770s and 1780s. They were also aware that theatrical publics had mixed, quite contrary to the regulations of 1769.

The reduction in cost of boulevard and fair tickets at that time had not discouraged the interest of the social elite in popular theater. Nicolet and Audinot both shared the distinction of arranging performances before the court at Versailles in 1772. The *Fairground Almanac* took keen pleasure in exposing the aristocratic presence on the boulevard in the mid-1770s.[98] And in 1777 or 1778 Nicolet, for one, installed small boxes which for reasons of cost as well as fashion were occupied by "people of the highest quality."[99] At Sallé's somewhat socially inferior stage the bourgeois Joffet commissioned the entrepreneur to build him a small box within the hall "in order not to be confused with the populace."[100] According to the *Fairground Almanac* the "honest Bourgeois" was increasingly visible—and distinguishable—amongst the popular crowd.[101] The reduction in prices had, indeed, encouraged significant growth in the lower-class public:

> ... those whom one called the people under the old regime did not tire of going [to the minor theaters]; because they were hardly discriminating in their choice of pleasure, they found it at Nicolet's, in all genres and at every price.[102]

Police reports confirm this wide social presence through the 1780s. The association of social classes within theater halls was not, however, a democratic one. Both cost of ticket and manner of dress segregated students, servants, soldiers, merchants, artisans, bourgeois and nobility in hierarchical, if close proximity.[103]

Just as social elements formally proper to the great theaters attended the boulevard spectacles, those formally proper to the minor stage had begun to frequent the Opéra, the Comédie-Française and the Comédie-Italienne. Papillon de la Ferté suggested that since the development of the boulevard spectacles, to which he credited the stimulation of dramatic taste amongst the middle classes, "persons of a more considerable Estate" had been joined at the great theaters by growing numbers of the bourgeoisie. Moreover, in his study of Parisian theater audiences for this period, the historian John Lough concurs with some contemporary observation that even the lower-classes increased noticeably in their attendance at the Comédie-Française and Comédie-

Italienne between 1760 and 1789.[104] In the last decades of the eighteenth century great and little theaters actually shared certain elements of the theater-going population. Their publics, though not homogeneous, did include the same range of social groups. It is, of course, impossible to know with accuracy the proportions of any one class in the royal theaters or in those of the boulevard. Lough argues that the aristocracy still dominated in taste if not in absolute numbers the middle- and lower-class elements at the Comédie-Française or the Comédie-Italienne and, one might add, the Opéra.[105] And according to Grimm, the middle and lower classes dictated on the boulevard the gay theater enjoyed by all members of society: "The populace has its pleasures that it madly loves and the well-to-do, who never have enough, do not always scorn those of the people."[106]

For the classical mind the subtle transformation in theater publics bore—at least in theory—on the kind of dramatic art to be found on the great and minor stages of Paris. Much of Papillon's attack on the censorship of boulevard theater was based on this assumption; he sought to allow some improvement in dramatic quality on the boulevard to suit the middle class. He did not explicitly recognize, however, that the art of the royal theaters might also change, or that the boulevard censorship by the actors might serve as a conduit of popular dramatic culture. Yet a number of plays submitted for review to the French and Italian actors were never performed by the minor theaters for which they had been destined. The royal companies claimed these exceptionally promising plays for their own. The French actors pilfered from the boulevard in 1780 *The Hussar Wedding* and in 1784 *The Female Physicist,* this last in their estimation "characteristic of high Comedy."[107] For their part, the Italian actors acquired in the same manner at least two plays by the popular playwright Robineau de Beaunoir. Both *Fanfan and Colas* and *Friends of the Day,* intended for the Variétés-Amusantes, appeared on the Italians' stage in 1785 and 1786.[108] The Opéra did not exercise the same preliminary review of boulevard plays, yet it, too, was not above performing upon occasion from the popular repertory. *Alain and Rosette or the Naive Shepardess,* a pastorale performed at the Opéra in 1777, had been first produced at the Théâtre de Nicolet. "This miserable spectacle," commented the *English Spy,* "has had the glory of furnishing the premier theater of France with a play from its own repertoire."[109]

Much as the royal companies wished to distinguish their art from popular dramatic culture, they had, in fact, long borrowed from that popular culture much of its creativity and innovation. La Harpe realized this with respect to the fair theater of the early eighteenth century in his *Lectures on Literature,* published between 1799 and 1805:

> The amusing thing is that all the great theaters, which fought [the Fair Theater] with so much animosity, and heaped upon it so much scorn, have been able to imagine nothing better in an

> effort to counterbalance its success than to lower themselves to its level and appropriate its means and resources, farces, ballets and smut.[110]

Several scholars have subsequently agreed that throughout the eighteenth century the influence of the fair tradition upon great theater was far from negligible. As early as 1725 the Comédie-Française had begun to offer short plays featuring Arlequin in direct imitation of the fair theaters. The pantomime developed on the fair stage in the 1740s was soon picked up by the Comédie-Italienne. Of course, the single largest appropriation of popular forms was attendant upon the union of the Opéra-Comique with the Comédie-Italienne in 1762. Even the Opéra toyed with the new form of dance-mime first developed in the fairs and realized on the minor stages after 1750. Noverre, whose innovative style heavily influenced dance on the boulevard, was briefly accepted as ballet master at the Opéra between 1776 and 1781.[111] The introduction of popular genres and styles to the great stages met nevertheless with continual antagonism. Noverre never truly succeeded in influencing the Opéra's repertory of dance. Playwrights and men of letters such as Palissot did not accept the performance of *parades* and comic operas by the Comédie-Italienne. In 1769, in response to *The Talking Picture,* one of the first of plays in a popular form to be performed by that company, Palissot addressed a scathing satire of the fair genre and style to "my worthy friend Mister Nicolet":

> Illustrious Nicolet, your loss is assured . . .
> . . . .
> In order to revive a languishing and sickly taste,
> The hôtel de Bourgogne [the Comédie-Italienne] is staging
>   the *parade;*
> Clairval, displaying all the colors of a handsome Pierrot,
> Wears again the costume of his original profession,
> And his theater, proud of what it has stolen from you,
> Attracts all Paris with your company's wardrobe.[112]

Some twenty years later a similar criticism was leveled at the French stage by the *General Almanac for all the Theaters of Paris:* "The Comédie-Française, with its *Figaroism,* has fallen into the genre of the Boulevards."[113]

As Palissot made clear, it was more than the popular genre or repertory on the great stage that provoked his ire and that of later contemporaries. The Clairval whom he named was one of several actors who graduated from the Opéra-Comique to the Comédie-Italienne at the union of these two theaters. Quite naturally, they brought with them certain comic styles of acting and spectacular uses of costume and scenic display. Far from ignoring these crowd pleasing assets, the Comédie-Italienne in fact exploited them in response to competitive pressure from the remaining fair theaters newly-established on the boulevard.[114] It was the open acknowledgment by the Italian stage of the fair actors' value that must have prompted certain contemporaries to claim that the minor theaters of Paris were a testing ground for the talented and upwardly mobile artist.[115] In *The Idler* Mayeur de St. Paul pointed out that "*Grammont* did his apprenticeship at Nicolet's, la *Ruette, Clairval,* Madame *Trial* and others, such as *Bouret,* began acting on the fair theater that is anathematized."[116] Except for Grammont, all these actors who now performed at the Comédie-Française or Comédie-Italienne hailed from the Opéra-Comique disbanded in 1762. In the next two decades, however, the rise of boulevard artists—individually and without the compulsion of institutional amalgamation—met a great deal of resistance.

Although Grammont was accepted by the French actors two years after his debut on their stage in 1779, other actors and artists nurtured on the boulevard in the 1770s and '80s were not as fortunate. Lelievre of the Grands-Danseurs and Lolotte Delaire of the Ambigu-Comique failed to pursue their apprenticeships with the royal companies. The celebrated comic Volange created a huge scandal with his attempt at upward mobility. According to the *Secret Memoirs,* after Volange had scored a brilliant success at the Variétés-Amusantes in *Janot or the Beaten Pay the Price,* the French actors recognized him as the best farceur in France, and they were interested in claiming him as their own. It was the Comédie-Italienne, however, that succeeded in obtaining for Volange an order to debut. Whether Volange might have adapted his farcical style to the comic sophistication required by the Italian actors in 1780 can only be surmised; it is certain that latent antagonism between Volange and the royal actors led to his abrupt dismissal. A quarrel broke out over the attempted debut of yet another boulevard artist, the erstwhile director Parisau. The Italian actor Michu complained bitterly that "they are infecting us with all the buffoons of the boulevard." Humiliated, Volange sacrificed his career—and that of Parisau—to a vengeful riposte: "Monsieur Michu, if I did not respect your sex [the actor was a known homosexual] you would have business with me."[117]

Hostility towards the art and artists of the minor fair theaters did not prevent the boulevard from exercising an influence on great dramatic culture; some of the plays and genres and some of the popular artists were welcomed by the three royal companies of Paris. Similarly, repression of boulevard theater did not prevent seepage in the other direction. Since the late-seventeenth century the fair theaters had thrived on the comic parody of serious plays performed by the Comédie-Française or the Opéra. Though such parody became less frequent in the boulevard repertory in the last decades of the eighteenth century, it constituted nonetheless an important inlet of dramatic themes and styles from great culture. Minor theaters such as the Grands-Danseurs and the Ambigu-Comique parodied tragedies by Ducis and Voltaire, comedies by Sedaine and Beaumarchais and operas such as *The Curious Peasant Girl* and *Rosette.* They imitated great plays of exceptional interest, borrowed scenes and plots from classical repertory and adapted plays in forbidden genres to simple comedy and dialogued pantomime.[118]

The Théâtre des Associés, to take a most outrageous example, often presumed to change nothing more than the title of some of the best known pieces within the classical tradition before bringing them to the boulevard stage. "This Spectacle, so little known," noted the *Fairground Almanac* in 1776, "understudies the French and Italian Actors; at least it performs *Le Cid, Andromaque, Electra, Zaire, The Braggart, The Gambler,* etc., *Annette and Lubin, Silvain, Lucile,* etc. . . ."[119] With Paillasse, a stock character of the early boulevard, holding many of the leading roles, these masterpieces of the royal stages were of course quite disfigured—a fact which the director Sallé depended on in his bid for the indulgence of the royal actors:

> Messieurs, I will give tomorrow on Sunday a representation of *Zaire;* I beg you to be so good as to send a deputation of your illustrious company to see it; and if you recognize the play by Voltaire after having seen it performed by my actors, I will allow that I deserve your censure and will consent never again to have it performed on my stage.[120]

Prompted by their own mirth, the royal actors granted Sallé permission to continue with his unique productions of their own dramatic repertory.

Some years later in 1785 Nougaret observed of the Théâtre des Associés that "thus a Spectacle where the People formed an idea of the masterpieces of great theater was tolerated."[121] By this time, however, the royal actors tolerated a great deal more artistic license than they wished from other minor theaters along the boulevard. While governing officials in charge of the Opéra busily reorganized the boulevard economy, the lieutenant-general of police attempted to restrain the preliminary censorship of the boulevard repertory. According to Papillon de la Ferté, de Crosne haggled long and hard with the royal companies, especially the Comédie-Française, for a relaxation of their aesthetic and artistic prerogatives:

> The Magistrate of Police has not ceased in reassuring them of their fears that the little theaters have gained in importance, even leaving them authority to take all the plays they would find worthy of their own theaters, but rescinding their right to deprive the little Spectacles of plays they would not want to perform themselves, on the pretext of several scenes passably constructed . . .[122]

The register of censorship decisions[123] kept by the French actors between 1784 and 1789 indicates that de Crosne was in fact successful in his suit—after a year or more of wooing. In 1785, when under the aegis of the Opéra the boulevard spectacles had gained the status of theatrical privilege, the number of their plays reviewed by the actors rose dramatically. The largest part of these were destined for the Variétés-Amusantes, recently moved to an ascendant position at the Palais-Royal. Significantly enough, the number of suppressions also peaked in 1785, although in this as in other years the police did not honor many more than half the charges of artistic infringement made by the French actors. This heightened censorship subsided only slightly in 1786; after this year, however, complaints by the royal actors fell sharply, as did suppressions by the police, for each single stage and for the boulevard as a whole. (See Table 1.) The actors kept up their surveillance of the Grands-Danseurs and the Ambigu-Comique and eased that of the Variétés-Amusantes. But the assiduousness with which they had previously called for alterations and suppressions of boulevard plays had been relinquished—perhaps because censorship had, in the end, done little to prevent or forestall the intermingling of classical and popular art. The aesthetic barrier between great and little dramatic cultures had in reality proved as highly porous as economic and social restraints and by the late 1780s as obsolescent.

Boulevard Privilege and the Decline of Prosperity, 1784-1789

Over the course of years between 1769 and the mid-1780s the cultural gap between the royal theaters and the boulevard spectacles imposed by contemporary attitude had not prevented a pragmatic interchange of genres, plays, authors, actors and audiences. Nevertheless, the two dramatic cultures remained distinct entities, even if they were not wholly separate. The minor theaters grew and prospered economically and artistically because the popular pose first assumed in the 1760s protected their industry and their art from the competition and direct attack of the three great companies of Paris. As long as the dramatic culture of the boulevard and the fairground was supposed to be marginal, the little theaters and the little dramatic tradition flourished in a repressed and controlled economy.

Rather abruptly, the reorganization of the boulevard in 1784 to the economic benefit of the Opéra changed the conditions of prosperity for the minor theaters themselves. The integration of these theaters within the monopolistic confines of privilege had a paradoxical effect. A restrained economy in popular theater gave way to an increasingly competitive market. Those days were gone when Nicolet's stage alone had dominated the boulevard, surrounded by only a handful of sideshows, and gone, too, the probationary competition of the 1770s, when one by one the Ambigu-Comique, the Théâtre des Associés, the Variétés-Amusantes and the Théâtre des Elèves pour la danse de l'Opéra had settled by his side on the ramparts.

As early as 1781 the government's interest in the minor theatrical industry had promoted a substantial increase in the number of petty amusements—principally in the fairs. To these belonged the Wauxhall d'Hiver, a sort of dance hall at the Saint Germain Fair; the Redoute Chinoise, a pleasure ground with restaurant, cafés, games and spectacles, built at the Saint Laurent Fair; Fantocinni's marionettes; the Colisée or Cirque royal and the horse show of

Sieur Astley. After 1784 the Opéra's proprietary concerns in the boulevard and in the fairs positively encouraged an explosion of popular spectacles. A dwarf show directed by Dame Duchenne; fireworks by Ruggieri and others; physics exhibitions run by Sieur Girardin, Sieur Comus and M. de Léon; mechanical exhibits by Sieur Préjean and Sieur Lesage; the waterworks of Jean Michel Missel; Sieur Haller's optical show; sports tournaments; more marionettes; a Wauxhall d'Eté; yet another dance hall called the Panthéon; and an additional theater or two sprang up on the boulevard, in the fairs and in the Palais-Royal.[124]

In order that the spirit of economic monopoly be upheld—the Opéra was after all leasing portions of its privileges—all these minor theaters and petty amusements were theoretically one of a kind. A certain Melan signed a contract with Opéra officials whereby he held an exclusive privilege to the amusements in his Wauxhall d'Eté. Antoine Colon, future entrepreneur of the Théâtre des Délassements-Comiques, petitioned successfully for dramatic forms and publics not formally exploited by other minor entrepreneurs:

> Moreover, I consent to represent nothing but marionettes, short comic plays, shadow shows and pantomimes without the Harlequin role or that of Pierrot... the simple form of [these pantomimes] to approach in no way those of the great spectacles of the boulevards, and to serve only for the relaxation of the least well-to-do class of people...[125]

Old-timers such as Nicolet and Audinot capitalized upon the farces, pantomimes, comedies, music and dance that had characterized their theaters in the early 1780s. Yet, none of these petty entrepreneurs truly exercised a monopoly of one amusement or another. The proliferation of minor spectacles had made this all but impossible. Nicolet and Audinot held privileges to the Grands-Danseurs and the Ambigu-Comique respectively, not to the genres or dramatic forms produced on those stages. Melan's "exclusive privilege" was hardly exclusive, since he was forced to compete—albeit on separate days—with other firework spectacles throughout Paris.[126]

This fragmentation of privilege on the boulevard, in the fairs and in the Palais-Royal extended throughout the theatrical order as a whole. Monopolies of dramatic genre no longer distinguished the great from the popular stage. Differences between one minor spectacle and another, between the great and the little theaters, were, rather, maintained by arbitrary device. Since the late 1760s, for instance, comic opera had been exploited solely by the Comédie-Italienne, which held the right to this genre from the Opéra. In 1784 the Opéra leased this same genre to a small theater in the Palais-Royal, but with the stipulation that the young actors of the Beaujolais mimic on stage what others sang for them in the wings. Given these simple constraints comic opera performed by the minor theater was judged different from that performed by the royal company. Two years later a new boulevard theater, the Bluettes established by Clement De Lornaizon, began to perform comic opera in the manner of the Beaujolais, but in order to separate these minor enterprises from each other, the Bluettes was forced to place a gauze curtain or scrim between the audience and the stage. Colon's Délassements-Comiques adopted this scrim to differentiate itself from the Associés, which in turn opened its show with marionette skits that symbolically bound to the fair its forays into the elite genres of tragedy and comedy.[127]

According to Millin de Grandmaison, in his critique of the Parisian theatrical order, this profusion of privilege created a complex hierarchy of dramatic industry:

> An understanding of the dramatic hierarchy was truly a science difficult to acquire; one learned to admire greatly the fecund genius of the minister of Paris in finding means of granting new privileges without infringing upon the old.[128]

For all intents and purposes the bifurcation of theatrical cultures elaborated in classical thought had been effaced. Indeed, the popular pose as such was no longer credible for many of the minor spectacles that thronged the theatrical market in the 1780s. Many filled the socio-cultural gap that contemporaries had long perceived between the royal theaters of the elite and the minor amusements of the people. Gaillard and Dorfeuille had raised not only the dramatic quality but the price of admission at the Variétés-Amusantes when they moved that theater to the Palais-Royal. Other newly-established fair spectacles also abandoned the popular classes who had filled the old boulevard theaters for 2, 6, 12 or even 20 sous. The Beaujolais, the Wauxhall d'Eté, the Redoute Chinoise, the Panthéon all charged between 30 and 36 sous and more. Only now, when the deceit was no longer necessary, the old fair theaters that had struck the popular pose in the 1760s and 1770s in order to protect their industry became more popular than ever before. As in the past, the Grands-Danseurs, the Ambigu-Comique and the Associés—joined briefly by the Délassements-Comiques—were not formally permitted to court any but a popular audience, nor to innovate beyond the traditional idiom of the fair and boulevard. In a crowded market of theaters financially suited to all classes of society, it was they who opened their doors wide to the "people and lower bourgeosie" still faithful to the traditional popular stage.[129]

Both Nicolet and Audinot, above and beyond all other minor entrepreneurs, had made their fortunes on the boulevard in the years after 1769. But by some cruel irony their legal integration into the privileged world of theater marked the waning of their industrial affluence as entrepreneurs in popular amusement. At first glance this would seem not to have been so. In absolute terms the productivity of the minor theatrical industry on the boulevard, in the fairs and the Palais-Royal continued to climb in the years after 1784. Officials of the Opéra estimated that the Academy received 41,568 livres from the fair spectacles in 1783-1784. Between 1784 and 1785 they expected an increase to 64,143 livres. A year or so later this amount was to rise to 111,376 livres, and in 1788 to 157,940 livres.[130] The hospitals of Paris also took advantage of the expansion of the fair industry to augment the receipts of their poor tax. They collected approximately 167,530 livres between April 1783 and April 1784. In the next fiscal year this amount jumped to some 188,185 livres. The overall productivity of the poor tax on minor spectacles subsided after April 1784, though, significantly enough, receipts from the boulevard alone continued to climb. Because the poor tax was based at least in part upon a percentage of theater receipts, the climb in its productivity on the boulevard after 1784 generally indicates there a thriving and prosperous industry. But as the number of minor theaters and spectacles increased, entrepreneurs such as Nicolet and Audinot realized smaller and smaller portions of the boulevard's profits.

The extent to which this was so can be seen in the accounts of expenses and receipts for the Grands-Danseurs, which afford a unique look at business on the boulevard in the years after 1782. (See Figures 2 and 3.) The reorganization of the minor theatrical industry in 1784 had a modest, depressing effect on Nicolet's income at the door, but in fact receipts had been in decline since the end of 1783, when the growth of fair spectacles had first begun in earnest. Not until the end of 1786, however, was it obvious that declining income no longer covered yearly expenses. Nicolet suffered a staggering loss of 23,000 livres—a catastrophe shared to some extent by his boulevard neighbor, Audinot. Both men complained to the hospital administrators that newly-licensed competition harmed their own enterprises:

> ... far from reaping profit from the revenues of their spectacles they suffer, on the contrary, considerable loss.... Their Receipts have been greatly diminished ... by the inattendance of a public that now goes as much to the Palais-Royal as to the new Wauxhall ...[131]

Indeed, there is reason to believe that Nicolet, if not Audinot, surveying the theatrical district they had both helped to shape, might have rued like the French actors in 1785 "the little spectacles that inundate the Capital."[132] His debt had increased by the end of 1788.

The two entrepreneurs harbored their markets as well as they were able. In cooperation with Audinot, Nicolet managed the temporary suppression of De Lornaizon's Théâtre des Bluettes and possibly that of the Délassements-Comiques, which in any case burned to the ground in 1787. Alone he quashed tight-rope dancing at Astley's circus. Nor did he allow acrobats and rope-dancers to perform anywhere in the city of Paris but on his own stage. The contract between Nicolet and the Opéra did not permit the entrepreneur to take action "prejudicial to the other spectacles of the Boulevards,"[133] nevertheless, to suits of protest against the "tyrannic weight" of Nicolet's privilege the

Academy of Music turned a deaf ear: "The committee cannot get involved in the question of Mister Nicolet, who has a Lease."[134] Privilege alone, however, did not ease the economic slump that plagued the Grands-Danseurs in the late 1780s. Nicolet clearly chose to combat increased competition and a dwindling market by an aggressive courtship of the public's favor.

Nicolet's deficit in 1786 had been caused by a fall in income, costs in that year holding a fairly steady course. Rather than curtail expenses in the following year, however, he boosted expenditures by some 79,095 livres, thereby increasing his debt. The cost of upkeep increased dramatically from 19,642 livres to 46,120 livres; perhaps Nicolet renovated his dark and dingy boulevard hall. Equally important were increased expenses for actors (an additional 29,835 livres) and costumes and props (an additional 6,000 livres). In the following year of 1788 these variable costs were augmented by smaller, though no less significant, amounts spent on soldiers and extras for spectacular pantomimes and on the purchase of new plays. Nicolet was not alone in improving his stage; Audinot had embarked upon an enlargement of his theater hall, and he joined Nicolet in August 1788 in yet another successful appeal to the hospital administrators for a reduction in the poor tax:

> This favor [the deferral of the quarter tax on several shows] is based this year, according to their memoirs, on the augmentation of expense occasioned for their theaters by a multitude of new plays as well as by the engagement of different persons and actors capable of responding to their needs and contenting the public.[135]

For Nicolet, and no doubt for Audinot, the improvements in the quality of theatrical productions had a noticeable and desired effect. After the low point at the end of 1786, receipts at the door climbed within the year higher than they had been since the end of 1784, and by the end of 1788 Nicolet's income once again matched his expenses. Yet even as these entrepreneurs regained their equilibrium in a highly competitive market, Paris was pitched into disarray by economic crisis and the political ferment of revolution. The long, cold winter of 1788, the scarcity of bread and the soaring prices of food crippled public attendance of amusements along the boulevard. Political agitation and popular protest, building in intensity from the spring through early summer, disrupted theatrical business.

"The severity of the times" and "the troubles of the Capital" obliged Nicolet, Audinot and others to close their doors for weeks at a time—most notably during the municipal revolution of mid-July.[136] Nicolet's income in 1789 fell by some 48,000 livres, the most precipitous decline he had yet experienced. When he and Audinot filed a request for respite from the quarter tax, the hospitals granted both directors dispensation through October. It was not enough. Nicolet barely managed to keep his expenses in line with lowered receipts; Audinot plunged rapidly into deficit. Unlike years past, the hospitals'

Plate 7. The boulevard between 1788 and 1790, altered by competitive improvements such as the new façade of the Ambigu-Comique pictured here. Gouache by Jean-Baptiste Lallemand. Photo: Office du Livre, Fribourg.

alleviation of the poor tax, "in order not to discourage the entrepreneurs who are all making an effort to sustain their enterprise," had none of its former, equilibrating effect on the boulevard economy. A balance sheet drawn up by hospital administrators revealed that in the last nine months of 1789 Nicolet's income had fallen 66,294 livres below that of the year before. The receipts of the Ambigu-Comique had similarly declined by 107,089 livres and those of the Variétés-Amusantes in the Palais-Royal by 88,327 livres.

In the course of 1790 the taxes that had long weighed upon the theaters of the boulevard and the fairs were collected for the last time. The Opéra lost hold of its theatrical farm; the hospitals could no longer enforce the full quota of their privileged levy. Nicolet's quarter tax in 1790 came to no more than six percent of his income,[137] and of his lease for 24,000 livres with the Opéra he paid no more than 2,000 livres. He even threatened not to pay the firemen annually assigned by the police to service his theater. The privileged control and restraint of the boulevard economy, in decline since at least 1784, fell apart almost of its own volition in the years 1789-90.

This breakdown prefigured the liberation of theatrical industry in January 1791, but it could hardly have inspired liberal ideology. Despite relief from the excessive taxes of the Opéra and the hospitals, the Grands-Danseurs continued for the next two years at least to plunge into economic decline. Not until the end of 1792 did Nicolet manage to pull out of deficit by the drastic reduction of all his costs. Nicolet's experience and that of others along the boulevard who undoubtedly shared in some measure these effects of economic and political dislocation had significance. Popular enterprise and the minor, commercial market of theaters elaborated under the aegis of privilege did not strain for release in 1790-91. Boulevard theaters such as the Grands-Danseurs, the Ambigu-Comique or the Associés limped into revolution.

Part II

The Dramatic Idiom and Literature of the Boulevard Stage

Prelude: An Afternoon at the Theater

> "The crowd teems [on the boulevard]; and that is one more reason to examine the attraction that draws the multitude towards these theaters, which everyone claims to despise, and which everyone frequents..."
>
> —Louis Sebastien Mercier
> *Tableau of Paris,* 1783

Towards the end of most afternoons in the later decades of eighteenth century Paris, idle young men, strolling matrons, demoiselles, domestics, valets, apprentices, shopgirls, artisans, master-craftsmen, well-off merchants and men of professional standing eased their way down the broad, tree-lined boulevard du Temple and gathered in clumps before the many small theaters along the avenue. Show-time was about to begin. In the 1760s and early 1770s the comic pranks of an Arlequin or a Paillasse, masked figures gesticulating in the balconies above the street, had served to draw the public from near and far. By the 1780s these balcony *parades* were no more to be seen, nor did the crowds need such supplication to throng around the ticket booths between the hours of four and five. Theater posters and daily journals had already announced throughout the city the marvels to behold in the boulevard halls: comedies, pantomimes, dances, military revues, and thrilling acrobatics! While the more genteel sent servants into the fray before the theater doors, others did not hesitate to press themselves for the limited number of places—all but the most expensive to be had for less than a livre. The pushing and shoving (for the French, as Mercier liked to observe, were neither orderly nor patient) presented ideal opportunities for an underworld of pickpockets. Here and there petty crooks jostled with the crowd, lifting gold watches, snuff boxes, even pocket books from the unsuspecting master-tailor, good bourgeois or well-placed valet.[1]

The tumult within the theater halls was hardly less than that without. Halls were of many sizes along the boulevard, but even the largest of these theaters were small, dark and dingy. On a good day at the Grands-Danseurs du Roi some 400 people or more might be packed into a squat space no more than 36

Plate 8. An acrobatic interlude at the Théâtre de Nicolet which drew the crowds to that stage. Photo: Bibl. nat. Paris.

feet across, 33 feet in length and perhaps 40 feet high. The glowing tallow candles that lit the entire hall did little to disperse the closeness of these quarters, rather adding to it with a black and grimy soot that clung to the walls and a heavy vapor that hung upon the air. Theater ushers and the French guard stood by to direct the unruly public to the places for which they had purchased tickets. Women of consequence and women of ill-repute, professional men and nobility incognito conspicuously occupied the most expensive seats in the house, or first loges, some of which were grilled over for modesty's sake. At nearly half the price, 18 or 20 sous, more common men and women were packed "like onions" on the long benches that lined the parquet. Despite the noisy complaints of these patrons, the French guard made sure, as at other Parisian theaters, that as many bodies as possible were squeezed side by side. Inside the boulevard hall there was no *parterre,* that open space in front of the stage in which gentlemen and students had traditionally stood at the Comédie-Française, but for 12 sous boisterous young lads and working men and women could crowd the amphitheater or second tier of loges that circled the top of the house.[2]

The impatient spectators were rarely, if ever, satisfied with their view of the stage or the crushing proximity of their neighbors. The guard coped as it might with those who sought better seats in an adjacent loge, with those who refused to remove their hats and with those whose tempers flared from real and imagined slights to their person. The physical intimacy of the crowd worked to break down the barriers of social reserve and rank. Insults between the better sort were hurled across the loges; servants and apprentices in the amphitheater quarreled with each other and with the guards. If tempers were short, manners were rude. At the curtain's rise, and the orchestra's first strains, the commotion subsided, but not entirely. Women continued to gossip in their box and, in the amphitheater above, an ill-taught lout, drunk perhaps or simple-minded, relieved himself over the rail upon the people below.[3]

Most of those in the crowded hall, however, did turn their eyes and minds to the splendid scene set before them. Sight and sound carried them beyond their cramped quarters into realms of the imagination. An orchestra of violins, cellos and clarinettes evoked a sweet and enchanting mood; backdrops and painted curtains depicted the mountains and trees of a deserted island; on the right of the stage there sat a straw-roofed cabin. SHHHH! *The Child of Nature* was about to begin! Actors and actresses took their places on the stage and played their roles with a natural and easy style that was quite unlike the classical elegance of the royal companies of Paris. Local color was copied in their dress and Nature imitated in their emotion. The young Mayeur, who played the part of the "natural man" abandoned far from a father and a society he did not know, wore his hair plainly and dressed in nothing more than a fur about his midriff. A certain "genius" of gesture and expression enabled him to peform the pantomime of a mute yet sensitive soul without trivial artifice or false ingenuousness. Mlle. Forest in the role of the young girl who joined the savage in sentimental love was less talented, perhaps, but beautiful and charming. Her studied naiveté and sensibility brought its own storm of applause. It hardly mattered that the learned critics should scorn what they considered feeble attempts to attain the noble tone and distinguished air of the royal stage. The boulevard audience was alternately titillated and touched, instructed and challenged by the story of natural virtue and social vice that unfolded before them.[4]

Of course, not all plays were of similar effect, or performed with equal talent or attention to theatrical detail. Not all theaters along the boulevard were capable of such a costly display of sounds and sights. The Grands-Danseurs itself, the very first to gain prominence, had struggled many years with a handful of musicians, actors and acrobats badly costumed and poorly educated in their art. The Italian playwright Carlo Goldoni, whose own comedies were produced at more prestigious theaters, attended a performance at Nicolet's in the 1760s. Much to his surprise, his own sword was promptly requisitioned for the Roman captain in *Coriolan,* the tragedy he had entered to see. So, too, was his forbearance:

> I awaited for a long while and with much impatience the play that had drawn me to this spectacle; the tightrope dancers gave me the shivers, the first two spoken plays put me to sleep...
>
> I saw actors poorly costumed, I heard verse poorly recited; but I realized that the play [,*Coriolan,*] was not without merit, and that the author had handled his subject very adroitly...
>
> I could say nothing of his style, because I guessed more than I heard: Nicolet's actors were not formed for this genre of representation, and [his] stage in general was still badly mounted; it is much better produced today. The small spectacles that have since been established have vied with [Nicolet], and have made it necessary for that director to provide himself with better actors.

The backwardness that had marked the Théâtre de Nicolet in the 1760s was still to be found some twenty years later on a very poor boulevard stage such as the Associés. Here the quality of production and performance so altered the masterpieces of classical theater that the royal actors themselves did not protest the ludicrous pillage of their repertory by Sallé and his troupe. The heroines of great tragedy dressed in tattered robes and flat shoes, the heroes in old togas that served for Orosmane as well as Gengis Khan. The simple addition of a fireman's bonnet and a corselet of golden paper had to suffice for the Greek and Roman roles. Untrained in the declamation of classical tragedy, these poorly dressed actors proffered sophisticated texts in unsophisticated, popular slang. The critical observer had not far to look to find on the boulevard a total ignorance of the "rules" of dramatic art.[5]

What many of these small theaters may have lacked in dramatic expertise of one kind, however, they made up for in another. Actors and actresses on the

Plate 9. Three plays performed at the Grands-Danseurs in the 1780s. On the left foreground a scene from *The Child of Nature.* On the right foreground a scene from *The Horn of Truth.* At the top an unidentified farce includes the stock characters Arlequin, carrying off the young girl, Cassandre pursuing, and Paillasse, hot on the master's tail. From Restif de la Bretonne, *Les Contemporaines,* (Paris: 1780-1785).

boulevard were adept at the idiom of the burlesque, a style of comedy, it was said, filled with coarse pranks, scandalous obscenities, lewd jokes, filthy allusions and unequivocal gestures. For the most part this comic talent was lavished on plays other than the sentimental piece in which Mayeur and Forest had starred. A short pantomime and perhaps a comedy would follow, though, in the day's performance. After a short interlude of acrobatics or of dance, an arlequinade, such as *Arlequin the English Cerberus,* filled the hall of the Grands-Danseurs with boisterous laughter. In sharp contrast to the graceful, emotional action in *The Child of Nature,* the well-loved characters Arlequin, Colombine, the old man and the lovers cavorted upon the stage, emphasizing their sparse dialogue with bodily expression. In this, Arlequin was particularly bright, versatile and funny. One *lazzi,* or complicated bit of comic mime, followed upon another. Howling with laughter, men and women held their sides and wiped their eyes to see Arlequin, disguised as a dog, lift his leg against the confused old man. *The Horn of Truth,* a successful and enduring comedy, though far less suggestive, delighted in much the same way. Servants and lovers set out to hoodwink the old Cassandre in such a tissue of lies, appearance and intrigue that the old man was lost but for the "horn of truth" he held to his ear. It was this horn, which dispelled conceit so that an inner truth could be heard, that saved Cassandre from giving his daughter to an unworthy man. In pleasing comically, the comedy moralized as well upon honesty in social relations and respect for paternal authority.[6]

What caught and held the attention of the public for hours at a stretch, day in and day out, was the extraordinary variety and vitality of the boulevard stage. Acrobats excited the spectators at Nicolet's with amazing jumps and flying leaps; child-actors now grown old touched the hearts of those at Audinot's; masked figures and marionettes delighted at many another minor theater. Each troupe along the avenue may have specialized somewhat in its own unique genre, but all participated in the theater of gaiety. Repertories mixed the comic with the sentimental, pantomime with drama, the marvelous with the naive. On the larger boulevard theaters of Nicolet and Audinot magnificent decorations, tasteful costumes, the use of theatrical machinery and of dozens of extras in military tableaux contributed to a deserved reputation for spectacular display. Playbills beckoned with a constant alteration of fare. Such tremendous attraction did the boulevard theaters exert in the last decades of the old regime that their number often could not satisfy the press of people at the theater doors. The public came because that gay theatrical culture engaged their hearts and relieved their minds. In the early 1770s ladies of condition and shopgirls alike had shouted with laughter at the crazy antics of Nicolet's ape, at the indecent skits and bawdy comedies upon the stage. In the 1780s they and their companions in the hall were moved to tears by the sentimental pantomimes and dramas performed at the Variétés-Amusantes, the Ambigu-Comique and the Grands-Danseurs du Roi. The curtain fell, the audience roared—here with bravos and the clapping of hands, there with catcalls and critical whistling. Whether some were disgruntled at the repetition of a well-worn play, or all were satisfied with the new adventures of a favorite hero, they would return to the popular stage. And so, with a little effort, may we.[7]

There are, of course, certain limitations to any journey into the past. Try as we may to reconstruct here the spontaneous, versatile and eclectic character of the boulevard stage, much has been obscured or effaced by the passage of time. Too little is known of acting styles on the boulevard—of the use of pantomime, acrobatics and improvisation, for example—too little known of stage design and costumes to attempt a thorough analysis of the theatrical reality of oral delivery and its aural and visual impact.[8] The texts of farces, comedies, pantomimes and comic operas that have survived two centuries in great number were, even at the time, a step removed from dramatic performance. There is evidence, for instance, that plays were reworked and altered during successive representations; and often what theater bills proclaimed as a pantomime in one act is found in print or manuscript as a comedy in two. Even if a text represented fairly what was performed on stage, there is no way of knowing what license actors were wont to take with the script before them.

Nevertheless, the written text is, for us, of immense importance. Plays written for the boulevard theaters represented at least a basic material from which dramatic reality took its shape. Moreover, this dramatic literature was unique in its combination of artistic elements and forms, of themes, attitudes and cultural perspectives. The character of this literature and the stage it served may be restored at least in part by looking to the fundamental elements and forms of the boulevard's dramatic literature and the traditions from which they originated, to the intellectual substance of popular plays and its relation to enlightened and revolutionary thought in the last years of the old regime and the first years of the new.

3

The Cultural Composition of the Boulevard Stage

The Complexity of Dramatic Tradition in Popular Theater

The minor Parisian stage of the late-eighteenth century seems to have occupied for contemporaries an ambiguous position between theatrical traditions of the past and great dramatic traditions of its own day. Critics of boulevard theater likened the minor dramatic idiom to obsolete and improvisational genres of the seventeenth century; champions of the boulevard stage tied that theater to a sophisticated and self-conscious imitation of eighteenth century learned style and thought. The critical position, most often held by those contemporaries tied by station or taste to the great theaters, emphasized the repressive gap between distinctly different learned and popular dramatic traditions. Those who viewed the world of theater from its bottom tended to focus upon the likeness and interaction of great and little dramatic traditions. Contradictory as they may have been, both sides in the debate had grounds upon which to stand. Minor theaters in the fairs and on the boulevard poached upon the artistic monopolies of the royal theaters with relative impunity. Great theaters harbored elements of the fairground idiom within their own art. But this did not mean that the two dramatic cultures were confounded one with the other. There was no official recognition of similarity in art or tradition. Moreover, contemporaries willingly acknowledged at separate times both facets of the boulevard stage—that it was artistically imitative of the royal theaters and that it was aesthetically obsolescent. Together these observations suggest that boulevard theater comprised an amalgam of traditions and styles, eclectically drawn from the past and the present, from the classical stage and fairground amusements.

Boulevard Masks and Role-Types

The disparate mix of characters to be found on the boulevard stage reveals much about the complex cultural pedigree of the fairground tradition. It is a very curious fact that actors and actresses in the eighteenth century were locked by talent and appearance into predetermined and invariable roles. At the Ambigu-Comique, for instance, the actor Mayeur always performed the part of "the Lovers and the Fools"; Moreau took "the Roles of Arlequin"; Picardeaux took "those of the Father and the Peasant"; and the actress Durand performed "the Roles of the Young Girl in Love and the Coquette."[1] Masked figures such as the eternal Arlequin, with his face mask, lozenge-patterned, multicolored habit and wooden baton rubbed shoulders with heartsick lovers, hoodwinked fathers, coquettish maids and amorous young girls.

Most of these standard roles on the boulevard—Arlequin, the lovers, the valets, the old men and women—could be found at the royal theaters as well. They had in fact originated from beyond the boundaries of the little dramatic tradition as it was known in eighteenth century France. Contemporary efforts to raise a cultural barrier between great and minor theaters could not conceal this evidence of common origins and common development for two supposedly separate traditions. The key to this dramatic heritage lay in the complicated growth of French comic theater, long before royal government monopolized great theater or sanctioned the bifurcation of French theatrical culture. During the tremendous renascence of the sixteenth and seventeenth centuries in France, the native, popular farce and the emergent stage of a humanist elite had both fallen under the profound spell of the *commedia dell'arte,* carried to Paris and all of Europe by roving Italian players.[2]

Despite its affinity with the learned Renaissance stage of Italy, the *commedia dell'arte* was an improvised theater, in which bodily expression, acrobatics and buffoonery took precedence over extemporaneous, sophisticated dialogue. Like other artistic forms characteristic of oral culture, the improvised *commedia dell'arte* depended upon stock elements to structure its spontaneity. Each scenario, or sketch for a play, relied upon a staple set of characters that consisted traditionally of two old men, two serving men, the Captain, a serving girl, pairs of lovers and some minor variant roles. Over the course of decades and centuries, the several types evolved into distinct masks. The serving men diversified as Arlequin, Scapino, Pulchinella, Pedrolina; the old men as Pantalon, Cassandre, or the Doctor. In the case of the lovers, the tendency to stylize was less pronounced, yet even here certain names became more commonly used than others; Isabella, Angelique, Léandro and Ottavio.

The ready acceptance of these roles and masks on French soil was clearly hastened by structural similarities between the Italian improvised comedy and French farce. The farce had long been peopled with figures characterized by both conjugal situation and profession; husbands, wives, peasants, millers, shoemakers, doctors, lawyers and merchants were reduced to their quintessential characteristics. Under the Italian influence it was not uncommon for French buffoons to borrow the mask and costume of an Italian type for their stock characters or to adopt the name of Pulchinella and the form, traits and person of Arlequin. Nor was it long before French humanist comedy, affected by the farce, the *commedia dell'arte* and classical theater, adapted for itself general types such as the old men, lovers, valets, soubrettes and old women.[3]

Throughout the sixteenth and much of the seventeenth centuries, then, both the native French farce and the humanist comedy experienced similar Italian influence, sustained by the permanent establishment of an Italian company in Paris after 1661. Moreover, these genres experienced the Italian influence commonly, since both were performed side by side on the same stage. This common development of popular and learned forms was gradually effaced, however, by the ostracism of certain native and oral elements from the neo-classical stage and great culture. After the Comédie-Italienne was banished in 1697—17 years after the Italians had become a royal company—both the *commedia dell'arte* and the Italianized farce went "underground," to thrive in the fairgrounds of Paris. But the classical split between learned or great and popular or little dramatic traditions was not clean. In 1716 the Comédie-Italienne returned to reintroduce a pure strain of improvised comedy to great culture, even as the Italian company looked increasingly to French authors and a literate form. Through mid- to late-century, the creation and performance of the traditional Italian repertory on the royal stage flagged intermittently.[4] In contrast, Italian masks still figured prominently at the fairs and later on the boulevard. Though great and little theater no longer developed in common, the minor stage had remained constant to the dramatic heritage at one time fully shared by great theater.[5]

In the second half of the eighteenth century the greatest measure of that legacy was the number of traditional Italian and native French masks still in use in the fairs and on the boulevard. Mezetin, the cunning cheat; Scaramouche, lively, vain, without scruple; Pantalon, one of several lecherous old men; these, like Arlequin, were traditional masks of the *commedia dell'arte.* Other stock characters such as the hoarse and hump-backed Polichinelle and his naive companions Gilles and Pierrot, though probably French in origin, had developed as imitations or close relatives of the Italian masks. Moreover, the general types of old man, lovers, valet and soubrette—common as well to classical comedy—were characterized on the boulevard a great deal of the time by other figures of the *commedia dell'arte.* Cassandre, a ridiculous and amorous old man; the Captain, braggart and coward; Colombine, soubrette; Léandre, elegant and pleasing lover; Isabelle, a young girl—all these became on the boulevard stage stock characters very much like the masks Arlequin or Scaramouche.

The general types of the *commedia dell'arte* had been at all times characters of the urban middle and upper classes. This tradition was not altered on the boulevard, where Cassandre, Isabelle, Léandre and other less stylized re-creations of the old man and lover types invariably represented merchants, bourgeois, their sons and daughters. The masks Arlequin, Scaramouche or the stock character Colombine were not themselves members of the upper orders but served them closely in the capacity of valet or lady's maid. The urban middle classes and their servants, however, did not completely dominate the boulevard stage. Peasants and villagers also walked the boards, as did lower-class tradesmen, craftsmen and petty laborers. These types and the stock roles provided for them had no part in the urban world created by the *commedia dell'arte.* Their cultural origins were quite distinct from—if at times confused with—the Italian stage.

The peasants and villagers of rural setting had their roots in certain pastoral and sentimental developments of comic opera, a genre nurtured by the fair theaters of the early-eighteenth century. Originally this form had relied almost exclusively on Italian masks and stock characters.[6] With less frequency, oriental vizirs, gods and goddesses, troops of shepards and shephardesses—all associated with the marvelous and tragical themes of the Opéra and Comédie-Française parodied by the minor theaters—made their way into the fair tradition. Yet except for these bands of shepards, the peasant or bailiff figured very rarely, if at all, as major roles in comic operas written before 1740. The maturation of rustic types within the fair tradition depended on sentimental tendencies given shape in mid-century by Charles-Simon Favart.[7] With his *The Young Girl in Search of Soul* (1741), he brought to the stage in a definitive way the types of naive peasant and simple peasant girl and abandoned completely the masks and satire of the *commedia dell'arte* style of comic opera for a "gallant and comic genre."[8] He was followed in this almost universally.

Characters of the urban lower classes were also developed at the fair theaters in the first half of the eighteenth century. The use of cobblers and other minor tradesmen on stage apparently depended on the fitful influence of the *poissard* or billingsgate slang, a realistic reproduction of popular Parisian speech and life that first surfaced in late-seventeenth century burlesque literature.[9] By the late 1600s this bawdy dialect was to be found at the Comédie-Italienne. Because of the burlesque's passage on the Italian stage, at the early fair short sketches known as *parades* combined billingsgate speech with the standard masks of the *commedia dell'arte* rather than with popular characters.[10] The appearance of urban lower-class characters really suited to the bawdy dialect did not occur until much later. In the 1720s and '30s several marionette shows inaugurated a strong tradition of urban, lower-class puppets, but the use of cobblers and other minor tradesmen in comic operas at the fair was rare until the 1750s. In that decade Jean-Joseph Vadé, known to his contemporaries as the creator of the billingsgate genre,[11] brought fishmongers, laundresses, soldiers and wigmakers prominently and with great success to the Fair Theater, or Opéra-Comique.

After the union of the Opéra-Comique with the Comédie-Italienne in 1762, many of the roles associated with the comic opera passed with that genre to the boulevard as well as to the royal stage. The particular history and influence of the Fair Theater must account on the boulevard at least for standard roles as diverse as Cupid, Peasant Girl, Niais or Fool, commingled with the Arlequin, Léandre and Isabelle inherited from an even earlier tradition of Italian theater. Even after the comic opera was prohibited to the minor theaters in 1764, these many different characters and types remained to people the *parades,* farces and comic scenes that passed through the dramatic censorship of the boulevard. The Comédie-Italienne and the boulevard theaters made use of the same constellation of characters—with one important exception. Lower-class characters do not appear to have passed as new and original roles to the Comédie-Italienne in 1762.

The influence of Vadé and his billingsgate figures on that stage had in fact been cut short, both by his untimely death (1757) and by the overwhelming preference of the late Fair Theater and the Comédie-Italienne for the sentimental comic opera and rustic characters of Favart.[12] Yet the billingsgate type did figure as a standard role on the boulevard, even if it was scorned by the more refined companies of Paris. In the tradition of Vadé, the former fair actor Toussaint Gaspard Taconet carried the billingsgate slang and character from the Fair Theater to the boulevard when he joined the Théâtre de Nicolet in 1764. Indeed, the cobblers, fishwives and especially the "roles of Taconet" prominently featured at the Grands-Danseurs commemorated this comic genius whose successful farces and veracious rendition of the humble and untutored cobbler had first brought to the boulevard stage "naive paintings of the adventures of the People."[13] Somewhat later, in 1778, Fleury de l'Ecluze, another former fair actor whose works in billingsgate slang were often confused with those of Vadé, established on the boulevard a theater—later to become the Variétés-Amusantes—wholly dedicated for a number of years to the lower-class genre and its characters. The billingsgate character alone of all other types had become the boulevard's special province.

The many role-types that hailed from a variety of cultural sources and entered the little dramatic idiom at several points in time in the seventeenth and eighteenth centuries still commanded the boulevard stage in the years 1785-1794. There were, to be sure, new elements such as savages, turks and fairies, but these characters figured sparingly in a repertory heavily larded with the established types of old man, lovers, Italian masks, peasants, artisans and tradesmen.[14] Since these traditional roles continued to govern the minor stage, it is possible to assess, in their proportionate use, something of the cultural disposition of the little dramatic tradition in the last years of the old regime. Of 260 characters that appeared in 75 plays on the boulevard between 1785-1794, 60 percent belonged to the classic types of lovers, parents and servants first brought to French soil by the Italian practitioners of the *commedia dell'arte.* Partly because by the eighteenth century these characters were to be found throughout Europe and at the great theaters of Paris as well, the Italian

Plate 10. The boulevard's plebeian role-type was memorably represented by the naive apprentice Janot in *The Beaten Pay the Price*. Photo: Bibl. nat. Paris.

nationality of such types had long been erased. Italian comic influence was, however, still noticeably felt on the boulevard, since at least 5 percent of the characters onstage were masks of Italian inspiration. In contrast to these role-types, originally foreign to the popular dramatic tradition in France, about 34 percent of boulevard characters had been developed indigenously on the early Parisian fairgrounds.

The distribution of role-types on the boulevard stage reveals more about that popular theater than simply its dramatic origins. The characters reveal something of the socio-cultural inclinations of the boulevard idiom, its interest and its intended audience. First and foremost these boulevard types belonged to a domestic world. This is obvious in the case of the lovers, parents, servants and masks. Significantly enough, peasants, tradesmen, even the bailiff were simply redundant versions of the basic domestic types in rural or plebian dress. Secondly, that world was of a predominantly urban and Parisian cast. Less than a quarter, or 21.5 percent, hailed instead from the rural villages of France. Finally, it was a middle- and lower-class world. Though certain of the role-types—the old men and women, the lovers and servants—were shared by the Comédie-Française and the Comédie-Italienne, a classical aesthetic distinguished between their use on great and little stage by their social realization. Through the mid-1780s the boulevard was constrained by censorship to portrayals of none but the Third Estate. Middle-class bourgeois shared the minor stage in roughly equal proportions with tradesmen, servants and peasants.[15]

Judging from these simple statistics, in the minds of contemporaries trained to the classical aesthetic the boulevard stage possessed very broad, generalized appeal to that large social category known under the old regime as "the people." D'Aubignac had long ago taught that the characters on stage might be appreciated and understood only by spectators of similar condition. Indeed, bourgeois, servants, tradesmen, peasants—or at least ex-peasants—all these might have been found seated in a boulevard hall. That is not to say that significant numbers of the well-to-do and upper classes were not also included in the boulevard public, since we have found their attendance there keenly resented by the royal actors.[16] But so long as censorship constrained role-types to the middle and lower classes, it was believed that boulevard dramatic culture could not reflect the aristocratic presence. As far as contemporaries were concerned, the roles that the boulevard stage inherited from farcical and pastoral traditions of the past and the social realizations allowed them by censorship firmly bound these little theaters through the 1760s, 1770s and early 1780s to a Parisian popular culture.

The taste and influence of fashionable, upper-class spectators did eventually penetrate the boulevard stage, but not until the fragmentation of privileged monopolies in the 1780s weakened the institutional control of genres and censorship. By the mid-'80s the development of new roles on the boulevard increasingly reflected the aesthetic authority of the great companies of Paris. Most noticeable was the introduction of upper-class characters to the predominantly popular stage. Attempts to raise the quality of theater on the boulevard in the 1780s resulted in an emphasis on middle-class and, when censorship by the royal actors grew lax after 1785, on upper-class roles at the expense of lower-class characters.

Other, more subtle changes had already been underway. After 1775 the use of the masks and stock characters of the *commedia dell'arte* in newly-written plays declined noticeably. Instead of employing the old man Cassandre, for instance, with his stylized characterization of the bourgeois parent, boulevard playwrights turned towards individualistic, hence more realistic, portrayals of the general type father. Though it belonged to the traditional role-type of father, lover or servant, peasant or artisan, the individualized character differed fundamentally from the mask or stock character. The latter had been encouraged by the tradition of extemporaneous performance and oral transmission found in the *commedia dell'arte* and, to a lesser extent, on the early fair stage. The art of the great theaters, conceived and transmitted in written form, discouraged the development of masks and stock characters.[17] Rather, a learned concern to avoid plagiarizing artistic genius, growing in intensity over the course of the eighteenth century, tended to protect the uniqueness of individual characters. By the late 1770s and 1780s the many young girls, old men or peasants created as individualized characters on the minor stage also differed one from the other in nuance of character and personality. Except for the old Italian masks and types, none of the characters created on the boulevard in the years 1785-94 were held as common coin to be passed from one play to another.

None, that is, except the very few whose début upon the stage had captured the imagination of the Parisian public. The valet Figaro, first conceived by Beaumarchais in *The Barber of Seville* (1775) and revived by the author in 1784 in *The Crazy Day or the Marriage of Figaro,* is an important case in point. After the second, triumphant appearance of the unforgettable valet at the Comédie-Française, "Figaro" turned up in a spate of plays destined for the boulevard. At three of the minor theaters no less than seven "Figaro" plays—written by at least four different playwrights—were first performed in 1784 and 1785.[18] For a short period of time, "Figaro" very nearly became a stock character on the boulevard stage. In their parodies and imitations boulevard playwrights willfully transposed "Figaro," along with his entire supporting cast and their jealousies, loves and intrigues, to other times and places. Yet despite the costume "à la figaro" to be found in one boulevard theater's inventory, the individualized character never generalized as the mask Figaro. This was perhaps due to the fact that the Comédie-Française attempted to prevent the use of its individualized character by any theater other than itself. In their grievance to the police the actors cited what they called the property rights of the author and the acting company to the "new [in other words, original] character."[19] The actors only managed, however, to suppress the names, not the characters, of the original play. Under guise, Beaumarchais' "Figaro" went on to inspire directly the prominent portrayal on the boulevard stage of the clever, socially critical and unservile valet. An individualized character originally brought to life on the great stage had reanimated in its own image the characterization of an old role-type on the boulevard.

Other successful figures, notably those originating on the boulevard itself, did become stock characters to a far greater extent than "Figaro," whose imitation in newly-written plays died out after 1785. The naive apprentice Janot, the Pointu family, the brave but simple peasant Nicodème, and to a lesser extent the chimney sweep Barogo and the Père Duchesne—all but one manifestations of the billingsgate role special to the boulevard—appeared again and again in the corpus of boulevard plays.[20] Janot, for example, first presented at the Variétés-Amusantes in Dorvigny's *The Beaten Pay the Price* of 1779, recurred in at least 22 separate plays between 1779 and 1807; the Pointu family appeared in some seven plays from de Beaunoir's original *Jerome Pointu* of 1781 through to 1794; and Nicodème, created by Cousin Jacques in 1790, figured prominently in at least seven plays in the coming decades. Though these popular heroes had been born of a literate theater, the measure of universality with which they were endowed suggests the development on the boulevard, however transitory, of a French *commedia dell'arte,* in which Arlequin and other Italian characters were replaced by stock types of the Parisian lower classes.[21]

Heavily laden in the early 1760s with the dramatic baggage of the early fairgrounds, the boulevard slowly moved away in coming decades from the masked figures of improvisational, comic skits towards the individualized characters of literate theater. Originally constrained to middle- and lower-class types, the boulevard broadened its representation in the 1780s of well-to-do and aristocratic characters. At the same time the boulevard stage experimented with stock characters of a French and plebian cast. To some extent these developments appear contradictory. Yet in the 1780s the boulevard reflected more faithfully than at any previous time the social composition and cultural interests of its "popular" public. For decades before and after 1760 repression and censorship had confined the little theaters to aging masks and lower-class characters, even while the public may well have been predominantly of the well-to-do and fashionable classes. The boulevard continued to cater to this public through the 1770s and '80s with its efforts to raise the quality of its theater and match the social status of its characters to that of its clientele. At the same time, the low prices for seats forced upon the little theaters in 1769 had allowed for growth in the attendance of a lower- and middle-class public. Their tastes and interests stimulated the maturation of the popular hero of tradesman or serving stock.

The casual alliance of stock figures and individualized characters, of upper- and lower-class roles, on the minor stage of the 1780s suggests how easily a diverse public sat together in boulevard halls, despite social distances in old regime society between one rank and another. It suggests also how well the boulevard adjusted old dramatic forms to new, how well it integrated elements of the traditional fairground stage with elements of great theater. The boulevard reflected in its lengthy roster of masks, role-types and individualized characters an eclectic dramatic heritage and the social and cultural diversity of the Parisian populace that comprised its audience.

Traditional Plot Formulas and Their Sentimental Transposition

The evolution of role-types in little theater did not occur independently of important structural changes in the organization of dramatic action. Rather, the kind of character portrayed upon the stage, whether mask or individualized character, was integrally bound to the plot. The traditional roles of father, lovers and servants had been originally suited to a very particular form of dramatic action—the love intrigue. In the *commedia dell'arte* the traditional masks and stock characters improvised for three acts and more a complicated intrigue that turned upon a small number of themes and conventional resolutions.[22] The young, with the aid of their servants, triumphed over parental obstacles in the path of true love and gained not only each other but the full pardon of their elders. Throughout the years 1660-1760 French classical comedy also depended heavily on a love intrigue derived from, amongst other traditions, Italian improvised comedy. What E.J.H. Greene calls the "Formula" consisted primarily of one action in which "the spontaneous loves of the young, traversed by the old, are aided and abetted by the servants."[23] This same formulaic intrigue dominated the fare of the early boulevard theater.

The Italian influence was readily acknowledged on the boulevard. The love intrigue was at first closely associated with the Italian masks and stock characters. Moreover, a number of plays were referred to in manuscript as "canevas," written scenarios whose action and dialogue were to be improvised on stage. Though many of these so-called "canevas" were in fact fully elaborated plays, they had willfully borrowed themes and intrigues from scenarios of the old Italian theater.[24] One such, a "pantomime" written in 1772 and performed with great success through the 1780s and '90s, was Placide's *Arlequin the English Cerberus*[25] (also referred to as *Arlequin Entombed* or *The Lover Entombed*). Contemporary comment on the dramatic action and the style of that pantomime suggests that it remained true to Gherardi's original outlines of dramatic plot sketched in the late-seventeenth century.[26] The comic interest and excitement of the improvised play had depended on the acrobatics and mime indicated at various points throughout the text. The rhythm of speech was to be broken constantly by stylized routines such as "the *lazzi* [or pantomime] of asking for a fifteen sou piece" or "the *lazzi* of urinating" in which a premium was placed on clever physical movement and obscene innuendo. To judge by certain reports of the immoral and degrading postures of Arlequin in Placide's play, the boulevard imitation had copied the physical style of the Italian stage as well as the plot.

Though very much in the tradition of the Italian improvised art, Placide's *Arlequin the English Cerberus* differed in an important way from most of the love intrigues written in later years for the boulevard. At its professional height, the Italian scenario had tended towards the visual elaboration of complicated imbroglios, to the detriment of the intrigue itself.[27] Arlequin's pantomime as a dog, for instance, embellished his courtship scene with Colombine in a manner wholly extraneous to the love intrigue. The dramatic plot more typical of boulevard theater was stripped of all elements that confused or obscured the love intrigue and its formulaic progression. In this austerity, though not in its acrobatics and stage business, the boulevard love intrigue more closely resembled the "Formula" enacted upon the great stages of Paris.

It is important to remember that although little theater shared with great theater an emphasis on the love intrigue plot, its realization on the boulevard displayed none of the sophistication and complexity of the "Formula" at the Comédie-Française or Comédie-Italienne. The actors, it must be remembered, were entitled to prohibit anything in the fairs and on the boulevard that closely resembled their own art and genres. For the Comédie-Italienne this undoubtedly meant the too-clever imbroglio; for the Comédie-Française the too-skillful manipulation of the "Formula." On the minor stage the number of acts was, perforce, cut to one or two and the subjects were trivialized. Within these limitations the boulevard perfected a very simple love intrigue, the formulas of which consisted in one coherent action, one obstacle to true love and one neat resolution.

The bare skeleton of the boulevard love intrigue is simply drawn. (See Figure 4.) Three "generations" or ranks of individuals—the parents, lovers and servants provided for by the traditional role-types—participated in the dramatic action. Bonds of filial or servile duty tied these generations into so many familial or domestic hierarchies. In those love intrigues not strictly of a domestic nature, the same hierarchy was nevertheless maintained. The bourgeois, the seigneur, the bailiff or their female equivalents simply occupied the position of ultimate authority in the social hierarchy. Common artisans, peasants or servants filled in the appropriate roles of old, young and servant according to their proper social rank or status. Two, perhaps three, families or social units would then become implicated in a simple imbroglio of crossed purposes and desires that revolved, in each case, upon love and marriage.

In a limited sense, boulevard theater revealed in its manipulation of the love intrigue what some have called a "paradox" of oral culture.[28] It is common to find in folk tales and folk songs based on the spontaneous repetition of a circumscribed set of linguistic and thematic formulas, for instance, that the same "text" is duplicated differently and different "texts" are essentially the same. This is largely true, on a structural level, of the boulevard plays. The plot structures of three plays, written at nine- and six-year intervals and produced at three different boulevard theaters have been drawn as illustration of this point. (See Figure 4.)

Without question, each of these several plots may be superimposed upon the basic structure of the love intrigue, although in no case is a full complement of character elements made use of. The generations are nearly complete in *The Furnished Room,* but in the other two plays the servants are dismissed altogether—and so, too, the young man in *Jean Who Cries and Jean Who Laughs.* Nor are the characters engaged in the same configuration of conflicting desires. If *The Furnished Room* is mainly concerned with the love of the young, *Jean Who Cries and Jean Who Laughs* exposes the ridiculous lust of two old widowers for each other's daughter, and *The Rustic Evening* presents a round-robin of love stimulated by the unnatural desire of a wealthy widow for the young miller in her employ. Yet despite the unique "story" of each play, these different texts are structurally the same. The young have invariably formed amorous ties prior to the opening of the play and without their parents' consent. Adelaide loves Léandre; Sophie and Victorine have lovers of their own; Blaise and Babet wish to marry. The parents, or those who stand in their place, soon raise some kind of obstacle to the consummation of young love. In *The Furnished Room* it is the social pretension of Madame Hautaine, who declares Adelaide too good for her suitor; in *Jean Who Cries and Jean Who Laughs* it is the pact between the two old men to take each other's daughter to wed; in *The Rustic Evening* it is the bailiff's refusal to match his niece with the apprentice Blaise and then the bold courtship of that young man by his own mistress, the widow Gervais. To break the tension of generational conflict and resolve dramatic action, some kind of trickery—disguise, deception, or coercion—is perpetrated in favor of the young. Very much in the Italian tradition, it is Scaramouche who engineers the social deception of Madame Hautaine by masking Léandre as a wealthy prince; Sophie and Victorine alter their personalities to discourage their old suitors; and the bailiff consents to his niece's marriage in order to gain Madame Gervais for himself. The dramatic movement of each play is thus based upon the same pattern of formulas, enumerated simply as love and revolt of the young, parental obstacle, and trickery. Though the texts are different in particulars, they are essentially alike.

As long as the production of boulevard plays depended upon an endless variation of the basic formulas of the love intrigue, the little dramatic corpus resembled an oral literature much like a corpus of folk tales. But if boulevard theater possessed artistic structure similar to oral literature in this instance, so, too, had the great stages of Paris. Through the first half of the eighteenth century this same love intrigue in somewhat more sophisticated style dominated 50 to 85 percent of the comedies performed by the royal companies.[29] Indeed, the likeness of classical and folk literature has been argued by a number of literary critics and historians, and been recently summarized by Lionel Gossman.[30] These scholars generally agree that the aesthetics of folk and classical literatures were identical in assumption and purpose. Both assumed the collective expression of social values and social order. As in folk literature, there was "no genre, no written work of classicism that [did] not suppose collective consumption, akin to speech . . . it [was] a product conceived for oral transmission."[31] The highly formulaic love intrigue on the great stage and on the boulevard is but one more indication that both high and low theatrical cultures in eighteenth century France shared a dramatic bond with each other and with folk traditions of the past.

Significantly enough, on the great stages of Paris the traditional love intrigue declined in use after mid-century. Greene argues that the "Formula" dropped off sharply in the 1750s, from 50 to 85 percent to 10 to 20 percent.[32] In comparison to such change on the royal stage, boulevard theater remained much more conservative. The simple love intrigue was written and performed throughout the years 1770-1794; not until 1780 or so did the dramatic action of a great many new plays become increasingly more complex in imitation of developments in great theater. From 1780 on, but not before, more and more theatrical interest focused upon supplemental themes, extraneous or not to the love intrigue, such as social equality, nature and sentimental love. In early boulevard plays dramatic action was almost entirely formulaic and physical; in later plays, written after 1780, the action was increasingly emotional, if not intellectual. Only after a lag of 30 years or so did the boulevard stage, too, begin to shift away from the love intrigue and the formalism of an oral-like dramatic literature.

Greene makes no attempt to explain the dissolution of the formulaic love intrigue on the great stage, yet it seems likely that its death knell was sounded by intellectuals and playwrights anxious to improve upon a stale classical theater with meaningful contemporary drama of their own.[33] The most important of experimentations with new forms and purpose—at least in its ultimate effect upon the boulevard stage—was the *drame* or bourgeois drama. The drama was meant to be a vehicle of moral education, tied to the secular philosophy of the Enlightenment. Like the fantastic imbroglio of the old *commedia dell'arte,* the intellectual baggage of that Enlightenment tended to obscure and alter the love intrigue. In the exposition of nature, social morality and sensibility, the comic formulas of obstacle and intrigue were abandoned for a sentimental pathos that combined the subject matter of the comedy with the dramatic actions of the classical tragedy.

The bourgeois drama's first success occurred on the privileged stage. *The Philosopher in Spite of Himself,* the first of the great dramas, was performed at the Comédie-Française in 1765; by 1771 the genre was well-established within that theater's repertory. In those same years the drama took firm hold at the Comédie-Italienne as *opéras-comiques larmoyantes,* lachrymose and sentimental comic operas.[34] This tremendous innovation in form on the great stages was, at first, formally barred from the boulevard theaters. The royal actors harshly excised from minor theater any comedy that suggested either literary or intellectual merit. The comic opera, a secondary vehicle of the drama, was prohibited to the minor stage after 1769. Nonetheless the bourgeois drama did reach the boulevard—and rather quickly—in the form of parody.

The satirical imitation of great theater had long been part of the fair tradition and it was inevitable that the bourgeois drama as well as comedy or opera should have been parodied on the boulevard. In late 1774 Voltaire commented again and again in his voluminous correspondence on the unusual circumstances in which the same subject (and a noble one at that) cut through the dramatic boundaries of Parisian theater: "It is said that Henry IV is going to appear at one and the same time at the Comédie-Italienne and at the French [Theater], as well as on the pont neuf [where street singers gathered]."[35] While the royal companies offered *Henry VI or the Battle of Ivry* and *The Hunting Party of Henri IV,* the Ambigu-Comique and the Grands-Danseurs both performed pantomimes said to have been direct imitations of the great dramas.[36] With satirical intent Voltaire slyly allowed that the most successful—and pleasing—of these plays was probably to be found at Nicolet's. Even so, the sentimental influence of the bourgeois drama on the themes and structure of plays written for the boulevard did not really make itself felt until the very late 1770s and early '80s. For this reason, the diffusion of the drama outside the great tradition may well have depended largely on the aesthetic propaganda of men like Nougaret and Mercier. Both men had reasoned long and hard that the moral mission of the drama might be advantageously directed towards the socialization of the lower classes of Paris. Mercier, in fact, seems to have tried out—or at least tolerated—one if not more of his own dramas at the Théâtre des Associés, one of the poorer and lesser known boulevard theaters.[37]

There was yet another factor, besides the direct link between traditions created by parody or efforts to inspire a moral theater, that stimulated the development of the boulevard drama. That was the determination on the part of at least one boulevard director to raise his theater in quality to the level of sophisticated culture.[38] Tired of learned scorn for an unrefined popular stage, Audinot, director of the Ambigu-Comique and himself an author of pantomimes, introduced on his stage in late 1780 one of the first of popular dramatic pieces to explore a world of sentiment. With *The Black and White Prince,* a "fairy-play in 2 acts, mixed with dialogue, music and dance," Audinot shook off the heavy arm of censorship by the royal actors with an auspicious innovation in dramatic form. In this play Audinot sought to unite the spectacular physical effects of the traditional boulevard stage with the moral suasions of the drama, enlightened ideas and sophisticated manners:

> Far from allowing indecencies in the Plays of his theater, he sought all means of uniting the delights of coup d'oeil and the appeal of the *Pantomime* to the attractions of the Melo-Drama, to the delicacy of ideas and the purety of Dialogue.[39]

Indeed, *The Black and White Prince* revealed in its structure a subtle alteration of the formulas and dramatic action typical of more traditional boulevard plays. Since *The Black and White Prince* had not abandoned the subject of frustrated love, certain of the love intrigue formulas—parental obstacle and revolt of the young—were to be found in the pantomime. The decrees of an oracle stood between Zulica and the young girl he loved, Rosine, but in spite of any and all fairy-obstacles, he awakened Rosine to the feelings of his heart. Unlike the traditional love intrigue, with its emphasis upon the inappropriate marriage schemes of the old parent or the mischievous shenanigans of the servants and masks, Audinot's sentimental pantomime concentrated upon the nature and development of emotional ties between the young. And it was this sentimental emotion, rather than any attempts to hoodwink parental authority, that overcame parental obstacles and resolved dramatic tension. Rosine unwittingly transformed Zulica into a monster; she pleaded to be made ugly rather than renounce him forever. Touched by the young girl's sentiment, the fairy restored Zulica to his former self and the oracle was forgotten.

In a great number of plays written around 1780 and after, sentimental love ties and other enlightened themes were roughly grafted upon the traditional love intrigue with somewhat less innovation than that achieved by Audinot. For the most part, this meant that all the basic formulas of the love intrigue—parental obstacle, love and revolt of the young, and trickery—still structured the main action of the play. In *The Wise Gardener or Lison Was Scared* (1780), for instance, the author tacked on to his simple and customary intrigue an enlightened exposition of natural love that was irrelevant to the resolution of dramatic action. It was, nonetheless, an indicator of sentimental emotion. Yet despite the "wise gardener's" arguments that his niece should follow her heart rather than heed the authority of the Baroness in her choice of marriage partner, the young girl's fate was sealed not by her choice but by a physical tussle for her bouquet between two young rivals for her hand.

In other plays, sentimental action was often more perfectly integrated within the love intrigue. Though enough of the traditional plot was employed to identify these plays as love intrigues, the penultimate trick was often noticeably altered. The action of *Père Duchesne,* written and performed in 1789, was nearly identical to the love intrigue of *The Wise Gardener,* replete with parental obstacle and revolt of the young. The young servant Lucille's

Plate 11. Scene from *Sleeping Beauty*, a sentimental pantomime at the Ambigu-Comique akin to *The Black and White Prince*. Photo: Bibl. nat. Paris.

desire to marry the chimney sweep Duchesne, whom she knew to be a kind and honest man, was threatened by her masters' low opinion of Duchesne's blustery, bawdy manner of speech. It was, however, the sentimental perception of his true character on the part of the Marquise—and not some coercive deception—that finally convinced her to consent to Duchesne's union with Lucille. *Blaise the Ill-Tempered,* written in 1782, had already incorporated this sentimental twist within a traditional plot. The mean old farmer Blaise mistreated his family and stood in the way of his daughter's marriage until they all resolved to leave him. Whereupon his heart was softened and his eyes were opened to the necessity of sentimental emotion.

A great number of plays were written which cannot be considered traditional love intrigues, or even sentimental love intrigues, for they were largely devoid of all customary formulas or dramatic action. In these sentimental plays one character or more acted emotionally on another or others, appealing to his or her natural feelings and inner sense of morality. Sentimental emotion in these plays comprised a far wider range of personal interaction than love or desire between the young. In *The Virtuous Courtesan* (1782) a young man recognized his sensitive sister in a hardened courtesan and successfully arranged her reconciliation with their father. For much of the play, however, Constance feared to act upon her chastened feelings, and it was her brother who finally persuaded her to return to a virtuous life. Similarly, in *The Officious Friend or the Return from Slavery* (1785) Sainville pleaded the case of a husband, long lost and presumed dead, before a woman who had already planned her second marriage and resisted welcoming to her arms a man she had not seen for many a year. Sentimental plays such as the three on *The Baron of Trenck* (1788), *The Cavalry Sergeant* (1783) and *Crime is Punished Sooner or Later* (1788), whose subjects ranged from an old soldier's chance defense of a girl in danger to the pathetic communion of an imprisoned nobleman and a humble turnkey, articulated the virtues of friendship, honor, courage, loyalty and honesty between individuals unbound to one another by familial or amorous bonds.

Although the exposition of sentimental emotion and natural morality tended to liberate dramatic action from the love intrigue of the past, traditional plot structures did remain in vestigial form even in the most sentimental of plays. Unlike the sentimental love intrigue, in which dramatic formulas retained much of their former shape and function, the sentimental play transposed and often attenuated customary dramatic formulas. Obstacles to the flow of sentimental emotion were no longer, necessarily, parental ones. Both Constance in *The Virtuous Courtesan* and the widow in *The Officious Friend* themselves created the emotional blockages to sentimental action in those plays. The same was true in plays dealing with social hierarchies other than the family. The Baron of Trenck had at first scorned to recognize loyalty and goodness in a man far beneath him in social honor and dignity (*The Baron of Trenck or the Intrepid Lieutenant,* 1788). The obstacle formula now rested on the inability of major characters in the play to recognize or acknowledge the legitimacy of sentiment and natural morality. The revolt of the young, in those plays in which it did occur, was weakened in its impact, since the obstacle was to be overcome by emotional suasion. Neither the young Dumond in *The Good Mother* (1785) nor Dorsigny in *The Irascible Master* (1789) acted to undermine parental authority. They sought, rather, to persuade the parent that interference with the love match was unnatural and unnecessary. The final trick or resolution of sentimental intrigue did not lie in physical deception or coercion but in a moral recognition or transformation that dissolved all obstacles. In *The Beautiful Flower-Girl* (1790) the social tension created by a young nobleman's love for a local flower-girl was broken by the sudden revelation of the girl's gentle birth. The Baron of Trenck learned to recognize and trust in the moral worth of his jailor; the peasant woman in *Crime is Punished* (1788) found room in her heart to forgive the thieves who had held her and her child at bay.

In order to analyze the component parts and cultural origins of dramatic action on the boulevard stage in the late-eighteenth century, the relationship between the love intrigue and the sentimental play has been examined developmentally. However, the chronology of boulevard plays indicates that this development occurred in only the most general way. The purest form of love intrigue, tied to the Italian masks and characters, was most often to be found as an old piece dating from the 1770s. The first inroads of sophisticated style did not appear until 1780 or so, when individualized characters and sentimental emotion began to alter and transform the formulaic action of the traditional stage. Yet at this same point development seems to have halted, for the plays subsequently written in the 1780s and early '90s show no obvious and steady trend away from the old formulas and towards an increasingly sophisticated or learned style. Examined historically, rather than structurally, the new repertory on the boulevard stage in the late 1780s and '90s appears to have been a jumble of differing elements and styles, without a prevailing tendency towards either extreme of formulaic intrigue or sentimental action. In the years 1788-1789, for instance, innovative sentimental plays were introduced to the boulevard public side by side with traditional farcical intrigues. It is only the relative absence of masks in plays written in the later'80s and the relative growth of sentimental and philosophical themes after 1780 that mark the direction in which little theater was headed.

Indeed, the introduction of sentiment had significantly changed the nature of the boulevard stage and its dramatic literature. Unlike the love intrigue, the purely sentimental play had no formal structure or patterned actions as such of its own. Its principle identifying features were, rather, to be found in certain philosophical and moral themes elaborated emotionally at length throughout the play. Even in those plays in which sentiment was combined with old formulas, the form and thrust of dramatic action was no longer bound to the physical mime and stage business of the traditional intrigue. The fashion for sentimental emotion had tied the old forms in an innovative manner to the refined style of the great stage. As a result, more and more emphasis was placed upon the emotional life of middle- and upper-class characters. When woodcutters and seamstresses did appear upon the stage, it was not to indulge in the gay and bawdy antics of Arlequin or the fishwives of the early fair. Now they enacted morality stories and proverbs appropriate to the manners of their class but affective and tasteful in nature. On the late-eighteenth century boulevard stage the farcical comic plot, honed by decades of traditional dramatic custom in the fairs, stood but half the ground. The moral lesson, derived from the innovative literature of great theater and learned culture, stood the other.

Obsolescence and Innovation in Boulevard Theater: The Complexity of Tradition Understood

Like the tight-rope walkers at Nicolet's Grands-Danseurs du Roi, boulevard theater as a whole balanced between the opposing poles of past dramatic traditions and the contemporary authority of the great stages of Paris. The past was kept alive on the popular stage by a number of circumstances. It had been a matter of social and political policy in Paris during the 1760s and 1770s to maintain the continued association of boulevard theaters with the entertainments of the fair. Nicolet was apparently enjoined to lard his program with acrobatics and tight-rope walkers; each performance at the Théâtre des Associés required the opening pranks of Polichinelle and marionettes; Audinot was initially committed to a troupe of children.[40] The incorporation of sophisticated styles and learned themes within the boulevard tradition was severely hampered, both by the co-optation of the Opéra-Comique within great theater in 1762 and by the effective censorship of popular plays by the royal actors for nearly two decades after 1769. The actors enforced rigid distinctions between their classical stage and the fair idiom to which they held the boulevard theaters. Policy and censorship had their effects on the quality and form of little theater. Lacking alternatives, the boulevard initially relied heavily on the masks, characters and intrigues of the *commedia dell'arte,* an antecedent tradition which had long been the appanage of the fair. The masks carried onto the boulevard certain dramatic practices originally associated with improvised theater, such as acrobatics, pantomime, ribald humor and formulaic plots.

By 1780-1785 the socio-cultural environment that shaped the boulevard idiom had begun to change noticeably. Again, a number of complementary circumstances acted to integrate the traditional boulevard play with the dramatic styles of great theater. The social and political policy that had enforced the rigid separation of great and little theaters and theatrical art had begun to dissolve. The economic profits of the boulevard had secured for the minor theaters a legitimate position amongst the theatrical institutions of Paris; they gained thereby in artistic and aesthetic prominence. This subtle elevation of the boulevard stage, the result of enlightened public opinion and liberalizing government, had its result in the decline of effective censorship by the royal actors. The French and Italian companies were no longer able to monopolize sophistication in dramatic style. The bourgeois drama effected a transposition and transformation of the figures and formulas of the boulevard stage in keeping with learned practice. Italian masks and characters gave way to individualized characters; sentimental stories of many kinds offered new alternatives to the traditional love intrigue, which itself altered significantly under their impact.

It is no longer difficult to understand the ambiguity that surrounded contemporary reference to the dramatic styles and idiom of the boulevard theaters. At a fundamental level both great and little theaters shared in the predominant aesthetic of the time, one that confused distinctions between traditions of the past and the present,[41] between dramatic idioms of the folk and the fairground and those of the classical stage. It would have been impossible for contemporaries to distinguish, for instance, between oral and literate elements within theatrical art or to assign these categories, respectively, to the boulevard and the royal companies. It was possible, however, to discriminate between genres[42] and to confine the boulevard to dramatic forms of the past, such as farces and *parades,* or to genres such as the pantomime actually developed in the fairs. Due in part to the repressive function of privilege and censorship, the small theaters lagged decades behind the dramatic course charted by the three great stages of Paris. Many of the elements and styles of the boulevard theater were obsolescent, tied to traditions moribund at the Comédie-Française or the Comédie-Italienne.

What distinguished the great from the little stage at any one point in time in the late-eighteenth century was, simply, a matter of degree.[43] Both Italian masks and the formulaic love intrigue fell from prominence at the Comédie-Française and the Comédie-Italienne after mid-century. In the next 30 years these same elements were reinforced in the boulevard idiom. Until the 1780s, censorship and social policy forced the boulevard stage to resort heavily to the masks and intrigues no longer of interest to the great theaters. But the persistence of traditional styles seems also to have been a matter of choice on the boulevard stage. Even after the relaxation of censorship and the development of sentimental fare, the traditional masks and the love intrigue still appeared in newly-written plays. Moreover, for decades the boulevard repertory continued to feature prominently traditional plays of the 1760s and 1770s alongside recent sophisticated and sentimental popular dramas.

Even those contemporaries who likened the boulevard to great theater were unlikely to confuse the two. One was for the people; the other for the social elite. One for theatrical apprenticeship; the other for serious artistic endeavor. Moreover, in contrast to the original impulse of great theater, the boulevard was apparently of derivative motivation. Apparently, but not really. Despite the conservative impetus of dramatic idiom on the boulevard, the minor stage was not wholly dependent on great culture and its past or current traditions. There is reason to believe that in the development of the sentimental play in the late 1780s and throughout the 1790s the boulevard quite surpassed great theater in artistic and aesthetic innovation. Boulevard experimentation with sophisticated dramatic style and enlightened, sentimental philosophy had tremendous effects on traditional dramatic action. Theatrical artists along the boulevard were creative by virtue of the very fact that they were forced to distinguish their art from that of the royal stages. Sentimental pathos found its fullest expression not in the truncated comedies of the minor theaters but in the spectacular pantomimes long considered their special province. These dialogued pantomimes prefigured the melodrama, which in turn directly affected the birth of Romantic drama. It was that nineteenth century genre, moreover, which finally proclaimed an end to the classical aesthetic on the great stages of Paris.[44]

In sum, the minor theaters of late-eighteenth century Paris bridged two idioms and two worlds: the obsolescent dramatic traditions still alive in the fairgrounds and the sophisticated dramatic literature of great theater and great culture. Characters as diverse in their origins and in their actions as Arlequin, Figaro and Janot all walked the boulevard stage in the years 1785-1794. Yet such cultural interchange, perhaps at its greatest ferment in the last decades of the eighteenth century, did not mean for the boulevard complete dramatic dependence on traditions foreign to itself. The universality of the individual, lower-class character Janot, on the one hand, and the subtle transposition of formulas in the sentimental love intrigue, on the other, suggest that the boulevard stage was able to fashion from very different traditions an intermediate style and idiom proper to itself. The boulevard did not belong to great theater or to the fairground but to an urban popular culture.

4

Cultural Visions of the Boulevard Stage

The Traditional World of Familial Etiquette and Social Order

The theatrical horizons of the boulevard stage were broad. Spectators saw spread before them, in the painted backdrops of the stage and in the mind's eye, fairy lands and earthly country that ranged from France and the European mainland to deserted islands and the New World, from provincial town to urban Paris, from the past into the present. Actors upon the stage impersonated the European, the Turk, the Negro, the Savages of the Americas set in the primitive state of Nature or in civilized surroundings. Attention was turned now to wealth, now to poverty, to the many classes of society that gathered in the stylish drawing rooms, chateaus, busy street corners and country lanes set upon the stage. The boulevard theater looked out upon rich and varied worlds, yet at the heart of this imaginative complexity lay a simple cultural vision. Moreover, it was a relatively stable vision. The plays that will be used here to explore the world depicted on the boulevard span in dates of authorship and first performance the early 1770s to the 1790s. Yet all formed an important part of the popular repertory in the years 1784-1793 and helped shape the boulevard's evocation of the social environment.[1]

The stable masks and stock characters of the boulevard stage, indulging in gay, light-hearted love intrigue, belonged to a social world that was ordered and static in conception. Within the family a hierarchy of rank and status was determined by the domestic ladder of parent, children and servants. The same formal distance between familial ranks applied equally to the organization of groups and professions within society at large: nobleman, bourgeois, tradesman, peasant. Not only were characters principally defined by their position in the social matrix, as demonstrated by roles such as father, valet or peasant, but that position within the matrix determined the dramatic behavior and attitudes of each character. Interaction and relation between one character and another, between one group and another, was clearly monitored by a conventional etiquette implicitly assumed within the boulevard cultural vision. In the domestic unit, the primary focus of all traditional love intrigues, each character owed deference and duty to the master of the household. The familial head in turn commanded unquestioned obedience from children and servants alike. This parent-children, master-servant relationship served as model for authority and deference in the world at large, in social units that extended beyond the nuclear family. Depicted on the boulevard stage, the seigneur referred to local villagers as "children"; the petty laborer obeyed the neighborhood "bourgeois" as he would a master.

Importantly, these artistic patterns of authority and deference did reflect contemporary values, if not a contemporary reality. According to various articles appearing in the *Encyclopédie* between the years 1755 and 1765 the family was a civil society, founded in nature, of parents, children and domestics dominated and ruled by the male head.[2] By right of "paternal rule" and "the rule of masters" the male parent held full authority over the person and effects of his children and full title to the labor of his servants. Those subservient to the will of the parent and master were expected to respond with respect, love, gratitude, and fidelity. A similar paternalism was meant to characterize relations between the seigneur and those who lived and worked on his domain. Servants and peasants owed their master honor and fidelity in return for his protection and beneficence. The social etiquette affected on the boulevard stage was, thus, a real one in eighteenth century France.

In this ordered, paternalistic world laughter and comedy resulted when characters behaved out of keeping with their position, their duties, and their obligations and rocked with their actions the careful balance of family and society. Parents and masters abused their authority; young lovers intrigued against fathers and tutors; servants defied their masters. In the overwhelming majority of plays such delinquent behavior attended that most solemn of social activities, marriage. The family, as a foundation and model of all civil society, perpetuated its likeness through the wedding of its young. In contemporary theory, any deviation from an ordered recombination of succeeding generations, such as marriage between parent (the old) and child (the young), or the inequitable combination of rank and wealth, was considered repugnant to the natural disposition of things.[3] Yet in the boulevard play these unnatural deviations occurred pro forma, providing the material of comedy. Swayed by lust and foolishness, like the Captain and Cassandre in *The Wonderful Waistband* (Grands-Danseurs, first performed in 1773) or Jean qui pleure and Jean qui rit in the play by that name (Ambigu-Comique, 1781), the parent desired to marry his own pupil or the daughter of a friend. Swayed by considerations of wealth and rank, like M. Thomas in *Pierre Bagnolet* (Grands-Danseurs, 1782) or Harpagon in *The Miserly Tutor* (Théâtre des Beaujolais, 1787), he thought to marry his humble daughter or pupil to a man of wealth and prestige. In response the young, and often in their behalf the servants, struggled to break free from their bonds of obedience. The unnatural authority of the patriarch was defied and the stability of the family threatened.

It was not only the family that wavered precariously in these moments of adolescent revolt. The balance and perpetuation of the social hierarchy as a whole was at stake in the recombination of households, money and status. In *The Furnished Room* (Grands-Danseurs, 1772) Madame Hautaine refused to marry her niece, Adelaide, to the merchant's son, Léandre, because of her own pretensions to a higher status in society: "He is of inconspicuous family, the scum of the earth" ["C'est du petit monde, de la crapule"].[4] An obverse social conscience forbade Madame Dumond to allow the union of her own son and her pupil Hortense, whom she knew to be of noble blood (*The Good Mother,* Grands-Danseurs, 1785). These distinctions between common and gentle birth were echoed by differences in professional standing and wealth. M. Thomas, wine merchant, did not value the profession of soldier as highly as he did bailiff and lawyer, and for this reason he opposed the marriage of his daughter Therèse to the man she loved *(Pierre Bagnolet).* The gardener Simon broke off his daughter's engagement to the seigneur's valet Arlequin when he stumbled across 100 écus in the lane: "... it's the darned money that I found which turned my head and made me proud ..." ["... c'est le maudit argent que j'avions trouvé qui nous avait tourné la tête ça nous avait rendu fiar ..."] (*Contentment Surpasses Wealth,* Grands-Danseurs, 1776).

Although much of boulevard comedy depended on the irregularities of the old, the balance of both the familial and the social hierarchies hung upon the subsequent behavior of the young—in most cases, the young girl. It was expected on stage as in the real world that she should submit to her parent's or protector's will in all things: "Obedience is unquestionably the foremost duty that education imposes upon your sex ..." [L'obéissance est sans contredit le premier devoir que l'éducation impose à votre sexe ..."], Léonore was told in *The Dismissed Rivals* (Grands-Danseurs, 1788). And indeed, in many plays the girl freely admitted the parent's right to administer her material welfare. "It is true, you may dispose of my Property as you see fit ..." [Il est vrai vous pouvez à votre gré disposer de mes Biens ..."], Isabelle deferred to her tutor Cassandre *(The Wonderful Waistband).* At the same time, she reserved the right to marry whom she chose: "... but I alone have the right to dispose of my heart and my hand" ["... mais seule j'ai le droit de disposer de mon cœur et de ma main"]. This was not a social right for Isabelle; it was, rather, her personal expression of revolt against the values of the parent and society at large. The inherent importance of wealth and status in the alliance of households had made of marriage a social trade in which the girl was supposed to participate only passively. In the boulevard love intrigue the girl's active determination to marry for love potentially disrupted this trade. The wine merchant Thomas was delighted that the young man he had chosen for his daughter Therèse was the son of a lawyer and bailiff, and extremely rich. It would be, he announced, a "good marriage" ["un bon mariage"]. Therèse objected, "You mean a good bargain, my father; love cannot be bought or sold" ["Dites un bon marché, mon père: l'amour ne se vend, ni ne s'achète"] *(Pierre Bagnolet).*

The social values which the young girl's comic struggle exposed were real enough in contemporary life; her revolt was not.[5] In *The Tableau of Paris* Mercier wrote bitterly that marriages were arranged solely by considerations of wealth: "Beauty and virtue hold no value at all among us, if a dowry does not support them."[6] The young girl's pursuit of a love match on stage, in opposition to her parents, was in Mercier's estimation strange:

> Nothing is more deceptive in the depiction of our manners and customs *(mœurs),* than *our Comedy,* where love is made to *young ladies (Demoiselles).* Our theater lies on this point. Let the foreigner be not deceived here: one does not make love to *young Ladies;* they are closed up in Convents until the day of their wedding... [young girls] of secondary rank do not leave [the company of] their mothers, and girls in general haven't any kind of freedom or familiar intercourse [with men] before marriage. Only the daughters of the petty bourgeois, the simple artisan and the people have complete freedom to come and go and, consequently, to fall in love as they please...[7]

Modern historians of the family tend to agree with Mercier, though he may well have overstated the case. Jean-Louis Flandrin argues that from the beginning of the sixteenth century the authority of parents and their powers of coercion over the young indeed steadily increased.[8] Through the Middle Ages adolescents had been able to contract clandestine marriages. By contrast, French law in the 1500s and 1600s enforced the need for parental consent in order to guard, as the *Encyclopédie* suggested in the eighteenth century, against "disproportions of birth and of fortune in the union of individuals..."[9] Flandrin notes, however—and he is joined in this by Natalie Davis—that parents did not systematically ignore the courting inclinations of their children. Davis believes that old and young basically agreed upon marriage goals. The children, and especially the young girl, internalized the social values of the family and society.[10]

None of the compromise between parent and child found in real life was at first apparent on stage. Resistance to parental authority on the part of the young girl, unexpected and unapproved by the dominant values of society, was turned to comic play by the equally aberrant behavior of the young man and his servants. While the obstinate girl remained for the most part passive, the lover, and in many cases the valet or serving girl, indulged in active violation of parental authority. According to Mercier it was against all moral and social principles to seduce or carry off a young girl, yet it was often this that the lover attempted. The great majority of love intrigues contained some incident of masked identity, whereby the young man and his companions gained entry into the girl's home. In *Guzman d'Alfarache* (Grands-Danseurs, 1789), for instance, the valet Guzman arranged the kidnapping of Felicia by dressing himself as the important Marquis de Villambozascas and his master Dom Carlos as a simple valet. By means of such disguise the servants, or those who manipulated intrigue, gained the confidence of the old and their unwitting consent to familiar relations between the young lovers. Scaramouche had Léandre take a room in Madame Hautaine's boarding house as a simple commoner *(The Furnished Room).* The mask was doubled when Scaramouche "revealed" to Hautaine that her boarder was in fact a German prince.

Parental consent to the lovers' wedding was in other instances achieved by open coercion. The young stole from Harpagon his precious money—only to return it for his signature on the marriage contract between Lindor and Lucinde *(The Miserly Tutor).* Claude Bagnolet, the half-witted youth intended for Therèse, was tricked into entering the army by Cœur d'Amour, the soldier who had captured the young girl's heart. Cœur d'Amour demanded either money or Therèse's hand in marriage for the release of the unfortunate rival *(Pierre Bagnolet).* Arlequin, dressed as a soldier, threatened to reveal Simon's past desertion from the army. His price was the 100 écus Simon had lately found, and eventually the hand of Javotte *(Contentment Surpasses Wealth).* In each case the young man successfully overcame parental marriage plans for the young girl. Madame Hautaine signed the marriage contract between the young lovers, as did Harpagon. Felicia's brother and tutor acceded to the roguish artistry of Guzman and M. Thomas relented before the unceasing obstinacy of his daughter and Cœur d'Amour.

In appearance the dénouement of the love intrigue seemed to strike a blow at the patriarchal order and its social code. Both the young lovers and the servants had thumbed their noses at a figure of authority with relative impunity and had managed to replace the dominant marriage values with individual choice and aspiration. Yet, in fact, parental authority had been neither seriously nor permanently violated. No play came to an end without the parent's final consent to the love match or without the reparation of relations between the young and the old. Moreover, it was not parental authority per se that the love intrigue ridiculed but the abuse of that authority. The intrigue itself had been initially stimulated by gross actions of lust, avarice or social pretension on the part of the parent. More often than not the old used their position of power to override or pervert the social code. The Captain and Cassandre hoped to marry unnaturally into a younger generation; Harpagon wished to give his pupil to a wealthy old man who asked for no dowry, despite his obligation to provide Lucinde with a dowry within his means: Madame Hautaine scorned those of her own rank and curried favor with those she believed to be noble and wealthy. In all cases the defective authority of the parent was checked by the resolution of the intrigue. The young widow Gervais, in *The Rustic Evening* (Associés, 1787), ignored the social distance of wealth and position between herself and Blaise in order to rationalize an aggressive courtship of her own apprentice: "After all, why should I blush over the choice I've made? I am wealthier than Blaise, and that is all that places me above him; no, distance in rank does not hold me back..." ["Après tout, pourquoi rougirois-je du choix que j'ai fait? Je suis plus riche que Blaise, et voilà tout ce qui me met au-dessus de lui; non, ce n'est pas la distance des rangs qui me tient..."] But in fact that distance did constrain her actions. In the final scene the bailiff counseled Gervais to behave in keeping with her position: "Consider that this irregular marriage that you wanted does not suit you; I am more your kind..." ["Réfléchissez que ce mariage inégal que vous vouliez faire, ne vous convenoit point, je suis mieux votre fait..."].

What is important in these examples is that the social code was in fact reaffirmed by the shenanigans of the young. They had "internalized" the traditional values of family and society. The lines of rank and status were maintained in *The Rustic Evening* when Gervais consented to marry the bailiff. They were as well in *The Furnished Room.* Léandre was, after all, the son of a rich merchant, "an honest Merchant who has done very well by himself, and who is esteemed by his colleagues" ["un honnête Marchand qui a fort bien fait ses affaires, et qui est estimé parmi ses confrères"], and Madame Hautaine no more than a landlady. Despite their resistance to parental authority, the young's choice of marriage partner was never unacceptable within the social code. Instead of mismatching the old with the young or the rich with the poor, as the parent did out of consideration for unnatural lust, social pretension or avarice, the young loved according to rank and place within the family and society. Léandre and Octave, the chosen suitors of Isabelle and Nicette in *The Wonderful Waistband,* belonged like the girls to the generation of the young; Cœur d'Amour practiced a profession equally estimable to that of the wealthy peasant Claude Bagnolet; Lindor, in *The Miserly Tutor,* was as wealthy as the old man preferred by Harpagon for the young Lucinde.

The dramatic action of the love intrigue tended to confirm the social code of a traditional, hierarchical world. Indeed, as long as the love intrigue flourished on the boulevard, it emitted a strong influence in favor of a stable, ranked society by providing cathartic release for tensions between parent and adolescent and between households of varying wealth and status. Strangely enough, however, the same repertory of plays harbored a fascination for social mobility and mutability. This fascination most often found expression in the aspirations and ambitions of the lower classes. In *Garguille or the Crockery Mender* (Grands-Danseurs, 1787) the merchant Silène rewarded the handyman Garguille for his constancy by making him a store clerk, a "garçon de boutique." Garguille's love interest, the cook Louison, was likewise apprenticed to a seamstress. "A while ago I had much to complain about," said Garguille, "now see all the Good Fortune showered upon me..." ["J'étions tout à l'heure à plaindre, maintenant vlà tous les Bonheurs qui nous assomment..."]. Such dénouement, wherein certain characters actually did rise—even if modestly—in the social scale, seems to have been rare. Far more often in the boulevard repertory social aspirations of the rural peasant or urban journeyman were crushed and their motivations ridiculed. For a brief moment the gardener Simon in *Contentment Surpasses Wealth* thought himself wealthier and therefore "better" than his own kind. Yet he finally admitted to Arlequin that he had been happier in his old place:

> ...it [the money] brought me bad luck; ever since I found it I haven't had a moment of peace... take Javotte, I give her to you... take as well these cursed Ecus, they've done me harm. I prefer to live poor [and] content: because after all: Contentment surpasses Wealth.
>
> [...il [l'argent] m'a porté malheur; depuis que je l'avons, j'nons pas eu un moment de repos... prenais Javotte j'vous la donnons... prenais aussi ces maudits Ecus, ils m'avons causé de peines. J'aimons mieux vivres pauvres [et] contents: car après tout, Contentement passe Richesse.]

A sustained flirtation with mobility and mutability was more obviously tied to the role of the zany or feckless rogue, always of a subservient social station in the love intrigue. In nearly every important appearance upon the stage the valet or serving girl was called upon to recite his or her past history.[11] All revealed a checkered career marked by an amazing ability to adapt to social circumstance. This was most clearly expressed in *Like Father Like Son* (Grands-Danseurs, 1784), where Sans Souci and his son, Sans Souci fils, had been modeled on Beaumarchais' Figaro:

> Destiny will direct my path... dancing master here, professor there, valet in one city, poet in another, I will be able to climb or descend as circumstances warrant...
>
> [Le Destin dirigera ma route... Maître de Dance ici, Professeur là, Valet dans une ville, rimeur dans une autre, je pourrai monter ou descendre selon l'occasion...]

Sans Souci fils spouted these words in 1784. There is evidence that in the earlier plays of the 1770s the way up the social scale was considered more difficult to achieve and maintain. In *The Wonderful Waistband* Scaramouche complained that his unhappy birth forbade that he should succeed at anything presumptuous; his efforts to achieve enduring wealth by levying taxes on those who passed in the streets at night were too quickly cut short! Prior to his appearance on stage, Scaramouche had plunged once more down and out. Indeed, erratic swings up and down the social scale became de rigueur for his type. Guzman d'Alfarache, Pedro and Jacinthe (*The Dastardly Female,* Grands-Danseurs, 1785) all appeared as conniving servants who had in the past pitched violently, like Defoe's Moll Flanders, from the dregs to the heights of social existence. Just how high they might aspire by the 1780s, despite their lowly and subservient origins, was clearly stated by Arlequin the younger in *The Infatuated Old Man* (Grands-Danseurs, 1789):

Plate 12. Scene from *The Coppersmith* at the Ambigu-Comique, one of the many boulevard plays that focused upon the life and loves of the lower classes. Photo: Bibl. nat. Paris.

There are lackeys and lackeys. My friend, I was assured in Italy that there were no lackeys in Paris like the *Estaffiers*[12] in Rome. An *Estaffier* born rich is still an *Estaffier*. It's a chain that servitude reins in with a grip of iron, whereas in Paris a lackey has the *Barrières*, the *Bureaux*, the *Emplois*, important protectors. And he rides in a carriage which he ran after for twenty years. So you see, since this morning I have respectfully saluted all the lackeys I met. You can't tell what those people might become.

[Il y a laquais et laquais. Mon ami, l'on m'a bien assuré en Italie qu'il n'en était pas des laquais à Paris comme des Estaffiers à Rome. Un Estaffier naît riche est même Estaffier. C'est une chaine que la servitude retient avec une colle de fer au lieu qu'à Paris les laquais ont les Barrières, les Bureaux, les Emplois, les grandes protectrices. Et roule dans un carrosse après lequel il a couru vingt ans. Aussi as tu vu que depuis ce matin j'ai salué respectueusement tous les laquais que j'ai rencontré. On ne sais pas ce que les Gens là peuvent devenir.]

The zany's past or possible freedom from social restraint fostered on his part a resentment of his present subservience. Boulevard theater gave comic voice to this frustration and discontent, much of which was expected and indeed acceptable to the master. When Cassandre listened, through his "horn of truth," to the true feelings of his household servants for himself, he dismissed their scorn thus: "That's the way all valets think..." ["C'est ainsi que pensent tous les valets..."] (*The Horn,* Grands-Danseurs, 1772). Harpagon was equally complacent towards the insubordinate Nérine, who told her master he might not marry his pupil Lucinde to whomever he pleased: "Domestics are so poorly brought up that they say nothing but disagreeable things" ["Les domestiques sont si mal élevés qu'ils ne disent que des choses désagréables"] *(The Miserly Tutor).* In the early love intrigue this antagonism of servant and master was playfully expressed through the pranks of the valet or serving girl, who was careful to ingratitude him or herself with the hoodwinked master. In *The Wonderful Wasitband,* for instance, Scaramouche was recognized by the two young rivals as the valet who had duped them both in the past. He adroitly turned their intimate knowledge of him to good favor:

Pardon, Messieurs, both of you know my wit and cunning, both of you are in love. Both of you have need of me. (To Léandre in a low voice) He is your rival, I will work hard to supplant him... (To Octave in a low voice) He loves the same person as you, but we'll make him see the light.

[Et, grace, Messieurs, vous connoissez tous deux mon adresse et mon industrie, tous deux vous êtes amoureux. Tous deux vous avez besoin de moy. (à Léandre bas) Il est votre rival, je fait fort de le supplanter... (à Octave bas) Il aime la même personne que vous, mais nous luy ferons voir beau jour.]

Likewise Nérine asserted independence from an inferior and powerless role by acting surreptitiously to undermine her master's authority: "It will not be said that an intrigue conducted by Nérine won't succeed" ["Il ne sera pas dit qu'une intrigue conduite par Nérine n'aura pas de succès"] *(The Miserly Tutor).*

Certainly Nérine's mischievous plans came to fruition, as did those of Scaramouche and countless other domestics. The comic intrigue served to ventilate hostility of servant towards master without serious harm to social prestige. In the end all was joyfully forgiven and servant, master and young were bound in familial harmony.

It is significant that in certain plays written in the 1780s, those in which the servant, like Figaro, came to dominate the intrigue, his or her frustrations were more aggressively expressed. The valet l'Olive, in *The Dismissed Rivals,* stridently complained of his subservient role and the social prejudice that robbed his rank of dignity: "These Messieurs disparage us while they profit from our cunning. Ingrates, you despise the tree, but you eat the fruit" ["Ces Messieurs nous dénigrent tout en profitant de notre adresse. Ingrats, vous méprisez l'arbre, mais vous mangés le fruit"]. The plots and schemes hatched by the resentful servant were, correspondingly, more acrid and self-interested in tone. In *The Infatuated Old Man* Arlequin the elder and the younger schemed for their own monetary advantage in the courtship of Fleuridor and Madame Dorsin: "The Follies of the Masters ought to enrich the Domestics" ["Les Sottises des Maîtres doivent enrichir les Domestiques"]. Jacinthe's intrigue to unite the lovers and to aggrandize her own person in *The Dastardly Female* was so disruptive of domestic harmony that the serving girl was expelled in the end from the family circle.

The resentful servant vented his latent hostility towards the master in a general dissatisfaction with the ranked hierarchy of the social order. Florinette, the soubrette in *The Infatuated Old Man,* asked, "What difference is there between a woman of condition and her maid? None but that placed there by chance" ["Quelle différence y'a-t-il d'une femme de condition et sa suivante? Aucune que celle qu'y met le hazard"]. Chance alone, she believed, dictated one's birth and subsequent station within society. The valet l'Olive boldly dreamed of a social order in which such accident was corrected by the personal merits of the individual. His vision, moreover, dominated the opening lines of *The Dismissed Rivals:*

> One fact must be granted, people are very unhappy in this world! The Philosophes say some very pretty things about that. Me, without breaking my head with vain reasoning, I say that it all comes from men not being in their proper place. No notice is taken of this, which, in the physical as in the moral, is the source of all abuse. I have wit, schemes and cunning; I'm nothing but a miserable valet. An insignificant gentleman has neither wealth nor energy; he is my master. Change the order of things, put the embellished clothing upon the Valet, the Livery upon Monsieur, everything takes a new face... the Master rolls in money and the Domestic pockets frequent gratuities...
>
> [Il faut convenir d'un fait, on est bien malheureux dans ce monde! Les Philosophes disent de fors belles choses là-dessus. Moi, sans me casse la tête en vains raisonnemens, je dis que cela vient de ce que les hommes ne sont pas à leur place. On ne prend pas garde à cela; c'est

pourtant au physique comme au moral, la source de tous les abus. J'ai de l'esprit, de l'intrigue, de l'adresse. Je ne suis qu'un misérable valet; un petit gentilhomme n'a pas de biens, pas d'énergie, il est mon maître: changez l'ordre des choses, mettez l'habit brodé au Valet, la Casque au Monsieur, tout prend une nouvelle face... Le Maître roule sur l'or et le Domestique empoche les fréquents pourboires...]

For l'Olive the trappings of birth and wealth were more readily appropriated than their substance. Nevertheless, he did achieve, at least temporarily, the cathartic reversal of status which he desired. Wearing his master's cloak, l'Olive became a master himself for one brief comic scene: "How appearance commands respect!" ["Comme l'extérieur en impose!"] Servants, of course, had impersonated their betters in many popular plays, but it was not until the 1780s that this act of disguise was linked on the boulevard stage to strong ridicule of certain social values. In *Polichinelle Protected by Fate* (Grands-Danseurs), an episodic farce written in 1786, the hump-backed mask engaged in sustained mockery of a social order based on birth and wealth. Fortune favored Polichinelle with a purse that never emptied of money, and he set off to buy the world. A genealogist offered him background and nobility; a poet offered glory; a gentleman offered his daughter in marriage. Like L'Olive, Polichinelle was quite aware that these social honors veiled, but did not alter, his true character: "My personal valet gives me my character each morning with my suit of clothes..." ["Mon valet de chambre me donne mon caractère le matin avec mon habit..."]. Nevertheless, he aped not only the appearances of high rank but the prejudices. Those that petitioned him for money and aid, he curtly dismissed for their laziness. The irony was clear; Polichinelle had done nothing himself to merit wealth and position.

Despite the trenchant criticism of the social hierarchy proffered by the resentful soubrette, valet or mask in the last years of the old regime, theirs was not a liberating critique. The chance determination of her fate did not prompt Florinette to alter her servile status; rather, she used it to justify private disrespect for the master class and participation in the mercenary schemes of Arlequin the elder and Arlequin the younger *(The Infatuated Old Man).* For all his adroit masquerade at the top of the social scale, Polichinelle was rudely thrown to the bottom of the ladder *(Polichinelle Protected by Fate).* In the final scene Fortune retrieved her purse and left the hump-backed mask penniless once more. Yet Polichinelle relinquished his purchased name, glory and social attention without remorse. His crazy antics had been meant to ridicule the parvenu, he who rose swiftly, and at times precariously, in the social scale: "It is not enough to possess a great fortune," concluded Polichinelle, "it is more necessary to know how to conserve it" ["Ce n'est pas assez de posséder une grande fortune, il faut mieux savoir la conserver"]. To this end, the appearance of status had come under attack, not the substance of status. Despite his brief but persuasive sally into the world as an imposing marquis, Polichinelle could not change his true self and social place. He remained the zany born to the lower ranks of an ordered society. Even l'Olive did not question the need for place and rank. Although, in contrast to Polichinelle, he did not relinquish the notion of social mutability, neither did he argue to eradicate the social lines that separated servant from master. He asked only for a reversal of status between himself and the man he served. L'Olive's espousal of individual merit and achievement was perhaps more bold and sincere than that of a Florinette or a Polichinelle, but his personal revolution would not destroy rank and place. It was, at any rate, a pipe dream. Like the others, he remained the servant he had always been.

Natural Order and Sentimental Morality: The Impact of Enlightened Thought

Where unusual emphasis had been placed on the zany of boulevard comedy, there occurred in the 1780s a subtle shift in tone from comic acceptance of the social order to an ambiguous challenge of that hierarchy. Ideas and themes characteristic of learned thought and art in the age of the Enlightenment had penetrated popular theater. Nougaret, outspoken champion of the boulevard, repeated again and again that the little theaters might bring enlightenment to the people with the motto, "to instruct in amusing them."[13] Just so, the character l'Olive made reference to the philosophes, iconoclastic men of letters whose intellectual spirit had spread beyond the literary salons to the streets of Paris.[14]

On the boulevard stage this diffusion can be traced most obviously in the imitation of themes and genres with which many philosophes and men of letters gave expression to a "philosophy of sentiment."[15] Sentimentalism in literature and the arts had long roots in the eighteenth century, but it waxed in fashion towards the last decades of the old regime. By that time philosophes such as Diderot and Rousseau had tied refined emotionalism to enlightened themes of humanitarianism, nature and natural moral law.[16] The most obvious vehicle of this enlightened sentiment from elite circles to the popular stage was the *drame,* or drama, developed by certain philosophes and playwrights to give expression to their moral code of sensibility and natural virtue. The popular stage also drew sustenance from the novel, the moral tale and the sentimental press. The adaptation of sentimental stories to the boulevard stage meant the appropriation of much of the intellectual baggage of the Enlightenment. Popular theater not only embraced the more obvious features of the new philosophy, such as the glorification of nature and the natural man, but more subtle, generalized attitudes that shaped new perceptions of familial and social relations.

The sentimental play reflected the impact of Enlightenment philosophy on the boulevard tradition in both conspicuous and profound ways. The noticeable movement in contemporary playwrighting from stylized stock characters to the individual personality, whether the humble tradesman or "father of his family," corresponded to a slight but significant de-emphasis within the sentimental love intrigue and sentimental play of socially prescribed roles. Rank alone no longer implied the duties or obligations expected of any one individual within the family. Addressing his son as an equal in *Like Father Like Son,* Sans Souci explained that the love and gratitude he expected as a father depended not on abstract notions of filial duty but on his own fulfillment of paternal obligations:

> My friend, the firm manner in which I raised you formed your mind and your judgment: since I have no fear that you abuse my benevolence, I can reveal it to you in its entirety. My heart is open to you, and, were it possible to be more than a father, I would be for you more than anyone could be.
>
> [Mon ami, la manière ferme dont je t'ai élevé t'ai formé l'esprit et le jugement: comme je ne crains point que tu abuses de ma bonté, je puis te la montrer, tout est entier. Mon cœur t'est ouvert, et je serais pour toi plus que tous ce qu'on peut être, si l'on pouvait être plus qu'un père?]

The behavior of parent and young traditionally found in the love intrigue had been radically modified. The *Encyclopédie* had insiduously argued that despite the natural foundations of the domestic hierarchy, each family member was also in nature master of his own person.[17] Two differing conceptions of nature—one a social and one an individual construct—were superimposed one upon the other. Paternal authority was thus to be mitigated by an emotional consideration of the young's natural, individual rights. Dolmon, the complacent father in *The Love-Crazed Madman* (Grands-Danseurs, 1787), would not stand in the way of his daughter's choice of marriage partner: "I am not one of those fathers unworthy of the name" ["Je ne suis point de ces pères indignes d'en porter le titre"]. Bonds of affection, and not domestic rank alone, determined patterns of willing deference and restrained authority within the sentimental conception of the family.

The sentimental code of behavior and thought depended upon an emotional life responsive to the natural law anterior to the social order and its prescribed duties and obligations. The gardener Gervais resisted the will of the Baroness to arrange the marriage of his niece Lison because long years in the garden had taught him that nature must choose its own course. Lison had to be allowed to follow her individual inclination in love (*The Wise Gardener,* Grands-Danseurs, 1780). Natural morality did not just imply an individual freedom from social restraint, however, but an honesty and immediacy of emotional feeling and expression. When Dinval asked his lover Julie to speak sincerely of her love, she told him to heed her eyes and not her words: "I let my heart speak, it is my most cherished language" ["Je laisse parler mon cœur, c'est mon plus cher langage..."] (*The Fop Punished,* Grands-Danseurs, 1786). The mute communication of emotion was wholly pure because it was believed to be more closely tied than speech to the natural order of things. In *The Child of Nature* (Grands-Danseurs, 1781) the savage had no need of language or social convention to express the spontaneous, unselfish love he offered the girl Zélie. The natural impulse of the eyes and the body sufficed.

Much of the intrigue in the sentimental play derived from the implied or real conflict between sentimental morality and the social code of the traditional order, a code that mirrored contemporary values. In *Père Duchesne* (Grands-Danseurs, 1789) the young servant Lucille preferred an older man to one her own age; in *The Virtuous Courtesan* (Grands-Danseurs, 1782) the girl Constance dishonored her father by living as a high-class courtesan; in *The Beautiful Flower-Girl* (Grands-Danseurs, 1790) the Chevalier, son of a count, fell in love with the gardener's daughter Babet. The dramatic action in each of these plays turned upon tensions between paternal authority and individual freedom, between social obligation and natural emotion. Lucille struggled with the authority of her employers, motivated in her choice of lover by a sense of freedom from paternal restraint; Constance relied on a natural emotion to supplant the social prejudice for a wayward adolescent; the Chevalier weighed the social obstacles to his union with Babet against the moral clarity of his feelings for the girl. These same conflicts were expressed widely throughout the eighteenth century literature of sentiment. It is impossible, however, to assess the direct influence particular Enlightenment tracts may have had on most sentimental plays written for the boulevard, since few explicitly acknowledged either source or inspiration. But because at least one play did make extended allusion to *The New Éloïse,* a novel by Jean-Jacques Rousseau widely known to the reading public of old regime France,[18] it is possible to study the intellectual relationship of one Enlightenment text to the popular stage.

The Good Mother, written for the Grands-Danseurs du Roi in 1785, was typical of many of the sentimental plays performed on the boulevard in the last decade of the old regime. The sensitive young Dumond fell in love with his mother's pupil Hortense, a girl of noble birth. The differences in their rank precluded all notion of marriage between the young lovers, yet the social code could not deprive Dumond of emotional ties to Hortense. He rejected his mother's stern reminder that only a husband might "adore" Hortense:

> And why so, Mother? St. Preux, whose story I have read, always loved Julie...
>
> [Et pourquoi donc, Maman? St. Preux, dont j'ai lu l'histoire a toujours aimé Julie...]

In *The New Éloïse* the young Julie, daughter of a wealthy Swiss, was seduced by her tutor St. Preux, a man with no apparent station in an ordered society. The young lovers were forcibly parted, however, by social dictum; Julie submitted to her father's authority and subsequently married her father's friend Wolmar. Rousseau reunited the lovers some years later, when St. Preux was engaged to tutor Julie's children as he had once tutored the mother. Yet despite the increase of social barriers between the two, their emotional bonds had not lessened. It was this prospect of continued love that enchanted the young Dumond.

According to the Rousseau scholar Jean Starobinsky, *The New Éloïse* was primarily a prolonged meditation upon the opposition of social and moral values, presented in the language and imagery of obstacle and transparency, of veiled and limpid vision.[19] Increasingly, as social obstacles placed Julie and St. Preux beyond physical communion, their emotional life became more transparent and pure to themselves and others, unmarred by social appearance or hypocrisy. On the boulevard this complex emotional development was rendered simplistically. The subtle conflict between the artificial values of society and the natural values of the individual were presented bluntly, without the complexities of the masterpiece. Hortense was courted by two men at once, the sensitive young Dumond beneath her station, and the Marquis, a nobleman and a conceited fop. Despite the stark contrast between the two men, however, Hortense was unable to distinguish between the appearance and the reality of love. The maid Lucette cynically, but realistically, described for her love and marriage in contemporary society:

> One searches for a knight in shining armor; he comes by and by, abuses the rights we give him to our soul, laughs over the tears he causes and runs off to carry elsewhere a homage as light as it is insincere...
>
> [On cherche un vainqueur, il vient bientôt, abuse des droits que nous lui donnons sur notre âme, rit des pleurs qu'il fait berser et court porter ailleurs un hommage aussi léger qu'il est peu sincère...]

But Hortense could not reconcile the social game of courtship that the Marquis would play with her own inward, emotional turmoil. Madame Dumond needed to tell her that love did not follow upon the artificial laws of society, but upon the laws of sentiment and nature felt most strongly by the sensitive individual:

> ...at the moment when the mind begins to understand itself, at that same instant the soul breaks the bonds with which it was restrained, objects present themselves to its eye from a grander and nobler point of view. The Spectacle of Nature, up until then mute for [the soul], now stirs and amazes it; everything attracts the still indeterminate sensibilities of this young soul, it aches to fix itself...
>
> [...au moment où l'esprit commence à s'éclairer, au même instant l'âme brise les liens dans lesquels elle était retenue, les objets se présentent à ses regards sous un point de vue et plus grand et plus noble. Le Spectacle de la Nature, jusques-là muet pour elle et l'émeut et

l'étonne, tout aurait la sensibilité encore indéterminée de cette âme neuve, elle brûle de se fixer...]

It is significant that Madame Dumond asked her son whether he had read all of *The New Éloïse.* The answer was no; Dumond knew nothing of the penultimate temptations shared by Julie and St. Preux or of Julie's death at the novel's end. In fact, the tragic and sublime dimensions of *The New Éloïse* were of no interest on the boulevard. The popular stage remained, essentially, a comic theater. Neither *The Good Mother* nor any other sentimental play on the boulevard displayed the continued tension and sublimation of Rousseau's novel. Rather, the formulaic tricks central to the traditional love intrigue were used in innovative ways to break the tension and resolve the conflict between the social and moral orders. Whereas the love intrigue had relied heavily on masking, or enhancing, appearance, the sentimental play often turned upon the unmasking, or removal, of appearance. Of a sudden it was revealed that Madame Dumond's long-dead husband had been of noble birth.

The difference in dénouement between *The Good Mother* and *The New Éloïse* was more subtle than it was obvious. In both, the social order, its duties, obligations and values remained inviolate. Yet in the play all tension between that order and sentiment dissolved of itself, while in the novel that tension was transcended only with great difficulty. Julie and St. Preux overcame social violation through moral resistance and death; Dumond and Hortense overcame the same obstacle through social transformation. The young Dumond, now noble himself, was able to consummate his love for Hortense with no violation of the social code. Despite this mannered resolution of moral and social conflict, *The Good Mother* nonetheless suggested, like Rousseau's novel, the ultimate victory of sentimental morality over that of the traditional social order. The Marquis, guilty of social artifice in withholding knowledge of Dumond's true birth, encouraged the young lovers to steep themselves in Rousseau's natural philosophy:

...live, live out the Novel slowly, lovable children; I sought to deceive, I have been so in my turn.

[...filez, filez, lentement le Roman, très aimables enfants, j'ai cherché à tromper, je l'ai été à mon tour.]

The rather simplistic appropriation of Enlightenment themes by the popular stage evident in the comparison of *The Good Mother* with *The New Éloïse* was characteristic as well of a wider range of boulevard plays written in the 1780s. The Rousseauistic conflict in *The Good Mother* between individual freedom and social restraint, between natural emotions and social values, echoed the sentimental intrigue of a number of other plays obviously inspired by the new philosophy. In *The Virtuous Courtesan* the tension between natural and social values was plainly expressed in the emotional struggle of Constance, caught in the opposing pull of vice and virtue. On the one hand, her present lover Zero-neuf represented in his words and actions "the cruel morality" of physical, carnal need and illusory sentiment. On the other, her brother Delcour, a young "philosophe," spoke to her of natural virtue and moral honesty. The dramatic structure of the play, in which Constance confronted first one man and then the other, baldly emphasized that her choice lay with either of two extremes. Again, there was little of the emotional complication or compromise to be found in the masterpieces of high culture. The final victory of sentiment was complete. Constance not only begged but gained the forgiveness of her father.

The popular play gave voice to the same simplification of philosophical conflict and moral triumph with other "Rousseauistic" dichotomies between city and country, and nature and society. In *The Fop Punished* the paternalistic and chivalrous code of the old country nobility was starkly contrasted to the artificial values of the fashionable elite at court. The Marquis, newly arrived from Paris to woo Julie, disrupted the country way of life with his flagrant behavior and sweeping dismissal of what he termed "bourgeois" values:

> ... honor is a foolish fancy, reason a borrowed mask that is more the spirit of stupidity than of moderation, virtue a standard in which no one believes; as for fidelity, it is a term used by our forebears, an uncertain right praised by husbands, but for which people can no longer find use...
>
> [... l'honneur est une chimère, la raison un masque emprunté qui est plutôt l'esprit de la sottise que de la modération: La vertu un titre auquel personne ne croit; pour la fidelité c'est un terme de nos vieux parens, un droit fort incertain vanté par les maris, mais dont personne n'a pu trouver encore l'usage...]

For the Marquis life was nothing more than a social pageant, for which one prepared to seem what one was not. Julie's father, the Baron—very much the country gentleman—reacted to the Marquis' fashionable conception of life with a vigorous affirmation of the very same "bourgeois" values of honor, generosity, and sentiment that the Marquis had disparaged. The Baron's was a paternalistic world in which he as master sought to cherish and protect the "vassals" that depended on him.[20] Relationships within that world were emotionally stable and emotionally satisfying, for it was, above all, a natural world: "In our countryside, we breathe the perfume of Nature" ["Nous respirons dans nos campagnes le parfum de la Nature"].

That balm was even more pungent on the deserted isle of *The Child of Nature.* In an impossibly naive story, Johnson raised his son in a wooden cage, sheltered from all human contact and social corruption, only to release him on the island at the age of twenty-two. Johnson's purpose was, simply, to have his son learn from nature alone what it meant to be truly human:

> To demonstrate to men, by his example, that they are born good, sensitive, virtuous; that the most perfect education is not that which gives them what are called talents and virtues but that which removes from them the vices of society, which draws them near to nature and places them in its hands.
>
> [De montrer aux hommes, par son exemple, qu'ils naissent bons, sensibles, vertueux; que l'éducation la plus parfaite n'est point celle qui leur donne ce qu'on appelle des talens et des vertus, mais celle qui éloigne d'eux les vices de la société, qui les rapproche de la nature et les remet entre ses mains.]

The first experience of Johnson's son with the civilized Zélie and her father, shipwrecked on the same isle, proved that he was indeed a noble savage. He knew nothing of artificial intercourse or social prejudice but was direct and honest in his relations with others. The play was, in fact, a pathetic proposal that nature and natural law held prescriptive authority over the artificial mores of social man. In this, *The Child of Nature* expressed most clearly the fundamental precept of all sentimental discourse to be found on the boulevard stage. Those that lived closest to Nature were happy and good. For Constance natural emotion eradicated individual disorder; for the Baron sentiment reinforced a paternal and chivalrous order. Taken all together, the sentimental plays on the boulevard stage largely suggested that the moral law might simply, rationally, naturally prevail in harmony with the social world.

There was one important instance in many a sentimental play, however, in which the harmony of natural and social law threatened to break down. Beyond the ties of love and friendship centered upon the family, there existed a network of obligations to others in the social hierarchy, in both superior and inferior rank. The most visible and constant of these was the relationship between master and servant. The presentation of this relationship in the sentimental play differed significantly from the wit and prejudice to be found in the love intrigue.

Rather than accent the frustrations of an intelligent domestic such as l'Olive, the sentimental play emphasized the rights of even the most simple of servants and the sentimental, egalitarian vision of their masters. In *The Irascible Master* (Grands-Danseurs, 1789) the peevish gentleman M. de Préval had threatened to beat his servants more than once. The valet André learned that there was, by law, monetary compensation for him should this happen:

> If ever your master, who is very rich, said [a certain man of the law], and who owes nothing, breaks your arm or a leg, come find me; I will immediately institute, in your name, *criminal* proceedings that will bring you at least [two hundred écus in annual income].

> [Si jamais votre maître, qui est fort riche, dit on [que'quezun de justice], et qui ne doit rien, vous casse un bras, ou une jambe, venez me trouver; sur le champs, je lui intenterai, à votre nom, un procès *criminel* qui vous raportera, au moins [deux cent écus de rente].]

André gained little from this legal protection of his person, however, for try as he might, he could not provoke his master to strike. De Préval in fact had a heart of gold—something that yet another of his servants, the maid Lisette, was able to see clearly. De Préval was touched:

> . . . but you, born to an obscure rank; of uncultivated mind; in short, you, wholly ignorant of high society; you understand my character better, and you offer me more justice, than my cousin, my wife, my friend.
> [. . . mais toy née dans un rang obscur; toi dont l'esprit n'a pas été cultivé, toi enfin, que ne vit pas dans le grand monde, tu connais mieux mon caractère, et tu me rends plus de justice, que ma cousine, que ma femme, que mon ami.]

The point was, of course, that moral sympathy of servant for master and master for servant did not respect or succumb to obstacles of social rank. Moreover, the creation of sentimental ties up and down the social ladder acted to mitigate the distances of rank and status. In *The Love-Crazed Madman* the sensitive young man Volsers told his servant:

> Are you not my fellow, are you not a man like me? What separates individuals are games of chance, results of varying circumstances; virtue is but one whole, and the difference is for fools . . . men vain of your titles and your name, tear off the blindfold of pride that covers your eyes; and see that there are no ranks for wisdom.
>
> [N'es-tu pas mon semblable, n'est-tu pas homme comme moi? Ce qui sépare les individus, sont des jeux du hasard, des résultats de circonstances qui varient, la vertu n'est qu'une, et la différence est pour les sots . . . hommes vains de vos titres et de votre nom, arrachez le bandeau de l'orgueil qui vous couvre les yeux; et voyez qu'il n'est point de rangs pour la sagesse.]

Significantly enough, Volsers' words matched closely the opening lines spoken by the valet l'Olive in *The Dismissed Rivals.* In that play there had been no sentimental appreciation of the servant's natural merits or equality, and l'Olive had grown bitter and discontent. In the sentimental play the servant was more nearly disarmed by the sentimental visions of the master. The presentation of master-servant interaction in the sentimental play closely matched the description of the domestic economy of Clarens, the home of Julie and Wolmar in *The New Éloïse.*[21] Julie and her husband managed their household in such a way that their servants did not fret under their bonds of servitude. What they did they did gladly, with a feeling of true compliance and freedom. In his study of this novel, Starobinsky writes that notions of equality for the inhabitants of Clarens lay not in the abrogation of social rank but in the sentimental communion of those individuals. For Rousseau this was most fully achieved during the collective fraternity of the summer festival attended by the people of Clarens. Yet as Starobinsky states, the sentimental transcendence of rank and place did not menace the social order of paternalistic authority and subservient obedience.[22] Rousseau's egalitarianism posed a subtle compromise of the social order, not its radical rejection. Social transformation was unnecessary as long as the sentiment of equality was possible; in Starobinsky's words: "All takes place as if the essence of equality consisted in the sentiment of being equal."[23]

The expression of egalitarianism on the boulevard, in many senses broadly Rousseauistic, did not achieve the intellectual sublimation of *The New Éloïse.* No matter how sweetened by consideration, the sentiment of equality remained a "luxury of the master."[24] There were no festivals in boulevard plays to stimulate true or lasting feelings of fraternity. Lisette's reasons for accepting her master the way he was in *The Irascible Master,* for flattering his desire for approval and understanding, were purely expedient. She needed to remain "in service" ["en condition"]. Indeed, the boulevard stage manifested a keen sensitivity to hypocrisy on the part of the master, the seigneur and the upper classes of society. Expressions of equality were at least as forthright, if not more so, amongst those of inferior rank as amongst those of superior status. The chimney sweep Duchesne told the Marquis that, after all, neither he nor Lucille had need of the nobleman's permission to marry *(Père Duchesne).* The farmer Bagnolet claimed that the peasant was the equal of the idle rich, even of the industrious bourgeois, since it was he "who nourished them both" ["qui les nourrit tous deux"] *(Pierre Bagnolet).* In *Blaise the Ill-Tempered* (Grands-Danseurs, 1782) the irritable farmer Blaise refused to manage the seigneur's lands; he preferred to remain his own master:

Blaise: "...when one attaches oneself to the powerful, one becomes a serf...
Bailiff: "But no. One gets protectors."
Blaise: "Not at all. One gets masters."
Bailiff: "One procures friends."
Blaise: "There are no friends except among equals..."

[Blaise: "...quand on s'attache au puissant, serf on devient...
Bailli: "Mais non. On se fait des protecteurs."
Blaise: "Non pas. On se donne des maîtres."
Bailli: "On se procure des amis."
Blaise: "I n'y a des amis que quand on est égal..."]

On the boulevard, Rousseau's intellectual resolution of social inequity had been radically simplified and inverted. For Rousseau the moral law and sentimental emotion gave rise to an equality of spirit that soared beyond the shackles of social place. In the popular play this transcendence shared by individuals did not happen without a prior transformation of social place. For Blaise, and any number of outspoken characters, social equality had first to be procured before members of society might truly interact according to the laws of sentiment and nature. The boulevard stage neatly resolved conflict between moral and social worlds by proffering the sentimental notion that society, in make-believe at least, might conform to men's just deserts.

A Dualism of Social Codes: Radical Potential and Traditional Norms

At the start of this chapter the cultural vision of boulevard theater in the last half of the eighteenth century was explained as a simple one. Yet a tremendous ferment of innovative genres and new ideas on the popular stage complicated perceptions of the social world in the last years of the old regime. There were, in fact, two perspectives that sighted the length and breadth of the social hierarchy, two compasses that measured the rights and duties of the individual in society, two conceptions of social man that may be distinguished one from the other in the dramatic literature of the boulevard stage.

The love intrigue surveyed in comic style two main concerns of an ordered, hierarchical society—marriage and mobility. Both phenomena, by implying the movement of individuals and the changeability of status, potentially disturbed the stability of the social system. The choice of a marriage partner, presented on the popular stage as a confrontation between parent and adolescent, bore heavily on the perpetuation of rank and status in society at large. Master and servant gingerly explored the unequal relationship of subservience and authority that maintained the hierarchy of place in that society. The social code that determined the "acceptable" behavior of the characters on stage was one that mirrored closely the contemporary values of the boulevard public. Within the family all members, including the head of the house, were expected to honor the extent—and the limitations—of paternal authority over children and servants. Households were to be united in marriage according to reasonable assessments of wealth and status. All were to respect the permanence of place and the social distance that separated one rank from another.

The aristocratic and paternalistic code of the love intrigue was matched on the boulevard stage by the sentimental vision of those plays inspired by certain emotional strains of enlightened thought. Though the social world and social concerns of the sentimental play were very much the same as those of the love intrigue, it was not the social code, or its abuse and neglect, that drew the attention of dramatic action in these plays. It was, rather, nature and natural behavior, anterior to society and social etiquette and therefore of ultimate prescriptive authority. Armed with notions of natural, honest emotion and the natural equality of all persons, the sentimental characters on the boulevard stage sought to mitigate paternal authority, to match individual inclination to social demand, to ameliorate the inequities of rank and place. The etiquette of social conduct confirmed by the love intrigue was challenged by a natural standard of behavior that emphasized individual right and dignity. The result, in the resolution of sentimental intrigue, was a certain relaxation of the social code. Socially prescribed attitudes and behaviors became pliable under the influence of natural emotion. The sentimental play did not reflect or approve traditional values; it sought rather to teach the boulevard public a moral law and a moral behavior that might ease the injustice and inequities of contemporary society.

The comic love intrigue and the pathetic sentimental play differed greatly in their description of social behavior, but both agreed in the prescription of a paternalistic and ordered society. The dramatic situations clustered about the themes of marriage and mobility in the love intrigue initially called to account the social conventions of that society, yet their comic resolution tended to reaffirm the order itself. When the young revolted against parental control, it was to challenge the abuse of paternal authority, the excessive valuation of wealth and status that marred the social rights of the adolescent. The wild fortunes and discontent of the servants criticized a perversion of social values in which the false appearance of wealth or status took the place of respectable substance. In their words and in their actions, however, both the young and the servants voiced the legitimacy of a regenerate, traditional world. The sentimental critique of unnatural attitudes and behaviors did not menace the hierarchical order of unequal status and stable rank. The patriarchal structure of the family as well as the social hierarchy, both characterized by restrained authority and willing deference, were founded in nature—and as such, to be naturally honored in society.

The two distinct perceptions of a cultural vision—the one traditional and the other enlightened—were compatible in yet another instance. Both defended a degree of personal freedom for the individual within the confines of social duty and obligation. In the love intrigue this was recognized, for instance, in the young girl's right to choose her mate—albeit from a pool of socially suitable young men—and in the servant's light-hearted machinations against the master of the household. Within the sentimental play, individual freedom was broadly defined for all persons as the right to follow one's natural emotion and inclination. This sentimental amelioration of social restraint was understood in fact as complete, since the laws of nature did not thwart, but justified, the social order rightly perceived.

Yet the question of individual freedom within society at large steered the vision of both love intrigue and sentimental play towards unsafe ground. L'Olive's bold statement of personal merit and his vehement apology for social mutability were neither ridiculed nor retracted by the course of dramatic action. The valet's aspirations threatened to isolate him from a satisfying or stable social life. Polichinelle's attitude towards his own comic escapade as a wealthy Marquis was equally precarious. With only a slight change in emphasis he might have criticized a ranked order of birth and wealth and society's subservience to its false value. Similarly, in many sentimental plays the lack of necessity for moral sublimation in order to overcome social restraint skewed the thrust of enlightened expressions of equality. The moral law only triumphed in *The Good Mother, The Beautiful Flower-Girl* and other plays because traditional social obstacles had been miraculously removed. Without such social peripeteia, as the liverish farmer recognized in *Blaise the Ill-Tempered,* the moral vision of equality only frustrated those of subservient, inferior rank.

Did boulevard theater sow the seeds of a revolutionary discontent with ordered society among a broad and even plebian public? If so, it did not do so in isolation from dramatic culture as a whole. Due to the royal censor and the police, nothing of political import passed on the boulevard that had not already passed on the great stages of Paris.[25] The socially pugnacious valet in popular theater took his cue from Beaumarchais' Figaro at the Comédie-Française. Likewise, sentimental visions of fraternity and equality among men, as drama, developed first among the philosophes and the great theaters they served.

Nor did popular plays of social criticism and enlightened sentiment dominate the boulevard repertory. Certain sentimental plays, such as *The Fop Punished, The Love-Crazed Madman* and *Perè Duchesne,* were not performed more frequently than traditional love intrigues. Equally successful through the last decades of the eighteenth century were farces first performed in the 1770s, such as *Contentment Surpasses Wealth* and *The Horn of Truth,* or plays in that old style written in the 1780s, such as *Pierre Bagnolet and His Son Claude Bagnolet* and *Gusman d'Alfarache.* The valet l'Olive and the mask Polichinelle did not walk the boulevard stage more frequently than the sentimental masters Volsers and De Préval. Indeed, of all the plays considered here, *Contentment Surpasses Wealth* seems to have been by far the most successful in the years 1785-1794.[26] Moreover the message, neatly summed up in the title of that intrigue, was clear. Long into the 1790s Simon, and the boulevard repertory as a whole, preached acceptance of place in society and rejection of social aspiration.

Yet despite the fact that acrid servants and sentimental masters did not dominate the boulevard stage, nor inhabit it to the exclusion of great theater, nevertheless they did harbor in themselves the potential of enlightened philosophy. In the act of distilling the major themes of natural order and sentimental equality, these characters experimented in brief and perhaps insignificant moments with radical statements before a general, even untutored, audience. Boulevard characters did not, however, necessarily speak of revolution to come. For the bitter valet l'Olive, as for the plaintive lover

Dumond in *The Good Mother,* the social values of an ordered, traditional world were not expected or desired to change. What was desired to change, what did change on stage and in the mind's eye was the individual's apparent place in that society.

Through the 1780s and for some years beyond the full power of that pipe dream still lay dormant. In play after play, dramatic action tended to mitigate the impact of protest. Moral vision, that "luxury of the master," undermined the lowly Duchesne's defiance of Lucille's noble master in one of the most successful "revolutionary" plays of 1789.[27] Dramatic, revolutionary events in the real world—the fall of the Bastille, of absolute monarchy, and the jeopardy of the old order—took the popular stage by surprise. Much that was potentially radical in the boulevard repertory had yet to be drawn out and developed. Though written in 1782, *Blaise the Ill-Tempered,* with its outspoken advocacy of social before sentimental equality, did not reach the peak of its success until 1794. But that is to anticipate five years of social and ideological upheaval. In the midst of the Revolution's second year boulevard actors still sang not of political change but of moral resolution to social conflict and a return to the stability of the traditional social order. The alarm bells, or tocsins, of popular discontent and riot might yet be silenced by the sentiment of equality:

> It had always been the same,
> The big guys ate the little.
> Then there came to pass a change
> That restrained that appetite.
> Little guys decided that
> Things could go on no longer.
> Little guys are not so dumb,
> They turned the world upside down.
>
> . . . .
>
> Brothers all we now must be,
> United without deceit;
> Living as sincerest friends,
> Shunning pride and etiquette.
> Lords, your manners should be sweet;
> In your looks put less disdain:
> Only then you'll not hear the tocsin.
>
> It is just each has his place,
> So as not to break the ranks.
> But scorn not the little guy
> Who would sit among the great.
> Noble he who smiles with grace,
> Who soothes the poor man's distress:
> Only then he makes mute the tocsin.

[Tout alloit comme j'te pousse:
Le gros mangeoit le petit:
V'la-t-y pas qu'une secousse
Met un frein z'à c't appétit.
L'petit se met dans la tête,
Qu'les chos's n'alliont put d'travers:
L'petit qui n'est pas si bête,
Vous r'tourne l'monde à l'envers.

....

Il faudroit être tous des frères
Unis par la simplicité;
Vivre tous en amis sincères,
Sans étiquette et sans ficrté.
Bachas, ayez douces manières:
Dans vos regards moins de dédain:
Vous n'entendrez jamais le tocsin.

C'est juste qu'chacun ait sa place:
Il n's'agit pas d'brouiller les rangs:
Mais, sans faire aux p'tits la grimace
On peut s'asseoir parmi les grands.
Noble qui sourit avec grace,
Du pauvre adoucit le chagrin:
Et v'la c'qui fait taire le tocsin.]
(*The Carpenter of Bagdad,* 1789)[28]

Part III

The Boulevard Profession and Social Turmoil

Prelude: The Lure of a Boulevard Street Show

"Nature in secret lent you her brush;
Your soul furnished the model;
Genius traced there faithful expression;
And your wit *without doubt* finished the rest.

—On Ribié, anonymous verse in
Pierre Jean Baptiste Nougaret,
Fairground Almanac, 1787.

Ever since he could remember, he had been drawn to the little theater on the boulevard. While milling crowds gathered and then dispersed around him, Ribié would keep to his high post on the fence by the tree savoring every detail of the short skits performed on the theater balcony. Dogs barking, children whining, men chattering around him—he heard none of these but the sound of blade on blade as the actors on their outdoor stage challenged one another in mock combat. Parry and thrust, parry and thrust. Ribié crowed with delight and nearly lost his balance as the hero gained the advantage. The actor's every gesture, his every telling move of body, hands and face fascinated the boy. He seemed never to get enough of the mannered postures, busy pantomimes and funny dialogue that filled the street before showtime. Often he remained, hanging loosely about his tree, long after the actors had retired inside and passersby had moved on. The strains of music, punctuated with whistles and catcalls, reached him from within the theater hall. Disconsolately, the boy kicked his shoes in the dust. If only there were a way to get inside! Ribié edged up to the entrance and cautiously peered around the door. The ticket taker, watching the stage from the hallway, quickly glanced in his direction. "Scat, boy!," he hissed. Ribié scampered away.[1]

Louis-François, for that was the boy's name, had been born and baptized in Paris in the year 1758. The registers record that his father was a puppeteer, or "merchant-sculptor of wooden figures," and his godfather a carpenter. Ribié's childhood was a hard one of poverty and want, and he took pains in later life to cover his origins. He received little if any education except in his father's calling and in the ways of the streets. Left to fend for himself at the early age of fifteen, Ribié turned naturally to the fairgrounds. Eventually he found employment at Nicolet's Grands-Danseurs as factor of sorts, barker and ticket seller. Perhaps for the first time, he made his way to the inside of a theater hall. Certainly in the next three to five years he seems to have trained a natural gift for acting as if by osmosis. He may have worked briefly for Beauvisage at the Théâtre des Associés; by 1777 or so Nicolet allowed him to try his skill on the balcony. Where once the boy had thrilled vicariously to the comic play and gay laughter of the outdoor skit, the young man moved his body and sounded his voice so as to make that gaiety his own. An earthy energy surged through him and over him, encompassing those who had paused on the street below. Many believed he recaptured the spirit of that infamous boulevard buffoon, Taconet.[2]

Convinced of his abilities, Ribié pressed Nicolet sometime in 1781 to allow him a debut inside the theater as Arlequin in *The Great Banquet of Stone.* Eying him from head to foot, the director tried to dissuade him from the reckless attempt. When Ribié persisted, Nicolet relented, providing that the boy ask the old Arlequin, Constantin, for his blessing and consent. With some anxiety Ribié sought the old clown up three flights of a dark and tortuous stairway. He found him in the middle of his morning shave, a napkin around his neck and soap over half his face. Constantin bade Ribié enter and returned to his small mirror hanging by a bit of string near the window. When the last of the soap had been scraped away, the old man turned to the aspiring actor and asked what he knew of artistry for the part. Ribié observed suavely that he relied on Constantin's advice. The clown willingly demonstrated a number of *lazzi* that had long served to make spectators laugh. Above all, the old man cautioned, you must be careful not to burn yourself when you mix the salad with your fingers. In the dinner scene of *The Great Banquet of Stone* Arlequin first seasons the greens with one of the oil lamps that light the stage! The old man went on and on, but the morning's tutelage stood Ribié in good stead. So great was his success as Arlequin that the young actor was engaged by Nicolet at 4,000 livres. And in years to come he became known as one of the best comic actors on the boulevard.[3]

Indeed, Ribié was a young man of many talents. Well before he secured a place in theater, Ribié had joined the mountebank Second in various sideshows that included the drinking of boiling oil. Not only was he an excellent juggler, but Ribié also tried his hand as charlatan selling unguents, balms and efficacious stones. In 1778, while he drew the crowds to Nicolet's with comic antics on the outdoor stage, he worked his own marionettes in the fairgrounds. These were almost more ribald than the mores of the time could allow, a police officer having admonished him "to no longer show in his spectacle a small figure that was indecent, that pissed before the spectators and had all the parts of a man and very visibly..." Some seven or eight years later, even after his promising start inside Nicolet's theater, Ribié advertised himself throughout town as master of a more "learned" entertainment. His "Beautiful White Living Rabbit, Prestidigitator" moved its head and clapped its paws when questions were asked of it. The result, Ribié claimed with a risible effrontery, of "a science... that consists *in algebraic combinations.*"[4]

As confidence man and as actor Ribié was described as "remarkable," "varied in all genres." But his aspirations did not end there. Ribié turned as well to the writing of plays. Because of his lack of education, jealous rivals accused Ribié of stealing manuscripts or, in a somewhat kinder vein, of dictating his ideas to collaborators. Yet there is reason to believe that the man who so easily absorbed the necessary skills of the actor also mastered those of the author. Chits and promissory notes that were certainly in his hand improved in grammar and fluency over the course of a decade and more that he spent with Nicolet. Between the years 1782 and 1808 he penned over 40 plays by himself or in association, many of them among the most successful and repeated of boulevard repertory. Ribié apparently had few illusions about his facility with words and scenes or his motives as a playwright. In *Cupid Astrologer,* a play he wrote for Nicolet in 1785, the Poet shocks Cupid with his pragmatic outlook on life:

> The public applaudes and that's the main thing. I'm looking to get rich and who cares how?... A new tragedy crops up, I pull the play to pieces, decompose it and make a parody of it or a travesty. People laugh, I earn a few écus and everyone is happy.... I'm only trying to make a living: more money and less honor, that's the motto of the day.[5]

Ribié as Poet was perhaps too modest and his notion of honor a matter of degree, for the man was hungry for the rewards of life. Ribié's ambitions drove him to the top of boulevard theater through the last years of the old regime and those of the Revolution. Yet very little is known of the career path he chose to pursue at the bottom of the Parisian theatrical hierarchy. Contemporary prejudice for the little theaters and the passage of time have obscured professional conditions for actors, actresses and authors in popular theater and, too, the impact of revolutionary change on the boulevard métier. Yet it is possible, in the study of group behavior from the 1780s through the early 1790s, to reconstruct in part professional lives and political activity for the minor artist. With respect to the minor playwright it has, in addition, been feasible to contrast professional conditions and individual careers for boulevard men to those for the minor writers studied by Robert Darnton. Darnton suggests that lowly literary men, frustrated by marginal status and social immobility in the

Parisian world of letters, formed the radical intelligentsia that rose to positions of power after 1789 and turned the cultural world upside down. Were boulevard artists subject to the same harsh environment of the literary low life? Did they reveal the same psychological profile of the radical revolutionary? And did they rise to political or theatrical dominance in the year II? Men such as Ribié made up the stuff of boulevard theater in its passage from the old regime to the Revolution. It is time to know them better.[6]

5

The Boulevard Profession—Actors and Actresses

The Artists' Life: Discipline and Insubordination

Sometime around 1777 the French actors composed a memoir in which they complained bitterly of the contempt excited by their calling: "[the profession] of the actor is thankless, above all others; we are drenched with loathing. . ."[1] Indeed, a long history in France of exclusion for those who chose the acting life was symptomatic of social intolerance for their métier. According to a deep-rooted prejudice strongly felt throughout the seventeenth, eighteenth and much of the nineteenth centuries, the profession and its practitioners were licentious and without honor. The hostility of the Church placed most actors beyond the pale of civil and religious law. The flagrant effects of excommunication were experienced by the French actors, who were not only barred like all other actors from a citizen's rights in life but notoriously denied Christian burial in death.[2] Nevertheless, although the French actors suffered from religious opprobrium and royal actors in general from civil ostracism and social snobbery, their lot was considerably ameliorated in the course of the eighteenth century by their growing acceptance in the salons of "the great" and, in the late 1780s, by their regular reception at court.[3]

There were those actors and actresses, however, for whom prejudice would not be breached. Des Essarts, writing in 1777, had been careful to distinguish between the royal actor, who deserved social esteem, and the lowly mountebank or buffoon, who did not.[4] These latter, relegated to the fairs and after 1750 to the boulevard as well, did not fail to draw a full measure of scorn for their profession and their persons throughout the remainder of the eighteenth century. Indeed, prejudice was doubled for the boulevard actor, "the most vile of Paris,"[5] engaged in "the most abject of all professions."[6] When the Italian actors erected a new theater on an outlying avenue adjacent to the boulevard du Temple, they took care that the building fronted not the boulevard but a side street "in order that it not be said that these Gentlemen were actors of the Boulevard."[7]

Contemporaries were apt to believe that the ethical value of dramatic fare reflected on the morals of the actors involved in its production.[8] For those who saw on the boulevard stage nothing but license and degradation, the minor actors was unquestionably reprobate. Yet intolerance for the boulevard actors and actresses had for its foundation not only a moral righteousness but the social discriminations of an ordered society. One pamphleteer hostile to the minor theaters claimed that without exception the boulevard actors had begun their careers as clerks, soldiers and valets.[9] Another concurred that many of the actresses at these same theaters had sprung from the lower classes. He regrettably admitted, however, that a number of girls of higher station also performed on the boulevard stage, so that one found there "clerks, milliners and other daughters of the Bourgeoisie . . ."[10] Unfortunately, in contrast to our extensive knowledge of the royal actors, comparatively few biographies may be reconstructed for boulevard actors and actresses, who for the most part remain unknown figures.[11] The social origins are known certainly for only a handful. Some came from families of professional connection such as "lawyer in Parlement" or "tax inspector." Some had parents who styled themselves "bourgeois of Paris" or practiced trade as "master-merchants." Others came from the artisanal and wage-earning class of cobblers, locksmiths, domestics and day-laborers. The meager biographical data suggest that contemporary observation of both popular and bourgeois elements on the boulevard stage was essentially correct.

Social prejudice decreed that once the sons and daughters of a prosperous middle class had voluntarily mixed with hoi polloi on the minor stage, they were lost to their families forever.[12] If they had not been born to the lower orders of society, actors and actresses along the boulevard willingly embraced their rank and place. Given the low social status of the boulevard profession, its attraction was puzzling. The same pamphleteer who worried about the dissipation of bourgeois youth on the boulevard claimed to have questioned hundreds of young girls on their passion for theater: "all assured me that they only looked for a protector with sufficient position and influence to place them in a theater along the Ramparts."[13] He failed, though, to relate or understand their reasons for wanting things so. Young men who chose the minor stage, especially those of "respectable family," were assumed to have fallen long ago into a debauched way of life and to work on the boulevard only to support their immoral habits. With somewhat more sympathy for these sons and daughters of the middle and lower classes, it is possible, however, to ascribe motives of independence from family and, more importantly, dreams of economic fortune.

Such was the religious and legal ostracism of the stage that those who acted were not only estranged but immune from the claims of society. The theater, whether great or small, was a place of asylum for young men and women from the absolute authority of their parents and families.[14] Economic well-being, at least on the minor stage, was less readily attained and depended, in any case, upon the individual's perception of comparative affluence. According to the playwright and songwriter Charles Collé, an actor at the Comédie-Française at one time "hardly got enough to live on, and it is certain that the mountebanks of the fair and the actors of the little theaters were truly poor devils."[15] Indeed, by late century the boulevard actors might well have been considered poor in comparison to the royal actors, who decidedly earned commanding incomes. In 1786 the average yearly salary of an artist at the Grands-Danseurs du Roi, the most prosperous of boulevard theaters, was 1,920 livres, as opposed to the average yearly share of 22,590 livres at the Comédie-Française. (See Table 2, Part I).

If the figure of 1,920 livres as an average salary is probably somewhat inflated for the remaining theaters along the boulevard, it is also true that an individual income could deviate widely from that mean at the Grands-Danseurs. (See Table 2, Part II.) Perhaps three-quarters of Nicolet's actors and actresses earned this amount or less, while the lovers and arlequins, for fear of competitive offers by other entrepreneurs, were undoubtedly paid more than the average. Indeed, the *Idler or the Boulevard Spy* charged that Nicolet provided the dancer Rivière with 10,000 livres in the early 1780s and biographical lore has it that Ribié, one of the best comics on the boulevard, was hired at the Grands-Danseurs at 4,000 livres a year, his salary rising in a few short years to 8,000 livres in 1786.[16] Even at 8 or 10,000 livres, however, the stars of the minor theaters realized only about half the average income of a royal actor. But in comparison with their fathers many, no doubt, had reason to feel proud. The lowest salaries on the boulevard fell no lower than the higher incomes of the wage-earners of Paris.[17] On the eve of revolution the average salary at the Grands-Danseurs du Roi was about six times that of a manual laborer and at least one and a half times that of a sculptor or goldsmith earning 100 sous a day.

Despite a certain measure of economic affluence, the life of an actor on the boulevard stage could be unstable and severe. Unlike the royal actors, who after a successful debut were accepted as life-long members of the Comédie-Française or -Italienne with a share in the company's profits, actors on the boulevard were forced by custom and law to engage in limited contracts of no more than a year in duration.[18] Unfortunately no written contract that passed between boulevard actor and entrepreneur under the old regime has survived to this day. Police records suggest that the actor's salary was agreed to verbally, though written statements may have existed. The actual terms of these wages are therefore only imperfectly known, but much of the actor's lot may be reconstruced from police and theater records and from written contracts passed in later years. In exchange for his yearly salary the artist was closely bound to stated theater regulations.[19] Actors and actresses agreed to accept the director's distribution of roles and to attend all rehearsals and performances without fail. Insolent behavior or a tardy appearance was to be penalized with standard fines, usually of six livres. To the director's authority in these things actors and actresses were allowed no formal protest—even the contract could not be broken. The artist was locked into a subordinate status without recognized rights or privileges.

In contrast, the director's prerogative to govern his company and to coerce recalcitrant artists was supported by officers of the law. If and when an artist failed to comply with any one of the theater regulations or to respond to rebukes and fines, the director hauled him or her before the local commissioner of police. In 1778 Lécluze, entrepreneur of the newly-established Variétés-Amusantes, had had more than one occasion to complain of the actor Toussaint for creating disturbances on stage. When Lécluze brought him before the police in August of that year, Toussaint had already been penalized twelve livres, six for having missed a rehearsal and six for having performed in a drunken state. Now Lécluze demanded not only a stiffer fine but imprisonment for Toussaint, for

> instead of correcting himself of the fault [of drunkenness... Toussaint] arrived at the theater to perform his role more drunk than the time before and even took it upon himself onstage to poke fun at his fines, which had no bearing on his role at it should have been performed...[20]

What Lécluze had in mind for Toussaint was a short stay in the For l'Evêque, the prison used for the detention of defiant actors from all the theaters throughout Paris.[21] While the director could apply as he saw fit fines already stipulated by police rulings, it was the police who determined in each case whether an actor might be thrown in jail. Again and again in the late 1780s an irate Nicolet, Sallé or Arnould, an associate of Audinot, demanded the Force, the prison that had replaced the For l'Evêque in 1780, for their actors who "came too late to the theater which caused great Commotion," or for those believed to have contracted with other theaters.[22] The boulevard actors Mayeur, Durancy, Ribié, Pierret, Varenne, Mercerot—each had an intimate knowledge of that prison in the last years of the old regime. From their point of view, wrote one Dumont, "The Actors of the Boulevard go [to jail] for little or no cause as long as they are subject to the despotism of the Entrepreneurs. I was there myself—and for having lacked the profound respect I was expected to show for the Director, who, at that moment, owed me consideration."[23]

What Mague St. Aubin, himself an actor at varying times at the Grands-Danseurs du Roi and the Ambigu-Comique, wrote of theater directors in general applied without rhetorical flourish to directors along the boulevard: thinking themselves "minor minister[s], [they] treated... the actors like slaves"[24] With the police behind him the director was in fact master of the artist's fate for the duration of the yearly contract. A contemporary scandal sheet attributed to a long-time actor and author for the Grands-Danseurs had it that the boulevard director's rule could be—and often was—rapacious. In *The Idler or the Boulevard Spy* Mayeur de St. Paul charged that Pierre-Germain Parisau willfully spoiled his artists to his own advantage. The fledgling director pilfered manuscripts, short-changed actors and saddled with debt the Théâtre des Elèves de l'Opéra in a matter of months.[25] Records of the Hôtel-Dieu Hospital and of the Royal Household confirm Mayeur's story[26] and suggest that the pamphleteer was not unfair in his allegations. Mayeur claimed as well that the director of the Ambigu-Comique had also made himself hated by his artists and neighbors. Audinot was known to be an inflexible master, unjust and rigorous in his direction of the stage. An anonymous poem reprinted in the *Idler* characterized him as a "tyrant" who gained an easy livelihood at the expense of demanding study and work on the part of his artists.[27]

The director of the Grands-Danseurs, in contrast, acquired something of a reputation for lax discipline. In the *Idler* Mayeur portrayed Nicolet as a man totally insensitive to the aesthetics of theatrical art, and, therefore, easy to please. During the rehearsal of a ballet, the scandal-monger claimed, Nicolet's criticisms might have been bothersome, but hardly exacting:

> . . . it took Nicolet's fancy, in wiping the tobacco upon his clothes, to find the dance step too long. He had the music stopped and ordered that a fourth of it be cut out. After some difficulties on the part of the ballet-master and the musicians they agreed that he was right, and that they were going to take out eight measures. The dancer took her place, and began again; the step was performed as before, without any changes, and Nicolet exclaimed: bravo! even asking whether it was not much better that way.[28]

In later years this same director's well-known indulgence of many of his artists drew comment from the press on "his paternal attachment and affection for those who for a long time had belonged to his theater . . ."[29]

Yet even Nicolet, "father" where Audinot was "tyrant," joined the other directors along the boulevard in a fundamental exploitation of actors, actresses, dancers and musicians. The many instances of insubordination, of missed rehearsals and of stalled performances reported by the directors to the police reveal that the artist's hours were long and tedious—an actor often performing in one or more different plays per day—and unrelieved for week after week. Directors were, in fact, meticulously jealous of the time and productivity of their artists. Another anecdote to be found in the *Idler,* though relayed by Mayeur for its absurdity, demonstrates that if Nicolet knew little about dance or music he, like the rest of his fellow directors, well understood his economic benefit:

> . . . a pantomime was being rehearsed. A musician waited his turn to play with his arms crossed. *Nicolet,* who caught sight of him, quickly ran up, stopped everything and asked why he sat there doing nothing while his comrades pegged away with all their might? This

Plate 13. Nicolas-Médard Audinot, known on the boulevard as a harsh master and sophisticated director. Photo: Bibl. nat. Paris.

Plate 14. Jean-Baptiste Nicolet, considered a kindly master, with an uncultivated taste and a shrewd mind for business. Photo: Bibl. nat. Paris.

musician, who played the viola, replied that he was counting measures—Do I *pay* you for counting measures? Play, Sir, I *pay* here so that one may play.[30]

Indeed, it is because boulevard entrepreneurs like Nicolet insisted on realizing their money's worth from the artists they employed that there is any information at all on the stringent regulation of artists on the boulevard stage. Moreover, the many acts of insubordination reported to the police expose how constant was the artist's frustration with and resistance to the autocratic rule of the boulevard director. Obstinately refusing to perform—or if coerced, performing badly—was the actor's only means of defying the theatrical institution run, in many ways, at his own expense. It should come as no surprise, then, that the actor Toussaint, of whom Lécluze complained in 1778, had planned in advance the "prank" of a drunken performance.[31]

Despite the rigors and frustrations of life on the minor stage the artist was constrained in more ways than one to continue his relationship with the boulevard director. All actors were legally bound for the duration of their annual contract; a good many of them were tied by economic dependence as well. It was not uncommon in this respect for the boulevard actor or actress to run up staggering debts with neighboring merchants, despite the fact that these "all believed themselves to be on their guard..."[32] By and large these debts were the result of an extravagance closely associated with theater in late-eighteenth century Paris, though in fact a constant expenditure for shoes, clothing and hairdressing, as well as for food and lodging, was expected and indeed required of the boulevard artist. At the Grands-Danseurs a regulation specified that, other than the costumes owned and distributed by the director, the actor or actress had to provide from his or her own pocket the shoes, white linen and coiffure necessary to an appearance on stage.[33] Even within a month's time expenses of this kind could run into quite a bit of money—60 livres for hairdressing and 12 or 36 livres for shoes—and if an artist fell sick for a month or two, losing income like the dancer Denoyant, these expenses were all but impossible to pay.[34] Upon occasion the indebted actor was imprisoned in the For l'Evêque or some other dungeon; if he was lucky, like the boulevard actor Dumenil, "[he] found the means of escaping from that house [of detention] and taking refuge at the Temple..."[35] Far more often the artist sought asylum in economic obligation to his director.

The most outrageous of big spenders was undoubtedly Ribié, a talented and crowd-pleasing actor who entered Nicolet's theatrical troupe at the age of nineteen. With a reported salary of 4,000 livres Ribié was, of course, among the highest paid of boulevard actors. "You might expect to see him raise the banner of economy," wrote another actor, Mayeur, in *The Idle Chronicler,* "but not at all... not only did he absorb his 4,000 livres, he duped as many people out of their money as he could."[36] Ribié had indeed plunged immediately into a vicious cycle of spending all he earned and borrowing on what he had not.

Upon Ribié's first arrival at the Grands-Danseurs Nicolet had agreed to advance the favored actor a sum of 72 livres—for an unknown reason.[37] Very soon the actor had wheedled from his employer more than 218 livres, a sum considerably higher than the average monthly salary at that theater. In the years that followed, however, Nicolet does not seem to have made the same mistake again. Rather than advance Ribié money—for the debts continued—and assume the role of sole creditor, Nicolet merely agreed to satisfy the actor's original creditors with monthly receipts from Ribié's salary. For the most part the apportionment of Ribié's monthly income seems to have been arranged informally, although there is evidence that some merchants had to take recourse to legal writs of attachment and to the police. A certain Decauquy, wine merchant at the Saint Laurent Fair wrote to the police in 1781

> that he had fed at the said fair Mister Ribié, one of the chief actors of Mister Nicolet, from the 5th of August to the 5th of September last [1780] and [Ribié] refusing to pay the sum of sixty livres ten sous that he owed, he [Decauquy] complained to Mister Nicolet, who also refused to honor the debt, saying that there were writs of attachment [on Ribié's salary].

It may have been this merchant whom Ribié avoided by fleeing the theater through a back door.[38] The efforts of both Ribié and Nicolet to forestall the wine merchant were, however, to no avail; before the stern eye of the commissioner Ribié was forced to agree to pay within a month.

What with five or more creditors at a time (this in 1785) and a propensity to rack up fines for failing his director and the public, Ribié would have been hard pressed for any income at all if it were not for the agreements between creditors and Nicolet to allow the young actor and his wife a small portion of the impounded salary for food, clothing and shelter:

> I, the undersigned, Monsieur Merle, Business Agent of the Creditors of Mister Ribié, for the Benefit of said creditors and to maintain Ribié in his Position, I consent in the name of said Creditors and give permission to Mister Nicolet to allow the said Mister Ribié a sum of three livres a day beginning today, October 21, 1782, for the board of him and his wife as well as for stockings, shoes, white linen, hairdressing and accessories relative to his role and for his wife, hairdressing, white undershifts and linen, . . . gauze apron, white stockings and shoes in accordance with theater regulations . . .[39]

Throughout the latter part of 1782 Ribié received no more than the small sums necessary for his food and upkeep—15 livres one week, 18 livres another. Though he still enjoyed considerably more than a typical laborer or journeyman, the arrangement must have been humiliating in some degree, as Ribié's promissory note suggests: "I acknowledge having Received from Monsieur Nicolet the sum of twenty-one livres for food, without which I would not be able to continue performing at the said theater . . ."[40] Indeed his obligation to Nicolet was no doubt intensely felt by both parties, since there is reason to believe that by accepting this position of middleman between merchant and actor, the director incurred upon himself some legal responsibility to honor the debt.[41]

The manner in which the director protected the actor from the full rigor of the debtor's law is an important illustration of the paternal relations between the two in late-eighteenth century Paris. By accepting writs of attachment on the artist's salary for which he too was liable the director was pledged, in effect, to the continued support of that actor or actress. For a great many pensioners at the Grands-Danseurs or the Ambigu-Comique and other small theaters, contracts were in fact renewed for years on end. This is not to suggest that all actors were in arrears to their director. Rather, director and actor fulfilled each other's needs in ways that reinforced their mutual support and dependence. Significantly enough, the fatherly or masterly role adopted by the director was reciprocated by irresponsible, even deviant, behavior on the part of many of his actors and actresses.[42] The boulevard artists' disregard for many of the social codes of society at large was an expression of their subservient relationship to the director. It was also a function of their marginal status in society.

The records of the police for the faubourg du Temple in the last years of the old regime disclose that as a group actors and actresses of the boulevard were poorly restrained by social etiquette and sobriety. Taconet, one of the earliest of boulevard actors, had been well-known as a drunkard, and many others followed in his footsteps, creating violent and abusive disturbances in the local cafés. In 1784 Despas, an actor at Nicolet's, was sent to the Force "for having kicked up a row at the Café Meziers and having uttered foul language to the sergeant... who arrested him..."[43] Ribié and Branchu, also of Nicolet's troupe, were picked up for a drunken spree at another wine merchant's on the boulevard and booked by the police for "having broken eight window panes and because they behaved very rudely towards the guard..."[44] In many of these cases the local community considered the director responsible for the actions of his actors. It was with less frequency, certainly, that he joined his pensioners in disturbing the peace. With a sense of horrified outrage the café owner Yon reported to the police in 1786 that Sallé, an old-timer from Nicolet's troupe and now director of the Associés, had accompanied his artists in a drunken brawl:

> [Mister Yon, Merchant-Dealer in Soft-Drinks]... said that on the occasion of the king's festival he had placed Chinese lanterns within his fence along the Boulevard du Temple yesterday night. Around 1:30 in the morning the said Mister Sallé, at the head of his troupe, climbed over the fence by the light of the Chinese lanterns... the said Pompée who was among the number and who held a bottle of eau de vie in his hand threw to the ground and broke the Chinese lanterns...[45]

Despite the protests of Yon and his wife, Sallé and his actors remained some three hours that early morning wreaking havoc upon Yon's café and spoiling his wine.

Personal quarrels between actors and actresses were often as violent and as public as the drunken comportment of the men. Nicolet reported two musicians for fighting in the orchestra pit and breaking a music stand.[46] In October of 1785 Adelaide Lessieur, actress at the Delassements-Comiques, lodged a complaint against Ribié, for what may have been the nasty outcome of a lover's quarrel:

> ... this afternoon at 4 o'clock the said Mister Ribié ... kicked her several times in the thighs, caned her on the left arm and boxed her on the ear twice with such force that he broke her earring ... Not content with beating her up the said Ribié threatened to whip her publicly on the Boulevard whenever he met up with her there.[47]

Such personal animosities could take on the proportions of vendetta. Marie Jeanne Desroyeaux, dancer at the Ambigu-Comique, came to the police in fear for her life at the hands of four other women dancers and their male companions. Three months previously these four had broken into Desroyeaux' make-up box and filled it with fecal matter. Severely reprimanded by the police at the time, they had been ordered to pay for the spoiled make-up and desist in their ill will. Yet they continued—publicly calling the young dancer "whore" and menacing her physically.

Desroyeaux' contribution to the longstanding quarrel is unknown, nor is it possible to ascertain whether she deserved the epithet "whore." It would not be surprising, however, if she had. Whether the minor stage initially attracted those who wished to be free of social mores or whether the profession enforced a dissolute way of life, many contemporaries agreed that the boulevard was rife with immorality. Some publicly remarked upon the general license of actors and actresses on the minor stage. Though these comments rarely—if ever—dwelt on specifics of behavior and thought, police records testify to a number of minor scandals fueled by sexual peccadillos of the actor, the actress and their director. Yet by far the most intimate and scurrilous look at the sexual relationships that riffled through the boulevard companies was proffered by Mayeur's "dirty book," *The Idler.*[48]

His purpose was to shock and titillate,[49] yet Mayeur was nonetheless persuasive that beneath an exterior of employer-employee relations and paternalistic association there ran a hard and fast current of masculine aggression and sexual jealousies. At the top of the pecking order stood the directors, men with the power and the money to buy the favors of young actresses by offering them position and income. Both Nicolet and Audinot apparently treated their young female artists as so many additions to a vast harem that was expensive and difficult to maintain. According to Mayeur, Nicolet lavished five times the average salary on his mistress Rivière; Audinot, too, was supposed to have spent great sums procuring the affections of one artist and then another. At one time charged with corrupting a child-actress, the director was forced to make substantial amends to her working-class parents:

> He reconciled the mother with a sum of money large enough to put her in the position of no longer having to work as a washerwoman, had the father accepted in the constabulary, and placed the young girl in a pretty apartment that he rented for her in the Marais.[50]

Despite their cost these relationships seem to have been highly unstable. Mayeur took delight in the evidence that it was the director's "destiny always to be the *cuckold*..."[51] The dancer Rivière apparently used her influence and position with Nicolet to support secondary affairs with a number of actors in the director's troupe; Audinot's young mistress did much the same thing.

Mayeur fairly crowed over the sexual exploits of his fellow actors—himself included—and obviously relished the public squabbles of actors and authors for rights to a desired actress. For their part, the women of the boulevard stage were expected to flit with abandon from one man to another. It is the inescapable conclusion of those who read Mayeur's book that boulevard actresses, as a whole, were akin to those other professional women who frequented the minor theater halls in search of clientele.[52] And if the question of choice or economic necessity is a real one in any study of prostitution, it applies as well to the minor actress. The actress, because of her sex, was saddled with a double burden on the boulevard. She was, like all boulevard artists, legally subject to the director's authority, liable to the vicious cycle of debt and economic dependence. For those women who gambled on the sexual interest of the director for quick advancement and worldly goods, their livelihood depended as well on sexual favor. The point is illustrated by Mayeur's biographical sketch of one Alphonsine. Starting at the young age of twelve as a dancer at the Ambigu-Comique, she passed as mistress through several hands until Audinot himself took an interest in her. The apartment he gave her did not long contain the young girl, however, and when Alphonsine's own interest in Audinot flagged in favor of another man, the director chased her from his theater. "*Nicolet* was her refuge;" wrote Mayeur, "she was pretty; he received her with open arms, slept with her around fifteen days, and passed her on to the *Chevalier de Séguer,* who maintains her well enough..."[53] Alphonsine either could not conceive or could not achieve professional advance and economic security as an actress without prostituting her body.

Not just actresses but actors were bandied about as entrepreneurs struggled with another sort of jealousy, that of professional competition between one theater and another. Although each theater along the boulevard had a hard core of longstanding artists, many actors and actresses were subject to a high degree of mobility on and off the small stages along the boulevard. By 1787 the Ambigu-Comique, for example, had lost all but four of the actors who formed part of the troupe of 35 to 37 men and women in 1777. In a decade's time the attrition of actors and actresses had reached 86 percent.[54] According to Mague St. Aubin, writing in 1787, actors seeking employment in Paris were so numerous "that each year at Easter [when theater contracts were terminated and begun], two or three hundred, maybe more, are without work and without hope of finding any for the season."[55] It is probable that boulevard directors annually refurbished their companies from this floating population of artists. But if entrepreneurs looked to actors and actresses newly arrived from the provinces or recently formed in the so-called "bourgeois theaters" or acting schools of Paris, they also coveted the more talented members of their neighbors' troupes. When his own first actress Diancourt briefly left the Ambigu-Comique, for example, Audinot lured away Nicolet's sometime mistress Rivière to fill his need for a popular and proven artist.[56]

At times professional competition of this sort between entrepreneurs spilled over into public dispute. In 1780 Parisau, director of the ill-fated Théâtre des Elèves de l'Opéra, protested in the *Journal de Paris* that Audinot had deprived the failing troupe of one of its most important artists by luring away the young child-actress known as l'Amour. In his own defense Audinot maintained, also in pages of the *Journal de Paris,* that he had hired the young girl at her own request and only at the end of her term with Parisau. At the heart of his argument lay an appeal to the perquisites of a free enterprise market:

> It is natural, undoubtedly, for an entrepreneur to seek the advantage for his enterprise: it is natural that any artist, any artisan, any worker prefer to attach himself to those who recognize and pay the best for the superiority of their talents. Neither law nor honor is wounded by the respective use of this natural right.[57]

Audinot specifically allowed that the "natural right" to a free and open theatrical market belonged to the actor as well as the entrepreneur. On the boulevard itself, the artist's ability to move from one stage to the next at contract's end went largely undisputed and was, in fact, his or her only major form of expressing approval or disapproval for the institutions that both succored and fettered. But in cases of a more outstanding mobility the actor was not quite the free agent that Audinot suggested.

Many contemporaries believed that boulevard theater was a testing ground for dramatic talent and, indeed, a number of actors and actresses apprenticed on the minor stages did rise to the top of the theatrical hierarchy.[58] But movement from the little to the great theaters did not depend on the choice or ambition of the boulevard actor or actress. It waited, rather, on an order for debut issued by the king's Gentlemen of the Bedchamber. The authority of these officials of the Royal Household superseded all other rights and prerogatives. In the case of the boulevard actor Volange, for instance, neither the actor nor the directors who vied for his services were able to act freely according to their "natural rights." In February of 1780 Volange had been ordered to appear at the Comédie-Italienne; by November his apprenticeship there had come to a disastrous end. In returning to the boulevard, Volange had thought to contract with the Grands-Danseurs du Roi, but the lieutenant of police Lenoir, resuming his jurisdiction, forced him to return to the Variétés-Amusantes, which had noticeably suffered from the actor's departure.[59] Within a year or so Volange was prevented from leaving Paris for a provincial stage. The hapless actor was held captive by his own comic talent and the conditions of his trade. Once on stage he did not have the right to quit it if the lieutenant of police or the officers of the Royal Household were opposed.[60] Like the great actors of Paris, the boulevard artists had no civil rights or professional existence other than those the king's ministers arbitrarily chose to grant.

Civil Status and Revolutionary Frustration

In December of 1789 the National Assembly resolved that actors should be admitted to equality and justice before the law. Hitherto ostracized by the Church and Roman law from rightful participation in civil society, actors were formally granted the rights of citizens, which included, notably, the right to hold or purchase public office and to participate in military service. Struck with this legal change in civil status, historians of theater have tended to investigate the newly-won civil—hence political—activity of actors during the revolutionary years that followed 1789.[61] Of necessity, their studies have dwelt on actors and actresses whose lives and politics were well-known, in other words the French actors and a handful of other artists from the more prestigious theaters of revolutionary Paris. We know in great detail, for instance, the conflicting political sympathies within the Comédie-Française and the schism they produced in that great theater in 1791. By and large, however, this kind of history has very little to do with the many anonymous figures who peopled the minor stage.

One is forced to admit, rather, that throughout 1789 and most of 1790 life for the faceless majority on the boulevard seems not to have changed at all. Directors had still to complain of the occasional actor or actress who failed to appear at rehearsals or performances; to demand redress for those of their artists who presumed to break contract; had still to reprimand their troupe for quarreling and fighting on stage and in the wings. None of the complaints—or vexatious fines and arbitrary jail terms imposed by the police—were new to the first two years of revolution. The formal acquisition of civil rights had done nothing to alter the interaction of actor and director or the actor's relationship to governmental authority. In return for his harsh discipline the director continued to receive a measure of obstinacy from his troupe; ultimate jurisdiction over the minor actor and regulation of his conduct still lay with the arbitrary justice of the lieutenant-general of police.

If the declaration of an actor's civil rights in 1789 had little discernible influence on the boulevard, the abrogation of traditional police regulations for the minor theaters less than a year later was more effectual. In mid-August of 1790 the governance of theater was transferred from the Crown's bureaus to those of the Commune. Municipal officers were enjoined in the decree on judicial organization of 16-24 August to maintain and execute current laws and ordinances of the police, but it is evident that, with respect to theater at least, many of the old regulations were allowed to falter. The new police did not officially recognize the fines and penalties upon which theater directors along the boulevard had long depended under the old regime to discipline their troupes. Without these means of reprimand, directors found themselves powerless to control their artists—or nearly so. In November and December of 1790 Nicolet and Audinot requested permission of the municipal authorities to annul contracts with two actresses, both of whom had willfully refused to perform on stage.[62]

During their long years on the boulevard Audinot and Nicolet had usually acted to prevent their artists from breaking engagements in mid-year, since it was to their advantage to retain the actor or actress for a complete term. Now, unless the police could be persuaded to supervise a working order in the theatrical troupes along the boulevard, the threat of expulsion was all that legally remained to discipline the unruly. Nicolet's manager, Constantin, explained to the police that the director "must count with certainty upon the subjects attached to his theater, because otherwise he would find himself compromised daily with the public without deserving it."[63] If the police would not sanction the director's annulment of contracts, insisted Audinot, they must allow the imposition of fines "according to the terms of the old regulations of the Police."[64] The new police, however, did little or nothing. They did not approve the director's abrogation of contract, for Mlle. Lacrois still performed at the Grands-Danseurs in 1791. Nor, apparently, did they authorize anew penalties and fines, though there is evidence that directors continued to impose them without the explicit approval or support of the police.

Before the Revolution the police had provided the director with one of his most important tools of discipline—the For l'Evêque. Without the threat of a prison term many artists no longer felt compelled to kowtow to the director in 1790 and 1791. No longer restrained by oppressive law and regulation, the actors' frustrations with the harsh discipline of the boulevard theaters blazed into unrest. Nowhere was this more evident than at the Théâtre des Associés. In December of 1790 Sallé's direction of the small theater had all but disintegrated in the face of mutiny.[65] Those of his artists who had been with Sallé for a number of years refused to work with new actors and actresses, forcing them from the stage and appropriating the best roles. The hapless director had been made to renew and augment contracts and salaries for fear of his losses without a full company. Tensions within the troupe and with the director came to a head when the actress Pompée aired her grievances before the public, and in the aftermath of that tumultuous performance Sallé's actors refused to honor their contracts. They had, in effect, gone on strike.

The actions of Pompée and others were not merely petulant and disobedient. Rather, they had taken on a larger significance. The random obstinacy of individuals had coalesced into the concerted resistance of a whole troupe to the authority and management of the theatrical entrepreneur. The actors of the Théâtre des Associés submitted a formal, written declaration to Sallé and to the police that they would no longer perform for Sallé. Their reason was, the police noted succinctly, to protest "ill-treatment by Sallé."[66] But that group protest was still, in many ways, as mute as individual rebellion. If the actors at the Théâtre des Associés had any clear idea of the rights and prerogatives for which they yearned, it was not transcribed in the records of the police. What was recorded were statements by directors and police officials alike that "insubordination" was fast becoming rampant among actors and actresses in all the little theaters along the boulevard du Temple.

The outbreak of such alarming insubordination was met by an equal determination of some boulevard directors to hold onto the discipline of the past. Audinot was one of these, despite the fact that the police no longer gave support to his authority. In February 1791 a certain Varenne, actor at the Ambigu-Comique, thought to document his refusal to act his role in *Pierre of Provence* with a certificate of ill-health from a doctor and a letter of explanation to the police. Audinot, however, rejected Varenne's excuses out of hand:

> ... that evening Mister Varenne had requested of Monsieur Audinot in the presence of Monsieur Gabriel, officer of the guard, that a pantomime with fighting scenes not be offered since his condition, which [Audinot] knew well, deprived him for a time of the facility [to perform those scenes] for fear that his health would be grievously endangered, but that he would perform any other play. Monsieur Audinot responded to this plea *that Mister Varenne was at his orders.*[67]

The next day, when Varenne failed to appear at showtime, the public gathered in the hall of the Ambigu-Comique would have none of the play hastily substituted for the vigorous pantomime. Spectators throughout the eighteenth century responded vociferously to their theatrical amusement and an unexpected change in the program, a bad performance, as well as scandalous allusions on stage, could send the audience into riot. On this particular occasion the police observed that

> the Public opposed [the change in program] with the greatest Uproar and demanded that they be told the contents of the Doctor's report. An officer of the guard took to the stage and said that the illness of Mister Varenne was real and that he had told Monsieur the

> Commissioner of Police about it this morning... The public seemed satisfied with this response and accepted [another] play... entitled the *Knight of Assas.* It was desired that the play accepted by the Public be performed and believed that it would have been performed in tranquility, but not at all, the tumult began again with even greater force and all hope of calm was lost...[68]

Audinot had gambled that the public, or the police, would censure Varenne for his refusal to perform, but he had been wrong. Instead, the public had accepted the actor's plea of ill-health. *Pierre of Provence* was performed that night, but only because two other actors calmed the spectators by offering to take parts in that pantomime for which they were not fully prepared. The actors as a group had gained a certain advantage over their director. Varenne's malady had been real, but for those who wished to irritate Audinot and challenge his direction with impunity, an example had been set. At the curtain's final fall the actor Damas took up Varenne's standard by refusing to play next day on "the vain pretext of having a cold..."[69] The guard mollified Damas and restored a temporary peace, but little else.

Relations between the hard-nosed Audinot and his truculent troupe did not heal; they festered. By May of 1791 order within the company had broken down almost completely. In a complaint meant to be heard not only by the local commissioner of police, but the departmental police and officials of the Commune, Audinot charged that 30 of his artists—at least half of his actors, dancers and musicians—had been disturbing for some time the regular operation of his theater. According to the commissioner who penned the police report, Audinot "may well complain of the insubordination that reigns at his theater, for it has been greatly detrimental to his interests and to the service of the public."[70] Indeed, because of misunderstandings between Audinot and his troupe the Ambigu-Comique opened and closed its doors to the public intermittently.[71] Similar agitation at other minor theaters of the boulevard reached such a pitch in this and following months that Audinot's troubles, and those of Sallé, no longer stood out as isolated incidents. In the last months of 1791 the police heard complaints as well from Nicolet; from Colon, at this time acting director of the Délassements-Comiques; and from Cauvin, entrepreneur of the Lycée Dramatique, a small stage newly established on the boulevard in May of '91. Actors on all these minor stages refused roles distributed by the directors, appropriated those given to others, or simply absented themselves from performance. A certain Guibert, actor at the Grands-Danseurs du Roi, justified his refusal to perform the role given him in *Money Means Nothing* with the assertion that he had no other will than his own.[72] Quite simply, the boulevard artist declared himself emancipated from the order and discipline of the past.

It is possible to see in the confrontations of director and actors a resistance on the part of the artists to rules and regulations that deprived them of responsibility and independence in their work. Likely enough, although the records are absolutely silent on these matters, boulevard actors were demanding with increasingly frequent, albeit disorganized, chorus for more control in the distribution of roles, more free time, and more lenient discipline. That they should have done so—and with obvious distress to their employers and the police—in 1791, and especially in the latter half of that year, is not surprising. George Rudé, in his study of the popular temper, has characterized the several months before the Champ de Mars affair of July 1791 as a period of "social upheaval and of revolutionary agitation."[73] The wage-earners and tradesmen of Paris, buffeted by growing unemployment and democratic ferment, were developing a political consciousness. Perhaps the boulevard actor was equally susceptible to a democratic ideology.[74] Certainly the insubordination of artists along the boulevard, many of whom had ties of blood, if not of interest, with the wage-earning classes, paralleled the movement of journeymen in some trades for higher wages and better working conditions. The similarity of means and purpose, however, may have been no more than superficial. Whereas radical democrats such as the Cordeliers largely sanctioned workers' protests and programs,[75] actors on the boulevard and throughout Paris remained unorganized and unsupported by those with political power. A few incidents of unrest on the boulevard stage were reported in 1792, 1793 and 1794, but there is no evidence that insubordination remained as widespread or as threatening as it had been in 1791. The boulevard actors' movement petered out almost as quickly as it had begun.

The failure of the boulevard actors to develop a program of demands and to act consistently suggests one or both of two things: that their unrest was not, at heart, ideologically inspired; that certain hardships and frustrations which might have fueled their insubordination were alleviated by less political means. It is believed that the rising prices and unemployment of the revolutionary years stimulated the radical political activity of Parisian wage-earners and tradesmen.[76] Hard times in theater may have been enough to aggravate the endemic frustrations of boulevard artists. The years 1789 and after were difficult for the theatrical businesses of private individuals. The larger boulevard theaters like the Grands-Danseurs du Roi or the Ambigu-Comique suffered great losses; smaller operations like the Associés, the Délassements-Comiques and newly-established enterprises such as the Lycée Dramatique or Théâtre-Français Comique et Lyrique struggled mightily to make ends meet. The impact on the actor was enormous.

By the second half of 1791 a number of smaller stages along the boulevard began to default in payment of artists' salaries. This fact is known because actors and actresses along the boulevard quickly learned to make use of the justice of the peace, recently created by the Constituent Assembly to judge civil cases of minor monetary value.[77] In July one Franchet, actor at the Théâtre des Associés, complained that he had gone without pay for two months. Toussaint du Jardin, a musician at the Délassements-Comiques charged before the same officer in September that the entrepreneurs Colon and de Neuilly had paid him only half his appointed salary. Less than two weeks later de Neuilly requested delay in payment of some 200 livres due the actress Catherine Girard, "it being impossible to pay her up to the present because of the poor season..." The same season forced Cauvin, director of the Lycée Dramatique, to agree with his artists that the theater's receipts would be sequestered by the police to ensure full payment of salaries.[78] Despite the best efforts of the justice of the peace to render equitable judgment, however, economic instability for the entrepreneur meant an irregular and uncertain income for the actor.

At the same time, the artist's access to the justice of the peace provided him with some hitherto unknown protection from the economic oppression of his employer.[79] Indeed, that court of law seems to have schooled the minor actor and actress in those civil rights that mattered most. More than one artist revealed, for instance, that his or her understanding of the theatrical contract was faulty. The actress Roselli demanded that Nicolet pay her 66 livres for a month's salary only to find her charge neatly contested by the director of the Grands-Danseurs. The engagement she thought had ended in March of 1791 had in fact extended through April, so that the month of work that she had believed to be in addition to her year's salary was in fact covered by her contract. A couple of actors from the Délassements-Comiques were apparently unaware that their signatures meant acknowledgment and final receipt of a year's salary at that theater. Corrainville had been expecting some 66 livres more with which to pay off an impending debt.[80] Although such complaints on the part of the artists were without recourse, the justice of the peace dispelled at least some of the ignorance about contractual obligations and binding signatures of which directors had unscrupulously taken advantage.

However, many artists were able to sue for other kinds of recompense that directors wished to dismiss. The actor Guillaumont, who had mistakenly claimed 81 livres in May of 1791, filed in November for payment of 24 livres "above and beyond the salary that [Nicolet] had engaged to pay [him]..."[81] The director had, it seems, refused to honor his agreement as a penalty for some infraction of theatrical regulations by the actor. In Guillaumont's favor, the justice of the peace found the fine unjustly heavy and ordered Nicolet to pay the actor 12 livres—in effect reducing the penalty from 24 livres to 12. A more considerable amount of money was won by the musician Rignant in 1792. The directors of the Délassements-Comiques had attempted to deprive Rignant of two months' pay, or 100 livres, on the grounds that he had not performed on 18 of the 306 (316?) days stipulated in the year's contract. Clearly recognizing that the musician had, at least, rightful claim to a month or more of salary, the justice of the peace ordered Colon and de Neuilly to pay him some 53 livres (or 62 livres?) for services rendered.[82]

Erratic payments, unjust penalties, withheld salaries, even ignorance of the law—these were not the only frustrations for which the boulevard artist was able to seek some redress before the justice of the peace. Perhaps the most important of all alleviations from total dependence and subservience to the director was the regulation of an actor's debt and its repayment. In contrast to the manner with which Ribié's debts were managed prior to the Revolution, the justice of the peace arranged these matters with a consistent regulation—and in such a way that the actor was protected from any tendencies towards economic vengeance. In August of 1791 Jansonne la Ville claimed that despite writs of attachment formed against his salary, Nicolet ought to be required to pay him a sum of 150 livres. La Ville was requesting the two-thirds of his salary recognized by law as not liable to distraint. Significantly enough, the law to which the artist appealed had been promulgated under the old regime. A declaration of 18 August 1779 had ruled that the salaries of actors attached to court spectacles "be free and discharged of all seizures, impounds, or writs of attachment up to the amount of two-thirds... reserved to provide for board and lodging..."[83] The ruling, however, was quite clearly meant to cover the employees of theaters and spectacles "connected to our courts," those that depended, in effect, on the Royal Household. The minor stages of the boulevard did not fall under this jurisdiction, but under that of the lieutenant-general of police, and there is evidence that the law of 1779 was not extended to the boulevard actor under the old regime.[84] Certainly there was no mention that Ribié, indebted as he was throughout the 1780s, was yet entitled to two-thirds of his salary.

The fact that the law of 1779 was admitted by the justice of the peace in 1791 and thereafter was, then, of double importance to the boulevard actor. Not only was the minor artist finally granted an equality of legal status with the great actors of Paris, but he was given the opportunity to limit his economic dependence and acquire some dignity before the law. It was Ribié himself who insisted in court that only a third of Forest's salary could be justly impounded by Nicolet for the actress' creditors. Even in those cases where the entire salary might be legally withheld from the artist—when, for instance, the debts were for food and lodging[85]—the boulevard actor could file suit for an adequate sum of his monthly income. In August of 1791 the justice of the peace awarded La Ville 50 livres of the 150 he claimed "for the provision of food"; in 1793 the same officer authorized the actress DuCharme "notwithstanding the writs of attachment... formed against her in the hands of Citizens Colon and Clergier to receive for the provision of food the sum of one hundred livres..."[86]

The actors' experiences with the justice of the peace proved that before the law in revolutionary Paris they in fact had rights that bore directly upon relations with the entrepreneur and society at large. The vague notion of natural equality and of civil rights declared in 1789 achieved an immediate value when the individual artist was enabled to contest at least some part of the director's rule or a creditor's claims. Indeed, one is tempted to conclude that arbitration by the justice of the peace disarmed protest amongst boulevard actors and actresses in 1791. Both complaints of insubordination and claims brought before civil justice reached their peak in 1791 and as rapidly declined in 1792. It is possible, of course, that the significant decrease in suits before the justice of the peace of 1792-94 after the high of 1791 may be explained by the novelty of that office in 1791. The subsiding of large-scale insubordination, however, needs another explanation.[87] If the volume of financial suits on behalf of artists did little or nothing to dispel their unrest, perhaps it was the relative easing of economic distress on the boulevard that relieved the causes of complaint before the police and the justice of the peace. In the short term, at least, Nicolet was able to break through the deficit that had plagued his theater through 1789, 1790 and 1791, and the average salary of artists at the Grands-Danseurs recovered in 1792 from its low point the year before. (See Figures 2 and 3 and Table 2, Part I.) Directors and actors at other of the small theaters along the boulevard may have been equally lucky.

There is one thing that did not affect the dissolution of protest and insubordination on the boulevard. The breakdown of traditional police authority over the minor acting troupes may have released pent up frustration and misdemeanor in 1791, but the curtailment of widespread insubordination in 1792, 1793 and 1794 had nothing to do with the reimposition of policing activity or government supervision. Police commissioners for the Temple section reiterated again and again in the course of 1791 the need for a general regulation of theater to be promulgated by the police. Such a code, however, was never implemented, either in 1792 or in the remaining years of the Revolution. A conflict of interest between the Commune and the central government over the role of theater in revolution, which grew sharply in 1792 and remained bitter through 1793-94, made this all but impossible. The boulevard was left to govern itself, and, except for the justice of the peace, actors, actresses and directors were left to their own devices. With very little modification, relations between artists and entrepreneurs subsided into the customary patterns of the old regime. Theatrical regulations still charged the actor to accept the roles that he was given, to appear at rehearsals and performances without excuse; individual artists still flaunted these rules with tardy or insolent behavior; whether contested or not, fines were still levied. In these matters the politics of revolution—and the actors' protests—were seemingly without influence.

It was not until 1794 that the records of the police, of the justice of the peace and of government reflected a renewed unrest on the boulevard similar to that of 1791. Directors of the more precarious theatrical enterprises, defaulting in payment of their actors and actresses, silently acknowledged their inability to maintain these artists within their troupes. Contract breaking became more frequent than it had ever been before. Like the rest of their compatriots, boulevard artists and their directors suffered greatly from the political uncertainties that closed theater doors and from the economic inflation that ravaged both profits and income. By June of 1793 prices of essential commodities in France as a whole were double or even triple what they had been in 1790.[88] The assignat fell to less than a quarter of its value in specie by the end of 1794.[89] For many in the wage-earning classes, the rise in prices was partially ameliorated by the doubling, tripling or even quadrupling of wages.[90] Salaries on the boulevard, however, remained nominally the same. The range of individual income, in both its higher and lower figures, had not changed since before the Revolution. The average salary at the Grands-Danseurs seems, in fact, to have been in slight decline since Nicolet's financial recovery in 1792. Inflation had, in effect, cut real income on the boulevard by one-half or two-thirds. (See Table 2, Parts I and II.)

The very highest paid of actors on the boulevard, receiving no more than 4,000 or 5,000 livres and probably less, had fallen in income below many of the journeymen and laborers over whom they had soared in the years before 1789.[91] There can be little wonder, then, that by 1794 boulevard artists—and especially the more poorly paid among them—should have grown bold in the demand for more income or for release from an inadequate salary. The musician Poulain declared his contract at the Ambigu-Comique "insufficient in stipulated salary to provide for his subsistence" and therefore null and void.[92] Salaries were indeed low at Audinot's theater; the average income of an actor in the contract year April 1793-94 was only 1,571 livres and well below the average salary at the Grands-Danseurs.[93] Audinot was forced to admit that Poulain's income, as a musician probably much lower than 1,571 livres, provided a meager living. Yet rather than agree to release the artist from his contract, as Lazzari and other directors were doing in 1794, Audinot insisted that the engagement be honored:

> ... [Audinot] realized readily that the stipulated wages were not sufficient for the subsistence of an artist but also that he [the artist] was only occupied three hours a day and that during the rest of his time he ought to be able to find enough work to meet his Needs. Anyway, he was no worse off than the artists of all the other theaters...[94]

Audinot clung perhaps too tightly to the director's advantages and prerogatives of the past. At the height of the Terror his own stubborn attitudes and unbending discipline led to another round of trouble at the Ambigu-Comique. This time the contestation between the director and his troupe passed directly to the Surveillance Committee of the Paris Department, which took a special interest in "the Subject of the difficulties that have arisen between the Directors and some of the Artists at the Théâtre de l'Ambigu-Comique."[95] The nature of these difficulties was never recorded in detail by the Surveillance Committee or by the police. It is clear, however, that sometime before the end of the theatrical year in April 1794 Audinot had attempted to alter the written contract he signed with each artist.[96] Throughout Paris concern for wages was mounting, and strikes for higher pay became increasingly frequent.[97] In order to protect himself from similar demands and from the breaking of contracts, Audinot tried to insert a new clause binding the actor who broke the engagement to an exorbintant fine of a month's wages. By this action, however, Audinot precipitated what he wished to avoid. Several members of his troupe apparently agitated for higher pay and the right to break contract without penalty. Perhaps this ruckus came to the attention of the Surveillance Committee when that body detained Audinot for several days in January 1794.[98] Because of the Committee's intervention three of Audinot's actors realized an increase in pay, and the new article was stricken from the contract and replaced with the right of either party to annul the engagement without penalty at three months' notice.

The Surveillance Committee's interference in the affairs of the Ambigu-Comique is the only recorded instance of the government regulating theatrical discipline on the boulevard in the years 1790-1794. Moreover, it was a stop-gap measure that addressed the particular problems of only one stage. The Surveillance Committee was unable to effect a general ordinance governing theatrical companies such as that demanded by the police in 1791, since this authority rested with the Commission of Public Instruction, created in 1794 to deal with matters of the Parisian stage. In the months preceding and following the fall of Robespierre and radical government, however, this Commission did not act. Mague St. Aubin, in a letter to the Committee of Public Safety in June of 1795, faulted the Commission for its failure to curb disorder among the minor actors of the boulevard:

> The Commission of Public Instruction has been charged with the police of theaters. I do not know whether it has concerned itself with those that one calls the great theaters; but it has forgotten the little ones.[99]

As testimony to this, Audinot's problems with musicians and one actor in particular continued to be tremendous. In May of 1794 three members of the orchestra missed an entire performance at the Ambigu-Comique.[100] In that and in following months the actor Roger systematically tested each provision of his contract. He missed performances, he came drunk, he quarreled on stage. More importantly, he demanded an increase in pay, without which he determined to leave the Ambigu-Comique at the end of the month. Audinot would not budge on any point, especially that of contract breaking, despite the written terms he had been forced to accept by the Surveillance Committee before the 9th of Thermidor:

> If artists have the right thus to break on their own whim an engagement legally contracted, it follows that the entrepreneur, who counts upon a group of artists in order to keep up his business, would be exposed to constant interruptions of his incoming receipts in order to

> replace absent artists, which would be absurd and completely unjust. For this reason the plaintiff [Audinot] asks that the citizen Roger be ordered by the court to Continue his engagement until its original expiration...[101]

Where directors and artists did not come to terms of their own accord in 1794 and after, insubordination was once again recognized as a problem of major proportions.

The actors' struggle for some form of emancipation from the director's harsh rule had been ill-fated from the start. The acquisition of civil rights had been only a first and cosmetic step towards liberation from the past. There had been no revolutionary law regulating the actors' commercial interaction with an open market of theater. Without such legal opportunity they had been unable to break from the paternalistic security of the director or the theatrical order of the old regime. The prolonged vacuum of power on the boulevard within which the actors battled erratically and often ineffectually to translate their civil rights into better working conditions turned to their disadvantage in the long run. Many of those who in 1789 had welcomed the elimination of prejudice for the actor felt disabused of this enthusiasm by years of uncontrolled insubordination and chaos on the minor stages of Paris. Mague St. Aubin was one of these, despite the fact that he was himself a long-time actor on the boulevard. In *The Reform of Theaters,* published in 1787, he had argued against the exclusion of all actors, whether high or low, from civil society. During the Revolution his fortunes changed temporarily, and he served briefly as director of the Théâtre-Patriotique (formerly the Associés) in 1795. In that year he acknowledged to the Committee of Public Safety that the revolutionary experience had proven the need for a severe discipline of the acting profession:

> The Revolution came; Actors were admitted into society, and unfortunately most of them apparently exerted themselves to justify by their immoderate conduct, by their swindles, by their vulgarities without number and of all kinds, the degrading opinion that one used to have of them. It even seems that, regretting the opprobrium from which national beneficence emancipated them, they wished to redouble their offensive efforts to secure that just opprobrium once more. No fidelity in the execution of contracts; no regard for the regulations which they themselves agreed to; no respect for the public.... In a word, these vile Beings, unworthy of liberty since they care only for licentiousness, have taken advantage of the apathy of the laws to violate them all and to dishonor their art more and more by troubling society.[102]

Mague strongly urged a return to the policing of theater that had characterized the old regime. The petty entrepreneurs of the boulevard must be protected and strengthened in their authority, he argued, and the mobility and independence of actors must be reduced. Contracts must be inviolate and imprisonment as well as fines imposed for infringement of theater rules. Mague's opinions gained ground.[103] The boulevard artists' erratic defiance of a theatrical organization that many found oppressive was placed in jeopardy under the Directory. With the advent of Napoleon and the end of the French Republic any gains they had made were forfeit by law. The year 1807 marked a return to the discipline of the past for all actors great and small:

> Any subject who shall cause disruption of a performance, either by refusing, without excuses deemed acceptable, to fill a role within his range, or by not being present at the indicated time for the performance, or, finally, by any other act of insubordination whatsoever towards his superiors, will be liable, according to the gravity of the case, to a fine or to an arrest.[104]

Except for a new civil status of little occupational benefit and a practical access to a civil court that granted the artist some economic protection, the boulevard experience had changed little for the minor artist before or after 1789. The cultural revolution in Parisian theater had no concern for the professional conditions and opportunities of the boulevard actor and actress at the bottom of the acting world.

6

The Boulevard Profession—Actor-Authors and Playwrights

Necessitous Men of Letters and Vocational Stability on the Boulevard

The boulevard stage, with its rapacious entrepreneurs and emotionally volatile actors, actresses, musicians and dancers, was very much a part of the Parisian literary world. Each minor theater had attached to it a number of prolific playwrights who provided the bulk of dramatic fare. Destival de Braban, Mayeur de St. Paul, Ribié, Dorvigny and Robineau de Beaunoir wrote constantly for the Grands-Danseurs; Arnould-Mussot, Audinot, Gabiot de Salins and again Dorvigny supplied the Ambigu-Comique. The smaller Délassements-Comiques had but one steady playwright, Plancher Valcour, and the Théâtre des Associés, apparently none at all. In addition, the minor theaters were served by a number of playwrights a good deal less productive but nonetheless well-known as boulevard authors: Parisau, Maillé de la Malle, Mague St. Aubin, Pompigny, Sedaine de Sarcy, and Fonpré de Francasalle.[1] There were also casual authors who now and again supplied the boulevard stage,[2] as well as an unknown number of anonymous playwrights.

In a way, those boulevard playwrights who did not scruple to sign their names to their work are as anonymous today as their more fastidious colleagues. As literary figures they are forgotten like their theatrical production. Indeed they had little reputation in Paris of the late-eighteenth century. The world of letters considered them unknown by virtue of the fact that they wrote for the minor stage—exclusively.[3] With very few exceptions none of these boulevard playwrights had ever seen the fruit of their labor performed on the great stages of Paris. This failure disqualified them from any literary pretension—most especially in the eyes of the French actors, who considered as "dramatic authors" only those playwrights who had had at least one play presented by that royal company.[4]

Yet boulevard authors did persist in believing themselves "dramatic authors" and men of letters. Gabiot de Salins, involved in a squalid dispute with Audinot and Parisau over the direction of the Ambigu-Comique in 1784, reminded his opponents and the public at large of his literary calling: "I was an Author, according to my view."[5] Some five years later this same Gabiot declared himself the equal of the likes of Michel-Jean Sedaine, an established dramatic author who had contributed over two dozen plays to the great theaters of Paris: "as an author, my rights are as sacred as his."[6] Men of boulevard letters well understood, however, that they did not frequent the same literary circles as Sedaine and his ilk. Gabiot carefully allowed that there existed an intellectual and social distance between Sedaine and himself, the one an Academician and the other "a literary man unknown outside of one theater..."[7] Similarly, Destival de Braban acknowledged openly that the boulevard author belonged to the bottom of the literary world:

> On Parnassus, as throughout the world, there are the shameful poor. How many Men-of-Letters have been forced to seek their livelihood in the meanest ways?...[8]

Most of the principal playwrights for the boulevard theaters in fact featured prominently in the world of hacks and would-be philosophes surveyed by the *Little Almanac of Our Great Men* in 1788. Destival de Braban, Mayeur de St. Paul, Dorvigny, Gabiot de Salins, Parisau, Maillé de la Malle, and Mague St. Aubin all figured amongst the dozens of poets that Rivarol and Champcenetz found in "the smallest nooks and crannies of the republic of letters..."[9] None of these boulevard playwrights enjoyed position in the established literary world, or as Destival called it, Parnassus, that mount of sinecure and status. They were as a group—by their own admission and contemporary critique—"necessitous," without secure and independent income.[10] Destival maintained that, unlike those at the top, the boulevard author was forced to turn his talents and his pen to mercenary ends:

> A Work of genius demands a considerable amount of time and one does not always have the wherewithal to publish at his own expense. Thus months pass by, years wear on and the Author is, without respite, tormented by necessity.
>
> What ought he to do? Must he die in misery because he hasn't an income of eight or ten thousand livres? No.. he must find, within himself, resources nimble and sufficient enough to ward off the hardship that besets him: he must write, therefore, *propter famen,* pending the time he may do it *propter faman.*[11]

For the playwright this meant deflecting his ambitions from the prestigious companies of Paris to the lowly theaters of the boulevard. Unlike the royal companies, these theaters did not scruple over the lack of reputation and connection from which so many aspiring dramatic authors suffered. Nor did they sit for months or years at a time on an accepted manuscript as did the French actors. An author did not wait long for a play to be produced on the boulevard, since the minor theaters thrived on large repertories and the fast turnover of dramatic fare. Indeed, for many a playwright the minor stage promised the theatrical career he might otherwise never have attained. Nougaret poked fun at such ambitions realized on the boulevard, but he, too, had taken advantage of the minor stage:

> The universe owes so many obligations to Mister Nicolet! He helped me over the barrier to theater, which is hardly easy to climb the first time.[12]

In turn, boulevard entrepreneurs took their advantage of the "necessitous" playwright. There is scant information on the amount a play might have earned on the boulevard in late-eighteenth century Paris, but what does exist suggests that the playwright who hoped to make money with his literary skill made precious little. A rare document—a note from the entrepreneur Nicolet to one of his most prolific writers—reveals the exploitive terms which boulevard director and author might generally have agreed upon in the later 1760s or early 1770s. On acceptance of his manuscripts, so many of which formed the most successful repertory of the Grands-Danseurs, Beaunoir was to be paid an inconsiderable sum of 18 livres each:

> Sir, the administration over which I preside has decided that in the future, as in the past, your works will be accepted without being read and you will continue to be paid eighteen francs per play; but you are asked not to present more than *three* per week. Nicolet.[13]

The plays that Nicolet bargained for so advantageously were probably no more than one-act farces or *parades.* But as the boulevard grew in prosperity and in artistic pretensions, the price for a two- or three-act farce or comedy rose precipitously. According to anecdotal evidence, in 1779 Dorvigny sold his farce *Janot or the Beaten Pay the Price* to the boulevard Variétés-Amusantes for 6 louis, or 144 livres.[14] The value of a boulevard play had apparently increased eight-fold in a decade's time. Rough estimates of the average price per play at the Grands-Danseurs for the last years of the old regime tend to confirm this rise, although it is clear that the average price of a play varied from year to year—as it did, no doubt, from theater to theater. (See Table 3: Average Cost of Plays at the Grands-Danseurs, 1786-1792.) In 1786 a manuscript accepted by Nicolet probably brought something around 120 livres; in 1788, the year in which Nicolet as well as his competitor Audinot sought to improve their repertories, the average price jumped to 153 livres. The mean for the years 1786 to 1790 was 125 livres per play.[15]

Despite the increase in the value of comedies written for the minor stage between the late 1760s-early 1770s and the late 1780s, boulevard playwrights were grossly underpaid for their work. While Beaunoir was receiving his 18 livres for many a successful *parade* or farce, a comedy produced at the Comédie-Française could be expected to pay at least several hundred livres, no matter how poorly it was accepted by the public. An extraordinary run of thirty performances on the royal stage would bring, on average, some 4,000 to 7,000 livres.[16] This was because the Comédie-Française or Comédie-Italienne rewarded playwrights with varying percentages of the receipts brought in by their plays. In contrast, boulevard authors were utterly cut off from a like share in profits from the performance of their plays. They had, in effect, sold to the entrepreneur not only the right of production but the right of property as well.

Upon occasion, boulevard directors were willing to concede that the author of an extremely successful play had been short-changed. Dorvigny's *Janot or The Beaten Pay the Price,* which reached 220 to 230 representations—unheard of at the time for any successful play whether on a great or a minor stage—was said to have made 150,000 to 200,000 livres for the entrepreneurs of the Variétés-Amusantes.[17] As a token of gratitude the directors awarded Dorvigny 288 livres, or twice the amount he originally received for the play. This was, however, small pittance compared to the 59,510 livres Beaumarchais received in 1787 from the Comédie-Française for the first 99 performances of *The Marriage of Figaro,* like *Janot* a phenomenal success.[18] Though the playwrights patronized by the royal stage had grievances of their own, their squabbles over money with the French actors were settled by government intervention and supervision. They had no need to beg, as did some minor playwrights, for even the most modest recompense. After the hundredth representation of *Annette and Basile* at the Théâtre de Beaujolais, a minor theater in the Palais-Royal, the playwright Guillemain humbly reminded the directors that he had little wealth: "[although] honor nourishes the arts . . . to honor I would wish to join a little money . . ."[19]

There was one other way the boulevard playwright might add to the small sum he could expect from the stage. Although he had sold the right to representation to the director, the author usually tried to retain the right to publication. A surprising number of comedies performed on the boulevard were in fact published—often within a year or two of their first representation. The practice was, however, only imperfectly accepted. Boulevard directors were apt to regard the plays for which they paid and which they produced as belonging to them exclusively. In his legal squabbles with Gaillard and Dorfeuille over the privilege to the Ambigu-Comique in 1787, Audinot demanded that the new directors be forbidden access to the Ambigu-Comique's repertory "seeing that [the plays] belonged to him exclusively, he having bought or composed them . . ."[20] Apparently, Audinot attempted as well to restrain at least one of his authors from publication. The playwright Parisau spoke out against Audinot's proprietary claims in a memoir of his own: "By yielding a play to the theater for representation, has [the author] lost the right to have it published?"[21] In March 1785 the question was legally decided in Parisau's favor: a director might not oppose the publication of a play "when the author has not ceded to him the ownership of it . . ."[22] The courts of the old regime had vaguely articulated a distinction between two forms of property interest in a dramatic piece—that of representation and that of publication.

Unfortunately, there is no direct information on the relations of boulevard playwrights and the booksellers of Paris; but neither is there reason to doubt that these lowly men of letters were as subject to the stingy terms of the book guild as some of their better-known colleagues.[23] In a semi-legal pamplet by Nougaret, who wrote plays for the boulevard as well as prose works for a general public, publishers were badly criticized for the harsh bargains they drove with unknown and needy authors:

> In vain one occasionally bows and scrapes to a Bookseller. He wants to have the manuscripts presented to him *gratis,* or at least, for very little. He dupes you, makes himself wealthy and the Author dies of hunger: *dies of hunger,* an exaggerated manner of speaking, which nevertheless comes close to the truth.[24]

It is tempting to believe that for the minor playwright, Nougaret did speak the truth—especially in the early 1770s when a low price on stage bespoke for the boulevard play an equally low publication value. Perhaps with the rise in cost of a boulevard play from the late 1760s-early '70s to the late 1780s—indicative of a more prosperous and competitive theatrical market—the minor playwright was able to strike a better deal with the bookseller.[25] The case of the publisher André-Charles Cailleau suggests at least that in these later years one Parisian bookseller was willing to specialize in boulevard plays. Cailleau, a printer-bookseller who seems to have published the vast majority of boulevard plays in print in the 1770s, '80s and early '90s, dabbled himself in the gay, billingsgate theater that had been cultivated by Vadé and others on the fairgrounds of Paris. Gripped by a passion for the stage that did not scorn the minor theaters, Cailleau apparently dispensed his large earnings, a fortune evaluated at 300,000 livres, in support of talented young authors without fortune:

> ... because of his profession and his taste for letters, he kept up relations for many long years with a multitude of authors, whom it pleased him to aid with his advice and, the more often, with his purse.[26]

If a single play brought little, either on stage or in the bookstall, a large number of them earned more. At the end of his career, Beaunoir estimated that over the years income from his hundreds of plays reached nearly 300,000 livres.[27] The economics of the boulevard placed a premium upon volume. But not all playwrights were as fecund as Beaunoir or as fortunate to have received carte blanche from a minor stage. Even on the boulevard reputation and a flair for comedy and farce determined who made money and who did not. It is easy to imagine eager playwrights haunting the theater halls and nearby cafés, grasping for dramatic tips and casual commissions. Certainly that was the case for Joseph Patrat, whose *The Englishman or the Reasonable Fool* was written in 1781 expressly for Volange and at the actor's suggestion.[28] Indeed, Volange was so apt at turning his roles to advantage that playwrights vied with one another to provide the star of the Variétés-Amusantes with plays—or so it was claimed in *The Idler:*

> Volange [is] surrounded by half-starved authors, who, for a bit of bread, write caricature parts for him which he performs quite well...[29]

The motivation strongly felt by the "necessitous," even starving playwright to sell as many plays as possible tended to exacerbate competition between authors on the boulevard in an ugly way. As a rule minor playwrights adapted for the stage songs, tales, fables and novels to be found in a wide range of published works, in the periodical press and in the Bibliothèque bleue. Their intense rivalry for reputation and sales, however, created a literary arena of ruthless and dishonest practices. It was commonplace that boulevard authors should crib from one another, steal ideas and blatantly plagiarize the work of others.[30] According to the *Fairground Almanac* "there pullulates a species of so-called Authors who cravenly attribute to themselves the plays of dead or living Writers..."[31] Certain of the boulevard playwrights were in fact repeatedly singled out for their obdurate plagiarism. Parisau, for instance, boulevard author and erstwhile director of the Théâtre des Elèves de l'Opéra, was accused of producing under his name the plays he purchased from others. He had, moreover, the audacity to submit one of these comedies to the Comédie-Italienne, where it was performed under his name in October of 1780. Gabiot de Salins also dodged charges of plagiarism throughout his career on the boulevard. It was his distinction, as well, to be known as "Le Cabaleur" or "Schemer" at the Ambigu-Comique where, due to his position in that theater's administration, he could vent his excessive jealousy for the success of others.[32]

It is impossible to determine the accuracy or fairness of the accusations of plagiarism and favoritism that echoed up and down the boulevard in the late-eighteenth century. What cannot be denied, however, were the rampant jealousies that stimulated continuous rounds of rumor and calumny. The author of a successful play no doubt expected as a matter of course that he would be charged with dishonesty of one kind or another. Hence the importance of the foreword to a play such as that Mayeur de St. Paul placed before the published version of *The Child of Nature*. There was every reason to suspect the author of foul play. The subject matter, taken from a novel by l'Abbé Baurieux, had already been treated for the minor stage by Baret de Villeancourt in *The Savage Tamed by Love*. Mayeur himself had taken the lead role in this play at the Ambigu-Comique. Now an actor at the Grands-Danseurs du Roi, Mayeur thought to translate his winning performance to

Nicolet's stage. In doing so, he claimed both the conventional right to draw literary sustenance from original sources and the indulgence of the public:

> Filled with desire to please [the public], I needed but several days to compose the Play that one is about to read, wherein I strictly followed the storyline of the Novel. . . . However, not a sentence of the other comedy will be found in my Play, though it be permitted to me, as to Monsieur Baret de Villeancourt, to copy, in certain places, the Dialogue of the Novel. . . . I would much rather create and be inferior than to seem a plagiarizer.[33]

The delicacy of the playwright's literary honor contrasted ludicrously on the boulevard with an indelicate profession.

It has been observed that late-eighteenth century France had not yet developed the literary market able to support men of letters in large numbers. Although it was increasingly possible for an occasional, highly successful author to earn a living by his pen, most writers and playwrights still depended heavily upon some form of patronage. Dramatic authors and littérateurs perched near the top of the literary world owed their affluence not to literary endeavor but to sinecure and government pension. La Harpe, for instance, one of the playwrights in hot dispute with the royal actors over property rights and percentages, earned his keep as editor of the *Mercure* at 6,000 livres per year. Successful men of letters filled the staff of this and other Parisian journals; they received gratuities and annual allowances from wealthy patrons; they depended upon generous subsidies that flowed from the coffers of the royal Treasury.[34]

By and large these sources of money and prestige were denied to the minor playwright of the boulevard. The point is made with the pension lists drawn up in 1785 by officials of the Contrôle général, a branch of government broadly concerned with financial and public administration. Calonne's ministry accepted requests for gratuities from, presumably, hundreds of writers, but no more than 147 of these were included on a master list. Only one applicant noted amongst these "Men of Letters Who Request Pensions" had written for the boulevard stage—and only in a manner of speaking. Madame de Beaunoir, "hardly fortunate," requested a pension in recognition of her authorship of *Fanfan and Colas,* a charming piece first performed at the Comédie-Italienne in 1784. But it was not she who had written *Fanfan and Colas,* it was her husband—or so he claimed in later years. Robineau de Beaunoir, that indefatiguable playwright for the minor stage, apparently had used his wife's name more than once to pass off his own plays at the Comédie-Italienne, otherwise scornful of a boulevard hack.[35] Possibly he used her name once more to elicit a pension from the government itself. His own name—or that of any other boulevard playwright—would have carried no weight with the ministers of the king, concerned to support what was already accepted and reputable within the world of letters.[36]

The fact that no boulevard author other than Robineau—and he by proxy—seems to have applied for a government grant in 1785 is more significant than the apparent hesitancy of Calonne's ministry to include Madame de Beaunoir on its list of pensioned authors. It is unknown whether she was granted a pension or refused. How then did boulevard playwrights support themselves? Although they were not to be found in the editorial offices of Parisian journals or in the anterooms of high society, most boulevard playwrights had no pressing need for royal favor. Nearly all of them were involved in the business of theater along the boulevard in capacities other than that of author. Some, like Audinot and Arnould, were directors; others, like Maurin Pompigny, Gabiot de Salins and Parisau (after his disastrous turn as director of the Elèves de l'Opéra) were employed as managers and prompters; the rest and by far the majority appeared regularly as actors on the minor stages. Destival, Fonpré de Francasalle, Mayeur de St. Paul, and Ribié performed at the Grands-Danseurs throughout the 1780s and early '90s; Valcour was at different times entrepreneur, actor and part-time director of the Délassements-Comiques through 1791; the intinerant Dorvigny and Mague Saint-Aubin acted at the Grands-Danseurs, the Ambigu-Comique, the Délassements-Comiques and the Associés. Of all the playwrights writing regularly for the boulevard in the 1780s only two—Beaunoir and Sedaine de Sarcy—did not hold a paying position with a minor theater. Sedaine's employment is unknown; Beaunoir, atypically, held a position with the Bibliothèque du roi. Unfortunately for this brilliant, though minor littérateur, his colleagues at the royal library looked with diminishing indulgence upon his boulevard career and Beaunoir was forced to resign his post sometime before 1787. Those playwrights employed on the boulevard, in contrast, had secured an institutional niche suited to their social reputation and profession.

Thus far we have explored some of the social and economic conditions that impinged upon the boulevard playwright, and in so doing, have discovered something of the form and substance of at least one "cranny" of the Parisian literary world. By contemporary definition and self-acknowledgment, the men who wrote for the minor stage were inhabitants of the very bottom of that world. The question arises, then, whether or not the boulevard authors, as a group, fit the psychological profile that Robert Darnton has drawn of the frustrated "Grub Street" hack, who, unable to rise in the world of letters, turned his bitterness at personal failure into hatred for the elite institutions and mandarins of the Parisian Parnassus.[37]

For Darnton, the psychology of failure had its roots in the stymied mobility of would-be littérateurs and philosophes into positions of power and prestige in salon, academy and royal sinecure. The "Grub Street" in which these hacks wallowed, he argues, was virtually without exit in the last years of the old regime. This was, by and large, true of the boulevard as well. None of the minor playwrights studied here significantly enhanced their social positions in the world of letters through the 1780s. Social mobility, however, was to a certain extent distinct from professional mobility. Some minor playwrights, though they remained in the long run tied to the boulevard, did achieve formal access to great theater. Five boulevard authors, Dorvigny, Parisau, Pompigny, Audinot and Beaunoir, had at least one of their plays performed by one of the great companies of Paris.

Because these playwrights did not find their way out of the boulevard in the 1770s or '80s, one might consider their brief receptions at the Comédie-Française or the Comédie-Italienne as windfalls in a theatrical world better known for its hierarchical severity. It is significant, however, that in these instances the imposing structure of privileged theater was in fact yielding to the persuasions of talent. After Dorvigny's tremendous success with *Janot* at the Variétés-Amusantes, the Comédie-Française claimed his new manuscripts for its own. The royal company wanted nothing more or less than a similar box-office success. But Dorvigny's plays failed miserably on the great stage. The boulevard author's gift for comic play was inconsistent; it did not sit well with a demanding and sophisticated public. According to the *Secret Memoirs, The Hussar Wedding* performed in January 1780 did not merit a second representation by the royal actors:

> ...it consists of an ambiguous gibberish that neither the spectator nor the author understands and it is all the more insupportable in that it goes on for four acts. The author, Mister Dorvigny, ought to return to the boulevard with his plays; it is the only arena that suits him.[38]

Dorvigny's example, or that of others welcomed, however briefly, at the royal theaters, was surely indication enough to playwrights of the boulevard that the market for their plays was open at the top of the theatrical world—even if the further road to permanent success and positions of prestige was blocked. The reality, of course, for the majority of minor playwrights was that professional mobility in the literary world would not be their lot. But it does not follow that all were subject to bitterness and hatred. The possibility of mobility, however tenuous, could encourage frustration; it could also relieve it.

Gabiot de Salins was one of those proverbial provincial lads of the eighteenth century who sought to make their fortunes in the Parisian world of letters. His, however, was the mortifying experience of rejection by the French actors, coupled with the necessity to seek employment as a school-master, which was incongruous with his literary ambitions:

> A powerful reason—necessity—forced me to take employment distasteful to my sense of delicacy. But I dare believe that I place myself above my profession by my manner of thinking, which is independent of rank and fortune...[39]

At length Gabiot found himself a sinecure of sorts on the boulevard, as prompter at the Ambigu-Comique. He became one of the most prominent of minor playwrights, but evidently he could not forget his humilation at the doorstep of the established, privileged world of letters. Given the very few personal statements of his that survive, Gabiot remained defensive of his boulevard calling and jealous of what he believed to be "literary Aristocracy."[40] Both attitudes seem very much in keeping with a man whose personal rivalries and ambitious schemes had earned him the sobriquet of "Schemer." Gabiot resembled closely the frustrated Grub Street hack of whom Darnton has drawn a social and psychological portrait.

More than one profile, however, must be drawn for the boulevard playwright. It is not true that other boulevard authors necessarily shared the full measure of Gabiot's grudges, although they knew as well the daily grind of the theatrical low-life. Very little is known of one Destival de Braban, except that he, too, hailed from the provinces of France; he, too, had been drawn by the promise of Paris. There is even indication that Destival, actor and author for the Grands-Danseurs, harbored literary pretensions of a higher sort. He wrote poetry as well as plays, and his attitudes and bearing spurred at least some of his fellows to criticize him as a "gigantic pygmy of the republic of letters, who takes jargon for taste, knowledge for intellect, and grandiloquence for genius..."[41] Yet this same Destival protested only a year before the outbreak of revolution that the minor playwright did not waste his time in envy of those littérateurs with 8,000 or 10,000 livres in royal pensions:

> No, it does not follow that he envies the lot of those who, by their talents, have the fortune to procure for themselves such an income...[42]

In the mid-1780s Destival probably earned around 2,400 livres a year on the boulevard. Coupled to what was apparently an average salary as one of Nicolet's actors, he seems to have made in any one year an additional 150 to 600 livres on his plays performed at the Grands-Danseurs.[43] Destival was content with his income and his position—perhaps because he believed that talent distinguished those at the top from those at the bottom, as he believed that the door to professional mobility was left open for playwrights of his class:

> Do not say that it is impossible for an Author who works for the Little theaters to work for the Great.... His ideas, dulled by a fairground pen, trace themselves the more strongly in his head; his mind, concealed with care, reveals itself when needed...[44]

It is not possible, then, to characterize the boulevard playwright of old regime France as necessary prey to bitter frustration with an inferior lot or to radical rejection of the established world of letters. The responses of boulevard playwrights to the professional and social conditions of the Parisian literary world were in each case unique and often mixed, scattered along the spectrum of public attitude and personal value. If the frustrated Gabiot could be—and was—cited for his sentimental affirmation of traditional values in the years before 1789, it was the complacent Destival who brought several outspoken, socially critical zanies to the minor stage.[45]

Why is it that boulevard men of letters did not display more prominently or uniformly the radical tendencies associated with other marginal members of the literary world? The hacks who worked the libelous and pornographic trade had no institutions, no corporate structures, no social location to call their own.[46] But boulevard men of letters did have their place, no matter how humble, in the literary world. And because the minor theaters in which they acted or worked were partially integrated within the privileged world, they were privy as well to some institutional and economic stability. As actors, administrators, directors and authors they had "made it" in a thriving enclave of theatrical industry tacitly promoted and protected by the ruling powers of the old regime.

The Professional Liberation and Political Experience of Popular Playwrights

The revolutionary emancipation of the boulevard playwright was in some ways more complete than that of the minor actor. The law of 13 January 1791 that liberated theatrical industry from the privileged confines of the past had resounding effects on the rights of dramatic authors. Articles 1 and 2 dismantled the monopoly of classical genres and classical repertory long held by the privileged French actors, thereby broadening the market for serious plays. Articles 3 and 4 transferred all property rights to dramatic work to the author during his lifetime. Regardless of whether a play had been previously performed or published, the author's written permission was now required for all future production. These terms were strengthened and clarified in a subsequent decree of July 19-August 6, 1791.[47]

This fundamental reversal of dramatic property rights as they had existed under the old regime was born of a long and heated debate among men of letters, the French actors and theater directors throughout 1790. It is well known that this debate culminated with La Harpe's *Address of Dramatic Authors to the National Assembly* in August of that year. La Harpe's petition, signed by a delegation of dramatic authors, demanded the abolition of dramatic privilege and the guarantee of author's rights that the National Assembly was, in fact, to resolve upon five months later. Perhaps because La Harpe and his colleagues won the day, it is less well known that another, less distinguished delegation of playwrights countered La Harpe's petition with one of their own.[48] Led by one Parisau, he who had been both director and author on the boulevard in the late 1770s and '80s, this second delegation contested the wisdom of liberating the theatrical industry of Paris. Although they, too, acclaimed an author's lifetime property rights, they could not agree with La Harpe and his co-petitioners that the hierarchy of theaters and genres—and especially the classical monopoly of the Comédie-Française—should be undone.

The most significant aspect of this clash between liberal and conservative points of view in late-1790 lies with the men who held them. Of the 19 men who signed La Harpe's petition all but one had had their work performed at the Comédie-Française. In contrast, only six of the 25 playwrights who signed Parisau's petition had had a play accepted by that august company. Almost half of these men, however, had written for the boulevard stage in the 1780s; six wrote more for the boulevard than for the great theaters of Paris. Only two members of La Harpe's delegation had ever written for the minor stage, and these sparingly.[49] Generally speaking, it may be said that those who clamored for the collapse of theatrical privilege in 1790 figured noticeably in the Parisian world of letters; were, in fact, among those whom even the French actors would have recognized as "dramatic authors."[50] Those who would maintain the rigid hierarchy of dramatic art and status were far less successful professionally. Most of them, although not outsiders to at least one of the three great companies, had no more than a precarious toehold in the privileged world of letters. In this case, then, the impetus for reform and liberation had come from inside certain circles of the literary elite, from the top of the literary establishment. What of the bottom of the theatrical Parnassus? Except for Parisau, who had left the boulevard for journalism in 1789, none of the hard-core boulevard playwrights of importance in the 1780s participated in this political wrangling over the liberation of theater and authors' rights. As individuals and as a group they had nothing to do with the legal renovation of the theatrical order in 1790-1791.

Nevertheless, they were affected by the declarations of theatrical liberty and authors' rights, most noticeably in the manner and amount of payment for dramatic fare. Change was slow in coming to the boulevard, however, as it was in fact to the great theaters of Paris. It was not until August of 1791, for example, that the more successful men of letters, led by Beaumarchais and others in the Bureau dramatique, came to new terms with the Comédie-Française.[51] For lack of an organized voice, playwrights on the boulevard were subject longer and sporadically to the same kind of agreements between themselves and directors that had characterized the old regime. Plancher Valcour, actor-author at the Délassements-Comiques in the 1780s, was said to have pulled down the gauze that separated the audience from the stage in response to the fall of the Bastille, crying "Long live liberty!"[52] Yet two years later and four months after the decree of 13 January 1791, Valcour still found himself entangled in the exploitive designs of the boulevard director. Since June of 1789 Valcour had lived and worked at the Délassements-Comiques as part-time actor, manager and author. Through April of 1791 he claimed to have presented on that minor stage 39 of his own plays. Sixteen of these he relinquished without fee, but for the remaining 23 he claimed payment. The directors Colon and de Neuilly flatly refused, and before the justice of the peace in April and May of 1791, tried their best to minimize their debt.

In a most ingenious manner, the unscrupulous entrepreneurs sought to take advantage of the January 13 law. That act designated that five years after the death of a playwright all private property rights to his work were rescinded and his plays became public property. By confounding this public domain with the body of published works, Colon and de Neuilly claimed that Valcour's plays were public property—not because he had had them published but because he had plagiarized the published works of another;

> ...among the number of plays for which Mister de Valcour demanded payment from them many were slavishly copied from the dramatic proverbs of Mister Carmontelle. They did not intend to pay Mister de Valcour for a play that by virtue of publication belonged to the public...[53]

Under the old regime directors had had little concern for the charges of plagiarism daily made on the boulevard. The sensitivity of Colon and de Neuilly was something new, in Valcour's opinion a ploy to rob him of the monetary value of his plays. He vehemently denied the allegations of Colon and de Neuilly, declaring "that the Plays have been performed many times at the Théâtre des Délassements without objection," and the justice of the peace ruled in his favor. Colon and de Neuilly were to pay Valcour, "according to the stipulated prices," 483 livres for 23 plays. But the playwright's victory was hollow. Not only did Valcour agree to a miserable price of 21 livres per play, he consented to relinquish to the directors all property rights to the representation of his bartered works.

During the interval between the January 13 law and that of 19 July-6 August 1791 it was still possible for an author to forfeit his property to the director—unwittingly in some cases—due to the ambiguous phrasing of article 4 in that first law. Authors were to retain all rights to the representation of their works, even those already produced "regardless of former regulation; *however, those acts which will have been passed* between actors [or directors] and living authors or deceased authors *within the last five years will be executed.*"[54] Accordingly, directors in charge of the many new, as well as old, theaters of revolutionary Paris presumed that customary agreements with dramatic authors would take precedence over the authors' rights. At the new Théâtre de la Liberté, established in 1791 at the Saint Germain Fair, one Dancourt had agreed to the production of his play *The Descent of Nicodème into the Brabant* for 72 livres per representation when the receipts exceeded 600 livres. In March of 1791 he complained to the police that the director Dupré refused to honor his promise, whereupon Dancourt withdrew his consent to the play's production. Fully cognizant of his newly granted rights, the playwright demanded "according to the terms of article 3 of the decree of the National Assembly" that the police seize and sequester the receipts of Dupré's theater.[55] Dupré argued successfully, however, that Dancourt had rescinded his rights under the new law by written agreement with the director:

> Dupré . . . made known . . . an act signed in duplicate between him and [Dancourt] the 16th of February last ceding the play on the part of Mister Dancourt in favor of Dupré and renouncing the right to dispose of it in favor of any other theater in the capital . . .[56]

In following years the property rights of the author recognized by the law of 13 January 1791 were respected more or less according to the latest decree. The law of 19 July-6 August 1791 clarified the ambiguities of January 13 by specifying that regardless of prior representation or publication, the playwright retained his property right. The following year, on 30-31 August 1792, the Convention revoked the authors' rights over plays printed or performed before January 13, 1791. On the first of September 1793 the Convention acted to guarantee once again the playwrights' property rights by repealing the 30-31 August law and reinforcing those of 13 January and 19 July 1791. This vacillation on a governmental level between old and new formulations of dramatic property rights was paralleled on the boulevard by a hesitancy between old and new terms of agreement between authors and entrepreneurs. In early 1791 the directors of the Délassements-Comiques were still buying the author's plays outright; by mid-1794, at least, they had seemingly changed their pratice to accommodate the playwright's claims.

According to a deposition with the justice of the peace, Louis Fonpré (formerly de Francasalle) had agreed with Colon and de Neuilly that his patriotic play *The Voyage of Cobourg* would bring him 24 livres when the receipts exceeded 200 livres and 12 livres when the receipts were less than 200 livres. Although this arrangement did not quite entitle Fonpré to a share in the profits—as authors received on the great stages of Paris—it did ensure him a fixed royalty of sorts for the duration of the play's production. But if Clergier, administrator of the Délassements-Comiques, found these terms reasonable for the theater, the entrepreneur Colon did not. At his behest the contract with Fonpré was broken and the playwright forced to accept a flat sum of 86 livres "paid in advance."[57] After what he believed to have been seven performances, Fonpré calculated that he had so far earned 100 livres under the terms of the first agreement; he had been forced to settle for 24 livres less in final payment. Regardless of national decree or the example of great theater, it was to the director's advantage to bargain for a fixed fee, whether or not the playwright retained his property right.

Under the direction of Colon and de Neuilly the Délassements-Comiques was known for the stingy compensation of minor playwrights. In 1792 the *General Almanac for all the Theaters of Paris* charged that these entrepreneurs in particular abused "the critical situation of an Author, by offering him three louis [72 livres] for a play in 3 acts."[58] The profits for Colon and de Neuilly, it was said, could run to one hundred times that amount. It is unclear, however, whether boulevard men of letters were better off dealing with any of the other theaters along the ramparts. The same *Almanac* claimed that Sallé, of all the directors on the boulevard, paid his playwrights the most, but how much is unknown. The only other information available on payments to authors during the revolutionary years is gleaned from the expense accounts of the Grands-Danseurs for 1791 and 1792. Through 1790 the average cost of a play in authors' dues at that theater was 125 livres. In 1791 and '92 this average cost dropped precipitously to 55 and 57 livres respectively. It is more than likely that in 1791 Nicolet abruptly altered his arrangements with playwrights in accordance with their new-found right to life-long compensation for the income of their dramatic fare. This meant, however, that in the first year of production the playwright realized—on average—less than half the amount that he had when forfeiting his rights to profits under the old regime.[59] The playwright's consolation for this reduced fee could only be found in the hope of continued royalties in coming years and the prospect of bringing his plays, after an exhausted run at the Grands-Danseurs, to some other theater in Paris or in the provinces.

Although the immediate value of a new play declined on the boulevard, there is reason to believe that some minor playwrights with a backlog of popular, successful plays actually realized an increase in income from their literary work. Correspondence on behalf of Robineau de Beaunoir reveals that this boulevard playwright—like Guillemain, an old author for the minor theaters of the Palais-Royal, or Dorvigny—took advantage of his renewed property rights to withdraw old plays from the Parisian theaters to which they had originally been sold under the old regime. Through the auspices of the Bureau dramatique, several of Beaunoir's plays were resubmitted for performance both in Paris and in the provinces. These well-worn plays commanded less than a new play, but nonetheless brought to the author hitherto unknown income. Boursault, entrepreneur of the Théâtre de Molière, a new theater established in 1791, was willing late in that year to pay Beaunoir no more than six livres per representation:

> ... he was not able, for Plays so old and so well known, to propose the same payment as he would for novelties. For other works of the same kind he had agreed with Mister Dorvigny to a sum of six livres per representation ...[60]

The appeal of Beaunoir's plays was such, however, that Boursault grudgingly agreed to pay 12 livres per representation—at least until the end of January 1792. During that time and for several months to come Beaunoir realized on *Jerome pointu,* a play he had written over a decade earlier, at least 152 livres, and probably more. He even received perquisites on old plays performed in Marseille, Maçon and Moulins, an income virtually unheard of under the old regime.[61]

It has been suggested that the writers and hacks at the bottom of the literary world formed the ranks of the radical intelligentsia that governed politics at the height of the Revolution.[62] That some leaders of the sans-culottes, such as Marat or Fabre d'Eglantine, had spent a literary past circulating just beyond the borders of elite Parisian salons, academies and royal theaters cannot be denied. But how many of their comrades on the outskirts of great culture in late-eighteenth century Paris followed their radical lead? The question of political sympathies and radical activity depends on an intimate knowledge of individual response to the political stimuli of 1789-1794. For those who populated the boulevard in the last years of the old regime, this information barely exists for a handful of actor-authors and playwrights—for those, in fact, whose literary skills had already placed them in the limelight of little theater before 1789. How did this select group of men, more vocal, talented and conspicuous in the records of history than scores of other boulevard artists, respond as individuals to the political and cultural upheaval of 1789-94? The first and most significant observation is that only a very few boulevard playwrights abandoned theater to participate more directly in the maelstrom of revolutionary politics. The second is that their activities embraced both ends of the political spectrum.

The first of the boulevard playwrights to reveal political sentiments were the conservatives, Parisau and Beaunoir.[63] Parisau, who had asserted as early as 1785 an author's proprietary right to publish his work, had taken a conservative position over the issue of theatrical repertories versus the public domain in 1790-1791 by leading the petition in support of the property rights of the royal companies of Paris. Other of his activities make clear that Parisau was attached to the politics of the old regime as well as to the cultural privileges of the three royal theaters. As a journalist, he wrote and produced the *Gazette à la main* or *Feuille du jour,* an aristocratic organ of apparently vulgar tendency. Parisau's journal was suppressed as counter-revolutionary in August 1792. Shortly thereafter he was imprisoned, only to escape miraculously the bloody massacres of 2-3 September. When once again at large, and as ever a monarchist, he continued his aristocratic writings clandestinely until denounced before the Committee of General Safety on September 11, 1793: "[he is] former author of the *Feuille du jour,* which is found every day in all the haunts of counter-revolutionaries . ."[64]

Parisau was arrested and incarcerated a second time. In the next nine months he made several attempts to justify his political innocence before members of government, but the obligation of all those detained to give an account of their political conduct since 1789 told against him:

> I swear to you that I have neither said nor done anything that might be cause to deny me my freedom.... Around the period of August 10th I did in truth operate a newspaper that displeased and I was made to feel that keenly because the journalist Gorsas had my furnishings, my papers, and my printing press pillaged at the time.[65]

On July 10, 1794 Parisau was arraigned as an accomplice in an assassination plot against certain heads of government. It was his journalism, however, and not these trumped up charges, in which the President of the Jury was interested: "Didn't you put in your newspaper that in France one planted trees of Liberty but that they were without roots?" No further evidence of royalist sympathies was necessary to the court, and without further delay, Parisau was sentenced to death.[66]

Parisau's militant monarchism was shared in less disinterested fashion by Robineau de Beaunoir.[67] After 1787, and a long career on the boulevard, Beaunoir had put his fortune and his energies in the direction of a new theater in Bordeaux. The eve of revolution, however, found him back in Paris and in financial ruin. It seems, at first, that Beaunoir willingly embraced the patriotic notions of his countrymen, for he briefly served as orator of the masonic Loge du Contrat social—but by the end of 1789 he had fled to Belgium. Beaunoir later gave two very different reasons for this flight: if it was not the pursuit by his creditors, it was the fall of the Bastille and the acceptance by the king of the Declaration of the Rights of Man that convinced the minor littérateur to leave France.

Regardless of his true motivation, once in the Austrian Netherlands Beaunoir hired himself out at different times as spy and informer to a number of the political factions that vied with one another for control of the revolution in Brabant. Beaunoir's initial services for the governor-general d'Alton, chief executive in Belgium for the Hapsburg monarch, were shortlived, since the Austrians relinquished their provinces in December of 1789. Yet even as Beaunoir courted first the Estates party and then the democrats or Vonckistes, his royalist sympathies showed clearly. In early 1790 he became entangled in the affairs of the French actress Dubuisson, whose salon was known to the Belgian patriots as a center of Austrian intrigue. The same year he involved himself with a certain Wildt in a betrayal of the democrats that redounded to the Austrians' favor. After the Hapsburgs restored their rule in Belgium at the end of 1790, Beaunoir occupied himself with several libelous pamphlets against the Belgian patriot Van der Noot and with the journal *Le Vengeur,* in which he flattered the Austrians and attacked the republican principles of the French

Revolution. Clearly realizing that he was persona non grata to his radical countrymen, the boulevard playwright-cum-political-spy retreated first to Germany and then to Russia when the sans-culotte army marched into the Austrian Netherlands in April of 1792 and again in July of 1794.

The closest the boulevard ever came to producing a radical leader of those sans-culottes was in Plancher Valcour.[68] As early as 1789 Valcour had given expression to notions of theatrical and cultural equality and freedom when he tore down that gauze curtain at the Délassements-Comiques. He remained on the boulevard as an actor and author, however, until some time in 1792 or early 1793. In the course of this second year he abandoned an acting career to participate in political affairs. Now calling himself Aristide, Valcour became an editor and then director of the radical *Journal de la Montagne,* or *Journal of the Mountain,* the official organ of the Jacobin society. His association with the Jacobins was cemented with a post in the bureaus of the Committee of Public Safety.

As a journalist and poet at the government's service, Valcour reported on the deliberations of the Jacobin society, composed revolutionary songs and delivered speeches on behalf of the Jacobin leadership. In Paris and in the provinces, he rallied his countrymen to the cult of the Supreme Being and educated them in patriotic fervor and symbolism.[69] The songs and plays he composed at this time were blatantly partisan in their exaltation of the Mountain and of the sans-culottes. In July 1793 he sang before the Jacobins,

> Friends, often and for too long,
> Under the frightful reign of the tyrants;
>   One celebrated the despots in song;
> Under that of Liberty,
> Of Laws and Equality,
>   Let us sing of the Sans-Culottes.[70]

These same sentiments were given full expression in the new plays Valcour wrote for the Théâtre de la Cité, one of the new and more radical stages of Paris. In *The You and the Thou,* which played with great success between November 1793 and July 1794, the young lover cried "Ah! live, long live the Sans-Culottes! long live these intrepid revolutionaries! Without them, without the august and sainted Mountain, the Republic would no longer exist."[71]

Parisau, Beaunoir and Valcour were the only three of the dozen or more men studied here who left any trace of explicit political activity outside of theater in the years 1789-94. Their disparate political activities and sympathies are suggestive of the range of private sentiments that were probably experienced by the playwrights they left behind on the boulevard. It can in fact be said generally of the playwrights who remained in theater during the years of revolution, or who dropped from sight altogether, that not many were willing to risk the positions they had gained in minor theater to become politically involved; nor were they actively interested in turning the cultural order of the old regime upon its head. Yet because minor theater was perceived by contemporaries to be closely tied to the revolutionary upheaval, the question must be asked of these men: how did they participate as members of a profession in the revolutionary turmoil of which Parisian theater, and specifically the boulevard, was a part?

Historians of revolutionary theater have already remarked that it is singularly difficult to evaluate the political activity of most actors and playwrights because of the tremendous pressures placed upon these men and women to proselytize the virtues of revolution and—after August '92—of republican France. It was the imposition of a theatrical censorship in 1793 and the later progress of the Terror, these historians argue, that brought to an end the golden age of liberation for both actors and playwrights.[72] In fact, the men and women of theater had been subject to political pressures throughout 1792 and even earlier. The *Journal des théâtres* rued bitterly in April of '92 the bipartisan politics that had already shattered the French stage:

> In what position are the theaters? Always apprehensive, agitated, trembling; always a prey to cliques, to parties, to factions; always exposed to hear applied to themselves, by those interested in harming them, the vague and dangerous reproach of aristocracy...[73]

Increasingly, the demands of the public forced the actor and the playwright to assume a political radicalism he or she may not have felt. According to one theatrical almanac it was an actor's patriotism and not his talent that gained the approbation of an audience; according to another the same applied to the playwright: "Many authors have imagined that in making use of the civic oath or the national guard [in their plays], all would be said, and they would be excused any lack of talent..."[74]

By 1793 the exigencies of the theater-going public were sanctioned by radical government. Aristide Valcour, especially interested in the cultural revolution of the theatrical world, voiced the new regime's political interest in the expressed sympathies of theatrical artists and playwrights:

> Not only must known republican works be performed... patriotic men of letters must be engaged to work for the theater, to enlighten, sustain, perpetuate public spirit. Encourage authors, reward them, decree that the author of a good revolutionary work will have served the country well...[75]

At its own instigation the Commune re-established an official censorship of theater in September 1793. Municipal officers not only monitored the repertories of Parisian theaters, they kept sharp watch on the literary activities of individuals. One Antoine Vincent Arnault later recalled in his *Memories of a Sexagenarian* (1833) that his own willful abstention from theatrical patriotism had cost him a sharp reprimand from the police:

> The citizen Baudrais, to whom I had submitted my work, gave it back to me several days later. He had found nothing in it that was not innocent, which I had expected: "But it is not enough, he added, that a work be not against us, it must be for us. The spirit of your opera is not republican; the mores of your characters are not republican; the word *liberty!* is not spoken a single time. You must place your opera in harmony with our institutions."... I was made to understand, moreover, that all authors, like all artists, were to make their patriotic contributions in money struck in the coinage of the republic. Up until now I had not met this obligation.... It was incumbent upon me... to furnish the stage with a republican work.[76]

Arnault's experience suggests that the revolutionary output alone of any one boulevard playwright (for they, too, were equally subject to the surveillance of the police) would be an inadequate, even invalid, measure of the man's political sympathies. The lack of intimate records of any kind for these men makes it impossible to evaluate fully the motivations—whether of patriotism or of fear—that produced such homage to the Revolution. But homage it was. It is meaningful, that is to say significant of participation in theatrical radicalism, to distinguish therefore between those boulevard playwrights who wrote for the stage in 1792, '93, and '94 and those who did not write for the stage when the pressures for radical theater began to mount in those same years.

Those minor playwrights well-known to the boulevard under the old regime who continued to write for the revolutionary stage were political kin to Aristide Valcour in effect, if not intent. Despite his responsibilities to the *Mountain,* Valcour kept up a barrage of revolutionary plays. The titles of many suggest their radical import; for example, *Republican Discipline* (1794), *The Tomb of the Imposters, or the Inauguration of the Temple of Truth* (1794), and *The You and the Thou* (1794). Other boulevard authors, though uninvolved in a political career, followed his patriotic lead in theater. Maurin Pompigny had been employed in the administration at the Ambigu-Comique before moving on as actor and then director at the newly-established Théâtre de la Cité sometime after 1792. His theatrical work was apparently intermittent, since Pompigny simultaneously held an unknown position in the republican army. Distinguishing himself from the crowd of revolutionary playwrights as the "citizen soldier," Pompigny provided the Cité at the height of the Terror with several very radical plays, among them *The Republican Husband.* So extreme was that play in expressed hatred for aristocrats and clergy that the *Keeper of Republican Principles and Political Morality* singled out its author for his vigorous presentation of the "virile and touching lessons of civic virtues."[77]

Other members of the revolutionary press were less enthusiastic about Pompigny's patriotic efforts, citing the playwright's plagiarisms and dramatic mediocrity. This was not the case with Dorvigny, who earned praise as a model of the patriotic writer for his work in late-1793 and early-1794.[78] Believed to be an illegitimate son of Louis XV, this boulevard actor lived a romantic life of which novels are made. Captured by pirates in his youth, actor and author at the Grands-Danseurs and other of the minor theaters of Paris, an inveterate drunkard, Dorvigny was apparently in distress when the Revolution began. Whether from political conviction or new-found opportunity, Dorvigny revived his spirit and his literary career. In 1789 he wrote the immensely successful *Père Duchesne* and its sequel *The Wedding of Père Duchesne.* He signed a petition of musicians and men of letters in November 1792 demanding that the Convention assure the rights of "these harbingers of the Revolution . . ."[79] He gained momentary prestige in 1794 when the Commission of Public Instruction, composed of Robespierre, Barrère and Collot d'Herbois, chose one of his plays to inaugurate the Théâtre de l'Egalité. *Perfect Equality or the Thou's and Thee's,* a Rousseauistic vision of social relations in the new order, was officially commended for its excellent synthesis of political didactism and dramatic interest:

> There is none more patriotic, or which better attains the goal to which all works of this genre must tend—that of elaborating thoroughly upon the decrees that are celebrated [within the play], to make their spirit understood, to demonstrate all their advantages and to make them loved.[80]

Other of the boulevard playwrights must also be cited for their manufacture of patriotic theater in 1792, '93 and '94. Destival de Braban, who continued in these years as an actor at the Grands-Danseurs (now the Gaité), was chiefly responsible for what new fare was produced at that theater after 1789. It is more indicative of his own revolutionary ardor, however, that Destival collaborated with Aristide Valcour in the authorship of several patriotic pieces for the radical Théâtre de Molière in 1792, and in the process altered his name to Décius, more in keeping with republican taste. One of their joint plays, *Three Years of the History of France,* was lauded by the press for the "ingenious order in which the events that led up to, accompanied and followed the Revolution are made to pass before the spectator's eyes."[81] A year and half later in early 1794 Destival was recognized once again for his patriotic contributions to the stage when an officer of police censorship cited his play *The New Calendar or There are No More Priests* as an example for playwrights and theaters to heed. Fonpré de Francasalle, another actor in Nicolet's troupe from 1786 through 1792, turned his hand as well to radical theater. In 1793 he left Nicolet to become a dramatic coach at the Lycée des Arts and in 1794 became an administrator of some sort at the Théâtre de la Cité. At the same time, he brought his literary work to the more patriotic theaters along the boulevard. The Théâtre-Patriotique (formerly the Associés) produced in 1794 *Catherine Théos, or the Would-Be Mother of God* and *The Catholic, Apostolic and Roman Army Put to Rout;* the Délassements-Comiques the *Voyage of Cobourg.* Finally, Gabiot de Salins, too, took up his pen for revolutionary theater. Except, possibly, for a stint with the "Molière battalion" in 1792-93, Gabiot remained throughout the Revolution as manager of the Ambigu-Comique.[82] He wrote a couple of successful plays for Audinot in 1789 and 1790, one of which, *Paris Saved or the Failed Conspiracy,* was interpreted for political allusions in the royalist cause.[83] By late 1793, however, Gabiot was writing unequivocally with revolutionary spirit, as his *Café of Patriots,* calling for the explusion of aristocrats from these social and literary gatherings, made clear at the Lycée des Arts.

It would be a mistake to assume that Valcour, Pompigny, Dorvigny, Destival, Fonpré and Gabiot wrote nothing but patriotic plays in the years of revolution. Even Valcour and Destival, recognized for their republican efforts at the Théâtre de Molière, were chided by the press for falling, now and again, into their old ways:

> But shortly these authors, abusing their abilities, inundated the Théâtre [de Molière] with a quantity of plays that were not well received by the public...[84]

Much of this "quantity of plays" produced by Valcour, Destival and other of the old boulevard hacks, remains unknown—not only because the manuscripts have been lost or destroyed, but because a great deal of theater written and performed during the radical years of the Revolution seems to have been penned anonymously. Only the sentiments and ideologies of those in power could guarantee the acknowledged playwright safe passage in the stormy waters of revolutionary politics; all else, if Baudrais' words to Arnault are well understood, was suspect. By these standards, a number of boulevard authors may well have lived these years as recalcitrant citizens of the republican stage. There is no indication, for instance, that Mague St. Aubin, Sedaine de Sarcy, Maillé de la Malle, Arnould or Audinot signed their names to any patriotic plays in 1792, '93 and '94, though one or two of them may still have contributed anonymously to the "quantity of plays" for which the minor theaters were still known.[85]

In contrast to Destival or Dorvigny, these men participated little in the revolutionary world of letters. They may, perhaps, have been proud to boast like Robineau de Beaunoir in later years that "my pen is all that the Revolution was unable to take from me..."[86]

Both Arnould and Audinot, co-directors of the Ambigu-Comique through 1795, wrote sparingly for their stage if at all after 1792. Notice of two manuscript plays written in 1789 and 1791 is the only trace of the boulevard author Sedaine de Sarcy in the years 1789-94.[87] Mague St. Aubin, an actor who roved from stage to stage on the boulevard, found himself at the Associés in 1790. A play he wrote for Sallé in that year, *The Rattles,* seems to have been his last until the end of the radical revolution.[88] Mague left the Associés, now become the Théâtre-Patriotique, and moved to the Ambigu-Comique in 1792 and to the Variétés-Amusantes de Lazzari in 1793. He was during these and following years actor, part-time director and even bookseller, but not patriotic playwright. For reasons that may well have been those of Audinot, Mague and Sedaine, Maillé de la Malle, too, abruptly stopped writing for the minor theaters in 1789. Actor at the boulevard Variétés-Amusantes in 1782 and afterwards a dramatic coach at the Palais-Royal's Théâtre de Beaujolais, he disappeared from theater so completely that one scholar mistakenly believed him dead.[89] The year 1793, however, found him alive and, it seems, in hiding from patriotic theater. Yet even a humble citizen was forced to prove his revolutionary sentiments, or at least, to guard his political conservatism. In October of 1793 Maillé was denounced before the Committee of General Safety for an argument in a café over radical newspapers, respectable men and citizens' cards:

> Then this individual [Maillé] got up saying... you can take your papers and your card, because only damned beggars and rogues carry around a citizen's card... then this individual spoke very disparagingly and very insolently to them... when the Citizens asked him for his card, he answered them impertinently and in a manner reminiscent of the old regime, where is your own...[90]

Clearly, the playwrights who lived and worked the boulevard stage in the last years of the old regime did not form a cohesive political group at any point in the Revolution to come. Some chose to become politically involved in the revolutionary controversy, either in France or abroad; others—most—remained in theater. Some displayed frankly conservative or reactionary sympathies in their professional lives; others gave enthusiastic voice to the radical patriotism of the year II; the rest did or said nothing at all. Some, no doubt, merely adapted to the ideologies of the day without conviction; others, no doubt, were sincere. Thus, although a few boulevard playwrights—Valcour most conspicuously—dedicated themselves to the political renovation of Parisian theater, it would be incorrect to suggest that radicalism was a function of the pre-revolutionary boulevard milieu. Men who had shared the professional conditions of author and actor on the ramparts under the old regime scattered along the spectrum of political allegiance and political activity in the years 1789-94.

This was so in spite of the tremendous pressure placed upon boulevard playwrights—as on all playwrights in Paris—to pay their patriotic dues in radical theater. Yet so inadequate, so insufficient, was the response of old boulevard playwrights to the changing political clime that the minor theaters were increasingly forced to look to outsiders for political plays. In the first years of the Revolution perhaps one of the most successful of the boulevard's revolutionary plays, *Nicodème on the Moon,* had been written by Beffroy de Reigny, a newcomer to the Parisian popular stage. Three years or so later, during the same period that the police censor Baudrais chastized the likes of Arnault, different theaters along the boulevard turned to a certain Boullaut for *Brigands of the Vendée;* to Gassier St. Amand for *The Death of Marat;* to Briois for *The Taking of Toulon* and *A Day of the Vendée or the Death of Young Barra;* and to Bellement for *The Second Décade.*[91]

Little is known of these men, but what sources exist suggest that by and large they represented a new breed of playwright. There is evidence that they wrote their political plays as testimony to their revolutionary ardor—and to procure political advancement. In the year II Beffroy de Reigny formed the habit of sending texts of his patriotic plays to local sectional committees, hoping thereby to demonstrate his patriotic virtue and ward off in advance a political denunciation he apparently had cause to fear. He was in fact incarcerated for some two months in late 1793 and early 1794.[92] Jean-François Briois procured an attestation of civic faith from the Temple section in 1793 and presented it to the Surveillance Committee in hopes of gaining some employment. A year later he reminded the same Committee that he had in the meantime "proven" his patriotism with *The Taking of Toulon,* first performed at the Gaité in February 1794, and would continue to do so in two new plays, *The Death of Young Barra* and *The Heroism of Belperche.*[93]

Briois and his ilk, unbound by habit or training to the old ways of the boulevard, provide additional evidence for the case that the political radicalism to be found on the boulevard was not a function of that theatrical milieu, but, rather, a function of external revolutionary influences and social forces. Valcour, it must not be forgotten, also used his revolutionary plays as stepping stones in a political career beyond the boulevard. However, if old boulevard playwrights were not, as a group, the stuff of revolutionaries, that is not to say that they did not participate in an upheaval of the Parisian theatrical order. It is necessary to draw a distinction between their range of commitment to the Revolution, on the one hand, and their ready acceptance of new-found professional mobility and its material rewards, on the other.

The conservative Beaunoir, for instance, while offering his services to reactionary interests in the Belgian revolution, did not scruple to lend a hand in destroying old distinctions between theaters and dramatic cultures in Paris. He did this by withdrawing old successful plays from the Comédie-Italienne or the boulevard theaters where they were first performed and offering them indiscriminately to new establishments throughout the city. The release of the popular, pre-revolutionary repertories from their confines on the boulevard can in fact be largely traced by the diffusion of Beaunoir's old work and that of Dorvigny through Parisian theaters after 1791. Men of the boulevard such as Pompigny, Valcour, Destival, Dorvigny and Gabiot participated in the breakdown of old cultural barriers as well by bringing their new plays to a wide range of theaters established in revolutionary Paris. At least one among these boulevard playwrights, Dorvigny, reached the very pinnacle of success. The

Théâtre de l'Egalité, which produced his *Perfect Equality* in 1794, was for its short duration one of the most prestigious of Jacobin theaters.

The free and open market of theaters in revolutionary Paris seems to have provided opportunities for the minor playwright to improve and extend his career. Take, for example, the case of Ribié and Mayeur de St. Paul. Both men were longtime actors and authors on the old boulevard; both men took similar advantage of the liberation of theatrical industry to enhance their status as dramatic artists. In 1789 Ribié, if not Mayeur, greeted the Revolution with enthusiasm. Some believe him to have been one of the authentic vanquishers of the Bastille and to have been appointed for his valor Captain of the National Guard.[94] Both men are thought to have been editors of the first *General Almanac for all the Theaters of Paris,* a publication notable for its recommendation of a liberalized theatrical industry. By the end of 1790, or early 1791, however, Ribié and Mayeur left Paris together for the French colonies of Martinique and St. Domingue. Ribié, at least, had done this once before, in 1787, as a means of shaking off debts and creditors that had become too burdensome. Colonial insurrections this time cut short their journey and by the end of 1791 or thereabout, Ribié and Mayeur had returned to France. For the next year or so Ribié toured the provinces as an actor; Mayeur's actions are uncertain. It was surely by coincidence that in early 1793 both men took advantage of revolutionary circumstance to make a debut one step higher in the dramatic profession. In Bordeaux, Mayeur became the director of a theater soon known as the Théâtre de la Montagne; in Rouen Ribié opened up the Théâtre-Français, later called the Théâtre de la République.

As the patriotic names of these establishments would indicate, Ribié and Mayeur catered to the politics of theater in Rouen and Bordeaux, especially during the Terror in later 1793 and 1794. Directors on the make, they were in far more sensitive positions than they had been as actor-authors. Yet despite their civic efforts, both ran afoul of revolutionary government. Mayeur and his company were hauled in by the revolutionary tribunal of Bordeaux for the representation of what was considered an immoral play, though it was written by Aristide Valcour. Ribié was an active Jacobin organizer of popular fêtes in Rouen, but he, too, fell suspect to radical surveillance. Several weeks before 9 Thermidor the Committee of Public Safety in Paris ordered his arrest and removal to the capital. The reasons are unknown, but it took a certificate of civic faith from the Commune of Rouen to release the erstwhile director from jail.[95]

In later years, Mayeur and Ribié were able to keep something of the professional position they had briefly attained during the Revolution. Through the early 1800s they separately held positions as directors of the Gaité, the Théâtre de Louvois, the Théâtre de la Cité and the Théâtre-Olympique, all of them Parisian theaters. But willing and conspicuous participation in the new ways of the Revolution was not necessarily tied for Ribié, Mayeur and others like them, to advance—however modest—in the Parisian world of theater. Ribié's and Mayeur's theatrical directorships were interspersed with financial failure and their professional achievements were precarious. So it was that when the imprisoned French actors returned to their stage after 9 Thermidor, they removed Dorvigny and his *Perfect Equality* from their repertory.[96]. Likewise, when Pompigny applied in early 1795 to be included on the government's pension list of needy and deserving savants and men of letters, he was denied.[97] Pompigny, Destival, Gabiot, perhaps Fonpré, remained as they had begun—actors and authors of the minor Parisian stage.

Valcour alone of the boulevard radicals seems to have moved up in the professional order of Parisian theater. After a political career as a justice of the peace, he returned to his original profession in 1801 by joining the artists of the Théâtre de l'Odéon, a troupe initially composed of some of the best members of the disorganized Comédie-Française and thought to constitute in quality a second Théâtre-Français in Paris.[98] But it was not only radical involvement in the Revolution that subsequently resulted in upward mobility in the world of letters. Beaunoir, that arch conservative, also gained considerably in literary status on his return to France in 1801. He was, apparently, at the center of the Parisian literary movement, corresponding with European literati and writing once more for the stage. At the restoration he was finally awarded a sinecure in the literary division of the ministry of police.

And what of those boulevard authors who had avoided altogether involvement in revolutionary politics and revolutionary theater? If they had been more ambitious to leave their mark in the records of government or in the annals of theater, if they had been less anxious to remain anonymous and uninvolved in the maelstrom of revolution, we might be able to paint as fully for them as for their more radical or more conservative peers the pattern of their lives in the years 1789-1794 and after. It is indicative of their sentiments and their aspirations that we know so little. It may have been Maillé who was listed as an actor in Bordeaux in 1799. After the Théâtre de Lazzari burned down in 1798, Mague St. Aubin became an ambulatory actor, plagued by debts. In contrast, Audinot retired a reasonably wealthy man in 1795, the same year that his associate Arnould died. Sedaine de Sarcy and his manuscripts vanished completely.

Dorvigny, Pompigny, Destival, Gabiot, even Valcour, Mayeur and Ribié were among the playwrights who dominated with their literary production the little theaters of the boulevard and of Paris at large through the first decade of the nineteenth century.[100] The Revolution had had no catalytic effect upon their careers, for these same men had already made their mark on the minor stage of the old regime. So, too, had little changed in the harsh and erratic temper of their professional lives. Conditions had been altered by the acquisition of authors' rights but hardly improved for these men. Their conspicuousness as minor playwrights contrasted sharply with economic deprivation towards the end of their lives. The octogenarian Fonpré was seen begging on the Pont des Arts around 1812; in the same year Dorvigny, who had been forced to sell his clothes and his books for money, died in a poor house. Mayeur died impoverished, at the moment, supposedly, when he was to receive a gratuity as a man of letters.[101] "Ribié," wrote the publisher Barba, "used to have a four horse carriage, and yet he died in misery in a hospital in Martinique."[102] For most under the old regime, the professional life of an actor-author or playwright on the boulevard had been something of a bohemian existence—it had, in terms contemporaries might have understood, much of the precarious, contingent quality of the zany's calling. The same was still true for these men in the aftermath of liberation and turmoil in the Parisian world of letters.

Part IV

Boulevard Theater and Revolution

Prelude: Theater as Reactionary Institution and Revolutionary Instrument

> The theaters are still burdened with the debris of the last regime, with weak copies of our great masters, . . . with morals that are not our own. This chaos of objects must be swept away, as either strange to the revolution or little worth its sublime efforts; the stage must be disencumbered, so that reason may come again to speak there the language of Liberty.
>
> —Circular issued by the Commission of Public Instruction, June 1794.

March 1791. A man dressed in a simple vest presented himself at the ticket office of the Ambigu-Comique and requested entry to the theater's first and best seats. The ticket seller informed him that he would be unable to take a first place dressed as he was, but that he might seat himself in one of the second places. The man responded with some warmth that "he believed himself in the right since the new Regime to enter for his money in any and all places which it might please him to do dressed in any manner whatsoever." The police, who daily supervised theater operations and performances, supported the management's dress code and the social hierarchy it implied in the seating arrangements of the hall. "Decency demands that one be dressed in a coat in order to go to the first places," they admonished. Not to be daunted, the man persisted. "By what law or ordinance" do you decree how I must dress and where I must sit? To his indignation the theater seemed rife with the social distinctions and arbitrary ways of the old regime. The man would not be silenced, nor would he step aside from his stance in front of the ticket seller. Acting upon their authority to maintain the public peace, the police forcibly removed him from the premises. As they grabbed him by the arms, he continued his harangue. A second place was not what he wanted, he had the money for a first place seat! He did not cease in demanding "by what law?" when brought before the commissioner of police.[1]

September 1793. Latour-Lamontagne had a nose for sniffing out the anti-revolutionary perversions that undermined patriotic efforts to create a republican France. One of the many police spies who walked the streets and mingled with the crowds, Latour-Lamontagne felt it his special concern to warn the Minister of the Interior about the aristocratic infection that sapped the revolutionary stage. Even the most patriotic theater of all, the Théâtre de la République, did not completely escape the contagion. Latour-Lamontagne's careful scrutiny of actors and audience in the theater hall convinced him that far too often plays offered in republican faith still held traces of ridicule for the new regime. Such was *Mutius Scevola,* in which, despite strong statements of hatred for kings and love of liberty, the role of Porsenna depicted a human and generous monarch, worthy of esteem and admiration. How much more invidious were those plays written under despotic government! Indeed, for Latour-Lamontagne entire repertories were suspect. "They retrace for us in most flattering colors the old abuses of the feudal regime. The privileged orders reappear once more on the stage, hateful clothing wounds our eyes, the language of tyranny resounds in our republican ears and the counter-revolution takes place each day in our theaters." It was time, Latour-Lamontagne believed, to radicalize theater.[2]

August 1794. Mague St. Aubin cautiously tested political waters in the wake of Thermidor by sending his old book on the reform of theaters to be considered by the Commission on Public Instruction. Of prime importance in the repulican regeneration of theater, Mague insisted, was the purification of the morals of dramatic artists. "We must not allow virtue to be sullied by passing through impure canals; [we must not allow] the moralists to be immoral." When his book had first appeared in 1787 this task was all but impossible—"it was a waste of time to preach morals. *But now that virtue is the order of the day*..." As an old actor-author-director on the boulevard, Mague was surely aware that virtue had already, fitfully, cast its glance in the actors' direction. At the height of the theatrical Terror in January and February 1794 the Surveillance Committee of Paris had declared all actors responsible not only for their own private morals backstage but for those portrayed onstage. One Louis, actor at Lazzari's Théâtre des Variétés-Amusantes, was hauled before the Committee for taking a young girl from her home and living with her unmarried. The couple were admonished to regularize their relationship under pain of surveillance by the Temple Section's civil and revolutionary committee. The actor Picardeau and actress Juliette of the Ambigu-Comique were warned to modify their style of acting so that it might be more in keeping with the modesty of republican mores. The actor Thomas of the Gaité was jailed as a lesson to all that the actor was personally responsible for the roles he performed, not only in interpretation but in choice. All actors and actresses throughout the city were personally informed by the Committee of their duty towards a new and republican theater.[3]

What have these diverse scenarios concerning audience, plays and actors to do one with the other? It has been suggested elsewhere that because of the nature of its institution, theater, "enclosed by walls, bound by stages, and guarded by ticket takers," could never, "even with the cooperation of actors, managers, and playwrights," really become an instrument of revolution.[4] One of the most perceptive and misunderstood critics of the French stage realized this well before 1789. In his *Letter to M. d'Alembert on Theaters* Jean-Jacques Rousseau attacked the corrupting influence of social divisions encouraged by seating arrangements in theater halls, of scenes of unregenerate society described on stage, and of the moral alienation of the actor from the audience and society at large. All three were fundamental aspects of theater; all three were to haunt republican efforts to wipe out social memory of the old regime.

The investment of any individual theater in the institutional baggage of the old regime, measured in the hall itself, costumes, plays, stage machinery, artistic training and education, was often enormous even on the boulevard. Yet if certain contemporaries are to be believed, it was the boulevard, source of corruption in the breakdown of social and cultural rank, that "prepared the great revolutionary contagion."[5] The popular stage was thought to play a crucial role in the cultural turmoil that shook the theatrical world in the years of revolution. How effectively did revolutionaries shake off the institutional investments that bound theater to the old regime? Was the aristocratic hierarchy of theaters turned upside down in the years of revolution? In what manner? And did this have any effect on dramatic traditions or their customary social segmentation? Did the boulevard theaters that bridged the old and the new regime participate actively or passively in the republican renovation of theatrical culture? In answer we may find that if they did not entirely fashion of theater an instrument to their own ends, revolutionaries were nonetheless aware of the task that lay ahead of them.

7

The World of Theater Popularized

Liberation and the Hierarchy of Theaters

In the course of 1789 the dramatic privileges and censorship rights of the royal theaters dissolved. For all intents and purposes, the cultural segmentation that had marked the Parisian world of theater came apart at the seams. By law in January 1791 an imposing organization of theaters and dramatic genres was formally trampled underfoot. Contemporaries disagreed, however, over what would take its place. Liberal reformers such as Quatremère de Quincy and Millin de Grandmaison expected a cultural renascence, a flowering of the fine dramatic tradition in Paris and throughout France. They were forced to contend with conservative opinion that feared a free market would unleash the boulevard's dramatic idiom from its marginal confines. In the cultural experiment that followed, both fears and expectations were met.

The first and most obvious result of the liberal law of January 1791 was an immense explosion of theatrical industry such as had never before been seen in the city of Paris. In the preceding period of 1785-1788 no more than 11 theaters had at any one time opened their doors to the Parisian public. The addition in 1789 of the protected Théâtre de Monsieur at the Palais-Royal barely compensated in number for the temporary failure of two boulevard spectacles closed since 1787. In the course of 1790 the Théâtre des Bluettes and the Dèlassements-Comiques reopened; Mlle. Montansier, following the king, transferred her enterprise from Versailles to the Palais-Royal; and two more theaters opened doors in the Palais-Royal and the Place Louis XV. This gentle rise in the number of Parisian theaters between 1788-1790 took place, with only one exception, along the boulevard and in the Palais-Royal. Following the decree of January 1791, however, this pattern of slow and marginal development burst from its confines of rate and place. Almost overnight the number of theaters, closely reigned in at 15, more than doubled to 35. In 1791 20 theaters were established, and only five of these were to be found in those traditional areas of growth formerly allowed in the privileged economy of theater.[1]

The editors of the *General Almanac for all the Theaters of Paris* for 1791 welcomed the proliferation of theaters as a sign that "the old routine" of privilege and inequality in the theatrical world had been broken.[2] But the liberation of theater from the patterns of the past was deceptive. Within a year or so it became apparent that the marketplace meted out a crude justice reminiscent in its effects of government supervision and control before 1789. The number of performing theaters, 35, apparently remained constant between 1791 and '92, but 12 new establishments had come to take the place of as many defunct enterprises. In 1793, the count dropped to 24, despite five additional stages; and in 1794 these theaters dwindled to 19 or 20. The liberation of theatrical enterprise had created a Paris-wide explosion that rapidly peaked three-fold, and as quickly fell to a level commensurate with the pre-1791 rate of growth.

The high degree of instability amongst the many theaters of revolutionary Paris was largely restricted to those enterprises established after 1791. La Harpe recognized at the time that the ideological fervor of liberation, which he himself had helped to create,[3] had gotten the best of entrepreneurial prudence:

> Theaters proliferate every day, without adding either to talents or to good works.... Greed speculates without calculation; entrepreneurs in theater set themselves up without funds, resources, or necessary understanding and at the end of a year they go bankrupt. This will not fail to happen to several of our new theaters...[4]

A number of these barely-solvent theatrical ventures set up briefly on the boulevard. The Lycée-Dramatique, which opened once or twice a week in 1791, soon restricted itself to Sunday performances. Musicians for the orchestra were engaged by the week; proof, claimed one almanac, of the uncertain existence of that spectacle.[5] Indeed, the Lycée folded sometime in 1792. The Théâtre des Petits Comédiens Français was another stillborn boulevard stage, remaining open only intermittently from 1791 through 1793; so, too, was the Elèves de Thalie, which closed in early 1792 after no more than a year of business.

Although the petty enterprises newly established along the boulevard were highly susceptible to bankruptcy and failure, all Parisian theaters suffered from competition, inflation and dislocation. La Harpe observed in 1790 or earlier that "the revolution has ruined all the theaters..."[6] He meant to underscore particularly the hardships endured by the once-privileged companies of Paris. All three were menaced with enormous debts. The Comédie-Italienne, for instance, entered the revolutionary years already heavily in arrears.[7] Erratic receipts due to political agitation in the streets, heavy competition from the Théâtre de Monsieur and the flight of a wealthy clientele all contributed to the need for further borrowing. In contrast to the economic decline of the Comédie-Italienne and the other great theaters, La Harpe suggested in a fit of pique around 1790, "it is only the *little theaters* that have, with perseverance, prospered . . ."[8] Within a year or so more sober reflection led him to predict, however, that minor theaters on the boulevard and throughout the city, whether new or old, would surely fail in the intense theatrical market of revolutionary Paris:

> . . . besides, no talent whatsoever has as yet come to surface and as seats are sold so cheaply it is hardly possible that entrepreneurs can sustain the expense. Two years from now, almost all these theaters will have gone out of business for lack of resources.[9]

La Harpe's contrary moods as he considered the little theaters of Paris reveal much of the liberal condition after January 1791. Like many others who had supported the liberation of theatrical industry, he had implicitly assumed that the popular stage would disappear from an open and competitive market. Only the fine traditions of great theater would remain. It was believed, after all, that the despotic censorship of the little by the great theaters was responsible for the degraded dramatic idiom of the people; it was believed that theatrical talent and zeal alone would survive a truly competitive market.[10] But the little, popular theaters did not fail as a group—rather, they increased in number. La Harpe's predictions to the contrary, old boulevard theaters such as the Grands-Danseurs (which became the Gaité in 1791), the Ambigu-Comique, the Délassements-Comiques, and the Associés (which became the Théâtre-Patriotique in 1790) weathered the revolutionary years. So, too, did a couple of newcomers established there, the Bluettes, which reopened in 1790 as the Théâtre-Français Comique et Lyrique, and the Théâtre de Lazzari, opened in 1792. The discontinuity between expectation and experience in this instance stands as a kind of simile for the liberal experiment with theater as a whole. On several counts the decree on theater of January 1791 betrayed the liberal hope to shape by that law one fine dramatic culture. Harsh reality soured ideological fervor. The tenacity, indeed the growth, of popular theaters formed the first great disappointment of the experiment begun in January 1791.

Despite the liberal intentions of men such as Millin de Grandmaison, Quatremère de Quincy and La Harpe, a classical scorn for the popular stage as it had developed under the old regime had not been shaken. During the debate on theater in late-1789 and early-1790 all but the most zealous advocates of freedom had argued for the necessity to curtail the number of little theaters and to restrict by genre their artistic enterprise. As befit their conservative interest in a privileged order, the French and Italian actors had demanded that the Commune suppress every minor spectacle in Paris; Jean-François Cailhava, a recognized dramatic author, had called for the elimination of all but one popular stage in a revised edition of *The Causes of the Decadence of Theater* (1789); Nicolas-Etienne Framery, future agent of the Bureau dramatique, had allowed in his *On the Organization of Parisian Spectacles* (1790) only a few theaters to serve the people. Municipal commissioners themselves had proposed in March to lease theatrical privileges to no more than four little theaters: "a theater of song, one of tight-rope dancers, and two theaters of the spoken word, having as well the right to give pantomimes and dances."[11] Just one voice was heard in defense of the boulevard industry—that of a director who had been trying to establish an enterprise along the avenue since 1787.

In his *Address to MM. the Representatives of the Commune of Paris* (1790) Clement de Lornaizon deftly applied the principles of property rather than of privilege to the support of boulevard enterprise. He claimed that the minor spectacles had had juridical foundations equal to those of the royal theaters and that these must guarantee their position in the new regime:

> Under the old regime a royal decree [by which the great theaters were established] was nothing more than a ministerial order. It is ministerial authority that gave birth to the little as well as to the great theaters. They have thus a common origin and in this regard our proprietorship is as respectable as theirs.[12]

Yet despite the liberal appeal to property, a great deal of De Lornaizon's defense of the popular stage was like that of the police and the royal ministers under the old regime.[13] The minor spectacles could do no economic harm to the great theaters, argued De Lornaizon, nor aesthetic injury to the eminence of the classical repertory, precisely because the public and the fare of the great and little stage were essentially distinct. The minor theaters dealt in a product and a market ignored and scorned by the privileged and prestigious companies of Paris:

> We [the little theaters] live off the food that they [the great theaters] reject. . . . We present [it] to a class of public that digests very well these somewhat coarse leftovers. Without question it is unnecesary that all the inhabitants of a big city be conspicuous for their discrimination and refined taste for the beaux-arts. Less demanding in the choice of its pleasures, the people do not analyze, they feel.[14]

De Lornaizon insisted that all theaters have an equal right to enterprise; he maintained nonetheless that a hierarchy of theaters would still remain—one determined by dramatic idiom and public as well as economic means.

The little theaters eventually achieved entrepreneurial freedom because Quatrèmere de Quincy and his cohorts successfully declared that liberty and property rather than monopoly and privilege would shape the theatrical industry of Paris. These men did not include the boulevard stage in their lengthy arguments for an untrammeled market of theater. De Lornaizon's *Address* was publicly ignored. Yet, as De Lornaizon seems to have realized, most contemporaries, even those who supported the law of January 1791, were unwilling to concede that the popular stage might win by its persistence a place comparable to that of the more prestigious theaters of Paris. The *General*

Almanac for all the Theaters of Paris declared in 1791 that all theaters were free and equal. In 1792 the same *Almanac* explicitly denied that a liberal market was an egalitarian one:

> Although the Constitution decrees equality, there exist nonetheless between the theaters of Paris ranks irrevocably established by the natural inequality of talents and the personal resources of the Actors, the Directors and the Spectators; and though *Nicolet*, with his Dancers, may believe and call himself the equal of the Opéra, the throng of the best of Paris, the noted esteem that the judicious Public accords the good theaters to the prejudice of the bad, proves as La Fontaine said: "that a Rat is not an Elephant."[15]

The *General Almanac for all the Theaters of Paris* was essentially correct. The minor theaters along the boulevard and throughout Paris contrasted sharply with successful ventures established in competition with the Comédie-Française, the Comédie-Italienne and the Opéra. The Théâtre de Monsieur, established in 1789, the Théâtre Montansier established in 1790, the Théâtre Louvois, Théâtre de Molière and the Théâtre de Marais set up in 1791 and the Vaudeville erected in 1792, all, in the words of one historian, formed considerably healthy enterprises, based upon large amounts of capital and excellent troupes.[16] The directors of the Variétés-Amusantes in the Palais-Royal likewise took advantage of liberation to thrust their stage into a direct rivalry with the once-privileged Comédie-Française. Nearly all these prestigious competitors eventually sought and found subsidy from revolutionary government. In this they enjoyed something of the economic protection granted the royal companies under the old regime. The minor theaters of the boulevard had never received pensions from government; neither did the myriad petty enterprises that cluttered the boulevard, the Palais-Royal and other odd corners of Paris in the years 1789-94. In simple economic terms the distinctions that had separated great from little theater under the old regime were reflected in a like hierarchy of revolutionary theaters.

Similarly, the hierarchy of publics to which the many Parisian theaters catered remained roughly the same—though in fact many theaters made efforts to expand social access to their seats.[17] At the Comédie-Italienne, soon known as the Salle Favart, and the Comédie-Française, now the Théâtre de la Nation, income from the boxes, normally rented to the cream of wealthy and aristocratic society, fell precipitously through 1793. Evidently the high density of upper-class clientele at these theaters thinned out considerably as the Revolution progressed. Conversely, it seems likely that spectators of more modest social standing swelled in numbers as the once-privileged companies moved to attract a more democratic public than they had in the past. The Italian actors reduced the price of entrance to the pit to 24 sous in August of 1789.[18] In April 1790 the French actors announced plans to build 600 new seats priced for "the least well-to-do class of citizens."[19] This expense proved impossible, and in the following year the company reduced the gallery seats from 4 livres 7 sous to three livres and entrance to the pit from 48 to 36 sous. A number of new theaters priced their own seats comparably. The Théâtre de Marais, which La Harpe believed to be one of the best of the new stages, charged 2 livres 10 sous for all places; the Théâtre du Palais-Variétés seated the public for as much as 4 livres and as little as 15 sous.[20]

Despite the efforts of the French and Italian actors to open their theaters to a broader public, it is significant that the lowest of their prices still remained higher in 1791 than the highest of prices at the old boulevard theaters. Indeed there had been little change in the cost of seats at these minor spectacles since the police had lowered them definitively in 1776-1778. Audinot raised his grilled boxes to 3 livres in 1792, but his second tier of boxes had been lowered to one livre and his third tier of places maintained at 12 sous. Nicolet did nothing to raise his first places from 1 livre 10 sous and he lowered the price of tickets in the peanut gallery, or "paradise" as it was called by the French, to 8 sous. The Théâtre-Patriotique and the Délassements-Comiques offered seats that ranged in cost from 24 to 6 sous. The only deviation from these low prices was to be found at the Théâtre-Français Comique et Lyrique, where the best seats cost 3 livres and "paradise" went up from 12 sous to 1 livre 4 sous.[21]

The low cost of boulevard theater attracted "many classes of citizens" during the Revolution as in years before. At least through 1792 persons of the social elite and "the bourgeoisie, even those of wealth" continued to attend the popular stage in large numbers. Receipts for civic performances in December 1790 and April 1791 indicate that Nicolet sold more tickets for his boxes and first places than for his second, and cheapest, seats. This in contradiction to one historian's claim that with the fall of the Bastille the aristocratic and wealthy clientele of the boulevard left Nicolet to the populace. Yet the lower classes had been growing in size at the boulevard halls at least since 1785. The people, "few well-taught," filled the hall of the Théâtre-Patriotique and the Délassements-Comiques in 1792; they figured largely at the Gaité in 1794.[22]

Indeed in this last year, at the height of the Terror, the lower classes seem finally to have claimed the boulevard as their own. With some degree of pride the sans-culotte Perrière observed that the public promenade was no longer reserved for the wealthy:

> From one end to the other, the boulevards were stuffed with people . . . there were more heads of hair than hats . . . poorly dressed people, who would formerly have never dared show themselves in areas frequented by people of fashion, were walking among the rich, their heads held high . . .[23]

As under the old regime, the theaters of Paris, arranged in economic rank, still sketched out in gross form a social hierarchy of publics. Not until the later revolutionary years, however, were the lower classes finally represented in numbers more in keeping with their proportionate size. Boulevard theaters were, at the last, fully popularized in patronage as well as in name.

The Confusion of Dramatic Traditions

In the economic and social realms the boulevard theaters remained at the bottom of the theatrical hierarchy. If they were to be tolerated at all by the liberals of 1789-1791, they were to absent themselves from the cultural renascence so ardently desired by those early revolutionaries. For the editors of the *General Almanac for all the Theaters of Paris* the more prestigious theaters alone were to revive the dramatic excellence that had declined under the monopoly of the Comédie-Française; the boulevard and fair spectacles could have no part in the rejuvenation of taste and the great stage. Yet here the liberal reformers of 1789-1791 suffered their greatest deception. The liberation of theater had not eradicated the hierarchies of the past; more precisely, it had not eradicated the popular stage. It did eliminate the legal sanction of theater-types and repertory control. Aesthetic distinctions between theaters broke down when economic and social ones did not. All theaters could perform any genre or play indiscriminately, whether appropriate or not to their theatrical means or public. The *Almanac*'s outrage betrayed the reformer's sense of cultural violation:

> *Nicolet,* for example, imagines that in consequence of the Decree he can in future dispense with [new] plays; he no longer presents anything but the former works of the great theaters; but these works were destined to a sort of Public that does not go to Nicolet's theater... *Tartuffe* is as displaced on the Boulevard as *The Loves of Mr. Old-Hide and Madame Strong-Butter* would be ridiculous at the Théâtre de la Nation.[24]

Instead of the renascence of fine, classical traditions, the liberation of theater from the artistic restraints of the old regime had borne a dramatic confusion. In the aftermath of revolution, some would even say, like the near-contemporary and playwright J.B.A. Hapdé, that it had turned the cultural world upside down:

> ...revolutionary anarchy was bound to give birth to theatrical anarchy; *Brutus* and *Mahomet* were performed on the [popular] stages, the carmagnole was danced in the temple of Melpomène [the Comédie-Française].[25]

Some of the first historians of revolutionary theater reiterated this contemporary perception that an implicit order of theater and dramatic culture had been turned ruthlessly on its head. Hallays-Dabot declared that, in the wake of the January '91 law, "disorder only increased. All repertories were confused." In particular, he argued that the little dramatic tradition had been unleashed from its proper confines: "The Revolution triumphs over all the theaters. Everything is pretext for popular plays . . ."[26] Albert, too, observed "a universal jumbling," though he realized that change was not necessarily of the same kind for all theaters. While the little theaters pillaged plays from the great stages, he wrote, these in turn borrowed "the customary modes of action [i.e. genres], and sometimes even the plays" of the boulevard. Yet, with some contradiction, he further stated that "genres, noble and common, had not yet been confused, but all repertories were mixed together."[27] Albert's equivocation and Hallays-Dabot's vague notions of a popular theatrical anarchy suggest that the exact nature of cultural upheaval in theater requires examination.

The repertories of the Comédie-Française/Théâtre de la Nation and the Comédie-Italienne/Salle Favart in the years 1789-93 can be studied for the influx of plays that were unfamiliar or strange to the royal companies under the old regime.[28] Although it was rather uncommon for plays to be performed on more than one stage before 1791, the Comédie-Française had enjoyed the right, under the old regime, to appropriate successful plays within its aesthetic jurisdiction. With this prerogative, the royal actors picked up six plays first performed elsewhere in 1789 and 1790, well before the law of January '91. The liberation of genre and repertory restrictions, however, seems to have curtailed that company's interest in the dramatic fare of other theaters. The French actors borrowed no plays at all in the two years following the legal release of repertories, and only two plays from their companions the Italian actors in 1793. Of 59 plays first performed by the Comédie-Française between 1789-93, eight had previously belonged to the repertory of another theater. The once-privileged troupe had virtually no contact throughout the Revolution with boulevard plays or boulevard playwrights.[29]

The Italian actors proved only slightly less conservative. Of the 89 plays introduced on their stage in the years 1789-93, 21 had been performed elsewhere before 1789. Of these, two, possibly five, had figured briefly in the repertories of the Grands-Danseurs and the Ambigu-Comique. Measured play by play, the acceptance of the boulevard idiom by the Comédie-Française and the Comédie-Italienne was nothing short of severely restrained. Neither company, after all, had reason to abandon the artistic prestige of the classical repertory.[30] For other of the new theaters of revolutionary Paris, the appeal of boulevard plays seems to have been somewhat stronger. The Théâtre Montansier, for instance, produced 16 plays that had first belonged to the boulevard and fair theaters operating after 1750. Thirteen of these plays had appeared at the boulevard Variétés-Amusantes, one at the Grands-Danseurs. The Théâtre de Molière is known to have paid Dorvigny a decent royalty on *Janot or the Beaten Pay the Price,* that highly successful farce first performed by the boulevard Variétés-Amusantes. But only two other plays were borrowed from that theater and one, possibly, from the Ambigu-Comique. Other new theaters, such as the Variétés Comiques et Lyriques, the Théâtre du Palais-

Variétés, the Théâtre de la Concorde, the Marais and the Vaudeville, also chose sparingly from the boulevard repertory.[31]

The importance of the boulevard plays to the repertories of these newly-established theaters should not be overestimated. If the fare borrowed from the minor theaters is compared proportionally to the number of plays introduced on each stage in the years 1789-94, it becomes obvious that neither the Théâtre Molière, the Montansier or other revolutionary theaters allotted significantly large portions of their repertories to boulevard and fair plays, although in this they did surpass the once-privileged theaters.[32] Far greater portions were devoted to another kind of play that fell into the public domain after 1791—the comedies, tragedies, operas and ballets that had belonged to the royal theaters of Paris. Fully one-quarter of the plays performed on the Montansier were taken from the Comédie-Française, the Comédie-Italienne or the Opéra. At least 50 plays, or 43 percent, performed at the Théâtre Molière were similarly taken from the classical funds released into the public domain. Indeed, throughout Parisian theater the flow of repertory was almost entirely characterized by the plunder of plays that had once belonged within the great dramatic tradition.

This was true even on the boulevard. None of the new theaters that settled there after 1791 established any continuity of repertory with the older, popular stages of the old regime. Altogether the Variétés-Dramatiques, the Lycée-Dramatique and the Elèves de Thalie performed no more than three or four plays from the public funds of the Gaité or the Ambigu-Comique. Nor did the older boulevard theaters borrow very much from each other. Rather, the minor theaters of the boulevard chose consistently from the classical repertory. The new Lycée-Dramatique, which relied entirely on plays in the public domain, performed almost exclusively from the resources of the Comédie-Française and the Comédie-Italienne. The Variétés-Dramatiques leaned similarly towards classical fare, as did the Délassements-Comiques, first established in 1785. At this last theater 28 of the 31 plays taken from the public domain in the years 1791-94 had once belonged to the great theaters of Paris; altogether classical comedies and tragedies accounted for 30 percent of the entire revolutionary repertory of the Délassements-Comiques. The proportion was even greater, 48 percent, at the Théâtre-Patriotique.[33]

The classical tradition was well received on the boulevard. In 1791 the Gaité introduced nearly an equal number of new plays and classical comedies, but whereas only one of the new plays achieved some short-lived success, three from the classical fare enjoyed a consistent popularity throughout the next several years. The number of classical plays that were produced with success at the Gaité rose significantly in 1792, and performances of great comedy and tragedy nearly doubled from the year before. Historians have been struck with the enormous vogue on Nicolet's stage for the comedies of Molière. Contemporaries looked askance at his productions of Racine and Corneille.[34]

In fact, the Gaité performed from a wider range of the classical repertory. The most successful of these plays for 1791 comprised the comedies of Marivaux, Regnard and Dancourt as well as Molière, and in the following years works by Hauteroche, Boursault, Destouches, Legrand and Moissy were added. The range of classical repertory was even greater across all the little theaters of the boulevard, including as well works by Anseaume, Jean-Jacques Rousseau and Voltaire.[35]

Judging from the boulevard's broad enthusiasm for the comedies and tragedies of great theater, one might conclude that the liberals of 1791 had been correct in one thing—that the liberation of theater would promote the great dramatic tradition at the expense of the popular idiom. The liberal prophecy was true enough if one looked only at the transfer, from one theater to another, of repertory that had fallen into the public domain. The traditional fare of the boulevard gained little ground in comparison to that of the once-privileged theaters. The great theaters and those new ventures that imitated them remained relatively immune to the popular plays that had long delighted the boulevard public. In this respect, then, there was no popularization of repertories in the Parisian world of theater, despite the claims of Hallays-Dabot or Albert. Albert, Hallays-Dabot and their contemporary sources were, however, correct in another respect. During the course of the Revolution even prestigious theaters increasingly abandoned the classical genres of comedy and tragedy in newly written plays for dramatic forms similar to those first practiced on the boulevard.

One of the most ardent critics of this "aesthetic decay" was La Harpe. His position illustrates perhaps better than anything else that the liberal vision which he had helped to fashion in 1790 was also a classical one.[36] Although he himself had had an important hand in the liberation of genres controlled by monopoly, La Harpe was displeased by the mixing of forms. Sometime in 1789 the Comédie-Française co-produced Racine's *Athalie* with singers from the Comédie-Italienne. Tragic declamation alternated with sung chorus. Although the admixture of speech and song was by no means an innovation—this version of *Athalie* had been performed 20 years earlier at Versailles—it was in La Harpe's opinion unacceptable to the great dramatic tradition properly understood:

> One gets accustomed to this in minor pieces, such as comic operas; but nothing is more out of place in a great work such as a tragedy.[37]

The production was further marred, for La Harpe, by the impropriety of a comic troupe performing a serious play. The Italian actors who participated on stage had been trained to another genre:

> ...accustomed to excite laughter, [they seem] so inappropriate there... to those of good sense all this appeared to be the height of impertinence and bad taste.[38]

Other contemporaries had similar misgivings about the decay of pure classical genres and the mixing of forms on one stage. In 1791 the *General Almanac for all the Theaters of Paris* urged that the despotic weight of privilege be banished from the world of theater; in the same issue its editors deplored the introduction of non-classical genres upon the once-privileged stages of Paris. Obviously the *Almanac* had not abandoned traditional conceptions of high and low theater or of theater-types. The Opéra apparently produced a boulevard pantomime alongside classical operas, thereby provoking the *Almanac* to remark that "the public had with but one voice cried out that taste faltered more and more, and if this continued, works of opera would soon be performed on the stages of the fairs, and would not be out of place there..."[39] The implication was, of course, that by admitting boulevard pantomime-operas onto the once-privileged stage, the great theaters would come to imitate those fairground forms exclusively. In the opinion of the *Almanac's* editors, this had already occurred at the Comédie-Française:

> The Comédie-Française, with its *Figaro-ism,* even more than the Variétés, with its *Jeannot-ism,* has fallen into the genre of the Boulevards...[40]

The editors of the *Journal des théâtres* also joined in La Harpe's alarm for the corruption of dramatic taste and the breakdown of aesthetic order in theater. Indeed, in the first issue of November 1791 the *Journal* seemed to reveal an untoward hostility for the January law. Liberty in theater was said to menace dramatic art and taste, already corrupted by "the arrogant mediocrity of several would-be authors who write dialogued epistles in the manner of comedies and paquets of prose that they call dramas..."[41] In subsequent issues the attack on liberty was not repeated; still, the *Journal des théâtres* expressed concern not only for the degeneration of classical genres on the great stages but for the use of classical genres upon stages once limited to marginal forms. The *Journal* insisted that due to the paucity of good plays in the popular theaters of Paris, there would be little attention given in its pages to the boulevard stage. Yet the *Journal* harshly criticized the boulevard's Théâtre Comique et Lyrique for its obvious attempts to imitate the operatic productions of the Academy of Music:

> Entrepreneurs of theater cannot take too much care in order not to step out of the particular genre to which they have destined their enterprise, and, above all, not to rival [the great theaters].[42]

For some contemporaries there was a direct connection between the decay of theater-types throughout Paris and a huge outpouring of experimental genres in the early years of the Revolution. One literary historian has calculated that 24 different genre descriptions were applied to 225 serious plays written or produced between 1789-1799[43]—at least 11 of these genre descriptions were used before the end of 1794. Instead of tragedies, playwrights offered "historical dramas," "lyrical dramas," "tragedies based upon current events," "lyrical tragedies," "tragi-comedies" and "mimed and lyrical melodramas." New forms such as "patriotic panoramas," "patriotic scenes," "episodic plays," "historical events," "heroic tragi-comedies," "vaudeville operas," "comic operas" and "dramatic allegories" seemed to gain increasing ground on Parisian stages at the expense of the classical comedy and opera.

It was in the wake of reaction against the Revolution, of course, that the connection between experimentation in non-classical genres and the popular stage was drawn most clearly. In their *History of French Theater Since the Beginning of the Revolution* (Year X-1802), for example, Charles Guillaume Etienne and A.L.D. Martainville dismissed *The Husband as Director,* performed by the French actors in 1791, as a bastard form common to the fairs and boulevard:

> ... we will not honor [this farce] with the name of comedy... from then on the French stage was increasingly sullied by ignoble *parades*...[44]

Yet even at the time contemporaries were apt to interpret the decline in standards of dramatic art as a popularization of Parisian theater. According to the *Jounal des théâtres* the more prominent of revolutionary plays in early 1792, such as *Robert, Leader of Rogues* or *Mutius Scevola,* were most aptly described as melodramas, "a facile genre, that requires neither intrigue, nor unified action, nor experience of the stage."[45] Implicit in this review was the association of lack of rigor in dramatic art with the popular stage, an association current in French aesthetic thought since the mid-seventeenth century. La Harpe made similar allusion in his description in 1790 of new plays at the Comédie-Française and other prestigious theaters. His sarcasm and vitriol would have been directed before 1789 to the fair or boulevard stage alone:

> Another expedient within reach of everyone is to make up pantomimes of sorts based upon certain actions that in and of themselves have nothing to do with theater proper.... One or the other [event] is portrayed in one act, under the title of *Historical Episode,* for the authors themselves do not dare give dramatic titles to these sorts of sketches that are in effect monsters without name.[46]

Despite contemporary concern for the popular nature of dramatic experimentation, it cannot be assumed that all innovative genres in revolutionary theater had their origins on the popular stage. Some mixed genres in fact had precedent in the great dramatic tradition itself.[47] But at least two historians have argued with textual evidence at hand that the more important forms of the boulevard, in particular the dialogued pantomime, did in fact make sensible inroads into great theatrical culture during and after the

Revolution.[48] For Alexis Pitou that popular blend of sumptuous decor, music and ballet, of buffoonery and sentimentality, jumped from the boulevard to at least one prestigious rival of the Théâtre de la Nation in 1792. *Robert, Leader of Rogues* and *The Devil's Chateau,* both performed at the Théâtre Marais in 1792, comprised for Pitou the dramatic essential of the dialogued pantomime.[49] The popular genre spread even farther than Pitou imagined. *Robert, Leader of Rogues* gained such success at the Marais that the Théâtre de la République, formerly the Variétés-Amusantes at the Palais-Royal and now one of the premier theaters in Paris, performed Lamartelière's drama in April 1793.

According to some contemporaries the broad enthusiasm throughout Paris for genres hitherto confined to the boulevard had much to do with the commercial imperatives of the free and open market of theaters created by law in January 1791. The link between popular forms and an uncontrolled, unrestrained competition amongst theaters had been well established under the old regime by conservative proponents of the classical and privileged order. The conservative argument during the debate on theater in 1790 had repeated the classical warning that popular genres would thrive without monopolistic restraint. Critics of the revolutionary stage in 1791 and 1792 were forced to admit that the classical dictum had been correct. The *Journal des théâtres* blamed the proliferation of unformed genres and "monstrous" plays on the bitter rivalry for public custom between the once-privileged theaters and those established since 1790-1791:

> The theaters that have been established under the system of liberty have no other repertory than that which a decree of the Constituent Assembly allowed all to forage; but [these same theaters] have felt that with this repertory, as rich as it is, they could not possibly attract the public without offering new works.[50]

Since January 1791, if not before, the theaters of revolutionary Paris had been thrown into unrestricted commercial competition—not with one or two rivals of similar rank but with each and every other dramatic enterprise in the city. Such an arena placed a premium on economic survival and the theatrical novelties that guaranteed box-office success. If he had not believed the conservative argument in August 1790 when he read his petition for a free theater before the National Assembly, sometime in the course of 1791 La Harpe conceded that mercenary concerns had in fact popularized the dramatic art of the once-great stages of Paris:

> It is certain that the Revolution has harmed letters and the arts a great deal and for a long time to come...and one sees the torrent of bad taste spilling over into this prodigious multitude of productions in every genre... popular appeal, which has at least the merit of novelty, takes precedence over everything and destroys everything; for only a little while, it is true, but the plays follow upon each other so rapidly and multiply so easily upon twelve or

> fifteen theaters, that there is hardly a stupidity that cannot live a fortnight or so, and in consequence yield for the author much more than the work is worth.[51]

De Lornaizon's suggestion in 1790 that the dramatic cultures of the great and the minor theaters of Paris would remain as discrete in a free and open market as they had under the old regime proved to be false. Though it had hardly seemed likely in the first heady months of revolutionary reform, both liberal expectations and conservative fears attendant upon the liberation of theater had been ironically consummated. A young Pixerécourt remarked in 1795 that in the moment of revolutionary ebullition "a surprised Corneille mounted the stage at Nicolet's and Taconet in his grave did not despair of making an appearance at Le Kain's arena."[52] Boulevard theaters did perform the works of Corneille and Molière; great theaters did turn to the genres of Taconet and his fairground peers. Had the Revolution unleashed great dramatic culture, or popular dramatic culture? For many contemporaries there was ultimately little question. Those who deplored the use of popular genres at the Comédie-Française and other prestigious theaters were equally certain that productions of classical repertory on the boulevard had not raised the quality of the popular stage. At the Délassements-Comiques, observed the *General Almanac for all the Theaters of Paris,* the lead actor consistently disfigured *The Two Huntsmen and the Dairymaid,* first performed by the Italian actors in 1763:

> ... he appends, he excises, he minces; and that is not the genre of good comedy. This is precisely how bad buffoons spoil the Public taste, which habituates itself in such a manner to these detestable *parades,* that it can no longer suffer in others naturalness and truth.[53]

Boulevard buffoons and boulevard *parades* indeed made easy targets for those alarmed by revolution in Parisian theater. But in actuality the boulevard was less involved in that upheaval than many contemporaries were apt to believe. Despite the liberal law of January 1791 the little theaters along the ramparts had gained very little real status in the world of theater. They remained popular, socially, and poor, economically. Nevertheless contemporaries persisted in assigning the boulevard a catalytic role in the turmoil that swept the Parisian stage. They did so because the spread of non-classical genres and the consequent decline of dramatic standards and taste after 1789 seemed to have its origins in the origins of the boulevard itself—in the ill-advised leniency of a classical order that had weakened its own struts by allowing the marginal growth and development of unregulated, unformed theatrical activity. The aesthetic structure that had raised privileged theater to the heights of great dramatic culture toppled in revolution around the popular stage.

8

The Impress of Revolution on the Boulevard Stage

Political Circumstance and the Popular Dramatic Idiom

From the fall of the Bastille onwards the French Revolution made headway in the theaters of Paris. Indeed patriotic, political plays were in themselves revolutionary events. Under the old regime the censorship policies of the Crown had forbidden the stage to comment, even obliquely, upon current affairs and current kings. As this censorship faltered, theater moved cautiously and then with abandon into hitherto unexploited political waters. As early as 1790 the crusty La Harpe observed that "military apparatus, grenadiers' helmets, bayonettes, the catch words of liberty and patriotism are for the moment in the ascendance."[1] In the course of the next two years the presentation of patriotic fare was in fact to become a civic obligation.

In 1790 municipal government had authorized benefit performances for the poor during the lenten and other holy seasons, periods during which theaters had traditionally been closed. By 1792 monies raised in this manner went to the "widows and orphans of patriots" and the costs of impending war. Entrepreneurs considered these benefit performances as so many "proofs" given of "civic feeling."[2] Yet in and of themselves they came to mean little unless loaded with politically partisan plays. One enthusiastic entrepreneur claimed in 1792 that a new and patriotic duty had been fashioned for theater: ". . . a duty to present only those plays suited to guide public opinion well, enlighten minds, inspire patriotism and propagate the principles of Liberty and equality, which alone make for the Happiness of France and assure the success of the Revolution."[3] It was also in the year 1792 that the procurator of the Commune, one Manuel, pointedly urged Parisian theaters to demonstrate national independence from the Church of Rome by performing throughout Holy Week the politically charged *Death of Caesar*.[4] Theater had been reconceived as the temple of a civic religion, one that glorifed and celebrated the nation and revolutionary virtue.

In later years La Harpe was to imply that the boulevard had had some catalytic role in the upheaval that swept Parisian theater in the early 1790s:

> ... the Government committed a capital mistake in permitting for the people what are called *the little theaters*... which prepared the great revolutionary contagion that, for the last ten years, has infected almost everything.[5]

Certainly La Harpe believed there to be a link between the aesthetic popularization of the stage and the growing prominence of political themes and content.[6] Yet at the time contemporaries were more apt to criticize the little theaters for a stubborn adherence to old, even reactionary ways. In 1792 the *General Almanac for all the Theaters of Paris* singled out Nicolet, director of the newly named Gaité, for his constant devotion to the farces and pantomimes of the past:

> All Paris knows his genre; we have always regarded his theater as the school of bad morals... Mister *Nicolet* is an *old Stick-in-the-Mud* with old habits, old prejudices and old cronies; he would rather renounce life than abandon all that.[7]

Indeed Nicolet, as well as his neighbor on the boulevard, Audinot, continued to offer throughout the first five years of the Revolution a great many of the plays produced in the 1770s and '80s.[8] Some of the most successful plays in this period were *Contentment Surpasses Wealth* (1776), *The Dismissed Rivals* (1788), *The Cobbler's Household* (1771) and *Arlequin Entombed* (1778?) at the Gaité and *Musicomania* (1778), *The Deaf Man* (1780) and *The Cavalry Sergeant* (1783) at the Ambigu-Comique. Assuredly, these old plays had little relevance to current affairs, but the *Almanac* found many of them alien as well to the enlightened purpose of liberated theater. Nicolet's old repertory in particular was severely censored, as was even the newly written repertory at the Délassements-Comiques, for their continued reliance on the low comic idiom traditional to the boulevard:

> ... it is time to banish from all theaters the obscene ambiguities and filthy jokes that the profligacy of the last hundred years has sanctioned there... three-fourths of the plays performed on the boulevards, above all at Mister *Nicolet's* and even more at the *Délassements-Comiques,* have neither moral purpose nor propriety...[9]

Nevertheless, the minor theaters of the boulevard did not entirely withstand the political energy and force of the Revolution—even as the editors of the *General Almanac* took up their pens. After January 1791 the single most important source of new material for the minor theaters was the public domain of classical plays that had once belonged to the great companies of Paris. Many tragedies performed during the Revolution, above all those of Voltaire, questioned in historic guise contemporary social relations and political power.

Indeed revolutionaries invested more than a few with their own ideological significance. On the boulevard the radical potential of these plays was believed to be vastly increased, for the "people" were not trained to accepted interpretations of political and philosophical speculation. According to the *General Almanac for all the Theaters of Paris,*

> Voltaire did not create Brutus for the vulgar ears, but for Philosophers, who can grasp the true meaning of it without losing sight of its purpose; rarely does one see a Theater Hall filled with Philosophers, especially on the Boulevard.[10]

The *Almanac* would have preferred that the minor stage eschew "all plays that may awaken in the popular mind other sentiments than those of submission to thc laws and the love of peace."[11] To their consternation, the more zealous of boulevard theaters such as the Théâtre-Patriotique offered *Brutus* more than any other play in 1792. Others on the boulevard concentrated just as heavily on *Adelaide de Guesclin, Alzire, Atrée and Thyeste, Mohammed, Mérope, Nanine, Rome Saved,* and *Zaire,* all by Voltaire.

The editors of the *Almanac* were no doubt much happier with plays written expressly for the little theaters in the early years of Revolution, for many of these did in fact preach "submission to the laws and love of peace." Plays such as *The Carpenter of Bagdad,* written in 1790 and performed on the boulevard in 1791, and *Nicodème on the Moon or the Peaceable Revolution,* performed heavily at the Théâtre-Français Comique et Lyrique from 1790 through 1792 and beyond, were episodic plays in which the zany's calling was given revolutionary purpose. Both plays turned upon the same tensions between master and servant, the same fascination for mobility that had created dramatic interest in so many pre-revolutionary plays. Yet significantly enough, the naive valet Nicodème and the humble carpenter Hali, both of whom achieved the status and fortune traditionally craved by the zany, modulated the acrimonious tones and social snobbery associated with their kind. The carpenter Hali, trading places with his aristocratic master, sought to temper conflict between rich and poor, privileged and unprivileged, on behalf of the people:

> Come, wife, let's go prove to the Court, that men of the people are good, that it is wrong to do them harm...
>
> [Viens, femme, viens prouver à la Cour, que les gens du peuple sont bons; qu'on a tort de leur faire du mal...][12]

Landing his balloon on the moon, Nicodème caught the attentions of the indigenous emperor and his court. The zany proselytized this audience in the ways of peaceful revolution:

> There's the balloon, which left France because the revolution scared [my master]. . . . Ah well, he brought me to the Moon and just so the revolution starts here as well. . . . Oh! must be something in the air that communciates it. . . . Ah! it's the wind that brings revolution. . . . This Emperor is a good person, has sense, he has had the courage to spend four hours listening to me recount my voyage. . . . I told him how it is that the French wanted to ferret out the slavery in their country. . . .
>
> [V'là c'ballon, qu'est parti d'France, à cause qu'la révolution li a fait peur. . . . Eh ben; i m'amèna dans la Leune, et justement v'là qu'la révolution commence par ici. . . . Oh! faut qu'i'gnait queut'chose dans l'air, qui communiqu'ça. . . . Ah! c'est l'vent qu'est à la révolution. . . . Cet Empereur est eune bonne personne, qu'a du bon sens; il a eu l'courage de passer quatres heures à m'entendre raconter mon voyage. . . . j'lions dit comme quoi les Français aviont voulu faire dénicher l'esclavage d'leux pays . . .]

Boulevard playwrights deftly tied political circumstance and sentimental notions of revolution to traditional love intrigues as well. In some cases reference to the political and social events of the Revolution were in fact minimal, simply grafted upon customary themes as an afterthought. In 1792 Destival de Braban wrote for the Gaité a simple love intrigue called *The Soul-Seekers or How Girls Get Spirit,* a take-off on an old play by Favart of similar title. Rustic simplicity and pastoral morality did not disturb the traditional dramatic formulas of frustrated young love and parental obstacle. Not until the play's end did the character l'Amour turn to the audience with these final words: "Cupid is a Patriot, his true testament is Liberty" [L'Amour est un Patriote, son véritable testament c'est la Liberté]. *Vaporine and Furette or the Favorable Thunderclap,* an "opera" in two acts performed successfully at the Théâtre-Patriotique, dwelled similarly on dramatic interests of the past. A sentimental twist of fate overcame parental obstacles to the marriage of two young lovers. Only the reference to "assignats" and a rather ambiguous soliloquy to the public—"You will see flowers bloom there / despite the wind and peals of thunder" [Vous y verrez naître des fleurs / malgré les vents et le tonnerre]—placed *Vaporine and Furette* in the midst of the Revolution.

Other intrigues were more obviously political. In April of 1791, the Gaité performed briefly a "patriotic play" entitled *The Return of the Fédérés or Ça ira.* The comedy was an almost perfect blend of the traditional love intrigue and revolutionary circumstance, since it was the social revolution enacted in 1789 that destroyed the obstacle—in this case seigneurial—between the young lovers Janotin and Fanchette. But as the villagers prepared a patriotic reception for their former seigneur returning from Paris and the Fête de la Fédération, nearly every word spoken was of liberty, equality, and fraternity. The relevant titles of a number of other plays announced the public commitment of sponsoring boulevard theaters to ideas of revolutionary inspiration: at the Théâtre-Patriotique, *The Emigrants' Bawdyhouse, The Curé's Removal, The 14th of July,* and in 1792, *The 10th of August;* at the Théâtre-Français Comique et Lyrique *Life in State Prisons;* at the Lycée-Dramatique, *French*

Citizens or the Triumph of the Revolution; at the Délassements-Comiques *The Village Constitution, The Frenchman in Germany, The Military Discipline of the North;* at the Ambigu-Comique *The Day of Varennes.*

Despite the political influences of the early Revolution, however, the boulevard's dramatic mainstream continued viable and strong. The most successful plays in this period were indistinguishable from those written before 1789. At the Gaité *Père Duchesne,* and its sequel at the Ambigu-Comique *The Wedding of Père Duchesne,* owed nothing to revolutionary events and made no reference to political or ideological change. The introduction of explicit political content had as yet done little to alter the form or even the meaning of boulevard theater. Both Nicodème and the carpenter Hali pleaded for an end to social oppression, yet neither strayed far from the traditional message of the popular stage. Nicodème insisted that he was no more than a "poor country bumpkin"; Hali requested that his master be reinstated to his original position and that he, Hali, be allowed to return to a small house in the country. Nor had revolution changed traditional social relationships in the *Return of the Fédérés.* Upon his return to the village the Marquis asked the local people to drop antiquated forms of address in the name of freedom and brotherhood. The villagers persisted, nonetheless, in calling him "Seigneur" and begged him not to alter his customary paternalism. Egalitarian expression on the boulevard stage in the first four years of the Revolution stopped short of radical social upheaval. As long as traditional dramatic structures were not abandoned, boulevard theater did not move beyond the reaffirmation of rank and place and the sentimental sublimation that had characterized the pre-revolutionary stage.

Radical Censorship and Cultural Revolution

The response of Parisian theater to the abrogation of stage censorship in 1789-90 and the political incitements of the municipality in the course of 1792 aggravated tremendous conflict within revolutionary government. As early as June 1791 more conservative members of the municipal police had feared that several plays based on the king's attempted flight from France, among them the Ambigu-Comique's *The Day of Varennes,* would foment popular discontentment and riot in the streets. To avoid possible disturbances, the police wished to re-establish surveillance and censorship of theater, functions that had been annulled in 1789. Other factions in municipal government, however, proved highly tolerant of political ferment within theater halls and opposed any censorship of the stage. At issue was the struggle, first within municipal government itself and later between the municipality and national government, for control of theater and the ideological direction of the Revolution. The story of this struggle, which bears most directly on the more prestigious theaters of revolutionary Paris, has occupied almost exclusively the attentions of early historians of theater.[13] Suffice it to say here that the Insurrectionary Commune, consolidated in radical hands by the 10th of August, won the struggle on a municipal level in the late 1792. Resistance to the political manipulation of theater at a national level caused further conflict in the course of 1793.

Early in that year municipal representatives of the people advised the national Committee of Public Instruction to consider the revision of pre-revolutionary repertories in order to purge them "of all plays capable of corrupting republican spirit."[14] Now that the radicals of August 10th had control of the police and the Commune, they no doubt had in mind a nationally authorized surveillance to bolster that which they had already undertaken. At least since August 1792, the municipal police had been informally censoring the Parisian stage by means of skillful encouragement and thinly veiled threat.[15] In the months that followed, the Commune interfered with increasing frequency in the dramatic fare of Parisian theaters, especially the more prestigious of these, condemning whole repertories and engineering patriotic performances.[16] Parisian theater was to be republican; it was also to be popular—that is to say, available to the widest of publics. In a decree of June 18th, 1793 the municipality urged upon directors and theaters not only patriotic plays but the public's free entry to their performance.

Through the summer of 1793 Parisian theaters responded fitfully to the Commune's demands. There is evidence that at least some along the boulevard were reluctant to embrace republican theater wholeheartedly. As the political climate became increasingly tense, contemporaries came to interpret the persistence of traditional forms and themes on the boulevard as a cultural conservatism inappropriate to patriotic theater. The *Journal des spectacles,* a mouthpiece of public opinion on theater in 1793, revealed a swift surge of political intolerance for the traditional dramatic literature of the boulevard.[17] Between May and December of that year the *Journal* commented upon approximately 22 new plays performed on the boulevard. Thirteen of these were plays in the old style of the boulevard, with little or no reference to revolutionary politics or ideology. The *Journal* judged, in June and July, that plays such as *The Young Slave* (at Lazzari's Variétés-Amusantes) or *The Apple of Rambour* (at the Ambigu-Comique) differed little from the traditional fare of the boulevard but were acceptable nonetheless:

> Nothing new, some agreeable situations, a few pretty couplets, some very nimble remarks, some very bawdy moments, and many poetic and grammatical liberties, that's what characterizes *The Apple of Rambour,* which is a success . . .[18]

By August and September, however, similar situations and bawdy style in other new plays had become unacceptable. The *Journal des spectacles* now criticized the old boulevard genres for their predictability and their immorality:

"Whoever has seen one comedy-*parade* has seen almost all of them."[19] *Arlequin Mannequin* (at Lazzari's Variétés-Amusantes), which drew this criticism, was, like *The Two Magic Rings* (also at Lazzari's Variétés-Amusantes), in violation of a republican and Rousseauistic morality that daily increased in importance:

> It is the strict duty of a republican, and any honest man, not to make modesty blush, and not to place bad examples before the eyes of youth, who, similar to soft wax, receive bad as well as good impressions.... That's it for morality, that's it for the republic, if some remedial law does not hasten to sweep from theater the impolitic filth that pollutes it...[20]

Between June and October of 1793 the expressed attitude of the *Journal des spectacles* towards the traditional idiom of the boulevard had altered profoundly. Smutty gestures and indecent allusion on the popular stage had been criticized for over a decade, but now a heightened sense of republican mores invested the critique with political disapproval. Moreover, the political imperatives of mobilization and war with the enemies of France led the *Journal* to question and attack even the sentimental idiom of the popular stage. No part of the boulevard repertory was to be immune from republican purpose—a purpose that was lacking in *Cloris and Lycas,* a pastoral opera produced by the Théâtre-Patriotique in October 1793:

> But now that our theater teems, in a manner of speaking, with masterpieces, now that the most active passions stir in every heart, what interest can we have in the langorous loves of a shepard spurned by a cruel shepardess? None. When the trumpet of war and the call to arms sounds upon the ear, can we hear the soft murmur of rustic pipes?[21]

The *Journal des spectacles* was not the only source of republican opinion on revolutionary theater or on the boulevard stage in particular. Jacques René Hébert's *Père Duchesne* also turned against the traditional dramatic literature of the little theaters. In an issue late in 1793 Duchesne clearly warned his wife and the Parisian sans-culotte of the counter-revolutionary sympathies expressed by the popular theater of the past. Do they go to see the tight-rope dancers at Nicolet's? Duchesne's wife asks:

> No, Jacqueline, such a spectacle is unworthy of republicans. Only kings or their valets could amuse themselves with the sight of a poor devil laming himself and often breaking his neck in order to win a miserable Corset.[22]

The plots and formulas of the past were to be set aside in order to serve more important political ends. According to the *Journal des spectacles* boulevard theaters would do well to produce exclusively political plays such as *Alexis and Rosette,* performed by the Théâtre-Français Comique et Lyrique in August 1793:

> The gist of this play is as one can see quite trivial; but the author, ruled by the most ardent patriotism, joined to this sketch all that he believed would inspire love of the republic, and hatred of kings...[23]

It was just such a play that Duchesne suggested to the sans-culottes of Paris. At the Théâtre de la République, he informed his readers,

> you will see *The Last Judgment of Kings;* you will see all those crowned bandits with the rope around their necks, thrown upon a deserted isle; you will see the pope apologize, obliged to concede that he is only a juggler of goblets; you will see all the tyrants of Europe obliged to take off their clothes themselves, and be swallowed up at the end of the play by a volcano. Now there is a spectacle made for republican eyes.[24]

The rising tide of demand in 1793 for republican and political plays was reinforced at the end of the summer by the Convention's decision to ensure their production throughout the city. National government, which had since 1789 resisted censorship and the direct control of theater, weakened in its resolve with the execution of the king and the eventual expulsion of the moderate Girondins in June of 1793. By August the Jacobins, who had risen to leadership in the Committee of Public Safety, publicly adopted the Commune's demands for republican plays—and free performances—as their own:

> Citizens, the day of August 10th approaches; republicans have been sent by the people to deposit in the National Archives the minutes ratifying the Constitution.
>
> You would wound, you would outrage these republicans, if you allowed the continued performance in their presence of an infinity of plays filled with allusions harmful to liberty, and which have no other purpose than to deprave the public mind and morals...[25]

The Committee's proposal, adopted on August 2nd by the Convention, provided that for the next month theaters designated by the municipality would perform thrice weekly—once at the expense of the Republic—those "dramatic pieces that retrace the glorious events of the Revolution."[26] The Convention at large decided to stimulate "republican energy" at whatever cost. In a decree of 1-2 September the municipality was provided with the legal means to shape radical theater. Legislation that strengthened authors' rights to receipt of royalties provided for municipal registers of daily performances to be inspected and signed by officers of the police.[27] The Commune was not remiss in exploiting the intentions of the national government or the Committee of Public Safety. "No single law seemed to re-establish the censorship of theater," one officer of the police assigned to keep the Commune's registers observed, "however, since the law of September 2nd, which ordered the police of Paris to monitor theaters more closely, censorship has been just about re-established."[28]

The national government's hurried policies of subsidy and surveillance were not without effect on the boulevard, especially on those theaters such as the Gaité, the Ambigu-Comique or Lazzari's Variétés-Amusantes that had most noticeably dragged their feet in stubborn adherence to nonpolitical, traditional plays. By means of intimidation and interference, competing bodies shoved and pushed these minor theaters in more radical and republican directions. Hard upon the decree of August 2nd, ordering the free performance of republican plays, the Surveillance Committee of the Department of Paris[29] systematically summoned directors from the boulevard, as it did from all parts of Paris, to confer on matters of repertory for the coming month.[30] Nicolet, Audinot, Colon—none of these directors failed to appear before the Committee with promises to honor the fédérés gathered in Paris. Audinot's interview was typical:

> The citizen director of the theater called the *Ambigu-Comique* notifed the Committee that it is his desire to do nothing that thwarts the principles of the Committee, which are his own as well, and that he has already taken steps to offer patriotic plays.[31]

Nicolet, for his part, took it upon himself to submit in advance the list of plays he would produce in the coming weeks. He merely anticipated the Committee's designs. Throughout the month of August he and other directors were in fact required to report the plays and the costs for the free performances to be subsidized by the state.[32]

Of the 20 or so theaters operating in Paris at the time, 10 reported performances of those plays specifically commended by the decree of August 2nd—Voltaire's *Brutus* and Lemierre's *William Tell.* Two of these theaters—the Théâtre-Patriotique and the Délassements-Comiques—belonged to the boulevard. *Brutus* and *William Tell,* as well as Saurin's *Spartacus* and Chenier's more recent *Caius Gracchus,* were not, however, the sum total of the boulevard's patriotic efforts. A great many patriotic plays performed in the month of August had been fashioned for the boulevard itself. Most of these appeared on the minor stages which now plainly tended towards radical theater. The Délassements-Comiques offered *The Village Constitution, The Nun of Italy or The Cloistered Victim, The Happy Day or the 10th of August 1793,* and *The Girl National Guard.* The Théâtre-Français Comique et Lyrique produced *Alexis and Rossette or the Houlans,* a story of patriotic youth and Prussian deserters to the French cause; *Buzot, King of Calvados,* a political parody of the Girondins' disgrace; and the idyllic *Nicodème on the Moon.* Lazzari concentrated his political fare in a program that consisted of *The Death of Marat, The Prussian Deserters* and *The Speculator.* Sallé supplemented Voltaire with *Calas, or the Sad Effects of Fanaticism,* derivative of the philosophe's humanitarian concerns.

In November 1793 the *Journal des spectacles* would demand that in the radical effort expected of Parisian theater "all plays must be either patriotic or moral."[33] The boulevard proffered both kinds of republican drama in the programs of August. "Moral" plays in the republican theater of the boulevard deviated little from the basic formulas and themes of the sentimental love intrigue common before 1789. Yet in structure and content they revealed a syncretism of old forms and revolutionary purpose. Like *The Return of the Fédérés or Ça ira,* the Gaité's *The Lottery of Women* (or *The Departure of Patriots for the Frontiers)* relied heavily on the stock comic situation of elders courting the younger generation. But the central premise, that military service in 1793 had bereft a tiny village of all but one male, was neatly tied to revolutionary circumstance. The play, in the words of the *Journal des spectacles,* "gives proof of the patriotism of Mister d'Estival,"[34] the playwright.

The most "patriotic" of plays, however, represented something entirely new to the boulevard repertories. Plays such as *Alexis and Rosette* and *The Death of Marat,* both written by newcomers to the boulevard, sacrificed all traditional dramatic interest to concentrate on the rhetoric of revolution. There was no love intrigue, no parental obstacle, no deception or deceit by the young in these plays. Rosette did not complain that war kept her lover Alexis from her side. She rather rejoiced in her duty to inspire him to great deeds:

> If you wish to marry me, my friend, fight well,
> Scoff at cannons, brave everything, fear nothing,
> Other than shame and slavery.
>
> [Si tu veux m'épouser, mon ami, bats-toi bien,
> Moques-toi du canon, brave tout, ne crains rien,
> Hormis la honte et l'esclavage.]

The highpoint of the brief *Death of Marat* came, not with the patriot's decision to marry his mistress, nor even with the bathtub assassination, but with the funeral procession in which the French and then the goddess of Liberty vowed to avenge the death of the Fatherland's defender.

Nevertheless the most striking observation to be made of the boulevard's republican programs in August '93 is that little more than half of the plays chosen for performance were in fact republican. The remainder belonged to the apolitical fare of the past. With the exception of one or two plays of possible patriotic content,[35] Audinot weakened an already feeble political program with *End Against End,* an old comedy in the repertory of the Ambigu-Comique since 1782. The Théâtre-Patriotique balanced *Brutus* and *Caius Gracchus* with comedies of the old Comédie-Italienne and with its own traditional *The Rustic Evening,* first performed in 1787. On Nicolet's stage eight of the eleven plays produced for the subsidized performances of August '93 belonged to the Comédie-Italienne and only two had entered the Gaité's repertory since 1789.

It is improbable that all the old plays performed on the boulevard in August 1793, whether from the classical or popular repertories of the old regime, were invested with patriotic significance. Though in many new plays contemporary playwrights infused traditional formulas and themes with republican purpose, much of the pre-revolutionary repertory never achieved syncretic union with the patriotic stage. In the several months that followed the republican performances of August those with political power turned viciously upon old plays and the cultural conservatism in theater that they represented. In November the *Journal des spectacles* attacked past dramatic tradition lacking in moral or political relevance to the Revolution:

> Let us proscribe without pity these insignificant dramas, which have no other merit than that of style, and in which the purpose never was to inspire virtuous sentiment. Let us spurn with scorn the scandalous *farces* that outrage at one and the same time good taste and morals . . .[36]

The *Journal*'s offensive coincided with Hébert's public comment in *Père Duchesne* that the traditional idiom of the boulevard would no longer do for the sans-culotte. Hébert's opinion, among all others, was of the utmost consequence. He and his radical cohorts dominated the Commune, which since September 1793 had practiced tacitly a censorship of the stage. Hébert's actual role in the subsequent surveillance of Parisian theater is unknown, but his will to shape a sans-culotte and republican stage obviously influenced the direction of municipal censorship. In September the government agent and erstwhile playwright Latour-Lamontagne had advised his superiors in the ministry of police that no theater could escape corruption as long as the themes, formulas and plays of the past were permitted on stage:

> One must banish absolutely from the stage all that may recall to us our old errors. So that republican plays alone form the repertory of our theaters. So that the marquises cede their place to patriots. Burn, if necessary, the chefs-d'oeuvre of the Molières, the regnards, etc. The arts may lose something therein, but assuredly morals will gain by it.[37]

As if with the words of their agent in mind, the Parisian police readily administered a violent purge of repertories and plays.

According to a report submitted by the two censors Baudrais and Froidure in March 1794, the police had determined with careful scrutiny that all new plays submitted to them for approval conformed to the "new form of government [and] the most austere morals."[38] The censors claimed that in collusion with the Committee of Public Instruction, they pursued a more rigorous measure against the pre-revolutionary repertory as a whole—its simple suspension.[39] Vivien, the only historian other than Hallays-Dabot to have seen the municipal censorship records before their destruction in 1870, summarized their contents in an administrative study of theater in 1844.[40] In the space of three months, he wrote, 151 plays from the pre-revolutionary, classical repertory were examined. Thirty-three were rejected and 25 submitted to change. Many of the plays that had flooded Parisian theaters after January 1791 were now declared "bad":

> almost all the comedies of Molière, *Nanine, Beverly, The Braggart, The Game of Love and Chance, The Squanderer, The Gambler, The Fawning Lawyer,* and twenty other comedies.[41]

Corrections were required in many more—including, significantly enough, those plays commanded in August 1793 to honor the fédérés and the Republic:

> . . . in the *William Tell* of Lemierre, although as a kind of passport it was given as a second title *The Swiss Sans-Culottes;* the ending of *Brutus* and of *The Death of Caesar* had to be changed; *Mohammed* was forbidden as "a religious leader!"[42]

Despite this dramatic censorship classical plays were dropped from the repertories of Parisian theaters only sporadically or not at all. On the boulevard the Théâtre-Patriotique, as well as the Délassements-Comiques and Lazzari's Variétés-Amusantes, continued to rely heavily on the classical repertory through much of the year II.[43] Vivien's all too short examination of the censorship records makes no mention, however, that the radical press and local government had also moved decisively against the traditional repertory of the popular stage. Perhaps Baudrais and Froidure had not yet turned their attention to the boulevard. Others had. The two boulevard theaters which continued to produce most heavily from the traditional repertory of the popular stage, the Gaité and the Ambigu-Comique, fell under the intense scrutiny of the Surveillance Committee of the Parisian Department.

By mid-January 1794 the Committee struck out at the violation of republican morals in farces and comedies which had played on the boulevard, in some cases, for decades. Nicolet and his entire troupe were suddenly ordered to account for a very old and very successful piece called *The Lover Entombed.*[44] According to one member of the Committee this play was one of "the most obscene and the most filthy, proper for corrupting the morals of the most respectable, but little educated, portion of the people, who ordinarily attend this theater."[45] A comic piece of buisness in which Arlequin disguised himself as a dog offended the Committee, outraging their political sense of human dignity and decency. The actor Thomain, for his crude gestures, and Nicolet, for his tolerance of them, were both placed under several days' arrest.[46] The Committee now moved to interrogate Audinot and his company of actors for the continued performances of *The Apple of Rambour,* a somewhat licentious love intrigue reviewed favorably by the *Journal des spectacles* only six months before. Like Nicolet, Audinot was thrown in jail; his actors were released with the stern warning to interpret their roles more modestly.[47]

Alerted to a moral canker on the boulevard stage, the Surveillance Committee ordered that the directors of the Gaité and the Ambigu-Comique cleanse their repertories of offensive material. Directors and actors along the ramparts—and indeed throughout Paris—were called in company by company to face the Committee. All were generously invited to trace "the lofty deeds of our Brave brothers in arms and to inspire by the Representation of Good plays, the Virtues that exalt citizens to the heights they ought to reach..."[48] The Committee lectured artists and directors in their political and moral obligations to the cultural revolution that had still to be won:

> ...There remains to us a victory truly important to win; we must conquer ourselves.
> Purify our morals...and train us to the virtues that incline towards love and liberty.
> It is you, citizens, for whom it is specially reserved to carry out this new and glorious revolution.[49]

For the little theaters along the boulevard the Terror had become real. By March 1794 the close watch of the Surveillance Committee had been supplemented with the preliminary review of weekly programs. The municipal police organized a regular inspection of all plays in advance of their performance—thereby returning in principle to the theatrical censorship of the old regime. Little is known of this municipal activity, except that at least one director on the boulevard defied its imposition. Audinot's resistance quickly dissolved, however, before the disagreeable threats of the police. He hastened to submit his repertory, with the observation that "in all old plays, the word citizen replaces monsieur."[50] The municipal review of weekly programs in their entirety, rather than, simply, the inspection of newly-written plays, allowed the police to enforce a consistent revision of the old boulevard repertory in accordance with republican values and ideology. Republican titles of address became part of the dialogue in old as well as new plays, just as the tri-color cockade or the sans-culotte cap became part of any and all costumes. Liberty walked amongst the actors on stage and exhorted the French to brave deeds and republican ideals. Boulevard theater turned decisively from the gay idiom of the past to political discourse and patriotic concerns.

Radical government had forcibly and abruptly deflected many boulevard theaters away from traditional paths into more radical and republican directions. For boulevard directors the way was fraught with difficulties. Political plays were, if anything, potentially more dangerous than farces from the 1760s. Some entrepreneurs along the boulevard were more politically adventurous than the very conservative Nicolet, but his case illustrates well the sanctions they all faced. In late December 1793 the Convention, at loggerheads with the Commune over the pace of dechristianization, ordered the suspension of the anti-religious *Tomb of the Imposters* and all other plays tending towards the same goal.[51] At the Gaité Nicolet quickly suspended a play in imitation of Molière's *Tartuffe*—quite to the chagrin of its author Destival. Not until February 1794 was Nicolet convinced to produce *The New Calendar, or There are No More Priests!* By that time Destival had written to the censor Baudrais to complain of the delay and of his director's hesitations:

> You know my play entitled: The New Calendar or There are No More Priests! Up until now I have suspended its representation purely out of condescension to my fearful director, but I believe that there is no reason not to represent it, since there is nothing in it that touches upon the celebration of the so-called mysteries of religion, a just political consideration...[52]

But Nicolet had need of caution. Even a play as politically sound as *The Taking of Toulon* could and did become suspect. The Gaité's version of the French liberation of that seaport played for nearly two months before it drew the notice of the Surveillance Committee in April 1794. Why the Committee demanded the text of the play in unknown, but the act of review was full of portent in the political clime of the year II, as ideological currents shifted rapidly and often with little warning.[53]

The severity of the cultural revolution upon the popular stage may be assessed by certain rather dramatic shifts in repertory at boulevard theaters between 1793 and 1794.[54] Table 4, Change in the Repertory of Two Boulevard Theaters, 1789-1794, reveals that both the Gaité and the Ambigu-Comique moved at a sluggish pace (much more so at Nicolet's theater) in the incorporation of new dramatic material through 1793. Both Table 4 and Table 5, Change in the Boulevard Repertory, 1793-1794, make evident, however, that for these and other minor theaters an abrupt shift in emphasis away from pre-revolutionary plays, whether classical or popular, to plays written after 1789 took place between 1793 and 1794. In evaluating this sudden change in the boulevard repertory, it is, of course, necessary to avoid the generalization that all traditional fare performed on the boulevard (whether classical or popular) was counter-revolutionary and that all new fare was patriotic or republican in nature. At least through August of '93 a number of plays of the old regime were believed to express revolutionary aspirations. Conversely, many new plays were among those proscribed by the Surveillance Committee and municipal censorship in late 1793 and early 1794. Nevertheless it is possible to see in Tables 4 and 5 evidence of a conservative tendency in dramatic culture that was not modified on the boulevard until late 1793-1794.

Up until 1793 two boulevard theaters in particular, the Ambigu-Comique and the Gaité, relied heavily on plays written and performed before the Revolution. For other boulevard theaters such as the Théâtre-Patriotique and the Délassements-Comiques the link with the past consisted wholly in the performance of the classical repertory. The only newly-established boulevard theaters that survived through 1793 and '94, the Théâtre-Français Comique et Lyrique and Lazzari's Variétés-Amusantes, made somewhat less use of old, classical and popular reserves for their revolutionary repertories.

The tendency, more or less pronounced, of these boulevard theaters to conserve the plays and dramatic traditions of the old regime through the first five years of the Revolution faltered in late 1793 and 1794. For nearly every boulevard theater the repertory as a whole for 1794 showed significant decline in the use of traditional resources. Moreover, radicalization had a dampening effect on theatrical activity, for policial and republican plays did not grow in number to fill the vacuum created by the suppression of old fare. In fact, at every boulevard theater but two the number of plays performed that were written during the Revolution declined in 1794.[55] Plays of obvious political and ideological content rose in prominence in late '93-'94 simply because they alone remained viable at the height of the theatrical Terror.

After five years of revolution and five or more months of radical intervention and censorship a real transformation had taken place in boulevard dramatic culture. Most of the classical and popular plays that did remain in the repertory of one boulevard theater, the Gaité, were performed rarely in the first six months of 1794. The radical censorship and civic surveillance of the theatrical Terror had rid the boulevard stage almost entirely of plays offensive to the aims and ideology of the Republic. Not surprisingly, the few old plays that remained in favor were amenable to the patriotic and moral purpose of revolutionary theater. These did not include bawdy farces or love intrigues of the 1760s and 1770s; they did include sentimental intrigues of the 1780s. One such play, *Blaise the Ill-Tempered,*[56] was written by Dorvigny in 1782. In it the farmer Blaise maintained that there could be no natural justice in a world marked by socio-economic distinctions amongst men. The revolutionary implications of Blaise's outspoken egalitarianism may have lain dormant on the pre-revolutionary boulevard. Surely they did not in 1794. In company with plays such as *The Tyrants' Cake, The Civic Festival, A Day of the Vendée or the Death of Young Barra, The Unmasked Aristocrat, The Sans-Culottes, The Freedom of Negroes, The False National Guard* and *The Second Décade* the radical potential in *Blaise the Ill-Tempered* could not fail to come to the fore.

In both obvious and subtle ways the last years of the Revolution had profoundly altered popular theater on the boulevard. Shifting climates of opinion in 1793 and 1794 modified meaning and content in old, pre-revolutionary plays; they modified structure and purpose in new and republican plays. Through 1791 and 1792 the popular idiom had exerted its influence on the aesthetic condition of revolutionary theater. In 1793 and 1794 the Revolution took its effect upon the dramatic culture of the boulevard.

Postscript: The Jacobin Aesthetic and Republican Theater

In 1794 dramatic activity on the boulevard nearly came to a standstill. The Délassements-Comiques almost closed down after 1793;[57] the Théâtre-Patriotique persisted only feebly. Both the Gaité and the Ambigu-Comique curtailed plays and performances by around half. Nevertheless, under the aegis of a municipal police led by Hébert and his fellows the radicalization of Parisian theater came to a head. Between August and September of 1793 and March of 1794 a premium in theater was placed on political value alone;

dramatic rules and interests were sacrified for the quick, commerical response to changing events and ideological needs. Parisian theater had been popularized—in its use of unformed, undisciplined genres; in its appeal to the working class sans-culottes.

The republican course of Parisian theater altered perceptibly, however, with the fall of the Hébertistes in late-March 1794. Jacobin leadership, gaining immediate control over the crippled Commune, had equally severe—but different—conceptions of revolutionary theater. From the very moment of his appointment as the Commune's national agent, the Robespierriste Claude Payan harshly criticized the municipal censorship of Parisian theater. In one instance he even meddled with the radical mutilation of plays in the classical repertory, which had suffered artistically from the suppression of titles of address and costumes proper to the time and place of dramatic action. "Without doubt," he wrote to the Committe of Public Safety in May 1794, "one must find it as ridiculous to say *citizen* Catalina as to see Jupiter or Armide decorated with the tri-colored cockade."[58] The Committee of Public Safety, meanwhile, had lost no time in transferring formal control of the dramatic arts from the Commune to the Convention's newly-formed Commission of Public Instruction, to which Joseph Payan, brother to the national agent, was appointed head.[59] The two men thought alike. Neither the Commission nor its superiors on the Committee of Public Safety meant, however, to restore the old classical stage, "still encumbered with the debris of the last regime."[60] If anything, the political goals of republican theater were to be thoroughly and finally realized. But the Jacobins had far more grandiose schemes for the republican stage than had had the hapless sans-culottes. Together the Commission of Public Instruction and the Committee of Public Safety worked a vast plan for the French stage, "in order that reason return there to speak the language of Liberty, to throw flowers on the tombs of martyrs, to sing of heroism and of virtue, to make beloved the laws and the fatherland."[61]

To this end, Joseph Payan formulated the regeneration of dramatic art in contradistinction not only to the enervation of the arts under a despotic old regime but to the artistic mediocrity in which theater had wallowed since the onset of the radical Revolution. He reacted sharply to the popular and commercial appeal that had dominated radical theater at least since August-September 1793. For Payan the ephemeral and simplistic nature of many republican plays confounded all political intent. The commercial degradation of theater formed part and parcel of other, more obviously political, crimes committed by the vanquished Hébertistes:

> Ignorance, grossness, barbarity, in a word all that one may call hébertism of the arts, work for the counter-revolution by the degradation of thought, just as political hébertism does by plots, disorder and murder.... From this arises for the Commission the duty to take action against the stupidities of literature, just as the government crushed the crimes of Hébert...[62]

The Commission took seriously its appointed duty to raise the quality of republican theater. Though very little is known of the Commission's actual censorship, one historian has argued from what evidence exists that it was in fact as harsh as the Commune's had been. All plays were expected and required to conform to the "true principles of liberty."[63] A truly republican stage, however, would be born not of the political brutalization but of the political indulgence of Art. Taste became the byword of Payan's addresses and the search for genius the Commission's guiding light:

> ...it is a matter of establishing a public school, where taste and virtue are equally respected...
>
> * * * * * * * *
>
> The first laws that must be respected in a drama are those of taste and good sense...
>
> * * * * * * * *
>
> It is with pain that the Commission sees itself forced to mark its first steps down the pathway of taste and true beauty by severe lessons; friend and idolator of the arts, the regeneration of which is confided to it, [the Commission] will know how to recognize merit, search out talent, encourage its efforts, applaud its success...[64]

The Jacobin aesthetic gave no quarter to the popular dramatic idiom, such as it has developed in revolution, such as it had been known under the old regime. This was true despite the fact that of the known censorship policies and theatrical plans proposed or carried out by the Commission of Public Instruction in mid-1794, almost nothing concerned the boulevard. Such neglect, however, was not benign; the several reports and addresses of Joseph Payan provide glimpses of attitudes towards the traditional popular stage and its dramatic culture that were overtly hostile. Like the liberals of 1789-91, Payan had expected the little theaters to shed the popular idiom of the past in the first years of revolutionary liberation:

> Several of them, it is true, above all those that despotism had condemned to a deliberate nullity, to an offensive triviality, to a hideous immortality [sic] because they were frequented by that class of citizens which despotism called the *People*—and because it was not useful to despotism that the *People* suspect its dignity—several of [these theaters], I say, seemed to shake off their lethargy at the first strains of this Liberty, which recalled to their stage good sense and reason.[65]

Payan, like the liberals, was deceived in his hopes. But unlike the revolutionaries of 1789-91, Payan openly attacked the old routines, the prejudices against the popular stage, which he believed had stifled the artistic advance of the little theaters. Despite the legal declaration of liberty, throughout the Revolution theaters were tacitly ranked as great or small, and the serious artist still sought his glory in the prestigious theaters of Paris:[66]

> If their efforts [those of some popular theaters] have been in general more constant than happy; if, in spite of some transient sparks, some ephemeral phosphorescence, the dramatic career remains covered by treacherous darkness, we know the causes of it: the prejudices of authors, coddled by a certain public, accustomed to a certain kind of success; sentiments even lower still, explain well enough to the observer the momentary sleep of the Muses.[67]

Despite the radical maturity of the Revolution, Payan nevertheless shared in the aesthetics of the liberal prejudice at the same time that he deplored its social expression. His denunciation of political plays based on current events barely disguised an offensive upon the commercial and popular genres that had spread throughout Paris with the liberation of theater and increasingly political expectations of the stage:

> The writer who offers, instead of lessons, nothing but platitudes; instead of intrigue, nothing but pantomimes; instead of panoramas, nothing but caricatures; is of no use to letters, to morals, to the Stage, and Plato would have chased him from his Republic.[68]

The Jacobins had little difficulty justifying antagonism toward the popular stage of the old regime and its commercial forms—at no point during the Revolution had governing bodies looked with favor on the traditional dramatic culture of the boulevard. It was more difficult, however, to reconcile the fine theater implied by the Jacobin aesthetic with the popular ideals of the Revolution. In March 1794, responding to sectional petitions and untutored letters, the Committee of Public Safety established a Théâtre du Peuple (Theater of the People), "uniquely consecrated to performances given by and for the people."[69] The many companies of Paris were to share thrice-weekly performances of republican fare on the empty stage of the Théâtre de la Nation, closed by the Committee of Public Safety in September 1793. But within a month the Committee repealed its plans for the Théâtre du Peuple, reinstating the French actors of the old Comédie-Française-Théâtre de la Nation as the Théâtre de l'Egalité instead and shuffling the major companies from one stage to the next. By the same decree the Committee accorded the Opéra a grant of 200,000 livres for its "extraordinary service."[70] In following months both the new Théâtre de l'Egalité and the Théâtre de la République received as well subsidies of 25,000 and 50,000 livres respectively. These generous grants contrasted significantly with the meager 5,000 livres given the politically obsequious but less prestigious Théâtre des Sans-Culottes (formerly the Théâtre Molière).[71]

Jacobin leadership had openly shifted its emphasis from a popular republican stage to a great or fine republican stage. The stimulation of dramatic excellence had necessarily to precede its diffusion and command over theater of and for the people. As Payan declared, "soon we will go in search of the root of the evil... for the moment, it suffices to prepare the moral regeneration that is going to take place..."[72] Robespierre's Jacobins had returned, in part at least, to the vision of theatrical renascence first given shape by the liberals of 1789-1791. By bolstering the Opéra and the Théâtre de l'Egalité, the Committee of Public Safety reinvigorated the theatrical hierarchy that had all but toppled in 1792 and 1793. On the eve of Thermidor the Jacobins made their first efforts to build a world of fine, republican theater in which the popular stage, as it had been known under the old regime, would have no part.

Conclusion: The Boulevard Epitome

In many respects the study of boulevard theater in eighteenth century Paris is its own reward. The carnival atmosphere of the fairgrounds, the light-hearted comedies on stage, the bohemian cast of artists and entrepreneurs, all impart an especially delightful appeal to a world buried over 180 years in the past. But the history of the little theaters in the late 1700s has more serious purposes as well.

One of these has been to address the relations between dominant, classical traditions and excluded cultures in eighteenth century France. In the world of Parisian theater the three great companies of the king had been granted by law not just monopolies of theatrical industry but monopolies of dramatic art, artists and publics. By exclusion, the boulevard trade was inseparable from marginal publics, marginal artists and marginal art. The tendency has been strong in the historiography of old regime France to accept such formal distinctions in eighteenth century culture at face value, to argue that privileged and marginal traditions, whether they be of material, artistic or literary culture, split along a socio-economic divide between the governing classes of society and the people at large. Historians such as Robert Mandrou distinguish in this sense between elite and popular cultures. Yet in fact, theatrical publics were not nearly as discrete as the classical mind or ethnological historians might have it. Dramatic culture did not segment along the socio-economic barriers of society.

Throughout the last half of the eighteenth century boulevard theater attracted a mix of classes that ranged from one end of the social spectrum to the other. All members of society had access to the little theaters of the boulevard. With respect to this fact alone the segmentation of theatrical culture was characterized less by Mandrou's elite-popular gap than it was by the Burke-Redfield model of great and little traditions, which opposes a restricted social consumption of elite culture to a broad and unrestricted social consumption of popular culture. Yet even this model must be altered in order to reflect a more complex reality in Parisian theater. Access to the great dramatic traditions of the royal companies was not entirely limited to the social elite. Members of the middle and lower classes may not have dominated the audience of the Opéra or the Comédie-Française as they did at the Grands-Danseurs or the Ambigu-Comique, but their numbers increased noticeably at the royal theaters through the 1780s. Two cultural traditions, formally separated in legal rights, aesthetic license and dramatic appeal, were in practice socially miscible one with the other. An accurate model of pragmatic socio-cultural relations for Parisian theater in the last decades of the eighteenth century must pose an intersection of great and little dramatic cultures which describes the social diffusion of publics in both directions, albeit in greater and lesser amounts.

The same model must account for the diffusion of art and artists across the formal barriers erected by privilege between the great and the little stage. As the boulevard increased in economic importance and in public vogue in the late 1770s and early 1780s great and popular cultures converged. Though formally the comic vision of the boulevard theaters was a world apart from that of the royal companies, it was not practically so. Boulevard theaters parodied the repertories of the royal theaters, borrowed their themes and plots, and imitated their comedy and sentimental drama. In the same manner the royal theaters borrowed certain elements of the popular tradition. The phenomenal success of dialogued pantomimes and boulevard farces such as *Janot or the Beaten Pay the Price* prompted the privileged companies to imitate and engage the plays, playwrights and artists of the popular stage. Across a formal divide between privileged and non-privileged theater, great and little institutions engaged in a symbiotic exchange of dramatic culture, each borrowing, molding, adapting the art of the other and thereby their own art.

The classical mind had ostracized the fair and boulevard theaters to a shunned and marginal status. Yet the formal mechanisms of separation—social exclusivity, economic monopoly, aesthetic privilege—only hindered and did not prevent economic, social and artistic interaction between the great and the little theaters of Paris. Marginality, while it implies removal, implies as well that that which is removed also remains a part of the whole. The boulevard experiment in interaction between dominant and shunned sectors of society reflected for this reason many of the political and cultural forces that generally shaped the broad outlines of old regime France. A focus of stress in the last decades of the eighteenth century, the boulevard in its development may stand as a simile for a whole society moving towards dissolution and revolution.

The most striking observation to be made of this microcosm of the old regime is that a multiplicity of controlling powers each left their own expedient and idiosyncratic imprint on the boulevard, such that economic, cultural and social activity there resembled a mosaic of traditional and innovative patterns. In the 1770s and early 1780s the police and the hospitals of Paris encouraged a capitalistic growth of little theaters that contrasted, indeed conflicted, harshly with the privileged monopolies held by the three royal companies of Paris. This experimental marketplace atmosphere of the boulevard economy was eventually dampened, however, when royal ministers withdrew the commercial licensing of little theaters from the police and created for the benefit of the Opéra a traditionally organized franchise of popular entertainments. In the cultural sphere boulevard theater was initially constrained to obsolete genres and bawdy idioms by the heavy censorship policies of the French and Italian actors. Boulevard artists responded to these restraints by developing experimental dramatic forms through the 1770s. By the end of this decade the police and eventually the king's Household ministers pushed for the relaxation of censorship, thereby making way for the full flowering of the Enlightenment's moralizing influence in popular comedies and dramas. In the earliest years of its existence the boulevard, like the Comic Opera before it, catered quite openly to an aristocratic audience. At the combined insistence of the three great companies of Paris the little theaters were forced to develop new and different publics. Indeed the police protected and nurtured the boulevard theaters as a means of entertaining and educating the people, a class they believed to be rapidly expanding in size and in expectations. Altogether, royal ministers, police officials, entrepreneurs and artists on the boulevard worked out the integration of a commercial economy, a non-classical stage, and the popular classes within the social and cultural body of France.

It is significant that boulevard activity resembled a mosaic rather than an evolution of patterns. A great many of the salient influences on the boulevard milieu gave direction there to far-seeing experimental activity, but the boulevard did not pose a standard of reform for old regime France. Despite the economic innovations within the boulevard marketplace, moral and aesthetic innovations within the popular repertory and social innovations in the boulevard public, dominant economic, aesthetic and social sanctions had not been changed. Despite, or because of, the healthy vigor of the capitalistic economy of little theaters, the Opéra reasserted the primacy of traditional economic forms by leasing privilege on the boulevard as if the notion or appearance of exclusive monopoly would guarantee both market and profit. On the boulevard stage, the tenacity of old dramatic forms was such that new sentimental comedies, pantomimes and dramas meant to educate the people morally were simply incorporated within an enduring repertory of traditional, bawdy farces and love intrigues tied by classical theory and custom to popular theater. The little theaters provided entertainment to whole classes within the Third Estate hitherto denied ready access to the stage. Still, low prices and a steady growth in the number of middle- and lower-class spectators had not erased an upper-class interest and influence in boulevard theater. In all cases, what was new about the boulevard, whether a commercial economy, a didactic stage, or a popular public, did not replace the superior sanctions of economic privilege and classical taste or an aristocratic presence. Experiments in form had simply been attached helter-skelter to a preexisting framework, thereby altering in appearance but not wholly in substance its original shape and function.

To a very great extent, however, the economic, aesthetic and social accommodations that characterized the growth and eventual integration of what had once been a marginal milieu within the official order of eighteenth century France were incompatible with that order and had corrosive value in the breakdown of the old regime. This was so because in its essence old regime society was based upon exclusivity. By their very industry, little theaters violated the privileges of the three companies of the king. In their art, the little theaters violated classical taste and exclusive rights to theatrical performance. In their audience, the little theaters violated classical notions of dramatic publics and eroded the social distances upon which aristocratic society was based. Over all, the very notion of legitimacy in capitalist endeavor, in non-classical forms, in popular entertainment was anathema to a world that had long ago thought to exclude these things from its purview. On the brink of revolution conservatives alarmed for the old order discerned and condemned in boulevard activity a conspicuous reminder of other cultures, other economies, other social classes. Repentant revolutionaries later identified the boulevard even more clearly with the upheavals in theatrical culture that followed upon the fall of the Bastille—not because the boulevard itself gained cultural dominance, but because the republican stage reiterated its commercial imperatives and broad, common appeal. Yet despite corrosive incompatibilities the boulevard and its stage did not herald revolution, perhaps because the accommodation of popular theater within the theatrical world of old regime Paris was a stable one—at least until the very structures of privileged and aristocratic society were called into question. Significantly enough, only a handful of plays performed on the boulevard called for radical solutions to the inequities of rank and place. Over the 1770s and 1780s the popular repertory as a whole expressed affirmation of the social hierarchy and traditional values.

The general complacency of the boulevard stage largely reflected an identity of interest between the popular entrepreneur—and to somewhat less extent the popular actor and playwright—and the order of the old regime. The directors, actors and authors of the minor theaters were not only dependent on the commercial market of the boulevard. Even as marginal inhabitants of the world of theater they were enmeshed in relationships to society at large. Certainly the boulevard director depended upon the commercial appeal and success of his entrepreneurial venture to stay in business; there were no government subsidies to support the popular stage. But he depended equally on the many "despotic" bodies that controlled the commercial enclave of boulevard theater to sustain his theatrical activity. The police, the government, the hospitals and the Opéra protected the minor directors from privilege; they protected them as well from the full rigors of a commercial environment. That at least is the implication of the hospitals' lenient policy of rebating taxation. Once admitted to the boulevard community, entrepreneurs found a relatively secure niche in the theatrical world of late-eighteenth century Paris.

So, too, did many of their actors, actresses and playwrights. For these artists the boulevard director embodied aspects of both the aristocratic patron and the open market. The actor and actress depended on the director for his or her job, for protection from the debtor's law, for paternal indulgence and care. The playwright, who often doubled as an actor or stage manager, relied on the director to buy and produce his plays. In exchange for these forms of paternalistic support the director demanded a rigorous subservience to his administration and his commerical needs. Nevertheless he protected the boulevard artist in much the same way that the hospitals or Opéra protected boulevard enterprise. Though actor and author gained some success through audience recognition, neither directly depended for their livelihood upon the vagaries of public enthusiasm. It was, rather, the director who dispensed economic and professional security.

The ambiguous position of these minor artists, caught between the supports of an aristocratic and privileged system and the harsh liberation of a commercial market, must explain the range of political attitude and activity amongst actors and authors of the boulevard during the years of revolution. It cannot be argued that because boulevard artists were marginal to elite circles of privileged actors and playwrights, they necessarily resented the hierarchy of place in the world of theater or worked for its overthrow before and after 1789. Each individual artist, according to his own unique experience within the marginal world of Parisian theater, identified himself with the old regime or the new, with conservative or revolutionary theater. The activities of boulevard men in the 1790s scattered across the political spectrum, the degree of their involvement in political affairs and dramatic upheaval varying greatly. To characterize the group of boulevard artists by one individual psychology would therefore be grossly inaccurate. Rather, the complexity of their marginal status, excluded yet included within the theatrical profession as a whole, suggested to the boulevard artists many possible responses to the privileged order of the old regime and to the commercial order of the new.

The scattered distribution of response on the boulevard to the breakdown of the old order suggests a cultural revolution in the world of theater unlike that found by Robert Darnton for the literary underworld at large. Interpretative distinctions between Darnton's study and my own may be understood as the result of different methodological approaches to group behavior and sociology. Darnton begins with outstanding individuals involved in the cultural revolution of the year II and finds that certain common experiences before 1789 placed them in what he calls "Grub-Street." I begin with the literary milieu he defines—or at least part of it—and work with the widest possible range of men in that underworld. Darnton generalizes the "Grub-Street" experience from the rich records of a few historically significant individuals; I reconstruct the boulevard profession with over-simple data for a large number of personally insignificant men amongst many more anonymous ones. Darnton searches backwards for the origins of radical behavior; I trace forwards the dispersion of response to the Revolution. The institutional, social and professional strains between enlightened mandarins and lowly hack writers, between the official academies and underground clubs, which for Darnton triggered the mechanisms of cultural revolution, formed only part of a more complex reality in Parisian theater. The relationship of the artists studied in these pages—those for whom records remain—to the boulevard population as a whole may never be certainly known, but the data that do exist suggest that tensions between the high and low in theater were partially mitigated by a security of place, however, precarious, enjoyed by the boulevard entrepreneurs and their artists; by a professional mobility, however constrained, of actors and authors; and by an exchange, however limited, of dramatic culture between the great and the little stage.

Though it was part of the literary underworld, the boulevard did not rise in the years 1789-94, in tandem with the political ascendance of a Marat or a Fabre d'Eglantine. Very few of the minor authors who served the boulevard stage under the old regime became involved in revolutionary politics; not many more are known to have participated in radical theater. In its corpus of texts the boulevard revealed well into 1793 an ambiguous mood amongst its authors, actors and directors. The ideological direction of the cultural revolution in theater did not come from the minor stage. That direction, first shaped by the liberals of 1789-91, gained its proper velocity from outside the boulevard and even from outside the world of theater. It came from the imperatives of revolution itself. The enduring repertory of the popular stage only stood in the way of the radical theatrical politics starkly revealed in the year II. In order to consummate a republican theater, the revolutionaries of 1793-1794 had to neutralize and repress what they could of traditional dramatic culture. Far from celebrating the popular dramatic idiom of the boulevard, such as it had developed over many decades of the eighteenth century, the Revolution moved to destroy it.

Despite the popular context of revolutionary and republican theater a fundamental hostility for the boulevard stage had not been altered in the years after 1789. This was so because boulevard theater had not developed true reform in its cultural expression, had in fact remained attached to the idiom and forms of the past as Rousseau might have predicted. The most radical of revolutionaries sought to eradicate the reactionary nature of the institution in their terrifying, heavy-handed efforts to open up boulevard theater to close political influence and surveillance in 1793-1794. But like other stages that bridged old and new France, boulevard theater largely remained, in the words of one scholar, "the closed box of the old regime."[1] Pryed open and its contents spilled after a span of two centuries, the boulevard exposes facets of that old regime which have eluded containment elsewhere. Certainly the popular stage reveals the social and cultural alienation of the boulevard actor and author; the formal divisions in legal rights, dramatic arts, and social publics in the world of theater; the zany's potentially radical critique of rank and place. But the boulevard has also disclosed the minor artist's sense of security and complacency; a mixing of publics high and low, a continuity of dramatic traditions common and fine, and an integration of capitalist enterprise and privileged monopolies; as well as the dramatic expression and affirmation of traditional values; in a close, if hierarchical, association and symbiosis of classes and cultures. Well before 1789 a despotic regime had already evinced a guarded concern for popular culture and the people that was more than "benign neglect" and had extended them, on the boulevard at least, a protection that both eased and undermined the crushing weight of privileged, aristocratic society.

Tables and Figures

Table 1. Boulevard Censorship, 1784-1789

	Grands-Danseurs du Roi							Ambigu-Comique						
	1784	1785	1786	1787	1788	1789	Total	1784	1785	1786	1787	1788	1789	Total
Reviews/Year	4	16	16	7	13	8	65	10	17	20	9	15	7	78
Charges of Violation	0	2	2	0	1	0	5	3	1	5	1	0	0	9
Lesser Complaints	2	1	2	1	0	0	6	2	0	1	2	0	1	6
Actual Supressions	0	1	1	0	0	0	2	2	0	2	0	0	0	4

	Variétés-Amusantes							Theaters Unspecified						
	1784	1785	1786	1787	1788	1789	Total	1784	1785	1786	1787	1788	1789	Total
Reviews/Year	15	27	9	0	1	11	63	6	15	4	4	4	2	35
Charges of Violation	6	7	2	0	1	1	17	3	4	1	1	1	0	10
Lesser Complaints	0	3	0	0	0	0	1	1	0	1	0	0	0	2
Actual Suppressions	1?	3	0	0	0	1	4-5?	1-2?	3-4?	1?	0	0	0	4-7?

	All Theaters						
	1784	1785	1786	1787	1788	1789	Total
Reviews/Year	35	75	49	20	33	28	240
Charges of Violation	12	14	10	2	3	1	42
Lesser Complaints	5	2	4	3	0	1	15
Actual Suppressions	3-5?	7-8?	3-4?	0	0	1	14-18?

SOURCE:
Ms. *Registre pour les pièces des spectacles des Boulevards,* Bibliothèque de la Comédie-Française.
KEY:
Reviews/Year refers to the number of plays reviewed by the French actors and entered in the register of censorship kept by the royal company. Negative reviews resulted in one of two verdicts: *Charges of Artistic Violation* upon the repertory or upon the privilege of the French actors. Such a charge invariably called for suppression of the play.
Lesser Complaints, often accompanying permission to perform, involved requests for change, such as verse to prose.
Actual Suppressions reflects the number of those plays under charge of violation by the French actors which do not appear in my sample and are not listed as performed by C.D. Brenner in his *A Bibliographical List of Plays in the French Language 1700-1789* (Berkeley, 1947).

Table 2. Salaries of Artists on the Boulevard
Part I: Average Salaries at the Grands-Danseurs Compared to the Comédie-Française

Average Salaries, G-D	Average Salaries, C-F[x]
Jan - Dec 1786 101,751 livres / 53 artists[o] = 1,920	Apr 1786 - Apr 1787 519,577 livres / 23 artists[o] = 22,590* (19,557)[P]
Jan - Dec 1787 131,587 livres / 61 artists[o] = 2,157	Apr 1787 - Apr 1788 587,775 livres / 23 artists[o] = 25,555* (22,077)[P]
Jan - Dec 1791 102,252 livres / 63 artists[o] = 1,623	Apr 1791 - Apr 1792 288,671 livres / 23 artists[o] = 12,548* (10,737)[P]
Jan - Dec 1792 92,812 livres / 39 artists[o] = 2,379 (no musicians listed, figure may be high)	Apr 1792 - Apr 1793 150,794 livres / 23 artists[o] = 6,555* (5,050)[P]

[o] Artists are defined as actors, actresses, dancers of both sexes, acrobats, and musicians. C-F had only actors and actresses.
[P] These figures are the artist's share if only receipts of the door and the petites loges or boxes are taken into account. These figures are therefore more comparable to those for the Grands-Danseurs. See *.
* These figures are calculated from the entire share *(part entière)*, which consisted not only of a share of the proceeds from the door but included royal pension, boxes, interest on capital, appearance fees, etc. See [P].
[x] These figures are probably for the period mid-April to mid-April, since that is the period for which contracts were signed.

Note on Sources

Yearly expenses for actors, actresses, dancers of both sexes, tight-rope walkers, acrobats, and musicians, etc. at the Grands-Danseurs du Roi are taken from the "Etat de la recette et de la dépense . . ," Bibliothèque de l'Arsenal, Ms. 13002. These sums are divided by the number of artists (defined above) included in the employee listings of the Grands-Danseurs. These employee lists are to be found in Nougaret's *Les Spectacles des foires et des boulevards* (1773-1788) and *Almanach général de tous les théâtres de Paris et des provinces* (1791-1792). The result is the average salary for artists at the Grands-Danseurs during these years. These averages may be compared to the average share of actors and actresses at the Comédie-Française, as calculated from Claude Alasseur's Table 19, "Sommes Totales Versées aux Acteurs. Valeur moyenne d'une part entière," and Table 18, "Répartition du Revenu des Acteurs selon les sources du Revenus" (*La Comédie Française au 18e siècle*, 1967).

Table 2. Salaries of Artists on the Boulevard
Part II: Distribution of Salary on the Boulevard: Gaité (Grands-Danseurs) and Ambigu-Comique

	Gaité, 1795[+]	**Ambigu-Comique, 1795**[°]
5,000 livres or more	2	0
4,000 to 4,999 livres	1	1
3,000 to 3,999 livres	4	1
2,000 to 2,999 livres	7	1
1,000 to 1,999 livres	11	7
700 to 999 livres	7	4
	32 artists	14 artists
average salary	2100 livres	1650 livres

Sources

For the Gaité (Grands-Danseurs): Bibliothèque nationale, Ms. n.a.f. 3046. Papiers de la Gaité.

For the Ambigu-Comique: Archives nationales, BB[3]73. Correspondances, Comité de surveillance du Département de Paris.

[+] These income records for the Gaité, undated, are probably fixed in time to the transfer of that theater from Nicolet to Ribié, effected during the course of 1795. The inclusion of one Constantin, who died in 1795, places the records before the end of that year. It is assumed, therefore, that the salaries are for the contract year April '95 to April '96.

[°] These income records for the Ambigu-Comique are for the contract year April '94 to April '95.

Table 3. Average Cost of Plays at the Grands-Danseurs, 1786-1792

Year	**Estimated Number of New Plays Produced***	**Amount Paid to Authors**[P]	**Estimated Average Price per New Play**[+]
1786	31	3693 livres	119 livres
1787	20	2005 livres	100 livres
1788	25	3847 livres	153 livres
1789	26	3308 livres	127 livres
1790	28	3532 livres	126 livres
1791	20	1103 livres	55 livres
1792	13	753 lvires	57 livres

* The number of plays listed here is an *estimation* of the number of new plays produced each year as indicated in my sampling of the Grands-Danseurs repertory for the years 1785-1794. See [+] concerning the validity of these estimates.

[P] The amount paid to authors is from "Payements de pièces et pantomimes à differents auteurs," in "Etats de la recette et de la dépense. . .," Bibliothèque de l'Arsenal, Ms. 13002.

[+] These estimated averages conform closely to figures given in contemporary anecdotal sources (see discussion, chapter 6). In consequence, it is reasonable to assume that the estimated number of new plays produced each year is fairly accurate.

Table 4. Change in the Repertory of Two Boulevard Theaters, 1789-1794
Breakdown by Category of Plays Performed in the Successful Repertory*

Year	[P]Pre-Rev Rep	Borrowed Rep	New Rep	Total	**Old/ New
		Gaité			
1789	49 86%	0	8 14%	57	86%/ 14%
1790	43 74%	1 2%	14 24%	58	76%/ 24%
1791	40 70%	6 11%	11 19%	57	81%/ 19%
1792	31 61%	10 19%	10 19%	51	80%/ 19%
1793	38 68%	8 14%	10 18%	56	82%/ 18%
1794	22 61%	5 14%	9 25%	36	75%/ 25%
		Ambigu-Comique			
1789	22 69%	0	10 31%	32	69%/ 31%
1790	21 55%	0	17 45%	38	55%/ 45%
1791	13 33%	7 18%	19 49%	39	51%/ 49%
1792	12 36%	8 24%	13 39%	33	60%/ 39%
1793	19 54%	3 8%	13 37%	35	62%/ 37%
1794	9 31%	5 17%	15 52%	29	48%/ 52%

* Defined for revolutionary years 1789-1794 as those plays in the sampled repertory[+] (see key to table 5) which carried five or more sampled dates during the years 1789-94 and/or carried three dates in any single year 1789-94.

[P] Note on Categories: *Pre-revolutionary Repertory* includes all plays sampled in the years 1785-1788 and those sampled after that date but known to have been written and performed before 1788. *Borrowed Repertory* refers to all plays sampled in the years 1789-1794 and known to have been first performed on another stage before 1789 or borrowed from the public domain. *New Repertory* includes all plays sampled between 1789 and 1794, without history pre-1789 and/or known to have been written in the years 1789-94.

** Proportions are given between old fare, which included pre-revolutionary repertory and borrowed repertory, and new fare written during the years 1789-94. Much of the old fare, but not all, was condemned for its cultural conservatism in late 1793 and 1794. Some, but not all, of the new fare was republican in nature.

Table 5. Change in the Boulevard Repertory, 1793-1794
Breakdown by Category of Plays and Performances in the Sampled Repertories[+] of Boulevard Theaters

		Number of Plays		Number of Performances	
		1793	**1794**	**1793**	**1794**
Gaité	[P]Pre-Rev Rep	55 59%	24 44%	96 57%	72 56%
	Borrowed Rep	17 18%	10 19%	35 21%	15 12%
	New Rep	21 23%	20 37%	36 22%	41 32%
	Total	93	54	167	128
Ambigu-Comique	[P]Pre-Rev Rep	25 47%	11 24%	72 51%	29 23%
	Borrowed Rep	4 8%	8 18%	11 8%	27 21%
	New Rep	24 45%	26 58%	59 41%	71 56%
	Total	53	45	142	127
Théâtre-Patriotique	[P]Pre-Rev Rep	0	0	0	0
	Borrowed Rep	29 78%	6 55%	35 80%	6 55%
	New Rep	8 22%	5 45%	9 20%	5 45%
	Total	37	11	44	11

(Table 5 continued on next page)

		Number of Plays		Number of Performances	
		1793	1794	1793	1794
Délassements-Comiques	PPre-Rev Rep	0	0	0	0
	Borrowed Rep	16 59%	2	20 62.5%	2
	New Rep	11 41%	0	12 37.5%	0
	Total	27	2	32	2
Théâtre-Français Comique et Lyrique	PPre-Rev Rep	0	0	0	0
	Borrowed Rep	5 28%	5 42%	9 12%	7 41%
	New Rep	13 72%	7 58%	64 88%	10 59%
	Total	18	12	73	17
Variétés-Amusantes de Lazzari	PPre-Rev Rep	0	0	0	0
	Borrowed Rep	23 42%	20 33%	28 26%	31 25%
	New Rep	32 58%	41 67%	78 74%	91 75%
	Total	55	61	106	122

+ Based on a sampling of program announcements in the *Annonces* and other journals every eight days in the years 1785-1794. For other symbols, see key for table 4.

Figure 1. The Design of Theatrical Announcements in Parisian Journals in the Late Eighteenth Century

Annonces, affiches et avis divers (Petites Affiches)

→ **1785**	**1785-1789**	**1789** →
Académie royale de musique	Académie royale de musique	Académie royale de musique
———	———	Théâtre français
Théâtre français	Théâtre français	Théâtre italien
———	———	Variétés
Théâtre italien	Théâtre italien	Grands Danseurs du Roi
▬▬▬▬	————————	Ambigu Comique
Grands Danseurs du Roi	Variétés	
Ambigu Comique	▬▬▬▬	
Variétés-Amusantes	Grands Danseurs du Roi	
	———	
	Ambigu Comique	

Journal de Paris

→ **1785**	**1785** →
Académie royale de musique	Académie royale de musique
———	———
Théâtre français	Théâtre français
———	———
Théâtre italien	Théâtre italien
———	▬▬▬▬
BOULEVARDS	————————
Grands Danseurs du Roi	**PALAIS ROYAL**
———	Variétés
Ambigu Comique	————————
———	**BOULEVARDS**
Variétés-Amusantes	Grands Danseurs du Roi
	———
	Ambigu Comique

Note on Figures 2 and 3: Variable and Fixed Costs of the Grands-Danseurs, 1782-1792.

These figures are drawn from information as it is given in Ms. 13002. *Comptabilité du Théâtre des Grands-Danseurs, pour les années 1782-1792,* Bibliothèque de l'Arsenal. In other words, Nicolet himself broke down his total costs into the categories represented on the graphs: Actors, Dancers etc.; Costumes and Props; Authors; Daily Expenses; Soldiers; Upkeep and Renovations; Poor Tax; Opera Tax; etc. However, the categorization of these costs as either variable or fixed did not figure in the original "Comptabilité." Nevertheless, such distinctions allow us to comprehend more easily the economic conditions of a minor Parisian theater and the entrepreneurial decisions of its director. Note, for instance, that most of Nicolet's fixed costs, excluding upkeep, held a fairly steady course in the years 1782-1789—these were primarily imposed by the controlled economy of theater, which fell apart during the Revolution. Despite the drop-off in fixed costs, however, Nicolet was unable to pull out of debt after 1789 without a rather severe restraint of his variable costs as well.

Figure 2. Variable Costs of the Grands-Danseurs du Roi, 1782-1792

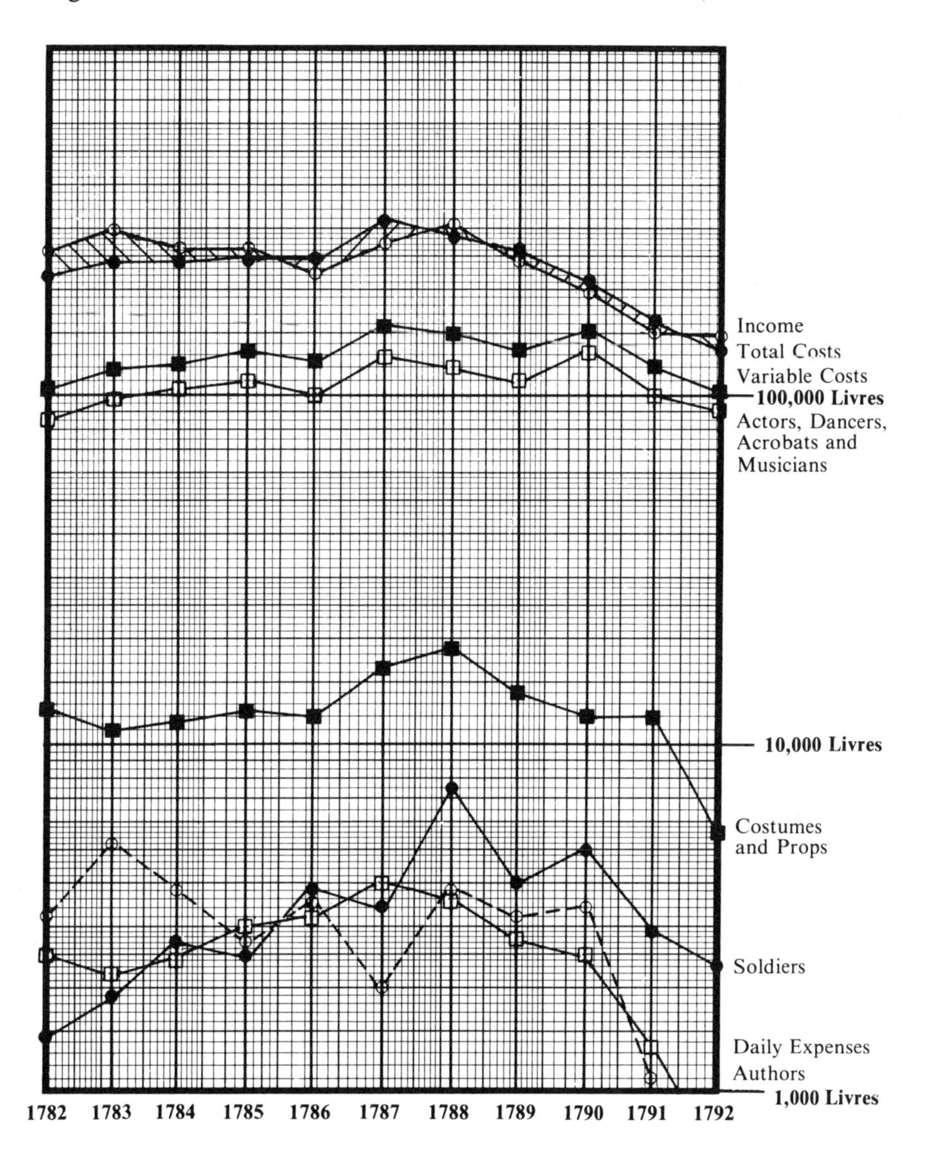

Note that this is a logarithmic graph.

Data for Figure 2
Variable Costs of the Grands-Danseurs du Roi, 1782-1792

	1782	1783	1784	1785	1786	1787
Income*	252,192	290,757	256,908	253,422	220,503	272,925
Total Costs	215,587	241,761	245,731	251,971	243,586	322,681
Total Variable Costs	106,349	119,637	126,644	134,113	125,239	158,970
Actors, Dancers, etc.	86,006	98,958	105,624	113,288	101,751	131,586
Costumes, Props	13,245	11,215	11,785	12,651	12,291	17,896
Authors	3,137	5,335	3,935	2,644	3,693	2,005
Daily Expenses	2,526	2,216	2,615	3,025	3,558	4,068
Soldiers	1,433	1,909	2,682	2,502	3,943	3,410
	1788	**1789**	**1790**	**1791**	**1792**	
Income	295,197	247,491	211,785	152,553	144,624	
Total Costs	289,617	259,095	212,959	157,388	134,591	
Total Variable Costs	152,105	135,879	155,861	119,620	102,103	
Actors, Dancers, etc.	117,219	111,645	134,473	102,252	92,812	
Costumes, Props	19,724	14,013	12,206	11,992	5,354	
Authors	3,847	3,308	3,532	1,103	753	
Daily Expenses	3,741	2,814	2,545	1,345	849	
Soldiers	7,569	4,096	5,101	2,925	2,332	

*Expenses in livres.

Figure 3. Fixed Costs of the Grands-Danseurs du Roi, 1782-1792

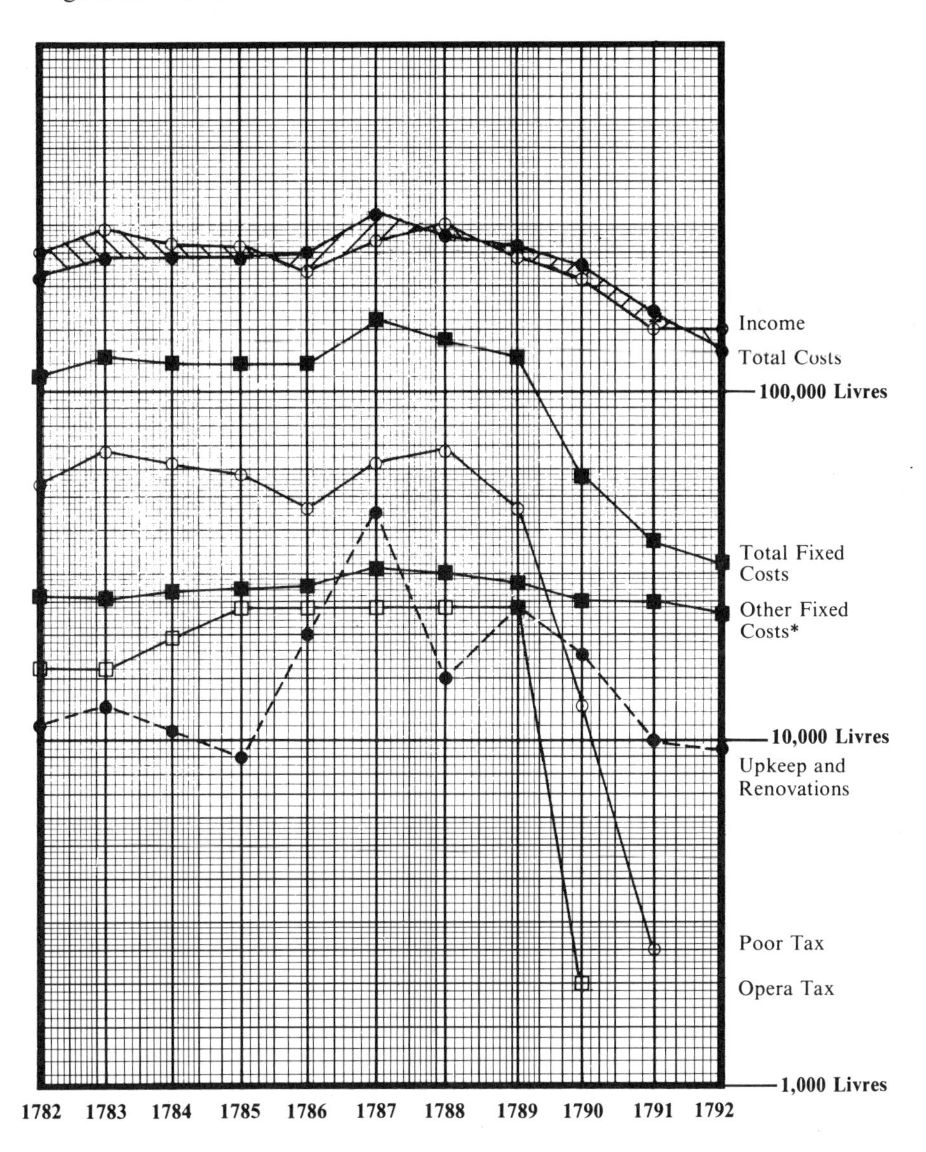

Note that this is a logarithmic graph.

*Payments for lighting; the Parisian guard; printing; and firemen.

Data for Figure 3
Fixed Costs of the Grands-Danseurs du Roi, 1782-1792

	1782	**1783**	**1784**	**1785**	**1786**	**1787**
Income*	252,192	290,757	256,908	253,422	220,503	272,925
Total Costs	215,587	241,761	245,731	251,971	243,586	322,681
Total Fixed Costs	109,238	122,124	119,087	117,858	118,347	163,711
Poor Tax	55,652	67,501	62,502	58,055	46,465	62,871
Other Fixed Costs**	26,192	25,678	26,498	26,903	27,644	30,720
Opera Tax	16,128	16,320	19,208	24,000	24,096	24,000
Upkeep and Renovations	11,266	12,625	10,879	8,900	19,642	45,120

	1788	**1789**	**1790**	**1791**	**1792**
Income	295,197	247,491	211,785	152,553	144,624
Total Costs	289,617	259,095	212,959	157,388	134,591
Total Fixed Costs	137,512	123,216	57,098	37,768	32,488
Poor Tax	68,163	46,718	12,131	2,488	———
Other Fixed Costs	30,356	28,061	25,300	25,274	22,909
Opera Tax	24,000	24,000	2,000	———	———
Upkeep and Renovations	14,993	24,437	17,667	10,000	9,579

* Expenses in livres.

**Other fixed costs include payments for lighting; the Parisian guard; printing; and firemen.

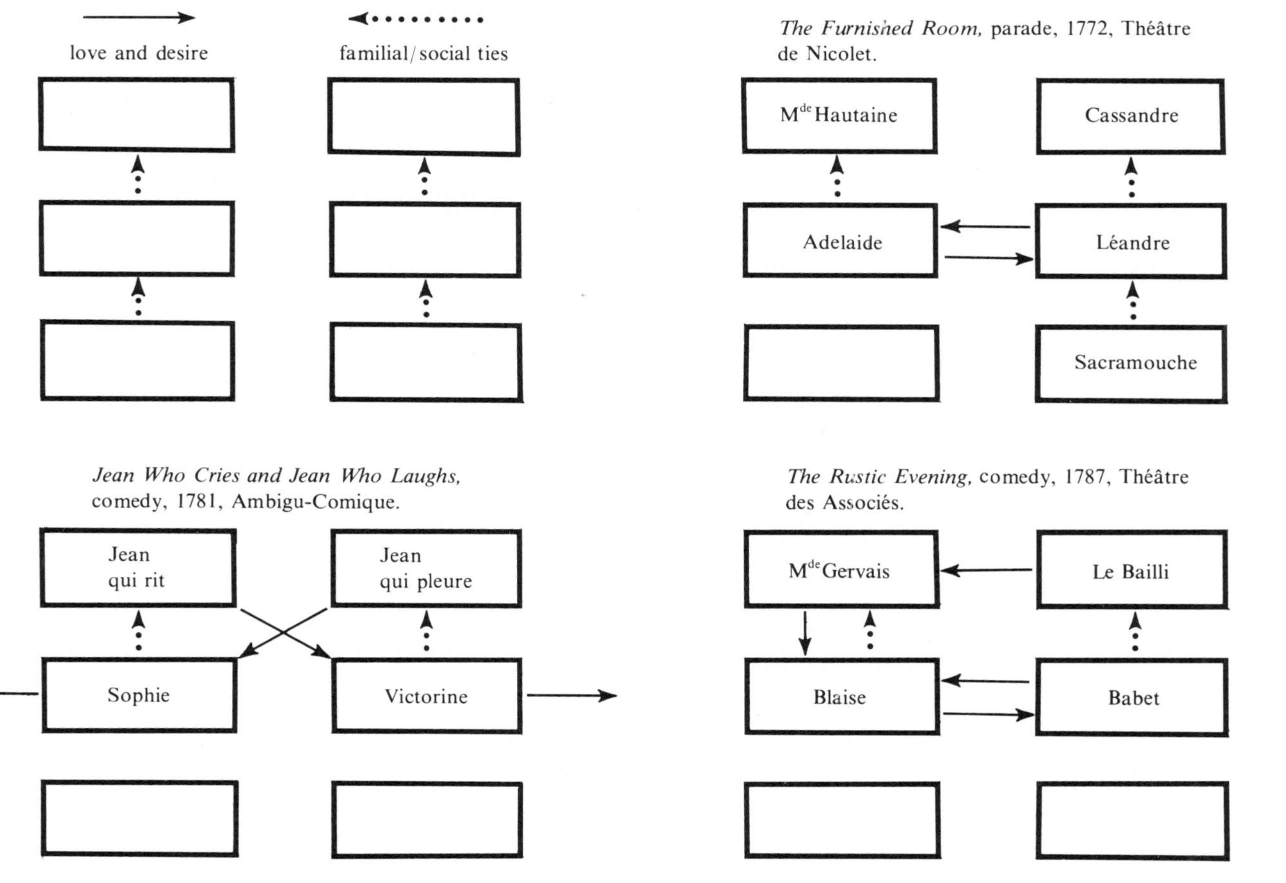

Figure 4. Schematic Drawings of Boulevard Plot Structures

Index to Boulevard Plays Studied and Cited

Notes

Introduction

1. Nicolas Brazier, *Histoire des petits théâtres de Paris* (Paris, 1838), preface.

2. [Nicolas-Joseph Sélis], *Lettre à un père de famille sur les petits spectacles de Paris* (Paris, 1789), p. 40.

3. Robert Mandrou, *La France aux XVIIe et XVIIIe siècles* (Paris, 1967), p. 135.

4. Mandrou, "Cultures populaires et savantes: Rapports et contacts," *The Wolf and the Lamb, Popular Culture in France,* Stanford French and Italian Studies, III (1977), p. 18.

5. Natalie Z. Davis, "The Historian and Popular Culture," *Wolf and the Lamb,* p. 10.

6. Note that in *La France aux XVIIe et XVIIIe siècles,* Mandrou states that his structural approach does not "reduce cultural life to these [social] cleavages. The exchanges, the interactions, are sufficient enough evidence that there is no need to insist" (p. 135). Still, he does insist that "ideological structures and social cadres are inseparable, no matter what the recognized inadequacies of this analytical plan" (p. 135). Reservations with Mandrou's interpretation of the *Bibliothèque bleue* are expressed by G. Bollème, *La Bibliothèque bleue, littérature populaire en France du XVIIe au XIXe siècle* (Paris, 1971), pp. 19-20, and by Peter Burke, "Oblique approaches to the history of popular culture," in C.W.E. Bigsby, ed., *Approaches to Popular Culture* (London, 1976), p. 73.

7. Mandrou, "Cultures populaires et savantes," p. 18.

8. Burke, *Popular Culture in Early Modern Europe* (London, 1978). Burke discusses the cultural model put forward by the social anthropologist Robert Redfield in the 1930s on pages 23-29, and offers crucial modifications.

9. Robert Darnton, "The High Enlightenment and the Low-Life of Literature in Prerevolutionary France," *Past and Present,* 51 (1971), p. 93 and *passim.* See also Darnton, "Reading, Writing and Publishing in Eighteenth-Century France: A Case Study in the Sociology of Literature," *Daedalus* (Winter 1971).

10. Darnton, "The High Enlightenment," p. 112 and n. 89.

11. Oscar G. Brockett, "The Fair Theatres of Paris in the Eighteenth Century: The Undermining of the Classical Ideal" in M.J. Anderson, ed., *Classical Drama and its Influence, Essays Presented to H.D.F. Kitto* (New York, 1965), pp. 251-70.

12. For instance, on p. 66 Brown accepts an erroneous interpretation of the *Cahier. Plaintes et doléances de Messieurs les Comédiens-français* (n.p., 1789) as, at face value, a document

submitted to the king and National Assembly. (See Maurice Albert, *Les Théâtres des Boulevards (1789-1848)* (Paris, 1902), p. 48). An attentive reading of the original "cahier" makes obvious its sarcastic tone and intended ridicule, not just of the royal actors but of the momentous events occurring in the National Assembly. The actors are depicted haggling over the means of voting—whether by estate (there being one nobleman among them) or by head. It being "*extremely dangerous* to opine by head, and in a single chamber... it was esteemed necessary to separate into two chambers,... the Tragedians would deliberate in the hall of Assembly, while the Comedians would go vote under the peristyle" (p. 7). Henri Welschinger, in *Le Théâtre de la Révolution, 1790-1799* (Paris, 1880), pp. 36-37 stated that he had found the *Cahier* in a collection of Pixérécourt papers and had understood it to be "a small satire and in which it delicately treats diverse grave questions of great momentary concern, among others the civil and political rights of actors." It would be a mistake to accept without independent corroboration the "facts" and "points of view" expressed in the document. Brown is also subject to errors of his own, such as translating *comédiens forains* incorrectly as "foreign actors" (p. 43) rather than, as it should be, "strolling," "street" or "fair actors."

13. Robert Isherwood, "Entertainment in the Parisian Fairs in the Eighteenth Century," *Journal of Modern History,* 53 (1981) p. 48. Isherwood uses Mikhail Bakhtin, *Rabelais and His World,* Helene Iswolsky trans. (Cambridge, 1968) on pp. 27-29.

14. Marvin Carlson, *The Theatre of the French Revolution* (Ithaca, New York, 1966), p.v.

Prelude I

1. Louis Petit de Bachaumont, *Mémoires secrets pour servir à l'histoire de la république des lettres en France* (London, 1777-1789), vol. 19, pp. 107-108 (28 June 1769).

2. Reprinted in François de Dainville, "Lieux d'affichage des Comédiens à Paris en 1753," *Revue d'histoire du théâtre,* III (1951), pp. 248-53.

3. Louis Sebastien Mercier, *Tableau de Paris,* nouvelle ed. (Amsterdam, 1783-1789), vol. 12, pp. 6-8.

4. *Cahier. Plaintes et doléances de Messieurs les Comédiens-français* (n.p., 1789).

5. *Mémoire et consultation sur la cause pendante en la Grand-Chambre du Parlement entre les Comédiens Français, le sieur Nicolet, et les autres Entrepreneurs des Spectacles Forains* (n.p., 1785), p. 11.

6. *Cahier... de Messieurs les Comédiens Français.*

7. Sélis, *Lettre sur les petits spectacles,* p. 40.

Chapter 1

1. The Comédie-Française and the Comédie-Italienne, both of which had been receiving annual pensions from the king since the late seventeenth century, were governed by the First Gentlemen of the Bedchamber until 1760. At this time their direction passed to the Intendents of Petty Entertainments (Menus Plaisirs), and in 1786 to the commissioners of the Royal Household. The Opéra received no regular pension from the king until 1780, although the royal academy was authorized to demand tribute from other stages for the use of song and dance. Throughout the eighteenth century, the Opéra passed erratically from under the direction of the city of Paris to that of the government and back again; in 1780 it was withdrawn once more from the city and placed under the direction of Papillon de la Ferté, Intendent of Petty Entertainments and royal commissioner attached to the Academy of

Music. For greater detail see Max Aghion, *Le Théâtre à Paris au XVIIIe siècle* (Paris, 1926) and Eugène André Despois, *Le Théâtre français sous Louis XIV* (Paris, 1894).

2. Joseph Nicolet Guyot, *Le Grand vocabulaire françois* (Paris, 1767-74), vol. 23, p. 313 (1772).

3. Nicolas Toussaint LeMoyne Des Essarts, *Les Trois Théâtres de Paris ou abrégé historique de l'établissement de la Comédie Françoise, de la Comédie Italienne et de l'Opéra* (Paris, 1777), p. 132.

4. Jules Bonnassiès, *Les Spectacles forains et la Comédie-française* (Paris, 1875), pp. 85-93.

5. The Hôtel de Bourgogne, founded in 1548, had a long history of exploitation, now by the Confrèrie, now by troupes of actors, cessionaries of the Confrèrie privilege. In 1675 the actors of the Hôtel de Bourgogne became legal titularies of the theatrical privilege long held by the Confrèrie. The Théâtre de Marais was established by provincial actors in the years 1600-1629. Molière's troupe settled in Paris in 1658. Italian players had a history nearly as long as the actors of the Hôtel de Bourgogne, first appearing in Paris sometime around 1570 and fixing themselves in a definite way in 1660. (Aghion, *Le Théâtre à Paris,* pp. 162-63). Spanish players were called by the Queen in 1660, and left in 1672. (Bonnassiès, *Les Spectacles forains,* pp. 85-96.) According to Emile Campardon, *Les Spectacles de la Foire* (Paris, 1877), 2 vols., it was at the end of the sixteenth century that the fairgrounds first began attracting actors and other forms of entertainment.

6. See Campardon, *Spectacles,* vol. 1, p. 179, article *Brioché* and Despois, *Théâtre français,* p. 85, citation of Colbert's correspondence for June 29, 1671, "that the king wanted very much to permit Brioché this exercise."

7. Quoted in Despois, *Théâtre français,* p. 80.

8. Pierre Clement, ed., *Lettres, Instructions et Mémoires de Colbert* (Paris, 1868), vol. 5, p. 551.

9. Despois, *Le Théâtre français,* p. 84, n. 1 cites this "unedited piece;" Campardon, *Spectacles,* vol. 2, p. 286, article Pygmées, corrects some mistakes of dating in Despois.

10. The ordinance is collected in *Recueil général des Anciennes Lois Françaises 420 à 1789* (Paris, 1821-1833), vol. 19, p. 253. Also as royal order (lettre de cachet) it is reprinted in Parfaict frères, *Histoire du Théâtre-françois depuis son origine jusqu'à présent* (Paris, 1747), vol. 12, p. 6.

11. Despois, *Le Théâtre français,* p. 82.

12. Clement, *Lettres de Colbert,* vol. 5, p. 551, n. 2.

13. Despois, *Le Théâtre français,* pp. 84-86; Campardon, *Spectacles,* vol. 2, p. 287, gives no date for suppression but suggests after 1678.

14. *Recueil des Lois,* vol. 19, p. 253.

15. A ruling or internal regulation for the king's troupe of Italian actors in 1684 indicates that these players, subordinate to the First Gentlemen of the Bedchamber, were considered a privileged company on the order of the French actors, who also received an order of internal regulation in 1684. See Campardon, *Les Comédiens du Roi de la troupe italienne, documents inédits* (Paris, 1880), vol. 2, p. 225.

16. *Mémoire sur la cause en la Grand' Chambre,* p. 14.

17. François Hédelin, abbé d'Aubignac, *La pratique du théâtre* (Amsterdam, 1715), reprinted in *Theorie und Geschichte der literatur und der Schönen Künste* (Munich, 1971) [pagination of the original], p. 65.

18. D'Aubignac appended to his *Pratique du théâtre* a *Projet pour le Rétablissement du Théâtre François,* a plan interrupted by the death of Cardinal Richelieu. D'Aubignac's later sentiments are quoted in Réné Bray, *La Formation de la doctrine classique en France* (Paris, 1963), p. 135, from d'Aubignac's *First Dissertation* (1663).

19. Bray, *Formation de la doctrine classique,* p. 132. For Bray, the classical doctrine, inspired by antiquity, was condemned by its essence to neglect "the ignorant people and the poorly-educated bourgeoisie . ."

20. Georges Duby, ed., *Histoire de la France* (Paris, 1970), p. 281 and Gustave Lanson, *Histoire de la littérature française,* 12th ed. (Paris, 1912), pp. 497-99.

21. D'Aubignac argued in his *Projet du théâtre,* p. 348, of *Pratique du théâtre* that these genres were closely tied to "an ill desire to please the little people." Boileau scorned the burlesque, a bawdy genre in vogue amongst aristocrats, as an irrational and trivial literature that had originated among the people.

22. If only less a friend of the people in his learned tableau,
He [Molière] had not had his characters grimace so often,
Had not quit, for buffoonery, what is agreeable and fine,
And had not shamelessly married Tabarin [king of buffoons in early 17th century French theater] to Terence.
— Nicolas Boileau-Despréaux, *Art poétique* in *Oeuvres complètes* (Paris, 1966), pp. 157-85 (translation mine).

23. Arthur Pougin, *Dictionnaire historique et pittoresque du théâtre* (Paris, 1885), p. 612, writes that the Pont-Neuf in the seventeenth century "was the rendezvous of all the street singers of Paris, who sold their merchandise there, and made audible to all passersby the facile and naive airs of their songs . . . thus when one wants to describe a flat, trivial melody without accent or color, one says scornfully: *It is a pont-neuf.*"

24. Boileau, *Art poétique,* Chant III (translation mine).

25. "Withdrawal" is the term used by Burke, *Popular Culture* and by Natalie Z. Davis, *Society and Culture in Early Modern France* (Stanford, 1965), to articulate, as Davis notes on p. 265, the process by which the "social and cultural distance between the learned and the people widened . . ."

26. E.B.O. Borgerhoff, *The Evolution of Liberal Theory and Practice in the French Theater 1680-1757* (Princeton, 1936).

27. Guyot, *Le Grand vocabulaire,* vol. 3, p. 115 (1768), article *Art.*

28. *Encyclopédie ou Dictionnaire raisonné des sciences, des arts et des métiers,* Denis Diderot and Jean le Rond d'Alembert, eds. (Paris, 1751-1765), article *Spectacles.*

29. Guyot, *Le Grand vocabulaire,* vol. 6, p. 253, (1768), article *Comédie.*

30. Des Essarts, *Les Trois Théâtres,* p. 135.

31. Campardon, *Spectacles,* vol. 2, pp. 250-85, resumé and reprints of documents pertaining to the early eighteenth century fair theater.

32. See Campardon, *Spectacles,* vol. 2, for particulars, including the transfer of ownership of the fair theaters to two Swiss Guards in the Royal Household so that the case, defeated in Parlement, might be carried out before the Provost of Town Hall, whose jurisdiction concerned cases of the Royal Household. Campardon also notes the intervention of the Cardinal d'Estrées, abbé of Saint Germain des Près, in favor of the fair theaters.

33. Campardon, *Spectacles*, vol. 2, p. 261, decision of Parlement, the 21st of March, 1708.

34. For this and the following, see Campardon, *Spectacles*, vol. 2, resumé and reprint of documents pertaining to the Opéra-Comique, pp. 191-202, and decision of the State Council (Conseil d'Etat), p. 285.

35. Campardon, *Spectacles*, vol. 2, pp. 191-202; Brockett, "Fair Theatres of Paris," pp. 251-70.

36. Ernest Boysse, ed., *Journal de Papillon de la Ferté* (Paris, 1887), 26 February 1769: "We have had some anxieties, these last days, over the subject of fair spectacles. The lieutenant of police having asked me, in order to avoid all these discussions in future, to name two royal actors to examine the plays of Nicolet, Audinot and others..."

37. The allegation of brutal censorship by the royal actors is found throughout the primary sources, for example: Mercier, *Tableau*, vol. 3, pp. 22-25, vol. 8, p. 35; Pierre Jean Baptiste Nougaret, ed., *Les Spectacles des foires et des Boulevards de Paris* (Paris, 1773-1788), 5th part, p. 75; Pidansat de Mairobert, *L'Espion anglais, ou Correspondance secrète entre MyLord All'Eye et MyLord All'Ear* (London, 1783-1784), vol. 10, p. 7. See also secondary sources: Campardon, *Spectacles*, vol. 1, p. xxxi; Bonnassiès, *Spectacles forains*, p. 64.

38. Bonnassiès, *Spectacles forains*, p. 64, cites one royal actor as having conceded privately that he refused several plays and cut several scenes that had been worthy of the royal stage.

39. Bibliothèque de la Comédie-française. Ms. Registre pour les pièces des spectacles des Boulevards. Although the Italian actors were included in the review of boulevard plays, as is evident from remarks in the register of the French actors, their decisions are not included, nor do they exist in a register of their own.

40. Ibid. Quotes and examples of censorship in this paragraph are taken from the French actors' register.

41. Ibid.

42. Ibid.

43. Mercier, *Tableau*, vol. 3, pp. 22, 25, 35 (1783). See also Nougaret, *Spectacles des foires*, 5th part, p. 75; and Thomas Rousseau, *Lettre à M*** sur les spectacles des boulevards* (Bruxelles et Paris, 1781), pp. 7-9.

44. Friedrich Melchior Grimm, *Correspondance littéraire, philosophique et critique* (Paris, 1877-82), vol. 3, p. 281.

45. [Sélis], *Lettre sur les petits spectacles*, p. 8.

46. Guyot, *Le Grand vocabulaire*, vol. 6, p. 253.

47. Louis Sebastien Mercier, *Du théâtre; ou, nouvel essai sur l'art dramatique* (Amsterdam, 1773), p. 3, n. a.

48. Luc-Vincent Thiery, *Almanach du voyageur à Paris* (Paris, n.d.), for 1783, p. 421.

49. None of the previous studies of boulevard theater in the eighteenth century—Maurice Albert, *Les Théâtres de la Foire (1660-1789)* (New York, 1970, original copyright 1900); Bonnassiès, *Spectacles forains;* and Louis Henry Lecomte, *Histoire des Théâtres de Paris, Les Variétés Amusantes* (Paris, 1908)—consider the integrating effects of the reorganization of theater in 1784-85, as developed below. Moreover, my concern for the legal structure of that reorganization distinguishes my analysis of the Variétés-Amusantes court case from the repetition of detail that Bonnassiès and Lecomte garnered from Bachaumont, *Mémoires secrets*, vols. 26-29, and several archival documents. Bonnassiès does devote a chapter to the

conflict in French political life between theatrical privilege and theatrical liberty, but his discussion is less an historical analysis than an impassioned plea for the virtues of a free stage.

50. Text of decree reproduced in Campardon, *Spectacles*, vol. 1, p. xxxv.

51. For text of lease and other documents pertaining to the Variétés-Amusantes in particular, see Lecomte, *Variétés Amusantes*, pp. 104-105 and *passim*. Much information on this court case comes verbatim from Bachaumont, *Mémoires secrets*, vols. 26-29.

52. Archives Nationales (hereinafter referred to as A.N.) Ms. H^2 2158. Bureau de la ville. Théâtres des Variétés-Amusantes et l'Ambigu, 1785-86.

53. Ibid.

54. Lecomte, *Variétés Amusantes*, pp. 106-107.

55. A.N. Ms. V^7 492. Conseil députés... pour juger en dernier ressort les contestations concernant les grandes et contravention du Tabac; Lecomte, *Variétés Amusantes*, p. 107.

56. Bachaumont, *Mémoires secrets*, vol. 30, p. 33 (26 November 1785); Bonnassiès, *Spectacles forains*, p. 79.

57. A.N. Ms. AJ^{13} 10. Redevances dues à l'Opéra, Copie du Bail passé... 22 avril 1786.

58. The Comédie-Française had summoned the Ambigu-Comique and Théâtre de Nicolet in 1778, the Elèves de l'Opéra in 1779 and the Variétés-Amusantes in 1781. In a memoir dated August 22, 1784, to Baron Breteuil, minister in the Royal Household, the French actors expressed regret for not pressing legal proceedings in past years out of deference to superiors in the ministry. Bonnassiès, *Spectacles forains*, p. 69, suggests that it is more likely that they knew their case would fail in the courts.

59. *Mémoire sur la cause en Grand'Chambre*, and cited in Bachaumont, *Mémoires secrets*, vol. 29, p. 115 (27 June 1785).

60. Bachaumont, *Mémoires secrets*, vol. 27, p. 44 (28 November 1784).

61. Grimm, *Correspondance*, vol. 14, p. 193 (August 1785).

62. *Mémoire en réponse et Consultation pour les Entrepreneurs du Spectacle des Variétés, contre les Comédiens françois*, cited at length in Bachaumont, *Mémoires secrets*, vol. 29, p. 169 (28 July 1785).

63. See pp. 20-21 citation of the ordinance of 1680. Note that this argument is similar in nature to that in the *Mémoire des entrepreneurs des Spectacles forains* against the Comédie-Française, dated 4 July 1785. In this memoir, cited by Bonnassiès, *Spectacles forains*, p. 76, the entrepreneurs claimed that the royal company's privilege was not a "patrimonial property; it is only a domanial good, perpetually under the eye of the Administration, which can modify the usufruct."

64. Bachaumont, *Mémoires secrets*, vol. 29, p. 169 (28 July 1785), p. 201 (14 August 1785).

65. Pierre Jean Baptiste Nougaret, *De l'art du théâtre* (Paris, 1769), vol. 1, pp. 123, 124, 131.

66. This concern for the moral utility of popular theater had its roots in a longstanding debate on the social influence of the stage that had raged in France during the seventeenth and early eighteenth centuries and had been renewed in 1758 by Jean-Jacques Rousseau's *Lettre à M. d'Alembert sur les spectacles*. But whereas Rousseau, and before him the Church, had condemned the stage for its false and immoral values, partisans of the stage since the early eighteenth century thought to grant theater reprieve in return for a moral purpose. After mid-century their arguments were applied to the popular stage. See Louis Bourquin, "La

Controverse sur la comédie au XVIIIe siècle," *Revue d'histoire littéraire de la France,* XXVI (1919), pp. 43-86, 555-76; XXVII (1920), pp. 548-70; XXVIII (1921), pp. 549-74 and Marguerite Moffat, *Rousseau et la querelle du théâtre au 18e siècle* (Paris, 1930).

67. Mercier, *Tableau,* vol. 3, p. 25 (1783).

68. Clement De Lornaizon, *Addresse à MM. les représentants de la Commune de Paris* [1790], p. 11.

69. Guyot, *Le Grand vocabulaire,* vol. 3, p. 115.

70. Nougaret, *Spectacles des foires,* 7th part, p. 75; Mercier, *Tableau,* vol. 3, p. 25.

71. Bachaumont, *Mémoires secrets,* vol. 28, pp. 5-6 (1 January 1785).

72. Bibliothèque Nationale (hereinafter B.N.), nouvelles acquisitions françaises (hereinafter n.a.f.). Ms. 3045. Papiers de la Gaité; Thiery, *Almanach du voyageur,* vol. for 1783.

73. [Mayeur de St. Paul], *Le Désoeuvré, ou l'Espion du Boulevard du Temple* (London, 1781 and 1782), p. 114. See also François Métra, et al., *Correspondance secrète, politique et littéraire, ou Mémoires pour servir à l'histoire des cours, des sociétés et de la littérature en France...* (London, 1787-1788), 19 December 1781, for similar observation of change and De Lornaizon, *Addresse,* p. 9, on the point that morals of the popular stage equalled those of the great stages. See also Mercier, *Tableau,* vol. 8, p. 35.

74. *Annonces, affiches et avis divers* (also known as *Petites Affiches*) (Paris, 1783-1811), April 1785, p. 990.

75. See letter to Baron de Breteuil and ruling of 25 March 1786 reprinted in Lecomte, *Variétés-Amusantes,* pp. 130-33.

76. Ibid.

77. *Annonces,* May 1786, p. 1141; August 1786, p. 2167.

78. Jacques A. Dulaure, *Nouvelle description des curiosités de Paris,* 2nd ed. (Paris, 1787), vol. 2, p. 353.

79. Ibid., p. 352.

80. Dulaure, *Description des curiosités;* Thiery, *Almanach du voyageur; Annonces;* [Pierre Jean Baptiste Nougaret], *Les Numéros parisiens, ouvrage utile et nécessaire aux voyageurs à Paris* (Paris, 1788).

81. *Les Spectacles de Paris et de toute la France; ou, Calendrier historique et chronologique des théâtres* (Paris, 1792), 41st part, avis préliminaire.

82. *Archives parlementaires de 1787-1860, Recueil complet des débats législatifs et politiques des Chambres françaises,* ed. M.J. Mavidal and M.E. Laurent (hereinafter referred to as *A.P.*) (Paris, 1862-1919), ser. 1, vol. 22, p. 214.

83. See *Actes de la Commune de Paris pendant la Révolution,* ed. Sigismond Lacroix (Paris, 1894-1914; New York, 1973-1974), vol. 4, pp. 512-13.

84. Ibid. p. 519.

85. A continual hesitancy between monopolistic privilege on the one hand and liberty on the other had characterized the regulation of French industry generally since the early 1700s, and most obviously in the years 1750-1770. See P.M. Bondois, "L'Organisation industrielle et commerciale sous l'ancien régime. Le privilège exclusif au XVIIIe siècle," *Revue d'histoire économique et sociale,* XXI (1933), pp. 140-89.

86. The ordinance of 1680 created the monopoly of the Comédie-Française "in order to render future representations of comedies more perfect." As for the Opéra, the ordinance of 30 April 1673 which regulated the number of musicans allowed to the French actors restricted their number in order that the Opéra "have all the perfection that it must hope for [with musicians]..." See *Recueil des Lois,* vol. 19, pp. 110, 253.

87. Grimm, *Correspondance,* vol. 14, p. 193 (August 1785).

88. *Figaro aux Parisiens, amateurs du bon goût, des arts, des spectacles et de la liberté* (Paris, 1790), pp. 10-11.

89. [Sélis], *Lettre sur les petits spectacles,* p. 18.

90. Etienne-Nicolas Framery, *De l'organisation des spectacles de Paris* (Paris, 1790), p. 214; [Sélis], *Lettre sur les petits spectacles,* p. 39-40.

91. Framery, *L'Organisation des spectacles,* pp. 87-88.

92. *A.P.,* vol. 22, p. 214.

93. Ibid., Article 2.

94. See De Lornaizon, *Addresse; Figaro aux Parisiens;* Framery, *L'Organisation des spectacles; Influence de la Révolution sur le théâtre français, pétition à ce sujet addressée à la Commune de Paris* (Paris, 1790); Millin de Grandmaison, *Sur la liberté du théâtre* (Paris, 1790); *Rapport de MM. les commissaires nommés par la Commune, relativement aux spectacles, du 27 mars 1790,* reprinted in *Actes de la Commune,* vol. 4, p. 515.

95. [Sélis], *Lettre sur les petits spectacles,* p. 35.

96. Ibid., p. 39.

97. Article 1. On interpretation of the Declaration of the Rights of Man and Citizen, see Albert Soboul, *The French Revolution 1787-1799,* trans. Alan Forrest and Colin Jones (New York, 1975), pp. 176-77; Albert Goodwin, *The French Revolution* (New York, 1965), revised edition, p. 75; and text of Declaration itself.

98. *Figaro aux Parisiens,* p. 9.

99. *Almanach général de tous les spectacles de Paris et des provinces,* attributed to Cousin Jacques, Mayeur de St. Paul, César Ribié and St. Aubin, eds. (Paris, 1791-1792), p. 5 (1791).

Chapter 2

1. I am indebted in my approach to the interaction between boulevard theaters and the privileged powers of eighteenth century French society to the "cultural" study of entrepreneurial activity developed by a group of economic historians, notably Thomas C. Cochran, W.T. Easterbrook and others, whose articles are compiled in Hugh G.J. Aitken's *Explorations in Enterprise* (Cambridge, Mass., 1965).

2. Dulaure, *Description des curiositiés,* vol. 1, p. 87: "la voule sur le verd gazon."

3. Brazier, *Histoire des petits théâtres,* vol. 1, p. 175.

4. Dulaure, *Description des curiosités,* vol. 1, pp. 86, 87.

5. Carlo Goldoni, *Mémoires de M. Goldoni pour servir à l'histoire de sa vie et à celle de son théâtre* (Paris, 1787), in Jean-François Barrières, *Bibliothèque des Mémoires,* vol. 6, p. 453.

6. Brazier, *Histoire des petits théâtres,* vol. 1, pp. 175-76.

7. Ibid., p. 175.

8. For what follows, see police records compiled by Campardon, *Spectacles*, vol. 2, pp. 111, 166-68; vol. 1, pp. 149-50, 366-68.

9. In 1759 Viarme de Pontcarré, Provost of Merchants, authorized billiards and taverns on the boulevard du Temple, a good indication that the locale had begun to hum with activity. See Bonnassiès, *Spectacles forains*, pp. 56-57.

10. B.N. n.a.f. Ms. 3045.

11. *Mémoire sur la cause en la Grand' Chambre*. Note that the spokesmen for the Comédie-Française place the date of the "revolution" at 1764.

12. According to Campardon, *Spectacles*, in 1762, Bienfait sold to Rossignol, who dropped from view; there is no record of Gaudon on the boulevard after 1767; Nicolet frère ran on hard times in the late 1760s and wandered the fairs until his death (?) in 1778.

13. Biographical material on Jean-Baptiste Nicolet appears in Campardon, *Spectacles*, vol. 2, pp. 151-64 and in Edmond Denis de Manne and C. Ménétrier, *Galerie historique des comédiens de la troupe de Nicolet* (Lyon, 1869).

14. It must be assumed that de Manne and Ménétrier, *La troupe de Nicolet*, are in error here. They claim that Nicolet succeeded to the marionette show of sieur Bienfait in 1756. Campardon, *Spectacles*, on the other hand, states 1) that Nicolet had held a puppet booth since 1753 and 2) that Bienfait II, in association with Pierre-Toussaint Martin, in fact held his own marionette show until 1762. Since Campardon based his account upon a scrupulous examination of police records as well as anecdotal sources of information, his history is preferred.

15. Bonnassiès, *Spectacles forains*, p. 57, writes that Nicolet settled on the boulevard in 1759-60 in order to perform a tight-rope dancing act. "Those were the limitations placed upon him, for the moment, by the act of authorization; he could neither sing nor speak." Unfortunately, Bonnassiès gives no direct or indirect evidence of the act of authorization of which he speaks. In all probability he refers to the suppression of speech on the minor stages, of which more below, in 1764, five years *after* Nicolet moved to the boulevard. For the years 1759-1764 his account differs significantly from those of de Manne and Ménétrier and Campardon, who argue that Nicolet moved to the boulevard with a marionette show. Brazier, a boulevard playwright of the early nineteenth century and full of misinformation himself, claimed that Nicolet succeeded to the tight-rope dancing spectacle of a sieur Restier in 1770 (in *Histoire des petits théâtres*, vol. 1, p. 1). This, too, is untenable, since it is known that Nicolet began to perform tight-rope dancing at least as early as 1762. According to Campardon, Restier II directed his troupe of tight-rope dancers at the Saint Laurent and Saint Germain Fairs at least until the fire of 1762 destroyed his hall at the Saint Germain Fair. It is possible, as far as such guesswork goes, that Nicolet purchased Restier's license at this time. This is claimed, at least, in *Recueil des Pièces qui ont eu le plus de succès sur les théâtres de la rue Richelieu, ci-devant des Variétés-amusantes, et théâtres du Palais-royal; sur celui des Petits Comédiens du Palais-royal, dits Beaujolais; sur celui de l'Ambigu-Comique, au Boulevart; sur celui de la Gaité, ci-devant les Grands-Danseurs du Roi; sur celui des Elèves de l'Opéra*, etc. (Paris, 1791), vol. 1, p. 2. It is also possible that both men held similar permissions at the same time. A certain Pierre Toussaint Gagneur, according to Campardon, formed part of Restier's troupe of tight-rope dancers in 1754; in 1762 he worked for Nicolet, and in the following year in 1763 he returned to Restier.

16. See the petition of the Italian actors to the lieutenant-general of police in 1762, reprinted in Campardon, *Les Comédiens de la Troupe italienne*, vol. 2, p. 285. See also de Manne and

Ménétrier, *La troupe de Nicolet,* p. 3; *Humble Mémoire du sieur Nicolet* (n.p., n.d.), reprinted in de Manne and Ménétrier, *La troupe de Nicolet,* p. 5n; *Placet aux Dames* (n.p., n.d.), reprinted in Campardon, *Spectacles,* vol. 2, pp. 158-64.

17. Quoted in Bonnassiès, *Spectacles forains,* p. 57.

18. Hubert Méthivier, *Le Siècle de Louis XV* (Paris, 1972), chapter 6.

19. This growth estimate appears in the contemporary source, B.N. fonds français (f.f.) Ms. 9557, fol. 2, *Spectacles inférieurs,* avril 1764. Modern scholars believe that of a Parisian population of some 600,000 or 700,000, an estimated 355,350 belonged to the laboring poor, perhaps another 100,000 need account for seasonal migrants. See Jeffry Kaplow, *The Names of Kings: the Parisian Laboring Poor in the Eighteenth Century* (New York, 1972), pp. 18, 32.

20. Méthivier, *Le siècle de Louis XV,* p. 60; Kaplow, *Names of Kings.*

21. Campardon, *Les Comédiens de la troupe italienne,* pp. 288-89.

22. Boysse, ed., *Journal de Papillon de la Ferté,* p. 74 (1 June 1762).

23. As a Gentleman of the Bedchamber the Maréchal de Richelieu held, along with three others, jurisdiction over the Comédie-Française and the Comédie-Italienne. In 1760 the First Gentlemen of the Bedchamber charged Papillon de la Ferté, Intendent of Petty Entertainments, with a more direct surveillance and management of the two companies. However, they continued, as is obvious in this affair, to exercise great authority themselves. See Boysse, ed., *Journal de Papillon de la Ferté,* p. 137 (February 1764).

24. Grimm, *Correspondance,* vol. 6, p. 100.

25. Probably by the police. See *Placet aux Dames.*

26. It is argued from internal evidence that B.N. Ms. f.f. 9557, fol. 2, *Spectacles inférieurs,* is a government document. The memoir suggests that the ministry will block the petition of the Comédie-Française and the Comédie-Italienne and that the Prosecutor-General will oppose the adjudication. Obviously the author was privy to the general commotion over the minor spectacles amongst officials in the Royal Household since February 1764 (see Boysse, ed., *Journal de Papillon de la Ferté,* p. 137 (19 February 1764). It seems likely that the police would have been in a position to know what the ministry was planning; moreover, as will become obvious below, it was the police who were anxious to protect the fair theaters from suppression, for precisely the reasons argued in *Spectacles inférieurs.*

27. B.N. Ms. f.f. 9557, fol. 2, *Spectacles inférieurs.*

28. These were obviously the cheapest of seats in Nicolet's theater before the ordinance of 1768. The author of the memoir carefully skirted the fact that the boulevard theater drew heavily upon a more prosperous citizenry for its audience as well—Nicolet's most expensive seats, at 6 livres, being comparable to prices at the Comédie-Française.

29. B.N. Ms. f.f. 9557, fol. 2, *Spectacles inférieurs.*

30. Ibid.

31. *Placet aux Dames.*

32. The most important arguments of the *Placet aux Dames* included those later developed by men of letters and playwrights in opposition to the property rights and dramatic monopoly of the Comédie-Française. In fact, the *Placet* served as a forum for certain specific grievances of those playwrights, whose discontent culminated in the mid-1770s and early 1780s in a limited reform of dramatic legislation regulating the remuneration of authors by the royal company.

See Jules Bonnassiès, *Les auteurs dramatiques et la Comédie française à Paris aux XVIIe et XVIIIe siècles* (Paris, 1874).

33. *Placet aux Dames.* Grimm's remarks in his *Correspondance,* vol. 6, p. 100, indicate an upper-class component of the audience at Nicolet's: "... his actors disfigure [the comedies of Molière] to the point of boredom and put all the partisans of the boulevard to flight." Only those who knew the performances of the same plays by the Comédie-Française would have been bored with the comparison; and the public at this royal theater was predominantly wealthy and notable.

34. *Placet aux Dames.*

35. A commissioner of police found the *Placet aux Dames* "an indecent critique against all the theaters of Paris and insulting towards Mister Nicolet..." Document reprinted in Campardon, *Spectacles,* vol. 2, pp. 157-158.

36. On this idea of theater as a school of virtue, see Borgerhoff, *Evolution of Liberal Theory,* and F. Gaiffe, *Le Drame en France au XVIIIe siècle* (Paris, 1910).

37. According to [Pierre Jean Baptiste Nougaret], *La littérature renversée, ou l'art de faire des pièces de théâtre sans paroles* (Berne and Paris: 1775), p. 45n., Lamoignon de Malesherbes pronounced the following discourse to the Académie française: "The public appointed itself as a Tribunal, independent of all Powers and which all Powers respect, that evaluates all talents, that pronounces on all kinds of merit.... This truth, which I expose to the assembly of Men of Letters, has already been presented to the Magistrates, and none have refused to acknowledge this Tribunal of the Public as the sovereign judge of all the judges of the land." I have been unable to verify whether or not the quotation is entirely accurate. John Lough, in *Writer and Public in France* (Oxford and New York, 1978) concerns himself with the formation of an influential public opinion. He quotes Duclos, who in 1751 recognized that the empire of intellectuals was most extensive, because "in the long run they form public opinion, which sooner or later masters or overcomes all kinds of fanaticism" (p. 244). In the 1780s Mercier assigned men of letters the sanction of law and morals in France. Thus, for Lough, "by the second half of the eighteenth century" men of letters claimed a social function, and "this claim was admitted by the general public" (p. 246).

38. Grimm, *Correspondance,* vol. 6, p. 101.

39. Mercier, *Du Théâtre.*

40. Documents reprinted in Campardon, *Spectacles,* vol. 2, pp. 157-58.

41. Text reprinted in de Manne and Ménétrier, *Troupe de Nicolet,* p. 5, n. 3 (dated 9 July 1764).

42. *Humble Mémoire.*

43. Ibid.

44. *Placet aux Dames.*

45. Response of Comédie-Française, reprinted in de Manne and Ménétrier, *Troupe de Nicolet,* p. 6n.

46. Grimm, *Correspondance,* vol. 8, p. 232.

47. Boysse, ed., *Journal de Papillon de la Ferté,* pp. 191-92 (19 August 1766).

48. Nicolas-Médard Audinot, destined to become one of the more important boulevard entrepreneurs and chief rival of Nicolet, had at this point opened a marionette show at the Saint-Germain fair. He did not move his theater to the boulevard until 1769.

49. *Mémoire sur la cause en la Grand-Chambre.*

50. Bachaumont, *Mémoires secrets,* vol. 4, p. 38.

51. Ordinance 14 avril 1768, reprinted in Des Essarts, *Les Trois Théâtres,* p. 142, n. 1.

52. Boysse, ed., *Journal de Papillon de la Ferté,* p. 236. The Maréchal wanted the Opéra "to close the Théâtre de Nicolet, although it had been agreed to the contrary some time ago with the lieutenant of police.... I don't imagine that the minister [Saint-Florentin] will fall in with the desires of M. le Maréchal on this subject" (12 December 1768).

53. E. Beatrice Abbott, in "Robineau, dit de Beaunoir, et les petits théâtres du XVIIIe siècle," *Revue d'Histoire littéraire de France,* XXXXIII (1936), p. 34, states that a ruling of the police (1768? 1769?) forbade song at the fair theaters, which necessitated the development of a new genre, the *parade.* There is no evidence of this ruling, but the Papillon diary suggests a mechanism for the suppression of song on the boulevard in 1768-1769—the pressures of the Maréchal de Richelieu.

54. Bachaumont, *Mémoires secrets,* vol. 4, p. 228 (9 February 1769).

55. Document reprinted in de Manne and Ménétrier, *Troupe de Nicolet,* p. 7, n. 5.

56. Ordinance 14 avril 1768, in Des Essarts, *Les Trois Théâtres,* p. 142, n. 1.

57. *Mémoire sur la cause en la Grand-Chambre.*

58. Ordinance 14 avril 1768, in Des Essarts, *Les Trois Théâtres,* p. 142, n. 1.

59. Boysse, ed., *Journal de Papillon de la Ferté,* p. 242 (30 January 1769).

60. Grimm, *Correspondance,* vol. 8, p. 232.

61. Bachaumont, *Mémoires secrets,* vol. 4, p. 228; Pidansat de Mairobert, *L'Espion anglais,* vol. 10, p. 11; Mercier, *Tableau,* vol. 8, p. 36.

62. The Registre des Déliberations du Bureau de l'Hôtel Dieu may be found at the Archives de l'Assistance publique in Paris. Some of the deliberations were reprinted by L. Brièle, *Collection de Documents pour servir à l'histoire des hôpitaux de Paris* (Paris, 1883), vol. 2.

63. A.N. Ms. Y12227. Archives des Commissaires. Police des Foires Saint Laurent et Saint Ovide à Paris, 1763-1783, document dated 1776. Archives de l'Assistance publique. Ms. Liasse 1438. Registre des Déliberations du Bureau de l'Hôtel Dieu, entry March 1774. See also Brièle, *Documents des hopitaux,* vol. 2, p. 70.

64. For example, in 1762 the Comédie-Française contracted to pay an annual 60,000 livres, an amount that dropped by some 10,000 livres with an act passed in May 1768. The figure 12% is arrived at in the following manner. According to the Register of the Hôtel Dieu, the Comédie-Française had contracted to pay the sum of 20,267 livres to the Hôtel-Dieu. This amount represented two-fifths of the entire poor tax, which would then have been 50,668 livres. Receipts at the Comédie-Française are listed in Claude Alasseur's Table 17, Décomposition de la dépense par poste, p. 155 in her *La Comédie-Française au 18e siècle* (Paris, 1967). In 1768-69 the receipts were 397,518 livres. In 1773, when the boulevard theaters first began paying the poor tax, the Comédie-Française was still paying about the same percentage, 12.54%. From 1773 through 1792-93 receipts at the Comédie-Française did not fall below the level of 1773 and in fact rose significantly. The highest receipts were those of 1784-85, 753,356 livres; in that year the poor tax measured only 6.72% of the royal theater's income.

65. Bibliothèque de l'Arsenal. Ms. 13002. Etat de la recette et de la dépense... Comptabilité du Théâtre des Grands-Danseurs, pour les années 1782-1792. This observation includes 1782 through 1788.

66. A.N. Ms. Y12227.

67. Archives de l'Assistance publique, Liasse 1438. Entries dated 9 août 1780, 11 juillet 1781.

68. The combined income from the major theaters was 64,049 livres. Note that the Hôtel-Dieu records represent only two-fifths of the total poor tax levied. These figures, therefore, reflect no more than one-tenth of gross receipts at the theater doors.

69. Goldoni, *Mémoires,* pp. 453-54.

70. Reprinted in *Catalogues de la Bibliothèque de l'Opéra. Le Cirque, Iconographie* (Paris, 1969).

71. Goldoni, *Mémoires,* p. 454.

72. Bachaumont, *Mémoires secrets,* vol. 8, 4 août 1775.

73. Nougaret, ed., *Spectacles des foires,* 1773-1778. For maturation of Audinot's troupe, see Roselyne La Place, "Des théâtres d'enfants au XVIIIe siècle," *Revue d'Histoire du Théâtre,* 32 (1980), p. 25.

74. Bachaumont, *Mémoires secrets,* vol. 7, p. 80 (7 November 1773).

75. Ibid., vol. 14, p. 260 (21 October 1779).

76. Ibid., vol. 7, p. 91 (7 November 1773).

77. Bonnassiès, *Spectacles forains,* p. 60, does not mention where resistance came from, although he speaks of it generally. Moreover, Bonnassiès mentions that some sources, whether primary or secondary is not specified, indicate that a transaction between Nicolet and the Opéra was passed at the same time as the one with Audinot. Below, I suggest that a contract with Nicolet was probably not passed until after the production of *The Abduction of Europe* or there would have been no complaint by the Opéra against that pantomime.

78. A.N. Ms. AJ^{13} 10, document dated 2 septembre 1779.

79. Aghion, *Théâtre au XVIIIe siècle,* pp. 194-207.

80. A.N. Ms. $0^1$615. Maison du Roi. Lettres de Baron de Breteuil. Letter dated 24 mars 1780, probably Amelot to Papillon.

81. Archives de l'Assistance publique, Ms. Liasse 1438. Entry dated 17 juillet 1780.

82. A.N. Ms. AJ^{13}10. Contract dated 1 mai 1780.

83. A.N. Ms. $0^1$620. Maison du Roi. Comité de l'Opéra. Compte que le Comité rend au Ministre de ce qui s'est passé en son assemblée du Mercredy 8 novembre 1780.

84. A.N. Ms. $0^1$620. Compte que le Comité rend au Ministre de ce qui s'est passé en son assemblée du Samedi 4 novembre 1780.

85. Ibid.

86. A.N. Ms. $0^1$620. Document dated 8 novembre 1780.

87. Bibliothèque de l'Arsenal. Ms. 13002. See Figure 3.

88. A.N. Ms. $0^1$618. Maison du Roi. Privilèges de l'Opéra. Rapports etc. sur les privilèges de l'Opéra.

89. A.N. Ms. $0^1$618. Redevances des Spectacles Forains; Bibliothéque de l'Arsenal. Ms. 13002.

90. Opéra privilege dated 18 July 1784, reprinted in Campardon, *Spectacles,* vol. 1, p. xxxv.

91. Bonnassiès, *Spectacles forains,* p. 68.

92. A.N. Ms. 0^{1} 618. Mémoire concernant la redevance des Spectacles forains, n.d., but after April 1784 and before May 1785.

93. Ibid.; A.N. Ms. 0^{1}845. Grands Officiers de la Maison du Roi. Grand Chambellan. Observations [sur les Spectacles forains], Papillon de la Ferté.

94. A.N. Ms. 0^{1}618. Mémoire concernant la redevance des Spectacles forains.

95. A.N. Ms. 0^{1}845. Observations [sur les Spectacles forains].

96. Ibid.

97. Ibid.

98. Nougaret, ed., *Spectacles des foires,* 4th Part, 1776, p. 9: "You came... *incognito.*"

99. Pidansat de Mairobert, *L'Espion anglais,* vol. 10, p. 9.

100. Document reprinted in Campardon, *Spectacles,* vol. 2, p. 378.

101. Nougaret, ed., *Spectacles de la foire,* 4th Part, 1776, p. vi.

102. *Coup d'oeil rapide sur les spectacles de Paris* (Paris, [1792]), p. 13. See also Métra, et al., *Correspondance,* vol. 7, p. 261 and *passim;* Mercier, *Tableau,* vol. 3, p. 25 and *passim;* and *Influence de la Révolution,* p. 12.

103. Wide social presence: based on records in the A.N. Y series, Archives des Commissaires, especially: Ms. Y15996-Y16009. Office de Vanglenne and Ms. Y16022. Rapports de la garde de Paris 1773-1790. Dress code: Document reprinted in Campardon, *Spectacles,* vol. 2, p. 157; Archives de la Préfecture de Police. Ms. A^{A} 239. Procès-verbaux des commissaires de police... Section du Temple, document 44 dated 31 mars 1791. Note that not until the end of the nineteenth century at cabarets like the Moulin Rouge was tacit seating by class disbanded in French entertainment halls. See on this Duby, ed., *Histoire de la France,* p. 502.

104. John Lough, *Paris Theater Audiences in the Seventeenth and Eighteenth Centuries* (Oxford, 1957), p. 218. Before this time the public of the great theaters had been almost entirely drawn from the aristocracy and the educated middle classes.

105. Ibid., p. 270.

106. Grimm, *Correspondance,* vol. 12, p. 437 (September 1780).

107. Bachaumont, *Mémoires secrets,* vol. 15, p. 45 (5 February 1780); Bibliothèque de la Comédie-française, Registre pour les pièces des spectacles des Boulevards. See also on *The Hussar Wedding,* chapter 6, p. 175.

108. Grimm, *Correspondance,* vol. 14, pp. 45 and 456. See also chapter 6, p. 173.

109. Pidansat de Mairobert, *L'Espion anglais,* vol. 10, p. 7n.

110. La Harpe, *Lycèe ou Cours de littérature ancienne et moderne* (Paris, 1813), vol. 11, pp. 230-31.

111. See Brockett, "Fair Theatres," *passim;* Marian Hannah Winter, *The Theatre of Marvels* (New York, 1964), pp. 40-43.

112. Reprinted in Grimm, *Correspondance,* vol. 8, pp. 359-60.

113. *Almanach de tous les spectacles,* p. 250.

114. C.D. Brenner, *The Theatre Italien, Its Repertory 1716-1793* (Berkeley, 1961), p. 12.

115. Nougaret, ed., *Spectacles des foires,* 8th part, p. 70.

116. [Mayeur de St. Paul], *Le Désoeuvré ou l'Espion du Boulevard du Temple* (Paris: 1907), p. 144. According to documents reprinted by Campardon in his *Spectacles* (see articles listed by proper names) Mlle. Deschamps, Rose-Pétronille Beauménard, Mme. Favart and Dorothée Luzy can be added to the list of artists who passed from the Opéra-Comique to début at the Comédie-Italienne or Comédie-Française. Josephe-Eulalie Audinot, Colombe, Damas, Daubigny, Joséphine Durand, Lelievre, Lolotte and Masson, all originally artists on the boulevard stage, made débuts with one of the royal theaters, three with great success.

117. Bachaumont, *Mémoires secrets,* vol. 16, p. 30 (18 October 1780); see also Métra, et al., *Correspondance,* vol 10, pp. 337-38 (25 November 1780).

118. For example, the boulevard theaters imitated the Figaro plays and *La Partie du chasse;* borrowed scenes for *l'Enlèvement de Proserpine* from *Proserpine de Quinault* and from Ghérardi's *Mezetin et Arlequin; Le Savetier avocat* retouched a comedy of Rosimond; *Le Ravisseur de sa femme* was adapted from a comic opera by Fuzelier. Much of this information comes from reviews of boulevard plays in Nougaret, ed., *Spectacles des foires*

119. Nougaret, *Spectacles des foires,* 4th part, 1776, p. 92; see also 7th part, 1786, pp. 149-50.

120. Brazier, *Histoire des petits théâtres,* vol. 1, pp. 56-57; anecdote must date from before the 1778 death of LeKain.

121. Nougaret ed., *Spectacles des foires,* 7th part, p. 149.

122. A.N. Ms. 0[1]845. Observations [sur les Spectacles forains].

123. Bibliothèque de la Comédie-française. Ms. Registre pour les pièces des spectacles des Boulevards. See discussion of this register in chapter 1, pp. 25-27.

124. Archives de l'Assistance publique. Ms. Liasse 1438. A.N. Ms. 0[1]618 Redevances des Spectacles Forains; Nougaret, ed., *Spectacles des foires,* for 1786 and 1787.

125. A.N. Ms. AJ[13]10, contract dated 24 avril 1786.

126. A.N. Ms. AJ[13]10. Melan contract.

127. Millin de Grandmaison, *Sur la liberté du théâtre,* pp. 49-53, n. 14.

128. Ibid.

129. A.N. Ms. 0[1]617. Maison du Roi. Lettres de Papillon de la Ferté. Réflexions en général: 1780-1790.

130. A.N. Ms. 0[1]618. Redevances des Spectacles Forains.

131. Archives de l'Assistance publique, Ms. Liasse 1438. Entry dated 3 août 1785.

132. *Mémoire sur la cause en Grand Chambre,* p. 3.

133. A.N. Ms. AJ[13]10. Contract dated 22 avril 1786.

134. A.N. Ms. AJ[13]10. Petition by Placide dated 12 octobre 1787.

135. Archives de l'Assistance publique, Ms. Liasse 1438. Entry dated 13 août 1788.

136. Ibid. Entry dated 12 août 1789.

137. Nicolet's last payment to the Hôtel-Dieu was 2,488 livres or 1.6% of his income—payments to the other Hospitals of Paris would have raised his contribution to around 6% of his total income. Note that after August 1790 the Grands-Danseurs, the Variétés-Amusantes and the

Ambigu-Comique, as well as the larger theaters in the city, refused to pay the quarter tax at all.

Prelude II

1. The impressionistic description of boulevard theater offered in the prelude to part II is based on a wide reading of sources—both printed and manuscript—of many different kinds. Although a collection of sources is given for each paragraph, no attempt is made, except where it is deemed necessary, to indicate particular references. For this paragraph, Brazier, *Histoire des petits théâtres. Parade,* showtime, and cost: Nougaret, ed., *Spectacles des foires,* 1773-1788. Theater posters and journal announcements: *Catalogues de la Bibliothèque de l'Opera. Le Cirque Iconographie; Annonces; Journal de Paris.* Crowd and pickpockets: A.N., Y16022; Mercier, *Tableau,* vol. 6, p. 121.

2. Size: *Architectonographie des théâtres, ou Parallèle historique et critique des ces édifices* by Alexis Donnet, Orgiazzi and Jacques-Auguste Kaufmann (Paris, 1837-1840) contains plans for the Ambigu-Comique and the Grands-Danseurs du Roi among other theaters. (See Plate 6.) Both plans represent subsequent improvements on the original buildings. The Ambigu-Comique was apparently renovated or rebuilt in 1791; in 1808 a "new" theater with three tiers of loges or boxes replaced the "old dark smoke-blackened building" that had been the original Grands-Danseurs (Brazier, *Histoire des petits théâtres,* vol. 1, p. 19). It is possible, however, to figure backwards what the dimensions of the original buildings might have been. The only way to expand on the boulevard was up. In assessing the height of the Ambigu-Comique and Grands-Danseurs, therefore, both the third tier of loges in the latter and the slanted roofs in both theaters were eliminated as subsequent additions. In both theaters the stage area was roughly equivalent to that left for seating—the Ambigu-Comique offering a slightly larger area for the audience than the Grands-Danseurs. The volume of the boulevard theaters was approximately one-fifth that of the new Variétés-Amusantes, built at the Palais-Royal in 1784-85. This illustrious building, which later became home to the Comédie-Française, was twice as big as the old Opéra which had burned down in 1781. Numbers: B.N. Ms. f.f. 7005, fol. 8. Recueil de pièces historiques sur la Révolution et l'Empire 1789-1815: Documents sur les théâtres à Paris (1790-1798). Candles: Brazier, *Histoire des petits théâtres,* vol. 1, p. 19; J.W. von Goethe, *Wilhelm Meisters Lehrjahre* (Stuttgart, n.d.), Book I, Chapter XV. Social Composition of Audience: A.N. Ms. Y16022; numerous pamphlets etc., for which see Chapter 2 discussion of audience. Also: Pidansat de Mairobert, *L'Espion anglais; Nougaret, ed., Spectacles des foires;* Mercier, *Tableau de Paris,* vol. 6, p. 121.

3. Public manners: A.N. Ms. Y16022. Occasionally the guard, lacking in military discipline, was responsible itself for the ever-present threat of riot and bloodshed in theater halls. (Bachaumont, *Mémoires secrets,* vol. 14, p. 71 (24 May 1779).

4. Two of the plays chosen for depiction on the stage, *L'Elève de la Nature (The Child of Nature)* and *La Corne de vérité (The Horn of Truth)* were pictured in an engraving accompanying the Dixhuitième Nouvelle of Restif de la Bretonne's *Les Contemporaines* (Paris, 1962; originally published 1780-85), vol. 3. The third, an arlequinade, cannot be identified; *Arlequin Dogue d'Angleterre (Arlequin the English Cerberus)* was substituted. Orchestra, scenery and acting: [Mayeur de St. Paul], *Le Désoeuvré;* B.N. Ms. n.a.f. 3046 Papiers de la Gaité; Mayeur de St. Paul, *L'Elève de la Nature (The Child of Nature),* published 1787; *Recueil des Pièces.* Critics: [Sélis], *Lettre sur les petits spectacles,* p. 13; Framery, *L'organisation des spectacles,* p. 225. Moralizing of audiences: Bachaumont, *Mémoires secrets,* vol. 14, p. 260. For what is perhaps the only consideration of acting style on the great stage of the eighteenth century, see: Dene Barnett, "The Performance Practice of Acting: The Eighteenth Century," *Theatre Research International,* 2 (1977), pp. 157-86; 3 (1977), pp. 1-19; 3 (1978), pp. 79-93.

5. Performance at Nicolet's in the 1760s: Goldoni, *Mémoires,* pp. 453-54. Associés censorship: Brazier, *Histoire des petits théâtres,* pp. 56-57—anecdote must date from before the 1778 death of LeKain. Costumes: Nougaret, ed., *Spectacles des foires,* 7th part, pp. 149-50 (1786), and 8th part, pp. 136-37 (1787). Criticism: *Influence de la Révolution,* p. 11.

6. Burlesque: Nougaret, ed., *Spectacles des foires,* 5th part, p. 142 (1776); *Influence de la Révolution,* p. 11; *Arlequin Dogue d'Angleterre (Arlequin the English Cerberus),* Placide, 1772—based on play of same title by Ghérardi (late 1600s). Police reports on, A.N. Ms. BB^{3}81. Comité de surveillance du Departement de Paris. Registres des séances. *La Corne de Vérité (The Horn of Truth),* Robineau de Beaunoir, 1772, 1776.

7. Bachaumont, *Mémoires secrets,* especially vol. 11, p. 91 (7 November 1773); vol. 14, p. 71 (24 May 1779), p. 130 (31 July 1779), p. 260 (21 October 1779) and vol. 4, p. 22 (9 February 1769).

8. See Winter, *Theatre of Marvels,* for an interesting but unacademic attempt in this direction for a slightly later period of popular theater in Paris.

Chapter 3

1. Nougaret, ed., *Spectacles des foires.* See the list of *emplois* in the 4th Part for 1776 or the 6th Part for 1778. These included the following: Males roles: Les Gilles, d'Arlequin, les Arlequins en second, les Amoureux, les Niais, Crispin, Soldat, Paysan, Père, Bailli, rôles de Taconet, les Savetiers, Caractères, Accessoires. Female roles: Amoureuse, Coquette, l'Amour, Duègne [rôle de vieille femme], Paysanne, Poissarde, Soubrette, les Caractères, Accessoires.

2. In this and the following consideration of the *commedia dell'arte* these secondary texts have been consulted: Gustave Attinger, *L'Esprit de la commedia dell'arte dans le théâtre français* (Paris, 1950); Raymond Lebègue, *Le Théâtre comique en France de Pathelin à Mélite* (Paris, 1972); Allardyce Nicoll, *The World of Harlequin, a critical study of the commedia dell'arte* (Cambridge, England, 1963); Constantin Mic, *La commedia dell'arte ou le théâtre des comédiens italiens des XVIe, XVIIe et XVIIIe siècle* (Paris, 1927).

3. Lebègue, *Théâtre comique,* pp. 29, 64-87, 144, 150 and *passim.* E.J.H. Greene, *Menander to Marivaux, The History of a Comic Structure* (Alberta, Canada, 1977), pp. 12-26, also considers the general influences of French classical comedy. Georges Doutrepont, "Les Types Populaires de la littérature française," *Académie royale de Belgique,* 2e serie, XXII (1926-28), Part i, pp. 177-205, discusses French types and their affinity to those of the *commedia dell'arte.*

4. *Notices sur les oeuvres de théâtre,* for 1755 and 1756, quoted in Attinger, *La commedia dell'arte,* p. 356: "One no longer wants arlequins or Scaramouches."

5. Attinger, *La commedia dell'arte,* pp. 281, 322, 439 and *passim.,* and Mic, *La commedia dell'arte,* p. 234.

6. Lesage and d'Orneval, creators of the comic opera in 1715, relied heavily on the farcical Italian masks and stock characters. This and the following observations on the use of role-types in the fair theater of the early eighteenth century are based on my research in the following collections: Le Sage et d'Orneval, *Le Théâtre de la Foire ou l'Opéra Comique* (Paris, 1721-1731), 8 vols.; *Oeuvres de M. Vadé ou Recueil des opéra-comiques, parodies et pièces fugitives de cet Auteur,* nouvelle ed. (à la Haye, 1785); and a pamphlet collection of plays by Favart at Princeton University.

7. Brockett, "Fair Theatres," pp. 262-63.

8. Paul J. Salvatore, *Favart's Unpublished Plays* (New York, 1935), p. 398.

9. This argument is developed at length by A.P. Moore, *The Genre Poissard and the French Stage of the Eighteenth Century* (New York, 1935).

10. This is entirely borne out in the *Théâtre des Boulevards ou Recueil de Parades,* 1st ed. (Paris, 1756), reprinted by Georges d'Heylli (Paris, 1881).

11. *Oeuvres de M. Vadé,* p. 2.

12. Emile Genest, *L'Opéra-Comique connu et inconnu* (Paris, 1925), pp. 102-105.

13. Nougaret, ed., *Spectacles des foires,* 4th Part, p. 9 (1776).

14. There is no record that savages or fairies were ever numerous enough to have become distinct role-types on their own; when Mayeur appeared as the savage in *L'Elève de la Nature (The Child of Nature),* it was pointedly remarked that this role did not match precisely the usual *emplois* of the actor, those of the lover and the fool. The roles of old men and women, lovers, peasants, and artisans were made to serve a broad range of characterizations. See *Recueil des Pièces,* vol. 5, Jugements et anecdotes for *L'Elève de la Nature.*

15. The lovers, parents, the Bailliff and some masks fall into the category of middle-class bourgeois; the "rôles de Taconet," the peasant, servants and some masks belonged to the lower order of "peuple."

16. See chapter 2, pp. 50-51 for example.

17. There were, of course, some exceptions. Crispin and Frontin, both conceived in the mid- to late-seventeenth century, were considered stock characters (without masks) on the great stage of the eighteenth century. The two types are perhaps evidence that the great tradition itself had still a great deal of oral impetus in the late 1600s and early 1770s. See Doutrepont, "Types populaires," discussion of these characters as well as Pougin, *Dictionnaire du théâtre.* Mic, *Commedia dell'arte,* p. 71, argues that the *commedia dell'arte* developed in an eclectic manner precisely because there was no copyright.

18. The following titles were found in my sampling of boulevard repertories:
    Le Repentir de Figaro, Parisau, 1784, Ambigu-Comique.
    Le Mariage de Cherubin, Gabiot de Salins, 1785, Ambigu-Comique.
    Figaro directeur de Marionnettes, 1785, Beaujolais (Palais-Royal).
    Le Voyage de Figaro, Esclave à Alger, Destival de Braban et Ribié, 1784, Grands-Danseurs du Roi.
    Le Retour de Figaro à Madrid, Destival et Ribié, 1784, Grands-Danseurs.
    Tel Père Tel Fils ou Figaro chez lui, Ribié, 1784, Grands-Danseurs.
    L'Enrôlement (L'Enterrement) de Figaro ou les Rencontres portugaises, Ribié?, 1785, Grands-Danseurs.
    Le Recontre de Cherubin, Grands-Danseurs du Roi. Same as *Figaro à Alger et le combat naval,* 1785, Grands-Danseurs.
    Almanzor, complement, Anonymous, Grands-Danseurs?, 1785, for opening of the Saint Laurent Fair.

    In his *Correspondance,* vol. 14, p. 74, Grimm remarked in November 1784: "What's more, it seems that all the theaters of the boulevards have been allowed to seize upon his [Beaumarchais'] *Marriage of Figaro* as a fund that belongs to them and to draw from it thirty different plays which have almost all succeeded..." See, too, Doutrepont, "Types populaires," pp. 435-56.

19. Costume inventory in B.N. Ms. n.a.f. 3045. Censorship efforts by the French actors: Bibliothèque de la Comédie-Française, Ms. Registre pour les pièces des spectacles des Boulevards.

20. See Discussion of Janot, the Pointu family, Nicodème and Barogo by Doutrepont, "Types populaires," in Part II, Chapter II (suite), IV., "Le transformisme, Types generaux." Also C.D. Brenner, *A Bibliographical List of Plays in the French Language 1700-1789* (Berkeley, Ca., 1947).

21. Moore, *Genre Poissard,* p. 361.

22. See n. 2 above for information on formulaic love intrigue of *commedia dell'arte,* for instance, Mic, *Commedia dell'arte,* p. 73.

23. Greene, *Comic structure,* p. 2.

24. According to notes in Nougaret's *Spectacles des foires,* these two plays—and no doubt more—borrowed from the old Italian theater: Beaunoir's *Le Mort Vivant,* 1773 and *L'Enlèvement de Proserpine* by Destival, 1786.

25. In this and following chapters bibliographical entries in the Index to Boulevard Plays Studied and Cited will stand instead of footnotes to the mention and citation of plays performed by the boulevard theaters.

26. Comment in A.N. Ms. $BB^{3}81$. Ghérardi play is available in manuscript at the B.N. Ms. f.f. 9329.

27. Greene, *Comic Structure,* p. 24; Attinger, *Commedia dell'arte,* pp. 28-29.

28. Burke, *Popular Culture,* pp. 124-25, 134.

29. Greene, *Comic Structure,* pp. 10, 153.

30. Lionel Gossman, "Literary Education and Democracy," in Richard Macksey, ed., *Velocities of Change, Critical Essays from MLN* (Baltimore and London, 1974).

31. Ibid., p. 10, quoting Barthes.

32. Greene, *Comic Structure,* pp. 10, 153.

33. For experimentation with new genres, see Borgerhoff, *Evolution of Liberal Theory,* chapter 3. On the bourgeois drama see, Gaiffe, *Drame,* especially p. 34.

34. Gaiffe, *Drame,* pp. 176-77.

35. For this and Voltaire citation below, see his *Correspondance,* Theodore Besterman, ed. (Geneva, 1953-1965), Letters 18089 and 18115.

36. Gaiffe, *Drame,* p. 199, n. 3, claims that Pleinchesne's *Le Charbonnier est maître chez lui ou la partie de chasse* at the Grands-Danseurs was an imitation of Collé's *drame.* The situation may well have been more complicated than that, given the lyrical drama at the Comédie-Italienne and the pantomime at the Ambigu-Comique *(La Partie de chasse ou le charbonnier est maître chez lui),* neither of which Gaiffe mentions. In fact, the pantomime at the Ambigu-Comique seems to have been written in 1769, 7 years after the original appearance of Collé's drama at a private theater, but 5 years before it appeared at the Comédie-Française.

37. Gaiffe, *Drame,* p. 200. On Mercier at Associés, see Nougaret, *Spectacles des foires,* 5th Part, p. 75 (1777) and [Dumont, comédien], *Le Désoeuvré mis en oeuvre ou le Revers de Médaille* (Paris, 1782), p. 43.

38. Luc-Vincent Thiery, *Guide des Amateurs et des Etrangers Voyageurs à Paris, ou Description raisonné de cette ville et tout ce qu'elle contient de remarquable* (Paris, 1786-1787), vol. 1, p. 609.

39. *Le Prince noir et blanc* (Amsterdam, 1782), Préface de l'editeur [Cailleau?].

40. *Almanach de tous les spectacles,* 1781, p. 200; Bonnassiès, *Spectacles forains,* p. 57.

41. Gossman, "Literary Education," p. 25, speaks of the "illusion of universality, the absence of a sense of history, in our meaning of the term, from the literary consciousness of the classical period . . ."

42. Gossman, "Literary Education," p. 22.

43. Burke, *Popular Culture,* p. 147, makes this same point: "If there is no difference in kind between the forms of learned and popular culture, there may still be differences of degree, arising especially from the fact that so much of popular culture was, and is, oral culture."

44. See on this Alexis Pitou, "Les Origines de Mélodrame français à la fin du XVIIIe siècle," *Revue d'histoire littéraire de la France,* XVIII (1911), pp. 256-96.

Chapter 4

1. Since the focus of this study is on the years preceding and during the French Revolution the 75 or so plays selected for examination in chapters 3 and 4 were chosen from a sampling in the *Annonces* and other Parisian journals of theater performances on the boulevard every eight days for the years 1785-1794. These plays were among the most successful fare on the boulevard, or written by playwrights constantly patronized by the minor theaters. Unfortunately, it was not possible to pick plays for study according to predetermined qualifications such as the number of times the play reappeared in the sampling; the theater in which the play was performed; the year in which the play was written or performed; or authorship. The dramatic literature that has survived two hundred years is riddled with lacunae, and for the most part is either unknown in origin or representative of the more prominent theaters on the boulevard. For these reasons, most of the plays examined in the following chapters were performed in the years 1785-1794 at the Grands-Danseurs du Roi, the theater that had dominated the boulevard since 1759. A number of plays from other theaters—a good many from the Ambigu-Comique, fewer from the Délassements-Comique, the Associés, etc.—have been included in order to assess whether or not trends on one minor stage might be said, generally, to apply to the entire range of boulevard theater. The plays are listed in the Index to Boulevard Plays Studied and Cited.

2. *Encyclopédie,* articles "domestique," "famille," "puissance paternelle," "puissance des maîtres," and "vassal" (vols. 5, 6, 13, 16 respectively). In the article "famille," the nuclear family was said to include parents and children. It is noted that in Latin the word embraced in its meaning the domestics of a household.

3. *Encyclopédie,* articles "mariage," vol. 10; "famille," vol. 6.

4. In this and other chapters bibliographical entries in the Index to Boulevard Plays Studied and Cited will stand instead of footnotes to the mention and citation of plays performed by the boulevard theaters.

5. It is worth pointing out that I disagree here with Greene's claim in *Comic Structure,* p. 160, that the artistic formula of revolt reflected a social reality: "It also appears clearly that F belongs to a period in France in which an upper bourgeois class had produced Young who want to make decisions themselves." The contemporary observations of Mercier and the historical studies of the family by Jean Louis Flandrin and Natalie Z. Davis, both cited below, suggest that parental control of adolescent behavior was strong.

6. Mercier, *Tableau,* vol. 3, p. 63 (1783).

7. Ibid., p. 86.

8. Jean Louis Flandrin, *Familles, parenté, maison, sexualité dans l'ancienne société* (Paris, 1976), p. 128.

9. *Encyclopédie,* article "mariage."

10. Natalie Zemon Davis, "Ghosts, Kin and Progeny," reprinted in Alice Rossi et al., *The Family* (New York, 1978), pp. 87-114.

11. This was true in *La Ceinture merveilleuse (The Wonderful Waistband)* (1773), *Tel Père Tel Fils (Like Father Like Son)* (1784), *Le Capon (The Dastard)* (1785), *La Caponne (The Dastardly Female)* (1785), *Polichinelle protégé par la fortune (Polichinelle Protected by Fate)* (1786), and *Guzman d'Alfarache* (1789)—to name some of the more obvious examples.

12. The Italian for footman is "staffiero." "Estaffier" undoubtedly belongs to the comic language developed by Italian actors in France, in which essentially French dialogue is laced with Italian words and sounds. See Judith Suther, "Harlequin on the Revolutionary Stage," *Washington State University Research Studies,* 43 (1975), p. 236 and Guy Boquet, "La Comédie-Italienne sous la régence: Arlequin Poli par Paris (1716-1725)," *Revue d'Histoire Moderne et Contemporaine,* 24 (1977), pp. 204-205.

13. Nougaret, ed., *Spectacles des foires,* 5th part, p. 75 (1777). Note that this opinion was repeated by Mercier, *Tableau,* vol. 8, p. 35: "The people who go to these little theaters are precisely those who have the greatest need of receiving some beneficial instruction..." and *passim.*

14. Darnton, "The High Enlightenment."

15. The term is Daniel Mornet's in *French Thought in the Eighteenth Century* (New York, 1929), translated edition. See Part IV. Since Mornet analyzed eighteenth century literature, a great deal of scholarly opinion has tended to identify sentimental thought as pre-Romantic, contending thereby that any linkage of *sensibilité* or sentimentalism with the Enlightenment is untenable. It is hard to believe, however, that sentimental and enlightened lines of thought, both originating just before or in the early 1700s, had no influence one on the other and no interaction. One has only to consider the sentimentalism of philosophes such as Rousseau and Diderot—the latter in his work on the *Encyclopédie* the epitome of *lumière.* Grenet and Jodry (see n. 16) seek to temper recent scholarly study of sentimental literature, "of what has been conveniently, but not always accurately, called Pre-romanticism..." Sentimentalism appears contrary to enlightened thought, they argue, but it is only an apparent paradox.

16. Louis Gottschalk and Donald Lach, *Toward the French Revolution* (New York, 1973), p. 133; André Grenet and Claude Jodry, *La littérature de sentiment au XVIIIe siècle* (Paris, 1971), preface and *passim.*

17. *Encyclopédie,* article "famille."

18. Though many of Rousseau's works were known to the public of old regime France, Mornet, *French Thought,* believes that *La Nouvelle Héloise* penetrated most deeply into the consciousness of Rousseau's contemporaries. It was, he writes, the Bible of sentiment in the eighteenth century (p. 218). *La Nouvelle Héloise* had a profound impact, running through 72 editions between 1762 and 1800 (p. 333). Mornet argues, however, that Rousseau had no influence on eighteenth century theater. This may be true in a study of structural or aesthetic innovation; it cannot be allowed in a study of attitudes and ideas.

19. Jean Starobinsky, *Jean-Jacques Rousseau, la transparence et l'obstacle* (Saint-Amand/Cher, France, 1971). The interpretation of the novel that is presented below is primarily Starobinsky's, although it is agreed upon in many particulars by both Mornet,

French Thought, and by Lionel Gossman, "The Worlds of *La Nouvelle Héloise*," *Studies on Voltaire and the Eighteenth Century*, XXXXI (1966), pp. 235-76.

20. "Vassals" is indeed the word the Baron uses, although in the play we see only his family members and servants.

21. See Part 4, letter 10 of *La Nouvelle Héloise*, on the domestic organization of Clarens.

22. Starobinsky considers other of Rousseau's political treatises, in particular *Considérations sur le gouvernement de Pologne*, in order to illuminate the importance of the festival or *fête* in his philosophical thought. In that treatise, Rousseau wrote that the means to equality was through participation in the *fête* "wherein ranks are distinguished with care, but wherein all the people take part equally..." (quoted in Starobinsky, *Rousseau*, p. 124). Starobinsky concludes that for Rousseau equality was not a social institution but a "state of the collective soul." Gossman, "La Nouvelle Héloise," pp. 265-66, differs somewhat from Starobinsky in this interpretation, arguing that Rousseau accepted and rejected the social order he painted in *La Nouvelle Héloise*. Rousseau, he claims, could not accept inequality, or the unhappiness of the individual in the social order, but was unwilling to believe in the transformation of society.

23. Starobinsky, *Rousseau*, p. 125.

24. Ibid., p. 122.

25. For a brief account of philosophical—and political—discourse on the great stages of Paris, see Robert Niklaus, "La Propagande philosophique au théâtre au siècle des lumières," *Studies on Voltaire and the Eighteenth Century*, XXVI (1963), pp. 1223-61.

26. According to my sampling of boulevard repertory performances in the years 1785-1794 the plays compared here were the most successful of those discussed in this chapter—success being measured as the number of times a play was performed in the ten-year sample period, three appearances over the ten-year period having been considered the cut-off between the successful and unsuccessful play. In the sample decade *l'Avantageux puni (The Fop Punished)* appeared in the sampling 13 times between 12/7/86 and 10/31/90; *Le Fou par amour (The Love-Crazed Madman)* 17 times between 3/13/87 and 10/21/94; *Le Père Duchesne* 15 times between 2/22/89 and 1/22/92; *La Corne de verité (The Horn of Truth)* 12 times between 1/29/86 and 12/13/94; *Contentement passe richesse (Contentment Surpasses Wealth)* 23 times between 8/25/86 and 8/15/94; *Guzman d'Alfarache* 12 times between 9/2/89 and 8/17/92; and *Pierre Bagnolet et Claude Bagnolet son fils (Pierre Bagnolet and His Son Claude Bagnolet)* 16 times between 6/3/85 and 2/28/91. L'Olive appeared in the sampling 9 times between 10/1/88 and 8/9/92; Polichinelle appeared 16 times between 3/18/86 and 8/28/90; Volsers in *Le Fou par amour* 17 times (see above) and De Preval in *Le Colérique (The Irascible Master)* 7 times between 5/29/89 and 10/15/90. While it is not suggested that these numbers reflect the actual number of times these plays were performed, they do provide estimates of frequency and bases for comparison between plays.

27. According to my sampling of boulevard repertory performances in the years 1785-1794, *Le Père Duchesne* must have had a prodigious run in 1789—for it appeared 12 times in the sampling for that year, where 3 appearances has been considered a cut-off between the successful and unsuccessful play. *Le Père Duchesne* was picked up three more times, once each in the years 1790, 1791 and 1792.

28. *Le Menuisier de Bagdad (The Carpenter of Bagdad)* was first performed by the Théâtre de Beaujolais in 1789, when that theater was still located in the Palais-Royal. On the 22nd of February 1790 the Beaujolais was forced to remove to an empty hall on the boulevard du Temple. In this location the comic opera was a great success from March of 1790 to

November, appearing 7 times in my sampling of boulevard performances for that year, where 3 appearances has been considered a cut-off between the successful and unsuccessful play.

Prelude III

1. Imaginative scene based on Gabriel-Jacques de Saint-Aubin: *A Street Show in Paris,* 1760. Canvas. London, National Gallery.

2. De Manne and Ménétrier, *La troupe de Nicolet,* entry Ribié; Henry Lyonnet, *Dictionnaire des comédiens français* (Geneva-Paris, n.d.), vol. 2, entry Louis-François Ribié; Joseph François Michaud, ed., *Biographie universelle, ancienne et moderne* (Paris, 1811-1862), 55 vols., entry César Ribié; Brazier, *Histoire des petits théâtres,* vol. 1, p. 10; Jean-Nicolas Barba, *Souvenirs* (Paris, 1846), p. 77.

3. Ribié's début, as told by the actor to Théophile-Marion Dumersan, "Histoire des Théâtres de Boulevart, Suite. Ribié (César), auteur et acteur," *Le Monde dramatique,* IV (1835-1841), pp. 241-42. For other biographical details, see sources in n. 2 above.

4. Puppet show: A.N. Ms. Y12227. Letter to the Commissioner Mutel, 21 août 1778; see also, Campardon, *Spectacles,* vol. 2, p. 320. Rabbit show: Nougaret, *Spectacles des foires,* 7th part (1786), p. 42. Sideshow and charlatanry: Campardon, *Spectacles,* vol. 2, pp. 316-17, entry Ribié.

5. Description of talents: Brazier, *Histoire des petits théâtres,* vol. 1, p. 10; *Recueil des Pièces,* vol. 2, "Jugement sur Pierre Bagnolet et Claude Bagnolet son fils"; Barba, *Souvenirs,* p. 77. Jealous accusations: Michaud, ed., *Biographie universelle,* entry César Ribié; Campardon, *Spectacles,* vol. 2, p. 318. Improved grammar: B.N. Ms. n.a.f. 3045-3049. *L'Amour astrologue:* B.N. Ms. n.a.f. 2860. Number of plays: Joseph Marie Quérard, *La France littéraire ou Dictionnaire bibliographique des savants, historiens et gens de lettres de la France pendant les XVIII*[e] *et XIX*[e] *siècles,* (Paris, 1827-1864), entry César Ribié and Brenner, *Bibliographical List of Plays,* entry César Ribié.

6. Historians have largely neglected the study of the acting profession in eighteenth century France. Most works have tended to be biographical and anecdotal. Notable exceptions are Gaston Maugras' examination of the social and legal sanctions that governed the professional life of the royal actor in *Les Comédiens hors la loi* (Paris, 1887) and Alasseur's reconstruction of the royal actor's salary and the economic life of the company in *La Comédie-française.* See also Henri Lagrave, "La Comédie-Française au XVIIIe siècle ou les contradictions d'un privilège," *Revue d'Histoire du Théâtre,* 32 (1980), pp. 127-41. Maugras, Alasseur and Lagrave have ignored altogether the minor artist of the boulevard. Concern for the impact of revolution on the actor and actress has been equally superficial. Maugras and Lagrave, unfortunately, have little to say about professional conditions after 1789. Maugras, as well as Ernest Lunel, *Le Théâtre et la Révolution* (Paris, 1911); Jacques Hérissay, *Le Monde des théâtres pendant la révolution* (Paris, 1922); Paul Reynoard, "Les Comédiens pendant la Révolution," *Annales Révolutionnaires,* VIII (1916), pp. 626-50; and Carlson, *Theatre of the French Revolution* all point to the civil emancipation of the actor in 1789, but only trace its effect in the political activities of a limited number of individuals, by force of documentation the great actors and actresses of Paris. The boulevard artist has had no place in this history. Equally, there are no studies of the minor playwrights per se and their relations with theater directors and booksellers, but because these men belonged to the literary world of Paris, some part of their history has been addressed by scholars such as John Lough, in *An Introduction to Eighteenth Century France* (New York, 1960), chapter 7: "Writer and Public in France" and by Darnton in "High Englightenment."

Chapter 5

1. Bonnassiès, *Auteurs dramatiques,* cited on p. 64.

2. Although all actors had a share in scorn and ostracism, not all were excommunicated. The Italian actors escaped the Church's opprobrium. See on this and preceding paragraph: Aghion, *Théâtre au XVIII*[e], pp. 407-408 and *passim;* Lunel, *Théâtre et Révolution,* p. 4; Adolphe Lacan, *Traité de la législation et de la jurispurdence des théâtres* (Paris, 1853), pp. 226-27; Alasseur, *Comédie-française,* pp. 16-18. In addition Lagrave notes that since the artists of the Opéra were constituted members of an Academy, they were not deprived of their civic "rights." The French actors alone, he claims, were considered no better than the mountebanks and buffoons of the fairs and boulevards. See Lagrave, "Comédie-Française," pp. 129-30. However, despite the fact that French actors and boulevard artists shared in a lack of civil status the differences in their respective positions within French society were manifest.

3. Aghion, *Théâtre au XVIII*[e], p. 412.

4. Des Essarts, *Les Trois Théâtres,* pp. 135-37, 153.

5. [Sélis], *Lettre sur les petits spectacles,* p. 22.

6. Thomas Rousseau, *Lettre sur les spectacles,* p. 46.

7. Métra, et al., *Correspondance,* vol. 10, p. 216 (26 September 1780). Many documents reprinted in Campardon, *Spectacles,* offer additional evidence of scorn for actors generally and boulevard actors particularly. For example, the religious scruples of one Ramponeaux prevented him from appearing on Gaudon's stage around 1760 (vol. 1, p. 365). In 1762 Dlle. Pichot complained about an acting school in her building that trained many for the fairs and boulevard because "it is not decent that comedy be performed in an honest house" (vol. 1, p. 146).

8. See for example, Plancher or Aristide Valcour, *Reflexions sur les spectacles,* reprinted in *Journal des spectacles* (1793-an II), vol. 2, no. 70, 23 fructidor II (9 September 1793); [Sélis], *Lettre sur les petits spectacles,* pp. 22-27; Thomas Rousseau, *Lettre sur les spectacles,* p. 6.

9. [Sélis], *Lettre sur les petits spectacles,* p. 22.

10. Thomas Rousseau, *Lettres sur les spectacles,* p. 46.

11. See for particular biographies that do exist: de Manne and Ménétrier, *La troupe de Nicolet;* Lyonnet, *Dictionnaire des comédiens;* Michaud, ed, *Biographie universelle;* Quérard, *La France littéraire;* among others.

12. Thomas Rousseau, *Lettre sur les spectacles,* p. 46; see also n. 14 below.

13. Ibid.

14. Maugras, *Comédiens hors la loi,* p. 217; Reynoard, "Comédiens," p. 627, quotes a list of grievances from Reims: "That in all cases, fathers and mothers, guardians and protectors be able to reassert their authority over children or pupils who would have been able to remain in the service of theaters without anyone being permitted to remove them thence . . ." Aghion, *Théâtre au XVIII*[e], p. 198, indicates that prostitutes in eighteenth century Paris attempted to get themselves enrolled in one of the artists' corps at the Opéra in order to escape the jurisdiction of the police. Regulation of artists at the Opéra, as at other royal theaters, depended on the Gentlemen of the Chamber and on the Royal Household.

15. Quoted in Aghion, *Théâtre au XVIII*[e], p. 413. Aghion provides no date. I have been unable to locate this statement in Collé's original works, and therefore have been unable to date it

accurately. The reference to the little theaters would seem to place Collé's remark after 1760, yet after mid-century the salaries of the royal actors had improved considerably over the early 1700s. (See Alasseur, *Comédie-française,* Table 19 "Sommes Totales Versées aux Acteurs. Valeur moyenne d'une part entière.") Thus, Collé's remark is perhaps most valuable as an expression of contemporary perception and expectation.

16. [Mayeur de St. Paul], *Le Désoeuvré* (1907 reprint), p. 76; de Manne and Ménétrier, *Troupe de Nicolet;* Michaud, ed., *Biographie universelle,* entry Ribié.

17. The lowest recorded salaries for boulevard artists are 600 livres at the Théâtre-Patriotique (Associés), 700 livres at the Ambigu-Comique, and 800 livres at the Gaité (Grands-Danseurs). Although these sums date from 1791-95, it is probable that they represent the lower ranges of the salary scales in the years 1785-89 as well, since, as Table 2: "Salaries of Artists on the Boulevard" indicates, salaries remained nominally the same throughout this ten-year period. Six hundred, 700 and 800 livres should be compared to the figures in George Rudé's Appendix VII: "Prices and Wages in Paris, 1789" in *The Crowd in the French Revolution* (Oxford, 1959), wherein a journeyman mason earned 508 livres per year, a journeyman locksmith or carpenter 635 livres per year and a sculptor or goldsmith 1,270 livres per year. Also compare to figure of 300 livres per year as salary of a manual laborer 1785-89 given by Alasseur, *Comédie-française,* p. 125, Table 9 "Comparaison du salaire du manoeuvre avec le revenu d'un acteur." My salary figures are derived from records of the justice of the peace as well as sources described in Table 2: "Salaries of Artists on the Boulevard."

18. A.N. Ms. $H^2$2158.

19. B.N. Ms. n.a.f. 3049. Papiers de la Gaité.

20. A.N. Ms. Y12227, letter to the Commissioner Mutel, 11 août 1778.

21. See Frantz Funck-Brentano, *La Bastille des Comédiens, Le For l'Evêque* (Paris, 1903). The Hôtel de la Force replaced Le For l'Evêque as a prison for actors in 1780, p. 307.

22. A.N. Ms. Y16022. Report of the French guard dated 5 June 1787. See also entire series A.N. Ms. Y15996-Y16009. Campardon, in his *Spectacles,* reprinted dozens of police reports documenting the imprisonment of boulevard actors in the 1760s, '70s, and '80s.

23. [Dumont], *Le Désoeuvré mis en oeuvre,* p. 14.

24. Mague de St. Aubin, *La réforme des théâtres, ou vues d'un amateur sur les moyens d'avoir toujours des acteurs à talents sur les théâtres de Paris* (Paris, 1787), p. 40.

25. According to [Mayeur de St. Paul], *Le Désoeuvré,* the authorities forbade the renewal of the license of the Théâtre des Elèves de l'Opéra because of Parisau's scandalous conduct and the numerous complaints of his creditors, p. 22 (in original), p. 44 (1907 reprint).

26. Archives de l'Assistance publique. Ms. Liasse 1438. Entry 9 juillet 1780. Hospital administrators confirmed that Parisau was in desperate financial straights: "That he is tormented by his creditors and that the entire proceeds from his Spectacle were seized . . ." Bachaumont, *Mémoires secrets,* vol. 15, p. 334, reported that the Théâtre des Elèves de l'Opéra was about to go bankrupt, the entrepreneurs being unable to satisfy their creditors or pay their artists. In A.N. Ms. $0^1$618, creditors who had backed the original director of the Elèves, Abraham, complained to ministers of the Royal Household that Lenoir had forced them to support Parisau when he arranged to take the Elèves from Abraham. By their account, "we were forced, by order of M. Lenoir, to lend [Parisau] money in order to pay his artists . . ."

27. Anonymous poem, reprinted by [Mayeur de St. Paul], *Le Désoeuvré* (1907 reprint), p. 128.

28. Ibid., p. 72.

29. *Spectacles de Paris* (1792), p. 23.

30. [Mayeur de St. Paul], *Le Désoeuvré* (1907 reprint), pp. 72-73.

31. A.N. Ms. Y12227, letter to the Commissioner Mutel, 11 août 1778.

32. [Mayeur de St. Paul], *Le Chroniqueur Désoeuvré, ou l'Espion du Boulevard du Temple*, 2nd edition (London, 1782-83), 2 vols., partially reprinted in Campardon, *Spectacles*, vol. 1, p. 269.

33. B.N. Ms. n.a.f. 3049. In 1762 one Claude Leclair received 300 livres as indemnity for his personal wardrobe lost in the fire that consumed the Théâtre de Nicolet at the Saint Germain Fair. (Campardon, *Spectacles*, vol. 2, p. 44. See also, vol. 1, p. 79, article Balmat.)

34. Archives de la Seine, Ms. D^6U^{39} 1791. Jugements. Justice de paix des arrondissements anciens de Paris: Section du Temple. No. 372 (8 November 1791). Note that the debts probably reflect some inflation over the pre-1789 period.

35. [Mayeur de St. Paul], *Le Désoeuvré* (1907 reprint), p. 132.

36. Quoted in Campardon, *Spectacles*, vol. 2, p. 317.

37. B.N. Ms. n.a.f. 3047. Papiers de la Gaité. Chits dating septembre 1777 and mai 1778.

38. A.N. Ms. Y12227, letter to the Commissioner Fontaine, on or before 6 August 1781. Also, [Mayeur de St. Paul], *Chroniqueur désoeuvré*, quoted in Campardon, *Spectacles*, vol. 2, p. 317.

39. B.N. Ms. n.a.f. 3049, chit dated 21 octobre 1782.

40. B.N. Ms. n.a.f. 3049, chit dated 9 novembre 1782.

41. Campardon, *Spectacles*, vol. I, p. 283, document II. Archives de la Seine. Ms. D^6U^{42} 1793-an II. No. 99 (29 December 1793).

42. For observation of actors' behavior as adolescent, see Joel Fouilleron, "Fabre d'Eglantine et les Chemins du Théâtre," *Revue d'histoire moderne et contemporaine*, XXI (1974), pp. 495-96. Sociological literature on deviance applies to the actor's position in eighteenth century society; for example: Richard Hawkins and Gary Tiedeman, *The Creation of Deviance* (Columbus, Ohio; 1975); Howard S. Becker, *Outsiders, Studies in the Sociology of Deviance* (New York, 1963); Don C. Gibbons and Joseph F. Jones, *The Study of Deviance, Perspectives and Problems* (Englewood Cliffs, N.J.; 1975); and Ronald A. Farrell and Victoria Lynn Swigert, eds., *Social Deviance* (New York, 1975). I have examined more fully the deviant behavior of the actor in "Moral Criminality Onstage and Backstage in Late Eighteenth Century Parisian Popular Theater," paper delivered to the Western Society for Eighteenth-Century Studies, April, 1982 and expanded and revised in manuscript.

43. A.N. Ms. Y16022, 21 août 1784.

44. A.N. Ms. Y16022, 27 juin 1789.

45. A.N. Ms. Y16000, 25 août 1786; also reprinted in Campardon, *Spectacles de la foire*, vol. 2, pp. 383-84.

46. A.N. Ms. Y16022, octobre 1787.

47. A.N. Ms. Y15998, 15 octobre 1785.

48. Campardon, in his *Spectacles,* reprinted several documents revealing among boulevard artists the irregular practices of fornication, adultery, homosexuality and prostitution. See for example, vol. 1, pp. 125, 153, 348, 365-66; vol. 2, pp. 29-31. See also sources indicated in n. 52 below. For public comment on boulevard immorality, see for example [Sélis], *Lettre sur les petits spectacles,* pp. 22, 27 and *Influence de la Révolution,* p. 11. Mayeur's "dirty book" is so described in the Archives des commissaires, entry 6 mars 1782, quoted in 1907 reprint of *Le Désoeuvré,* p. 17.

49. For these reasons one might wish to discount Mayeur's testimony. However, a pamphlet supposedly written as a corrective to Mayeur's account of the boulevard, [Dumont], *Le Désoeuvré mis en oeuvre,* does not deny—it rather confirms—the scandalmonger's allegations of sexual promiscuity and profligacy.

50. [Mayeur de St. Paul], *Le Désoeuvré* (1907 reprint), p. 122.

51. Ibid., p. 78.

52. Prostitutes formed a noticeable element of the boulevard audience, according to [Sélis], *Lettre sur les petits spectacles,* p. 31; Thomas Rousseau, *Lettre sur les spectacles,* pp. 7, 37; Pidansat de Mairobert, *L'Espion anglais,* vol. 2, p. 77; and the *Almanach de tous les spectacles* (1792), p. 298. The *Almanach* claimed that the Grands-Danseurs du Roi would never lack for customers "because *the girls* have free admission there, and the enterprises based upon the revenue of debauchery will never be lacking in a big city." Some boulevard actresses strengthened the association of their profession with prostitution by embracing both. See documents concerning Adélaide Dusseault, Marie Charlotte Becquet, Marie-Catherine Duhamel and Mlle. Cléophile reprinted in Campardon, *Spectacles,* vol. 1.

53. [Mayeur de St. Paul], *Le Désoeuvré* (1907 reprint), pp. 93-94.

54. This figure is based on the comparison of names in lists of artists belonging to the Ambigu-Comique to be found in A.N. Ms. Y12227, Etat des personnes qui composent l'Ambigu-Comique (in 1777), and in various almanacs of theater for the years 1778, 1786, 1787, 1791 and 1792.

55. Mague de St. Aubin, *Réforme des théâtres,* p. 30.

56. De Manne and Ménétrier, *Troupe de Nicolet,* p. 202.

57. Quoted in [Mayeur de St. Paul], *Le Désoeuvré,* p. 29; (1907 reprint), p. 51.

58. Nougaret, ed., *Spectacles des foires,* 8th part, p. 70. See chapter 2, p. 66-67 and chapter 2, n. 116.

59. Bachaumont, *Mémoires secrets,* vol. 16, p. 76; also [Mayeur de St. Paul], *Le Désoeuvré* (1907 reprint), p. 142. In this edition Mayeur claimed that Volange contracted with two theaters simultaneously for his own advantage. On his inability to leave the stage see [Mayeur de St. Paul], *Le Désoeuvré* (1782), p. 163.

60. On great actors, see Maugras, *Comédiens hors la loi,* pp. 215, 218.

61. See for example: Carlson, *Theatre of the French Revolution;* Paul d'Estrée, *Le Théâtre sous la Terreur 1793-1794* (Paris, 1913); Hérissay, *Monde des théâtres;* Lunel, *Théâtre et Révolution;* Maugras, *Comédiens hors la loi;* Reynoard, "Comédiens;" Welschinger, *Théâtre de la Révolution.*

62. This analysis is based on the Archives de la Préfecture de police, Ms. A^A239-240. Procès-verbaux des commissaires de police des Sections de Paris. 1789-1820. Section du Temple.

63. Archives de la Préfecture de police, Ms. A^A239, 1 décembre 1790.

64. Archives de la Préfecture de police, Ms. A^{A}239, 20 novembre 1790.

65. Archives de la Préfecture de police, Ms. A^{A}239, 21 décembre 1790.

66. Ibid.

67. Archives de la Préfecture de police, Ms. A^{A}239, 13 février 1791.

68. Ibid.

69. Ibid.

70. Archives de la Préfecture de police, Ms. A^{A}239, 10 mai 1791.

71. *Almanach de tous les spectacles* (1791), p. 181.

72. Archives de la Préfecture de police, Ms. A^{A}239, 19 novembre 1791.

73. Rudé, *Crowd in French Revolution,* p. 80; see for below pp. 82-84.

74. Rudé's Appendix IV, "Paris Trades and Insurgents of 1787-95," records that from the category of actors, artists and musicians etc. the Champ de Mars elicited the greatest response. Six actors etc. were recorded at that riot; two are known to have been involved in the August '92 disturbances, and one in the Grocery Riots of 1792-93. There was no record of actors at the Reveillon riots, the burning of the barriers, the Saint Lazare affair or the storming of the Bastille. The actor's political consciousness did not come until 1791 and then, weakly.

75. Rudé, *Crowd in French Revolution,* pp. 82-86.

76. Ibid., pp. 80-84.

77. According to Robert Chabanne, *Les Institutions de la France, de la fin de l'ancien régime à l'avènement de la IIIème République (1789-1875)* (Paris, 1977), the justice of the peace was the lowest rung of a very simple judicial hierarchy established by the Constituent Assembly. Justices of the peace were elected for two-year terms by active citizens, and aided by two assessors. The justice of the peace was primarily involved as the first and last resort in civil cases in which interest was below 50 livres; the first resort in cases between 50-100 livres. For cases involving monies above 100 livres, he had the role of conciliation, before the case was brought before the district tribunal.

78. For cases cited in this paragraph: Archives de la Seine, Ms. $D^{6}U^{39}$. No. 232 (2 July 1791), no. 332 (27 September 1791), no. 339 (8 October 1791); Archives de la Préfecture de police, Ms. A^{A}239, 28 octobre 1791.

79. Until the records of the Châtelet of Paris are searched, it will remain uncertain whether the minor actor or artist did in fact and/or in practice have recourse to the law in petty economic matters before the institution of the justice of the peace; whether in fact and/or in practice the Prévot de Paris prosecuted the minor artist for debt or regulated his financial satisfaction of creditors under the old regime. See n. 84 below. Campardon, *Spectacles,* vol. 1, p. 144, reprinted a document indicating that one Bidaine, dancer, did sue before the civil lieutenant-general at the Châtelet for two years of unpaid salary.

80. Archives de la Seine. Ms. $D^{6}U^{39}$. No. 201 (31 May 1791), No. 146 (30 April 1791).

81. Archives de la Seine. Ms. $D^{6}U^{39}$. No. 200 (31 May 1791), no. 363 (29 October 1791).

82. Archives de la Seine. Ms. $D^{6}U^{41}$ 1792. Jugements. No. 509 (28 April 1792).

83. *Recueil des lois,* vol. 26, pp. 153-55.

84. Lacan, *Législation et jurisprudence des théâtres,* p. 247, observes of the 1779 law: "It does not appear that the actors of other theaters participated in the same advantage, or that the rights of creditors over their salaries were limited in extent. There is at least no text bearing upon [the actor-creditor relationship at other theaters or on the boulevard]." It is possible, however, that the law of August 1779 did have an effect on the financial relationship of Nicolet and Ribié. If so, there is inadequate information to verify that influence. Note, in any case, that Nicolet was already acting as the middleman between creditor and actor before the promulgation of this law, as a chit signed by Ribié in December 1777 indicates: "I give full power to said Sir to take from my salary at Mister Nicolet's..." (B.N. Ms. n.a.f. 3047.)

85. Article 5 of the 1779 law declares "that in default of payment of said food and lodging, the entirety of said wages and salaries can be seized..."

86. Cases cited in this paragraph: Archives de la Seine. Ms. D^6U^{39}. No. 98 (26 March 1791); no. 280 (13 August 1791); Ms. D^6U^{42}. No. 76 (24 November 1793).

87. I do not believe the decline is a result of decreased reporting of directors to the police. Entrepreneurs do continue to complain of the insubordination of individual artists, although it is true they had less to gain now than before the Revolution.

88. Rudé, *Crowd in French Revolution,* p. 129.

89. Soboul, *French Revolution,* p. 436.

90. Rudé, *Crowd in French Revolution,* pp. 129, 135.

91. Compare the maximum salaries for boulevard artists with the hypothetical income of a sculptor or goldsmith. According to contemporaries cited by Rudé, *Crowd in French Revolution,* p. 135, those who used to earn 4 or 5 livres now earned 20 to 24 livres per day. The goldsmith would, thus, have an income of 5,080-6,350 livres per year; the journeyman carpenter, 2,540-3,175 livres per year. Although Rudé suggests a more modest increase in wage-earners' income, he allows that contemporary notice of quadrupled income "may not be greatly exaggerated."

92. Archives de la Préfecture de police. Ms. A^A241, 3 brumaire III (24 October 1794).

93. The salary figure for the Ambigu-Comique is derived from documents to be found in A.N. Ms $BB^3$73. Comité de Surveillance du Département de Paris. Correpondances. Salaries at the Grands-Danseurs are here figured on a January-January basis, due to the format of income records for that theater at the Bibliothèque de l'Arsenal, Ms. 13002.

94. Archives de la Préfecture de police. Ms. A^A241, 3 brumaire III (24 October 1794).

95. A.N. Ms. $BB^3$73.

96. Ibid. This contract for April 1793-April 1794 at the Ambigu-Comique, found in the records of the Committee of Surveillance, is the only written contract still extant known to have been passed on a boulevard stage in the years 1785-1795.

97. Rudé, *Crowd in French Revolution,* p. 134.

98. A.N. Ms. $BB^3$81. See Chapter 8, p. 226 discussion of this detention.

99. A.N. Ms. DXXXVII 3. Comité d'instruction publique. Théâtre et spectacles.

100. Archives de la Préfecture de police. Ms. A^A240, 6 prairial II (25 May 1794).

101. Archives de la Préfecture de police. Ms. A^A240, 23 thermidor II (10 August 1794); for Roger see also A^A240, 2 prairial II (21 May 1794) and 1 fructidor II (18 August 1794); A^A241, 11 thermidor III (29 July 1795).

102. A.N. Ms. DXXXVII 3.

103. For instance, Pixerécourt in 1795, in E. Estève, "Observations de Guilbert de Pixerécourt sur les théâtres de la Révolution," *Revue d'histoire littéraire de la France,* XXIII (1916), p. 558.

104. Article 12, law of 1 November 1807.

Chapter 6

1. Maillé de la Malle was also known as Maillé de Marencourt. Some authors used many different spellings of their names—Fonpré de Francasalle, for example. One spelling is adopted throughout for consistency.

2. Casual authors for boulevard theater included the following, many of whom are know today by their names only: Deville, Landrin, Renout, Beaubourg, Lebrun, de Berainville, Mension, Botasse, Lebailly, Crêton de Villeneuve, Vacherot, Derichard Dupin, Joly de St. Just, Boussernard de Soubreville, Hoffman, Guillemain, Brasle.

3. Framery, *L'organisation des spectacles,* p. 199.

4. Hérissay, *Monde des théâtres,* p. 51; citation of a ruling of 1780 governing relations between the royal actors and dramatic authors.

5. Nougaret, ed., *Spectacles des foires,* 7th part, p. 95.

6. Jean-Louis Gabiot de Salins, *Paris sauvé, ou la conspiration manquée* (Paris, 1790), preface or "avis aux auteurs dramatiques." Gabiot compared himself to Sedaine because that established author had influenced the royal censor Suard to withhold approval of Gabiot's play, *Paris sauvé,* which resembled closely a tragedy of Sedaine's.

7. Ibid.

8. *Recueil des Pièces,* vol. 5, preface to *l'Artiste infortuné* (1788).

9. Rivarol and Louis de Champcenetz, *Petit Almanach de nos grands hommes* (n.p., 1788), preface. See Darnton, "High Enlightenment," p. 95 for use of this same almanac in defining the citizens of Grub-Street.

10. Gabiot de Salins, quoted in Nougaret, ed., *Spectacles des foires,* part 7, p. 95; Nougaret, *littérature renversée,* p. x; [Sélis], *Lettre sur les petits spectacles,* p. 18.

11. *Recueil des Pièces,* vol. 5, preface to *l'Artiste infortuné* (1788). "Propter famen": because of or on account of hunger and poverty; "propter faman": for the purpose of reputation and fame.

12. Nougaret, *Littérature renversée,* p. xiv. On authors without reputation and the boulevard: ibid., p. x; on waiting for production, *Recueil des Pièces,* vol. 2, preface to *La Musicomanie* (1779).

13. A. Dinaux, "Les Masques arrachés," *Archives historiques du nord de la France,* nouvelle serie, V (1884), pp. 325-26. Note that Dinaux does not attempt to date the transaction.

14. Framery, *L'organisation des spectacles,* p. 197.

15. The figures given as average prices are provisional and possibly overestimations. They have been obtained by dividing Nicolet's "payements de pièces et pantomimes à differentes auteurs" (Bibliothèque de l'Arsenal Ms. 13002) by an estimation of the number of new plays produced each year as indicated by my sampling of the Grands-Danseurs repertory for the years 1785-1795. See Table 3: "Average Cost of Plays at the Grands-Danseurs, 1786-1792."

16. Lough, *Introduction to France,* p. 240; Lough, *Writer and Public,* pp. 218, 223.

17. Thomas Rousseau, *Lettre sur les spectacles*, p. 11n., gives 200,000 livres and the number of representations; Framery, *L'organisation des spectacles*, p. 197n., gives 150,000 livres.

18. Lough, *Writer and Public*, p. 223.

19. *Recueil des Pièces*, vol. 2, preface to *Annette et Basile* (1785).

20. Bachaumont, *Mémoires secrets*, vol. 29, p. 38 (18 May 1785).

21. Ibid., vol. 29, pp. 47-48 (23 May 1785).

22. Ibid.

23. Lough, *Introduction to France*, pp. 235-37; Lough, *Writer and Public*, pp. 201-203; Darnton, "High Enlightenment," p. 97.

24. Nougaret, *Littérature renversée*, p. x.

25. Lough, *Writer and Public*, p. 202; Lough, *Introduction to France*, p. 237. Lough sees a general rise over the century in booksellers' payments to playwrights.

26. Bibliothèque de l'Arsenal, Ms. 6758. Notice sur A. Cailleau by P.A.L.M. de Varenne.

27. Dinaux, "Les Masques arrachés," p. 326.

28. *Recueil des Pièces*, vol. 7, preface to *L'Anglois ou le Fou raisonnable* (1781).

29. [Mayeur de St. Paul], *Le Désoeuvré* (1782), p. 163.

30. For sources for plays: See reviews of plays in Nougaret, ed., *Spectacles des foires*, vols. 1-8; *Annonces, passim; Recueil des Pièces*, vols. 1-7; and *Le Journal des spectacles; contenant l'analyse des différentes pièces qu'on a représentés sur tous les théâtres de Paris* (Paris: 1 July 1793-7 January 1794). For allegations of plagiarism: Nougaret, ed., *Spectacles des foires*, is full of such references; see also A. Paer, ed., *La Confession d'Audinot* (Rouen, 1880; original: Geneva, 1774), p. 32.

31. Nougaret, ed., *Spectacles des foires*, 7th part, p. 160.

32. On Parisau, see [Mayeur de St. Paul], *Le Désoeuvré*, p. 21. On Gabiot, see *Almanach de tous les spectacles* (1792), p. 293.

33. *Recueil des Pièces*, vol. 5, preface to *L'Elève de la Nature* (1781).

34. Lough, *An Introduction to France*, pp. 231, 255; Darnton, "High Enlightenment," p. 98. Often these writers had more than one source of income. According to Darnton, p. 86, La Harpe not only earned income as editor of the *Mercure;* he received 3,000 livres for lecturing at the Lycée and 1,500 livres in pension from the government.

35. See correspondence on behalf of Beaunoir in the papers of one Froidure, A.N. Ms. T737 Papiers séquestrés. Alexandre Cioranescu, *Bibliographie de la littérature française du dixhuitième siècle* (Paris, 1969), lists "Mme de Beaunoir" as a pseudonym of Robineau de Beaunoir, with which he signed six plays before 1789. It is possible that Beaunoir and his wife may have in fact collaborated on those plays signed with her name. Contemporaries disagreed with one another over the question and apparently neither Beaunoir nor his wife ever set them straight.

36. On pensions of the *Contrôle général* drawn up by the ministry of Calonne, see Darnton, "High Enlightenment," pp. 85-88. This list is partially reprinted by Maurice Tourneux, "Un Projet d'encouragement aux lettres et aux sciences sous Louis XVI," *Revue d'Histoire littéraire de la France*, VIII (1901), pp. 281-311; Darnton notes that Tourneux' version of the list is missing 21 names that appear on the original list which he found in the Archives

nationales, F[17a] 1212. I have not seen the original list; however, I believe it is possible but not probable that other boulevard playwrights found their names included. Darnton, pp. 87-88, notes that "sound" opinions were a necessary qualification for a pension; moreover that the government chose to subsidize men with some standing in the world of letters.

37. For this and the following summary of Darnton's Grub-Street thesis, see his "High Enlightenment."

38. Bachaumont, *Mémoires secrets,* vol. 15, p. 42 (1 February 1780). On the claim of the French actors to Dorvigny's play, see ibid., p. 334 (19 September 1780).

39. Nougaret, ed., *Spectacles des Foires,* 7th part, p. 95.

40. Gabiot de Salins, *Paris sauvé,* preface.

41. *Almanach de tous les spectacles* (1791), p. 279.

42. *Recueil des Pièces,* vol. 5, preface to *l'Artiste infortuné* (1788).

43. Destival is thought to have had an average salary because of his position on a salary list to be found in B.N. Ms. n.a.f. 3046. See Table 2: "Salaries of Artists on the Boulevard." To this average salary is added an estimation of income from his plays accepted and performed for the first time in the 1780s (number of plays times the average cost of plays given in Table 3: "Average Cost of Plays at the Grands-Danseurs, 1786-1792"). It is probable that Destival had other sources of "hidden" income, since, for example, he worked and published as a poet as well.

44. *Recueil des Pièces,* vol. 5, preface to *l'Artiste infortuné* (1788).

45. On Gabiot, see ibid., vol. 4, preface to *l'Orgueilleuse* (1786); Destival penned these plays, discussed in chapter 4: *Le Capon ou le fourbe découvert* (1785?); *La Caponne ou l'intrigante confondue* (1785?); *Polichinelle protégé par la fortune* (1786); *Le Voyage de Figaro* (1784).

46. Darnton enumerates these qualities of the Grub-Street he studies as important contributions to the formation of a radical underworld of literature. See his "High Enlightenment."

47. *A.P.,* vol. 22, p. 214; vol. 28, pp. 442-43. Most historians of theater have already covered these laws and their effects on the Comédie-Française, as well as authors' relations with this great theater and to a lesser extent provincial stages. None, however, are concerned with the changes in professional conditions at the minor theaters of Paris. See, for an example of this bias, Hérissay, *Monde des théâtres.*

48. *Pétition des Auteurs dramatiques qui n'ont pas signé celle de M. de la Harpe* (Paris, 1790). To my knowledge only Hérissay, *Monde des théâtres,* of all theater historians cited in these pages, mentions Parisau's petition to the National Assembly. Albert, *Théâtres des Boulevards,* p. 65, appears to have been ignorant of Parisau's petition, which led him to misread in some part the import of La Harpe's petition for the boulevard.

49. Of the 19 men who signed La Harpe's petition, only Framery had not had a play performed at the Comédie-Française. Sedaine and Mercier both wrote sparingly for the boulevard theaters: Mercier had two plays performed at the Associés and one at the Ambigu-Comique; Sedaine had one play performed at the Théâtre de Nicolet. Of the 25 playwrights who signed Parisau's petition, Dancourt, Poinsinet de Sivry, Desforges, Desfontaines, LaMontagne and Parisau himself had at least one play performed at the Comédie-Française. Six wrote more for the boulevard than for the great theaters: Ducrai-Dumenil, Boutillier, Landrin, Dancourt, LaMontagne, and again Parisau.

50. According to Hérissay, *Monde des théâtres*, p. 51, the French actors questioned whether all who signed were in fact "auteurs dramatiques," and thus, presumably, worthy of deliberation with them. All who signed La Harpe's petition but Framery in fact fit the definition.

51. On the Bureau dramatique established by men of letters to negotiate financial terms with the great theaters of Paris, and on the percentages agreed upon in August 1791, see Hérissay, *Monde des théâtres*, pp. 65-66.

52. Lyonnet, *Dictionnaire des comédiens*, vol. 2, entry Valcour.

53. Archives de la Seine. Ms. D^6U^{39} 1791. No. 148 (30 April 1791). Note that Carmontelle did not die until 1806, so even his plays were not strictly within the public domain.

54. *A.P.*, vol. 22, p. 214.

55. Article 3 indicates that if a play was performed without consent of the author, it was "under pain of confiscation of the total proceeds of the representations to the profit of the authors." *A.P.*, vol. 22, p. 214.

56. Archives de la Préfecture de police. Ms. A^A166, 21 March 1791. Procès-verbaux des commissaires de police. Section du Luxembourg. .

57. Archives de la Seine. Ms. D^6U^{42}. No. 117 (7 June 1794).

58. *Alamanach de tous les spectacles* (1792), p. 303.

59. In my sampling of plays first performed at the Grands-Danseurs in 1791 and 1792 the average number of performances per play is three. With reference to Table 3: "Average Cost of Plays at the Grands-Danseurs, 1786-1792," this would mean that, at 55 or 57 livres a play, Nicolet was paying a royalty somewhere around 18 livres per representation and probably much less.

60. A.N. Ms. T737. Papiers Froidure. Letters Framery to Froidure dated November 1791? and Framery to Froidure 19 November 1791.

61. Lough, *An Introduction to France*, p. 254, on the fact that provincial theaters were notorious pirates.

62. Darnton, "High Enlightenment," pp. 98, 112-15.

63. The sources for all biographical sketches in this chapter are the following, unless otherwise noted or specified: Campardon, *Spectacles;* de Manne and Ménétrier, *Troupe de Nicolet;* Lyonnet, *Dictionnaire des comédiens;* d'Estrée, *Théâtres sous la Terreur; Nouvelle Biographie Générale* (Paris, 1853-66), 46 vols.; *Dictionnaire de Biographie française* (Paris, 1933-); and Michaud, *Biographie universelle.*

64. A.N. Ms. $F^7$4743. Police général. Comité de Surété nationale. Denunciation of Parisau by one Heron (11 September 1793).

65. A.N. Ms. $F^7$4774[63], Parisau letter to "les Citoyens composant l'administration de la police."

66. A.N. Ms. W411. Tribunal révolutionnaire. No. 945.

67. On Beaunoir, see also, Dinaux, "Masques arrachés;" L. Leconte, "Un pamphlétaire de la Révolution brabançonne," *Fédération archéologique et historique de Belgique*, Annales de Congrès 35e (1953), pp. 417-46; Abbott, "Robineau, dit de Beaunoir."

68. On Valcour, see also Charles Monselet, *Les Originaux du siècle dernier, Les Oubliés et les dédaignés* (Alençon, 1857), vol. 2, pp. 139-56; and Archives de la Seine. Ms. D34Z. Papiers Dereix.

69. François-Victor Alphonse Aulard, *Le Culte de la Raison et Le Culte de l'Etre suprême (1793-1794)* (Paris, 1892), p. 349; A.N. Ms. F[7]4775[37], dossier Valcourt (Aristide).

70. Aristide Valcour, *Chanson des Sans-Culottes* (n.p., n.d.).

71. Aristide Valcour, *Le Vous et le toi* (Paris, an II). Valcour's title makes reference to the revolutionaries' attempt to abandon class and rank distinctions in French between formal and familiar forms of address. Citizens were to address each other familiarly as "thou" or "toi."

72. d'Estrée, *Théâtre sous la Terreur,* pp. 280-82 and *passim;* Hérissay, *Monde des théâtres,* p. 205; Welschinger, *Théâtre de la Révolution,* pp. 28-30.

73. *Journal des théâtres* (Paris, 4 November 1791-23 June 1792), 20 April 1792, p. xxvi.

74. *Coup d'oeil sur les spectacles,* p. 17; *Almanach de tous les spectacles* (1791), p. 149.

75. *Journal des spectacles,* vol. 2, 9 September 1793; reprint of *Réflexions sur les spectacles* by Aristide Valcour first printed in the *Journal de la Montagne.*

76. Antoine Vincent Arnault, *Souvenirs d'un sexagénaire* (Paris, 1833), vol. 2, pp. 68-69.

77. *Conservateur des principes républicains et de la morale politique,* quoted in d'Estrée, *Théâtre sous la Terreur,* p. 262.

78. On Pompigny, see the *Feuille du Salut Public,* quoted in d'Estrée, *Théâtre sous la Terreur,* p. 261. On Dorvigny, see P. Fromageot, "Un Fils de Louis XV, Auteur dramatique," *Le Carnet,* XII (1902 Avril-Juin), p. 171, who quotes from *Moniteur* du 18 nivôse—also in preface to the play, published 1794; Barba, *Souvenirs,* pp. 170-73; and Monselet, *Les Originaux du siècle dernier,* vol. 2, pp. 89-113.

79. Fromageot, "Un Fils de Louis XV," p. 171.

80. Preface to *La Parfaite Egalité ou les Tu et Toi* (Paris, 1794), taken from *Moniteur* du 18 nivôse, quoted by Fromageot, "Un Fils de Louis XV," p. 171.

81. *Les Spectacles de Paris pour l'année 1793,* p. 281, cited by F.-A. Aulard, ed., *Recueil des Actes du Comité du Salut public* (Paris, 1889-1951), vol. 1, p. 72, n. 2.

82. A.N. Ms. F[7]4714, dossier Gabiot.

83. A.N. ADVIII. Bibliothèque administrative, Collection Rondoneau. Instruction publique. Théâtres et spectacles. 45. *Protestation de Messieurs de Mirabeau, Chapelier, Clermont-Tonnerre, etc.*

84. *Les Spectacles de Paris pour l'année 1793,* p. 281, cited by Aulard, ed., *Recueil des Actes du Comité de Salut public,* vol. 1, pp. 71-72, n. 2.

85. This observation is based on a thorough review of the bibliographical references provided by: Brenner, *Bibliographical List of Plays;* Cioranescu, *Bibliographie de la littérature française;* Quérard, *La France littéraire;* P.L. Jacob, ed., *Bibliothèque dramatique de Monsieur Soleinne* (Paris, 1843-44), 5 vols.; Charles Brunet, *Table des Pièces de théâtre décrites dans le catalogue de la Bibliothèque de M. de Soleinne* (Paris, 1914) as well as my own sampling of theatrical performances in *Annonces.*

86. B.N. Ms. n.a.f. 5052 [Papiers de Robineau de Beaunoir]. fol. 101, letter dated [1809].

87. Quérard, *La France littéraire,* citing J.S. Ersch, *La France littéraire contenant les auteurs français de 1771-1796* (Hambourg, 1797-1806), 5 vols.

88. Michaud, *Biographie universelle,* entry Mague St. Aubin, mentions *Les Hochets* as an indecent play. The play may, however, have been written by another author of similar name, Cammaille St. Aubin. See also on Mague St. Aubin: Alphonse Leveaux, "Mague de St. Aubin," *Bulletin de la Société historique de Compeigne,* II (1875), pp. 71-81.

89. Cioranescu, *Bibliographie de la littérature française.*

90. A.N. Ms. $F^{7}4774^{30}$, dossier Maillé.

91. Revolutionary calendars extended the seven day week to ten days and called it a *décade.*

92. A.N. Ms. $F^{7}4592$, dossier 5.

93. A.N. Ms. $F^{7}4618$, dossier 1. It is not known whether *The Heroism of Belperche* was ever completed or performed.

94. This may be erroneous. Fernand Bournon, *La Bastille* (Paris, 1893), reprinted the list of those recognized by the Commune as having full right to call themselves "Vainqueurs de la Bastille", neither Ribié's name nor that of any other pre-revolutionary boulevard playwright studied here appears. See also on Ribié, Barba, *Souvenirs,* pp. 76-77.

95. On Mayeur, see d'Estrée, *Théâtre sous la Terreur,* p. 347. On Ribié, see Claude Mazauric, "La Fête révolutionnaire manifestation de la politique jacobine, Rouen, 1793. An II," in Jean Ehrard and Paul Viallaneix, eds., *Les Fêtes de la Révolution Colloque de Clermont-Ferrand (June 1974)* (Paris, 1977), pp. 181-90; d'Estrée, *Théâtre sous la Terreur,* p. 346; A.N. Ms. $F^{7}4774^{91}$, $F^{7}4570$.

96. Fromageot, "Un Fils de Louis XV," p. 171.

97. A.N. Ms $F^{17}1213$. Instruction publique. Secours aux savants, artistes et gens de lettres; M.J. Guillaume, ed., *Procès-Verbaux de Comité d'Instruction publique de la Convention Nationale* (Paris, 1891-1957), vol. 5, pp. 359-60, 383-85; vol. 6, pp. 76, 89-90, 627-30.

98. *La Grande Encyclopédie* (Paris, 1886-1902), article "Odéon."

99. On Beaunoir's position in the world of letters see Michaud, *Biographie universelle;* Leconte, "Un pamphlétaire," p. 442; B.N. Ms. n.a.f. 3036. [Papiers de Robineau de Beaunoir] and Ms. n.a.f. 5052.

100. Brazier, *Histoire des petits théâtres,* vol. 1, p. 182. Over the period 1800-1825 Brazier saw that "a new generation of authors came to replace that whose brilliance had now faded. Arnould, Parisau, Gabiot, Dorvigny, Pompigny, Guillemain, Beaunoir . . . abandon the field of battle."

101. On Fonpré and Mayeur, see Lyonnet, *Dictionnare des comédiens;* on Dorvigny, see Fromageot, "Un Fils de Louis XV," pp. 173-74 and Barba, *Souvenirs,* p. 172.

102. Barba, *Souvenirs,* p. 77.

Prelude IV

1. Archives de la Préfecture de police. Ms. $A^{A}239$, 31 March 1791.

2. A.N. Ms. $F^{7}3688^{3}$. Rapport des Observateurs. Letters of Latour-Lamontagne dated 11 septembre 1793 and 18 septembre 1793.

3. Mague St. Aubin: A.N. Ms. $F^{17}1069$. Instruction publique. Théâtres 1791-1810. Letter in dossier of the Commision executive de l'Instruction publique dated 2 fructidor II (22 August

1794). Also reprinted in Welschinger, *Théâtre de la Révolution,* pp. 76-77. Actors: A.N. Ms. BB^{3}81, matin 13 pluviose II (1 February 1794); matin 27 nivôse II (16 January 1794); matin 26 nivôse II (15 January 1794). A.N. ADVIII 45. Circular of the Comité de Surveillance de Département de Paris, (21 January 1794).

4. Joseph Butwin, "The French Revolution as *Theatrum Mundi,*" *Washington State University. Research Studies,* 43 (1975), p. 142. Butwin discusses Rousseau's critique of theater on pp. 142-43.

5. Breakdown of rank: [Sélis], *Lettre sur les petits spectacles,* p. 40. Revolutionary contagion: La Harpe, *Lycée,* vol. 11, p. 131.

Chapter 7

1. The number of theaters in Paris throughout the period 1784-1794 and the duration of their enterprise has been determined with the following sources: Nougaret, ed., *Spectacles des foires; Annonces; Almanach de tous les spectacles; Spectacles de Paris; Journal des théâtres;* Carlson, *Theatre of the French Revolution,* "Chart of Theatres"; and Louis Henry Lecomte, *Histoire des théâtres de Paris, 1402-1904* (Paris, 1905).

2. *Almanach de tous les spectacles* (1791), pp. 4-5.

3. See discussion of La Harpe's role in liberating theater from privileged despotism in chapter 6, pp. 177-78.

4. Jean-François de La Harpe, *Correspondance littéraire,* (Paris, an IX 1801-1807), vol. 6, p. 93, letter dated from internal evidence from 1791.

5. *Almanach de tous les spectacles* (1792), p. 294.

6. La Harpe, *Correspondance littéraire,* vol. 5, p. 349, letter dated from internal evidence from 1790.

7. Arthur Pougin, *L'Opéra-Comique pendant la Révolution* (Paris, 1891), p. 12. By early 1794 the total debt of the Comédie-Italienne would reach 1,190,193 livres 18 sous, pp. 125-26.

8. La Harpe, *Correspondance littéraire,* vol. 5, p. 349, letter dated from internal evidence from 1790.

9. Ibid., vol. 6, p. 29, letter dated from internal evidence from 1791.

10. Millin de Grandmaison, *Liberté du théâtre,* p. 4; *Almanach de tous les spectacles* (1791), p. 5.

11. *Actes de la Commune de Paris,* series 1, vol.4, p.512. For petitions of the royal actors see ibid., pp. 164, 172. See also Jean-François de Cailhava, *Les Causes de la Décadence du Théâtre et les moyens de le faire refleurir* (Paris, 1789), pp. 41-42 and Framery, *L'organisation des spectacles,* p. 223.

12. De Lornaizon, *Addresse,* p. 14.

13. See B.N. Ms. f.f. 9557, fol. 2. and arguments of Papillon de la Ferté, from the later 1780s, chapter 2, pp. 62-63.

14. De Lornaizon, *Addresse,* pp. 7 and 11.

15. *Almanach de tous les spectacles* (1792), p. 95.

16. Pougin, *L'Opéra-Comique,* p. 40.

17. Lough, in his *Paris Theater Audiences,* pp. 223-224, was unable to describe with precision the changing composition of Parisian theater audiences during the years of the Revolution. He does quote Grimod de la Reynière to the effect that by 1797 the "people" frequented the great theaters in rather large numbers—yet Lough also suggests that contemporary sources such as Grimod often exaggerated the presence of the lower classes. The actor Fleury remarked in September 1793 that the audience at the Théâtre de la Nation recalled the select company which frequented that theater before 1789.

18. Brenner, *Théâtre-Italien,* pp. 34, 116.

19. C.G. Etienne and A. Martainville, *Histoire du Théâtre-Français depuis le commencement de la Révolution jusqu'à la Réunion générale* (Paris, 1802), vol. 1, p. 95.

20. On the Marais, see *Le Chronique de Paris* (Paris, 1789-1793); on the Théâtre du Palais-Variétés, see *Annonces.*

21. Prices for the little theaters of Paris are taken from the *Almanach de tous les spectacles* (1791 and 1792).

22. Many classes: Etienne and Martainville, *Histoire du Théâtre-Français,* vol. 1, p. 100; see also *Almanach de tous les spectacles* (1791), p. 6. Bourgeoisie: Etienne and Martainville, *Histoire du Théâtre-Français,* vol. 1, p. 182; Framery, *L'organisation des spectacles,* pp. 226-227; [Sélis], *Lettre sur les petits spectacles,* p. 35; *Influence de la Révolution,* p. 12; *Coup d'oeil sur les spectacles,* p. 13. Civic performance: B.N. Ms. f.f. 7005. Historian's claim: Henri Beaulieu, *Les Théâtres du Boulevard du Crime de Nicolet à Déjazet 1752-1862* (Paris, 1905), p. 8. The people at the Théâtre-Patriotique and Délassements-Comiques: *Almanach de tous les spectacles* (1792), pp. 35, 296. People at the Gaité: A.N. $BB^3$81. Séance 25 nivôse an II. A member of the Committee comments on "the most respectable, though poorly-educated, portion of the people who ordinarily attend this theater."

23. Albert Soboul, *The Sans-Culottes,* trans. Remy Inglis Hall (New York, 1968), p. 234.

24. *Almanach de tous les spectacles* (1792), p. 130.

25. [J.B.A. Hapdé], *De l'anarchie théâtrale ou de la nécessité de remettre en rigueur les lois et règlements relatifs aux differens genres des spectacles de Paris* (Paris, 1814), p. 1.

26. Victor Hallays-Dabot, *Histoire de la censure théâtrale en France* (Paris, 1862), pp. 163-64.

27. Albert, *Théâtres des Boulevards,* p. 78.

28. See repertories published by A. Joannidès, *La Comédie Française de 1680 à 1900, Dictionnaire général des pièces et des auteurs* (Paris, 1901) and Brenner, *Théâtre-Italien, Its Repertory.*

29. Only one of the plays picked up from a stage less prestigious than the Comédie-Italienne might have been considered a popular play. *L'Honnête criminel* had apparently been produced by the Théâtre de Beaujolais in the Palais-Royal. But Fenouillot de Falbaire could hardly have been considered a popluar playwright. In previous years all five of his plays had been performed at the court theater of Fontainebleau, by the Italian company or the French actors themselves. Other of the new playwrights welcomed at the Comédie-Française had offered a few plays to the Variétés-Amusantes in the Palais-Royal; none had had any work performed by the minor theaters of the boulevard.

30. Lagrave, "La Comédie-Française," p. 135, writes, "The Comédie-Française thus defined itself at the time as much a conservatory of national theater as a theater of creation."

31. For all theaters other than the Comédie-Française and the Comédie-Italienne repertory analysis is based on my own sampling of theater programs every eight days for the years 1785-1794 in the *Annonces* and other Parisian journals. The Variétés Comiques et Lyriques used eight plays from the boulevard in a repertory of 48 plays; the Théâtre du Palais-Variétés used nine out of 102 plays in its repertory; the Théâtre de la Concorde chose three plays from the little theaters of Paris and five from the great theaters; only one out of 73 plays in the repertory of the Marais came from a little theater (and that in the Palais-Royal); the Vaudeville likewise only chose one or two plays from the minor spectacles of Paris. Note that these figures are based on a sample of theater programs, and must therefore be recognized as approximate.

32. At the Théâtre de Molière compare four popular plays to 53 plays written for that theater in 1791 and after and to 59 plays borrowed from the great theaters of Paris. At the Montansier compare 16 plays to 74 plays written for that theater since 1790 and to 70 plays borrowed from the public domain. Note that these figures are based on a sample of theater programs and must therefore be recognized as approximate.

33. Note that these figures are based on a sample of theater programs and therefore must be recognized as approximate.

34. On Molière at the Gaité, see Albert, *Théâtre des Boulevards;* and Carlson, *Theatre of the French Revolution;* on Racine and Corneille, see *Almanach de tous les spectacles* (1792), p. 298.

35. Based on my own sampling of theatre programs every eight days for the years 1785-1794 in the *Annonces.*

36. Ferdinand Brunetière in *L'Evolution des genres dans l'histoire de la littérature,* 3rd ed. (Paris, 1898), vol. 1, pp. 161-62, portrays La Harpe as one of the last critical defenders of classicism in late-eighteenth and early nineteenth century France. La Harpe's allegiances to the classical dramatic tradition apparently did not interfere with the liberal position he embraced in urging the January law of 1791.

37. La Harpe, *Correspondance littéraire,* vol. 6, p. 89, letter dated from internal evidence from 1789.

38. Ibid., p. 91.

39. *Almanach de tous les spectacles* (1791), p. 17.

40. Ibid., p. 250.

41. *Journal des théâtres,* I, 4 November 1791. *The Journal des théâtres* originated in the bureau of the *Modérateur* and was edited by the same editor, Jean-Charles Le Vacher de Charnois. With the anonymous collaboration of Ducray-Dumenil, a prolific author of juvenile novels and literary editor of the *Annonces,* Charnois observed the revolution in theater from a rather conservative perspective through June 1792. In August of that year, due to his attachment to the royalist cause, he was arrested and imprisoned (Ducray-Dumenil had his own brush with revolutionary government for other reasons) and died in the September 2 massacre.

42. Ibid., V, 2 December 1791.

43. Brockett, "Fair Theatres," p. 268.

44. Etienne and Martainville, *Histoire du Théâtre-Français,* vol. 2, p. 24.

45. *Journal des théâtres,* XXVII, 27 April 1792.

46. La Harpe, *Correspondance littéraire,* vol. 6, p. 2, letter dated 1790.

47. The *tragédie-lyrique* and the *tragi-comédie,* for instance, had had a place in the seventeenth century work of Racine and Corneille. There had been as well more recent experimentation within classical theater—experimentation not always well received by the Comédie-Française or royal government.

48. Brockett, "Fair Theatres," pp. 268-70; Pitou, "Les Origines du Mélodrame," *passim.*

49. Pitou, "Les Origines du Mélodrame," pp. 272-73. Pitou's point is well taken that the dialogued pantomime had its greatest influence on great theater only many years after the Revolution. This boulevard genre evolved in the course of the 1790s towards the melodrama, which in the work of Pixerécourt, had definitive effect on the Romantic dramas of the early nineteenth century.

50. *Journal des théâtres,* XXVI, 20 April 1792; "monstrous" refers to *Robert chef des Brigands* in XXII, 16 March 1792.

51. La Harpe, *Correspondance littéraire,* vol. 6, pp. 105-106, letter dated from internal evidence from 1791.

52. Estève, "Observations de Guilbert de Pixerécourt," p. 552.

53. *Almanach de tous les spectacles* (1792), p. 305.

Chapter 8

1. La Harpe, *Correspondance,* vol. 6. p. 2.

2. A.N. Ms. F^{17}1069. "Demande de secours" by Langlois, entrepreneur of the Théâtre de Marais, to the Committee of Public Instruction, 12 January 1793.

3. Ibid. "Demande de secours" by Boursault, entrepreneur of the Théâtre de Molière, to the Committee of Public Instruction, 1792.

4. Circular addressed by Manuel, printed in the *Journal de Paris,* 28 March 1792, and reprinted by d'Estrée, *Théâtre sous la Terreur,* p. 70.

5. La Harpe, *Lycée,* vol. 11, p. 131.

6. Ibid. and La Harpe, *Correspondance,* vol. 6, p. 2.

7. *Almanach de tous les spectacles* (1792), p. 297.

8. According to my sampling of theater programs every eight days for these years in the *Annonces* and other Parisian journals.

9. *Almanach de tous les spectacles* (1791) pp. 197-98.

10. Ibid. (1792), p. 296.

11. Ibid.

12. Bibliographical entries in the Index to Boulevard Plays Studied and Cited will stand instead of footnotes to the mention and citation of plays performed by the boulevard theaters.

13. Because they are fairly well known and covered meticulously by many historians, the outstanding theatrical events of 1792 and early 1793, i.e. the affair over *l'Auteur d'un moment* at the Théâtre de Vaudeville and *l'Ami des lois* at the Théâtre de la Nation, are not discussed here. It is in the study of these events, however, and the positions taken on the issue of dramatic censorship of these plays by the police, the municipality and national government

(both the National Assembly and the Convention) that one learns how important theater was in the struggle for political and ideological control of the Revolution in 1792 and 1793. See Hallays-Dabot, *Histoire de la censure théâtrale;* Carlson, *Theatre of the French Revolution;* and Welschinger, *Théâtre de la Révolution,* pp. 380-409, where many documents dealing with *l'Ami des lois* are reprinted in their entirety.

14. d'Estrée, *Théâtre sous la Terreur,* p. 4.

15. Testimony of Pétion at Convention session 16 January 1793, reprinted in Welschinger, *Théâtre de la Révolution,* p. 404.

16. See, for instance, Hallays-Dabot, *Histoire de la censure théâtrale,* p. 179 on the Opéra's difficulties over *Le Siège de Thionville* and over a patriotic repertory for that stage.

17. The *Journal des spectacles* (1 July 1793-January 1794) was edited by Pascal Boyer, a relatively unknown musician and littérateur. His political leanings appear to have been republican and radical. The following page and a half relies heavily on this one journal for two reasons: it was the only journal at the time that commented at length on plays in performance and, because so many revolutionary plays are lost, it is an invaluable way to retrieve the subjects and plots of revolutionary theater.

18. *Journal des spectacles,* vol. 1, p. 181, 23 July 1793. See also vol. 1, p. 228, 29 July 1793 on *Le jeune Esclave,* whose situations, "though not very new, are nonetheless agreeable."

19. Ibid., vol. 2, p. 534.

20. Ibid., vol. 2, p. 693-94, 27 September 1793.

21. Ibid., vol. 2, p. 878, 30 Vendemiare II (21 October 1793).

22. Jacques-René Hébert, *Le Père Duchesne, 1790-94,* Albert Soboul, ed., (Paris, 1969), vol. 9, no. 310, p. 5.

23. *Journal des spectacles,* vol. 1, p. 285, 3 August 1793.

24. Hébert, *Père Duchesne,* vol. 9, no. 310, p. 7.

25. *A.P.,* vol. 70, p. 134. Speech by Couthon, 2 August 1793.

26. *A.P.,* vol. 70, p. 135, article 1 of law of 2 August 1793.

27. Guillaume, ed., *Procès-Verbaux du Comité d'Instruction publique,* vol. 2, p. 353.

28. Censors' report, March 1794, reprinted in Hallays-Dabot, *Histoire de la censure théâtrale,* pp. 189-90. Note that although d'Estrée knew about the censors' report, which declared that there had been no law of censorship, his interpretation of the 1-2 September law (and he never noted its contents) suggests that a preliminary censorship had indeed been directly sanctioned by the Convention: "The law of September 1st completed that of August 2nd, by according to the Commune of Paris that which it had desired for so long—the policing in its own hands of theaters in the capital—or, in other words, free rein to its animosities and its bitterness." (*Théâtre sous la Terreur,* p. 7). But the Convention did not mean the decreee of 1-2 September to settle the issue of preliminary censorship—that, at the subsequent request of Fabre d'Eglantine, was to be considered by the Committee of Public Instruction. (Guillaume, ed., *Procès-Verbaux du Comité d'Instruction publique,* vol. 2, p. 864.

29. The Committee of Public Safety or Surveillance of the Department of Paris, attached to the Department and not the Convention, was one of the prime instruments of the Terror in Paris. It was composed of members of the disbanded insurrectionaries that had directed the overthrow of the Girondins in June 1793. On this see Norman Hampson, *A Social History of the French Revolution* (Toronto, 1970, 1974), p. 183.

30. A.N. Ms. BB³81. Sessions 4-5 August 1793.

31. Ibid.

32. For government records of this see A.N. Ms. F¹⁷1294. Instruction publique. [Indemnités à raison des Représentations donnés de Par et Pour le Peuple Conformément au décret du deux août 1793.] This document is also reprinted in Welschinger, *Théâtre de la Révolution.*

33. *Journal des spectacles,* vol. 3, 30 brumaire an II (21 November 1793).

34. *Journal des spectacles,* vol. 1, p. 427, 24 August 1793.

35. These are *La Fête du Maire de Village,* possibly written by Pierre-Gaspard Chaumette, and *Les Chasseurs généreux,* anonymous and possibly the same as Anseaume's *Les deux Chasseurs et la Laitière.* Neither manuscript was available for study. The other play on the Ambigu-Comique's patriotic roster was *Le Masque de fer,* a highly successful pantomime first performed in 1790. This manuscript, also, has not been located.

36. *Journal des spectacles,* vol. 3, 30 brumaire an II (21 November 1793).

37. A.N. Ms. F⁷3688³. Observer report dated 11 September 1793.

38. Censors' report, March 1794, reprinted in Hallays-Dabot, *Histoire de la censure théâtrale,* pp. 189-90. By this scrutiny the censors meant to insure the politicization of all theater. See chapter 6 for one playwright's interview with Baudrais.

39. Ibid.

40. Vivien, "Etudes Administratives III: Les Théâtres," *Revue des deux mondes,* nouvelle serie, VI (1844), p. 399. Also in book form, *Etudes administratives* (Paris, 1852), vol 2, chapter on theaters. Note that these and other police records subsequently destroyed in 1870 have been inaccurately dated by those historians who worked with the originals. As Vivien would have it, the records at issue here represented the cooperative effort of the municipal police and the Convention's Commission of Public Instruction beginning in mid-May 1794. However, Guillaume, in a long "pièce annexe" to his *Procès-Verbaux du Comité d'Instruction Publique,* vol. 4, annex C. pp. 549-51, argues persuasively that municipal censorship was not implemented, as Vivien claimed, in accordance with the decree of 25(24) Floreal [14(13) May 1794] placing censorial functions within the jurisdiction of the Exectutive Commision of Public Instruction. "The decisions of these administrators [the municipal censors] were anterior to the regime that placed theaters under the direct authority of the Commission"—in other words before mid-May. I believe these records probably preceded in their entirety (three months according to Vivien) the fall of the Hébertists and the imprisonment of Baudrais and Froidure in late March. It was in mid-March that Baudrais submitted his report to the Commune, making strong references to the suspension of pre-revolutionary repertoire already underway. It is not impossible, however, that this record was completed by his successors, Faro and Lelièvre, whom Hallays-Dabot quoted as rejecting a play "filled with dukes, duchesses and abbots, and in which the national guard are represented like drunks" on 25 April 1794. (*Histoire de la censure théâtrale,* p. 192). Certainly, this censorship did not extend beyond early May, when Joseph Payan, head of the Commission of Public Instruction, began reversing the censorial policies of the Commune. Unfortunately, the historian's initial confusion has been passed from one study to another. Guillaume pointed out that the error of confounding municipal surveillance with that of the Commission of Public Instruction, which was first committed by Vivien and Hallays-Dabot, has been repeated by Welschinger and d'Estrée.

41. Vivien, "Etudes Administratives," p. 399.

42. Ibid.

43. A. Liéby, "La presse révolutionnaire et la censure théâtrale sous la Terreur," *Révolution française,* XLV (1903), pp. 306-53, 447-70, 502-29, XLVI (1904), pp. 13-28, 97-128, matched Vivien's censorship statistics with theater listings for the major stages and found, for example, that Molière's plays "continued to be represented on stage by a good part of his work in the year II" (vol. XLV, p. 521). Liéby also noted that the boulevard's Théâtre-Patriotique managed to conserve many of the classical tragedies that had been censured elsewhere through much of the year II (vol. XLV, p. 509).

44. This play, also referred to as *Arlequin au tombeau (Arlequin at the Tomb),* is the same as *Arlequin dogue d'Angleterre (Arlequin the English Cerberus),* discussed in chapter 3. Brazier, *Histoire des petits théâtres,* vol. 1, pp. 7-8, recalled that "*Arlequin the English Cerberus* used to create a furor, above all when Nicolet as a dog, having sniffed Pantalon's clothing, lifted his leg in the air. Pantalon shook his gown in such a comical manner that the whole audience would laugh and clap its hands."

45. A.N. Ms. $BB^3$81. Session 25 nivôse II (14 January 1794).

46. Ibid. Sessions 25, 26 nivôse II (14, 15 January 1794); A.N. Ms. $BB^3$73, dossier 38; A.N. Ms. $F^7$4774^{57}, dossier 3, Nicolet. Arrestation. 26 nivôse II (15 January 1794).

47. A.N. Ms. $BB^3$81. Session 27 nivôse II (16 January 1794).

48. Ibid., Session 5 pluviose II (24 January 1794).

49. Circular of the Committee of Surveillance of the Dept. of Paris, 21 January 1794, in A.N. ADVIII 45.

50. Quoted in Hallays-Dabot, *Histoire de la censure théâtrale,* pp. 160-61. Hallays-Dabot was wrong to place this evidence of municipal censorship in 1791. Liéby, "Presse révolutionnarie," p. 524, indicates correctly that the note accompanied Audinot's submission of repertory in germinal year II.

51. The political skirmish over *Le Tombeau des imposteurs* is discussed in many studies of revolutionary theater. See for example, Welschinger, *Théâtre de la Révolution.*

52. Destival letter to Baudrais, probably dated February 1794, reprinted in Welschinger, *Théâtre de la Révolution,* p. 104.

53. A.N. Ms. $BB^3$81. Session 25 germinal II (14 April 1794).

54. The following analysis is based on my sample of theater announcements, in which all performances were recorded every eight days for the years 1785-1794 as listed in the *Annonces* and other Parisian journals. See Table 4: "Change in the Repertory of Two Boulevard Theaters, 1789-1794," and Table 5: "Change in the Boulevard Repertory, 1793-1794."

55. The calculation of the number of performances as opposed to the number of plays changes the statistics very little. Even though in some instances a smaller number of new plays were performed more frequently (at the Gaité and the Théâtre-Patriotique), this did not alter greatly the relative emphasis on that category in 1794. Only at the Variétés-Amusantes de Lazzari did the number of performances noticeably increase emphasis on new plays, many of which, but not all, were republican in nature. See Table 5: "Change in the Boulevard Repertory, 1793-1794."

56. See chapter 4, pp. 128-131 for discussion of the play.

57. Certain documents in the Archives de la Seine suggest that the entrepreneurs of the Délassements-Comiques may have suffered bankruptcy at the end of 1793. That was certainly

the case for one of the "associates," Clergier—whose case may be pieced together at least partially with Ms. D^6U^144 objets divers, No. 3 Clergier faillite.

58. Quoted in Welschinger, *Théâtre de la Révolution,* p. 149.

59. Until the Commission's organization, the municipal police were to continue their surveillance as in the past; indeed, they stubbornly clung to their censorship of the stage long after the legal transfer of their authority. The Commission's request for theatrical repertories on 14 May 1794 may very well have been ignored altogether. In early June the Committee of Public Safety sternly reminded both police and theaters that the Commission of Public Instruction was "exclusively" charged "with all that concerns the regeneration of dramatic art." (Law of 18 Prairial, article 1). Some two weeks later the Commission once again ordered the transmittal of municipal registers and repertories. No doubt spurred by the new law of suspects (22 Prairial), the police complied this time with alacrity. See discussion by Guillaume, ed., *Procès-Verbaux du Comité d'Instruction publique,* vol. 4, pp. 549-52 of the complex series of events involved in the transfer of censorship authority from the Commune to the Convention.

60. Circular 5 Messidor. (Extracted from the register of decrees of the Committee of Public Safety.) A.N. Ms. $F^{17}1294$.

61. Ibid., pp. 4-5.

62. "Rapport sur les corrections de l'opéra de *Castor et Pollux,*" circular issued by the Commission of Public Instruction between July 5th and 25th 1794, reprinted in Guillaume, ed., *Procès-Verbaux du Comité d'Instruction publique,* vol. 4, pp. 714-16.

63. Quoted in Liéby, "Presse révolutionnaire," p. 113.

64. Circular 5 Messidor and "Rapport sur les corrections de l'opéra de *Castor et Pollux,*" both issued by the Commission of Public Instruction (A.N. Ms. $F^{17}1294$ and Guillaume, ed., *Procès-Verbaux du Comité d'Instruction publique,* vol.4, pp. 714-16, respectively).

65. Circular 5 Messidor, A.N. Ms. $F^{17}1294$.

66. The actress Louise Fusil remarked of the theatrical world in 1790: "There was at the time such a hierarchy of theaters throughout the kingdom, that the [French] actors would have believed themselves belittled (auraient cru déroger) by performing on a stage other than their own [the Comédie-Française]." *Souvenirs d'une Actrice, Mémoires de Louise Fusil (1774-1848)* (Paris, 1904), p. 143.

67. Circular 5 Messidor, A.N. MS. $F^{17}1294$.

68. "Fête à l'Etre Suprême," circular issued by the Commission of Public Instruction 29 June 1794 (approved and decreed by the Committee of Public Safety 13 messidor), reprinted in Romain Rolland, *Le Théâtre du Peuple* (Paris, 1913), pp. 186-90.

69. Decree of the Committee of Public Safety 10 March 1794, reprinted in Aulard, ed., *Recueil des Actes,* vol. 11, p. 626.

70. Aulard, *Recueil des Actes,* vol. 12, p. 614.

71. Ibid., vol. 14, pp. 170, 770, 259.

72. Circular 5 Messidor, A.N. Ms. $F^{17}1294$.

Conclusion

1. Butwin, "French Revolution as *Theatrum Mundi,*" p. 143.

Bibliography

Primary Sources in Manuscript

Archives de l'Assistance publique:

Ms. Liasse 1438. Registre des Déliberations du Bureau de l'Hôtel Dieu.

Archives de la Préfecture de police:

Ms. A^A 85. Procès-verbaux des commissaires de police des Sections de Paris. 1789-1820. Section de Butte des Moulins.

Ms. A^A 166. Procès-verbaux des commissaires de police... Section du Luxembourg.

Ms. A^A 239-241. Procès-verbaux des commissaires de police... Section du Temple.

Archives de la Seine:

Ms. D^6U^{39} 1791-D^6U^{42} an II. Jugements. Justice de paix des arrondissements anciens de Paris: Section du Temple.

Ms. $D^6U^1$44. Objets divers.

Ms. D34Z. Papiers Dereix.

Archives nationales:

ADVIII. Bibliothèque administrative, Collection Rondoneau. Instruction publique. Théâtres et spectacles.

Ms. AJ^{13}10. Perception des Redevances des Théâtres 1774-1787. Redevances dues à l'Opéra.

Ms. $BB^3$73. Comité de surveillance du Dept. de Paris. Correspondances.

Ms. $BB^3$81. Comité de surveillance du Dept. de Paris. Registres des séances.

Ms. DXXXVII 3. Comité d'instruction publique. Théâtres et spectacles.

Ms. F^7. Police général.

Ms. F^{17}1069. Instruction publique. Théâtres 1791-1810.

Ms. F^{17}1213. Instruction publique. Secours aux savants, artistes et gens de lettres.

Ms. F^{17}1294. Instruction publique. [Indemnités à raison des Représentations données de Par et Pour le Peuple.]

Ms. $H^2$2158. Bureau de la ville. Théâtres des Variétés-Amusantes et l'Ambigu, 1785-86.

Ms. $0^1$615. Maison du Roi. Lettres du Baron de Breteuil.

Ms. $0^1$617. Maison du Roi. Lettres de Papillon de la Ferté.

Ms. $0^1$618. Maison du Roi. Privilèges de l'Opéra.

Ms. $0^1$620. Maison du Roi. Comité de l'Opéra: Déliberations et comptes rendus au Ministère.

Ms. $0^1$845. Grands officiers de la Maison du Roi. Grand Chambellan, Comédie-italienne et française.

Ms. T737. Papiers séquestres. Emigrés et condamnés.

Ms. $V^7$492. Conseil deputés... pour juger en dernier ressort les contestations concernant les grandes et contravention du Tabac.

Ms. W411. No. 945. Tribunal révolutionnaire. Parisau.

Ms. Y12227. Archives des Commissaires. Police des Foires Saint Laurent et Saint Ovide à Paris, 1763-1783.

Ms. Y15996-Y16009. Archives des Commissaires. Office de Vanglenne.
Ms. Y16022. Archives des Commissaires au Châtelet. Rapports de la garde de Paris 1773-1790.
Bibliothèque de l'Arsenal:
Ms. 6758. [Pièces de A. Cailleau.]
Ms. 13002. Etat de la recette et de la dépense...,Comptabilité du Théâtre des Grands-Danseurs, pour les années 1782-1792.
Bibliothèque de la Comédie-française:
Ms. Registre pour les pièces des spectacles des Boulevards.
Bibliothèque historique de la ville de Paris:
Ms. 710. Voyage à travers une partie de la France et des Pays-Bas autrichienne, 1786.
Bibliothèque nationale:
Ms. fonds français (f.f.) 7005, fol. 8. Recueil de pièces historiques sur la Révolution et l'Empire 1789-1815: Documents sur les théâtres à Paris (1790-1798).
Ms. f.f. 9557, fol. 2. Spectacles inférieurs [de Paris] avril 1764.
Ms. f.f. 22085. [*Avis* de Delormel et fils.]
Ms. nouvelles acquisitions françaises (n.a.f.) 3036. [Papiers de Robineau de Beaunoir.]
Ms. n.a.f. 3045-3049. Papiers de la Gaité.
Ms. n.a.f. 5052. [Papiers de Robineau de Beaunoir.]

Primary Sources in Print

Actes de la Commune de Paris pendant la Révolution, Lacroix, Sigismond, ed. (Paris: L. Cerf, 1894-92 sic; New York: AMS Press, 1974), ser. 1, 7 vols; (Paris: L. Cerf, 1900-1914; New York: AMS Press, 1973), ser. 2, 8 vols.
Almanach forain. See Nougaret, ed., *Les Spectacles des foires et des Boulevards de Paris.*
Almanach général de tous les spectacles de Paris et des provinces, attributed to Cousin Jacques, Mayeur de St. Paul, Ribié and St. Aubin, eds. (Paris: Froullé, 1791-1792), 2 vols.
Annonces, affiches et avis divers, also called *Affiches de Paris* or *Petites Affiches,* (Paris: 1783-1811).
Archives parlementaires de 1787-1860, Recueil complet des débats législatifs et politiques des Chambres françaises, Mavidal, M.J. and Laurent, M.E., eds. (Paris: Paul Dupont, 1862-1919), ser. 1, 71 vols.
Arnault, Antoine Vincent, *Souvenirs d'un sexagénaire* (Paris: Duféy, 1833), 4 vols.
Aubignac, François Hédelin, abbé d', *La pratique du théâtre* (Amsterdam: J.F. Bernard, 1715), reprinted in *Theorie und Geschichte der literatur und der Schönen Künste* (Munich: Wilhelm Fink Verlag, 1971), pagination of the original.
Aulard, François-Victor Alphonse, ed., *Recueil des Actes du Comité de Salut public* (Paris: Imprimerie nationale, 1889-1951), 11 vols.
Bachaumont, Louis Petit de, *Mémoires secrets pour servir à l'histoire de la république des lettres en France* (London: Adamson, 1777-1789), 36 vols.
Barba, Jean-Nicolas, *Souvenirs* (Paris: Ledoyen et Giret, 1846).
Boileau-Despréaux, Nicolas, *Art poétique* in *Oeuvres complètes* (Paris: Editions Gallimard, 1966), pp. 157-85.
Boysse, Ernest, ed., *Journal de Papillon de la Ferté* (Paris: Paul Ollendorff, 1887).
Brazier, N., *Histoire des petits théâtres de Paris* (Paris: Allardin, 1838), 2 vols.
Brièle, L., *Collection de Documents pour servir à l'histoire des hôpitaux de Paris* (Paris: Imprimerie nationale, 1883), 4 vols.
Cahier. Plaintes et doléances de Messieurs les Comédiens-français (n.p., 1789).,
Cailhava, Jean-François de, *Les Causes de la Décadence du théâtre et les moyens de le faire refleurir* (Paris: Royez, 1789).
Le Chronique de Paris (Paris: 24 August 1789-25 August 1793).

Clement, Pierre, ed., *Lettres, Instructions et Mémoires de Colbert* (Paris: Imprimerie nationale, 1861-1882), 10 vols.
Coup d'oeil rapide sur les spectacles de Paris (Paris: n.d. [1792]).
De Lornaizon, Clement, *Addresse à MM. les représentants de la Commune de Paris* (n.p., n.d. [1790]).
Des Essarts, Nicolas Toussaint Lemoyne, *Les Trois Théâtres de Paris ou abrégé historique de l'établissement de la Comédie Françoise, de la Comédie Italienne et de l'Opéra* (Paris: Lacombe, 1777).
Donnet, Alexis, Orgiazzi, and Kaufmann, Jacques-Auguste, *Architectonographie des théâtres, ou Parallèle historique et critique de ces édifices* (Paris: L. Mathias, 1837-1840).
Dulaure, Jacques A., *Nouvelle description des curiosités de Paris*, 2nd ed. (Paris: Lejay, 1787), 2 vols.
Dumersan, Théophile-Marion, "Histoire des Théâtres de Boulevart, Suite. Ribié (César), auteur et acteur," *Le Monde dramatique*, IV (1835-1841), pp. 241-45.
[Dumont, comédien], *Le Désoeuvré mis en oeuvre ou le Revers de Médaille* (Paris, 1782).
Encyclopédie, ou Dictionnaire raisonné des sciences, des arts et des métiers, Diderot, Denis and d'Alembert, Jean le Rond, eds. (Paris: Briasson, 1751-1765), 17 vols.
Estève, E., "Observations de Guilbert de Pixerécourt sur les théâtres de la Révolution," *Revue d'histoire littéraire de la France*, XXIII (1916), pp. 546-61.
Etienne, C.G. and Martainville, A., *Histoire du Théâtre-Français depuis le commencement de la Révolution jusqu'à la Réunion générale* (Paris: Barba, 1802), 4 vols.
Figaro aux Parisiens, amateurs du bon goût, des arts, des spectacles et de la liberté (Paris: Goujon, 1790).
Framery, Etienne-Nicolas, *De l'organisation des spectacles de Paris* (Paris: Buisson, 1790).
Fusil, Louise, *Souvenirs d'une Actrice, Mémoires de Louise Fusil (1774-1848)* (Paris: C. Schmid, 1904).
Goethe, J.W. von, *Wilhelm Meisters Lehrjahre*, (Stuttgart, n.d.), Book I, chapter XV.
Goldoni, Carlo, *Mémoires de M. Goldoni pour servir à l'histoire de sa vie et à celle de son théâtre*, (originally published in Paris: Duchesne, 1787) in Barrière, Jean François, ed., *Bibliothèque des Mémoires*, vol. 6 (Paris: Didot, 1857).
Grimm, Friedrich Melchior, *Correspondance littéraire, philosophique et critique* (Paris: Garnier frères, 1877-1882), 16 vols.
Guillaume, M.J., ed., *Procès-Verbaux du Comité d'Instruction publique de la Convention Nationale* (Paris: Imprimerie nationale, 1891-1957), 7 vols.
Guyot, Joseph Nicolas, *Le Grand vocabulaire français* (Paris: C. Panckouke, 1767-1774).
[Hapdé, J.B.A.], *De l'anarchie théâtrale ou de la nécessité de la remettre en rigueur les lois et règlements relatifs aux differens genres des spectacles de Paris* (Paris: J.G. Dentu, 1814).
Hébert, Jacques-René, *Le Père Duchesne, 1790-1794*, Soboul, Albert, ed. (Paris: EDHIS, 1969).
Humble Mémoire du sieur Nicolet (n.p., n.d.), reprinted in Manne, Edmond Denis de and Menetrier, C., *Galerie historique des comédiens de la troupe de Nicolet* (Lyon: N. Scheuring, 1869), p. 5n.
Influence de la Révolution sur le théâtre français, pétition à ce sujet addressée à la Commune de Paris (Paris: Debray, 1790).
Journal de Paris (Paris: 1777-1811).
Le Journal des spectacles; contenant l'analyse des différentes pièces qu'on a representés sur tous les théâtres de Paris (Paris: 1 July 1793-7 January 1794).
Journal des théâtres (Paris: 4 November 1791-23 June 1792).
La Harpe, Jean-François de, *Correspondance littéraire* (Paris: Migneret, an IX 1801-1807), 6 vols.
______, *Lycée ou Cours de littérature ancienne et moderne*, nouvelle ed. (Paris: Lefevre, 1813, originally published an VII-an XIII), 15 vols.

Le Sage and d'Orneval, *Le Théâtre de la Foire ou l'Opéra Comique* (Paris: Etienne Ganneau, 1721-1731), 8 vols.
Mague de St. Aubin, *La réforme des théâtres, ou vues d'un amateur sur les moyens d'avoir toujours des acteurs à talents sur les théâtres de Paris* (Paris: Guillot, 1787).
[Mayeur de St. Paul], *Le Chroniqueur Désoeuvré, ou l'Espion du Boulevard du Temple*, 2nd ed. (London: 1782 and 1783), 2 vols.
[———], *Le Désoeuvré, ou l'Espion du Boulevard du Temple* (London: 1781 and 1782).
[———], *Le Désoeuvré, ou l'Espion du Boulevard du Temple* (Paris: E. Sansot, 1907).
Mémoire et consultation sur la cause pendante en la Grand' Chambre du Parlement entre les Comédiens Français, le Sieur Nicolet, et les autres Entrepreneurs de Spectacles Forains (n.p., 1785).
Mercier, Louis Sebastien, *Du théâtre; ou, nouvel essai sur l'art dramatique* (Amsterdam: E. van Harrevelt, 1773).
———, *Tableau de Paris*, nouvelle ed. (Amsterdam: [S. Fauche], 1783-1789), 12 vols.
Metra, François et al., *Correspondance secrète, politique et littéraire, ou Mémoires pour servir à l'histoire des cours, des sociétés et de la littérature en France, depuis la mort de Louis XV* (London: J. Adamson, 1787-1788), 12 vols.
"Millin de Grandmaison," [Aubin-Louis Millin], *Sur la liberté du théâtre* (Paris: Lagrange, 1790).
Nougaret, Pierre Jean Baptiste, *De l'art du théâtre* (Paris: Cailleau, 1769), 2 vols.
[———], *La littérature renversée, ou l'art de faire des pièces de théâtre sans paroles* (Berne and Paris: 1775).
[———], *Les Numéros parisiens, ouvrage utile et nécessaire aux voyageurs à Paris* (Paris: 1788).
———, ed., *Les Spectacles des foires et des Boulevards de Paris* (Paris: 1773-1788), 8 vols. Also referred to as the *Almanach forain.*
Oeuvres de M. Vadé ou Recueil des opéra-comiques, parodies et pièces fugitives de cet Auteur, nouvelle ed. (The Hague: Pierre Gosse, 1785).
Paer, A., ed., *La Confession générale d'Audinot* (Rouen: J. Lemonnyer, 1880, original: Geneva, 1774).
Parfaict, François and Claude, *Histoire du Théâtre-françois depuis son origine jusqu'à present* (Paris: Le Mercier et Saillant, 1734-49), 15 vols.
Petites Affiches. See *Annonces, affiches et avis divers.*
Pétition des Auteurs dramatiques qui n'ont pas signé celle de M. de la Harpe (Paris, 1790).
Pidansat de Mairobert, *L'Espion anglais, ou correspondance secrète entre MyLord All'Eye et MyLord All'Ear*, nouvelle ed. (London: John Adamson, 1783-1784), 6 vols.
Placet aux Dames (n.p., n.d.), reprinted in Campardon, Emile, *Les Spectacles de la foire* (Paris: Berger-Levrault, 1877), vol. 2, entry Jean-Baptiste Nicolet.
Protestation de Messieurs de Mirabeau, Chapelier, Clermont-Tonnerre, etc. (Paris: 1790).
Recueil des Pièces qui ont eu le plus de succès sur les théâtres de la rue Richelieu, ci-devant des Variétés-amusantes, et théâtre du Palais-royal; sur celui des Petits Comédiens du Palais-royal, dits Beaujolais; sur celui de l'Ambigu-Comique, au Boulevart; sur celui de la Gaité, ci-devant les Grands-Danseurs du Roi; sur celui des Elèves de l'Opéra, etc. (Paris: Belin et Valadé ainé, 1791), 7 vols.
Recueil général des Anciennes Lois Françaises 420 à 1789 (Paris: Belin-Le-Prieur, 1821-1833), 29 vols.
Restif de la Bretonne, *Les Contemporaines* (Paris: Editions les yeux ouverts, 1962; originally published Paris: Bélin, 1780-1785), 30 vols.
Rivarol and Champcenetz, Louis de, *Petit Almanach de nos grands hommes* (n.p., 1788).
Rousseau, Jean-Jacques, *La Nouvelle Héloise, Lettres de deux amans habitans d'une petite ville au pied des Alpes* (Amsterdam: 1761).
Rosseau, Thomas, *Lettre à M*** sur les spectacles des boulevards* (Bruxelles-Paris: 1781).

[Sélis, Nicolas-Joseph], *Lettre à un père de famille sur les petits spectacles de Paris* (Paris: Garnéry, 1789).

Les Spectacles de Paris et de toute la France; ou, Calendrier historique et chronologique des théâtres (Paris: Duchesne, 1754-1815).

Théâtre des Boulevards ou Recueil de Parades (Paris: Mahon, 1756), ed., Heylli, Georges d' (Paris: 1881).

Thiery, Luc-Vincent, *Almanach du voyageur à Paris* (Paris: Hardouin, n.d.), for 1783, 1784, and 1786.

______, *Guide des Amateurs et des Etrangers Voyageurs à Paris, ou Déscription raisonné de cette ville et de tout ce qu'elle contient de remarquable* (Paris: Hardouin et Gattey, 1786-1787), 2 vols.

Tourneux, Maurice, "Un Projet d'encouragement aux lettres et aux sciences sous Louis XVI," *Revue d'histoire littéraire de la France,* VIII (1901) pp. 281-311.

Valcour, Plancher or Aristide, *Chanson des Sans-Culottes* (n.p., n.d.).

______, *Reflexions sur les spectacles,* reprinted in *Journal des spectacles* (1793-an II), vol. 2, no. 70, 9 September 1793.

Voltaire, François Marie Arouet de, *Correspondance,* Besterman, Theodore, ed. (Geneva: Institut de Musée Voltaire, 1953-1965), 107 vols.

Secondary Sources

Abbott, E. Beatrice, "Robineau, dit de Beaunoir, et les petits théâtres du XVIIIe siècle," *Revue d'histoire littéraire de France,* XLIII (1936), pp. 20-54, 161-80.

Adam, Antoine, *Histoire de la littérature française au XVIIe siècle* (Paris: Editions Domat, 1954-1957), 5 vols.

Aghion, Max, *Le Théâtre à Paris au XVIIIe siècle* (Paris: Librairie de France, 1926).

Aitken, G.J., *Explorations in Enterprise* (Cambridge, Ma.: Harvard University Press, 1965).

Alasseur, Claude, *La Comédie-française au 18e siècle, étude économique (Paris: Mouton, 1967).*

Albert, Maurice, Les Théâtres de la Foire (1660-1789) (New York: Burt Franklin, 1970, original copyright 1900).

______, *Les Théâtres des Boulevards (1789-1848)* (Paris: Société française d'imprimerie et de librairie, 1902).

Attinger, Gustave, *L'Esprit de la commedia dell'arte dans le théâtre français* (Paris: Librairie théâtrale, 1950).

Aulard, François - Victor Alphonse, *Le Culte de la Raison et le Culte de l'Etre suprème (1793-1794)* (Paris: Felix Alcan, 1892).

Barnett, Dene, "The Performance Practice of Acting: The Eighteenth Century," *Theatre Research International,* 2 (1977), pp. 157-86; 3 (1977), pp. 1-19; 3 (1978), pp. 79-93.

Beaulieu, Henri, *Les Théâtres du Boulevard du Crime de Nicolet à Déjazet 1752-1862* (Paris: H. Daragon, 1905).

Bollème, G., *La Bibliothèque bleue, littérature populaire en France du XVIIe au XIXe siècle* (Paris: Julliard, 1971).

Bondois, P.M., "L'Organisation industrielle et commerciale sous l'ancien régime. Le privilège exclusif au XVIIIe siècle," *Revue d'histoire économique et sociale,* XXI (1933) pp. 140-89.

Bonnassiès, Jules, *Les auteurs dramatiques et la Comédie française à Paris aux XVIIe et XVIIIe siècles* (Paris: L. Willem, 1874).

______, *Les Spectacles forains et la Comédie-française* (Paris: E. Dentu, 1875).

Boquet, Guy, "La Comédie-Italienne sous la régence: Arlequin Poli par Paris (1716-1725)," *Revue d'histoire moderne et contemporaine,* 24 (1977), pp. 189-214.

Borgerhoff, E.B.O., *The Evolution of Liberal Theory and Practice in the French Theater, 1680-1757* (Princeton: Princeton University Press, 1936).

Bournon, Fernand, *La Bastille* (Paris: Imprimerie nationale, 1893).
Bourquin, Louis, "La Controverse sur la comédie au XVIIIe siècle," *Revue d'historie littéraire de la France,* XXVI (1919), pp. 43-86, 555-76; XXVII (1920), pp. 548-70; XXVIII (1921), pp. 549-74.
Bray, Réné, *La Formation de la doctrine classique en France* (Paris: Librairie Nizet, 1963).
Brenner, C.D., *A Bibliographical List of Plays in the French Language 1700-1789* (Berkeley, Ca.: 1947).
———, *The Théâtre-Italien, Its Repertory 1716-1793* (Berkeley: University of Calif. Press, 1961).
Brockett, Oscar G., "The Fair Theatres of Paris in the Eighteenth Century: The Undermining of the Classical Ideal," in Anderson, M.J., ed., *Classical Drama and Its Influence, Essays Presented to H.D.F. Kitto* (New York: Barnes and Noble, 1965), pp. 251-270.
Brunet, Charles, *Table des Pièces de théâtre décrites dans le catalogue de la Bibliothèque de M. de Soleinne* (Paris: Damascène Morgand, 1914).
Brunetière, Ferdinand, *L'Evolution des genres dans l'histoire de la littérature,* 3rd. ed. (Paris: Librairie Hachette and Cie., 1898).
Burke, Peter, "Oblique approaches to the history of popular culture," in Bigsby, C.W.E., ed., *Approaches to Popular Culture* (London: E. Arnold, 1976).
———, *Popular Culture in Early Modern Europe* (London: M.T. Smith, 1978).
Butwin, Joseph, "The French Revolution as *Theatrum Mundi,*" *Washington State University. Research Studies,* 43 (1975), pp. 141-52.
Campardon, Emile, *Les Comédiens du Roi de la troupe italienne* (Paris: Berger-Levrault, 1880), 2 vols.
———, *Les Spectacles de la foire* (Paris: Berger-Levrault, 1877), 2 vols.
Carlson, Marvin, *The Theatre of the French Revolution* (Ithaca, New York: Cornell University Press, 1966).
Catalogues de la Bibliothèque de l'Opéra. Le Cirque, Iconographie (Paris: 1969).
Chabanne, Robert, *Les Institutions de la France, de la fin de l'Ancien Regime à l'avènement de la IIIème République (1789-1875)* (Lyon: Ed. l'Hermès, 1977).
Cioranescu, Alexandre, *Bibliographie de la littérature française du dix-huitième siècle* (Paris: Editions du Centre National de la Recherche Scientifique, 1969), 3 vols.
Dainville, François de, "Lieux d'affichage des Comédiens à Paris en 1753," *Revue d'histoire du théâtre,* III (1951), pp. 248-53.
Darnton, Robert, "The High Enlightenment and the Low-Life of Literature in Prerevolutionary France," *Past and Present,* No. 51 (May 1971), pp. 81-115.
———, "Reading, Writing and Publishing in Eighteenth-Century France: A Case Study in the Sociology of Literature," *Daedalus* (Winter 1971) and in Gilbert, Felix and Graubard, Stephen R., eds., *Historical Studies Today* (New York: W.W. Norton and Co., 1972).
Davis, Natalie Zemon, "Ghosts, Kin and Progeny," in Rossi, Alice et al., eds., *The Family* (New York: Norton, 1978), pp. 87-114.
———, "The Historian and Popular Culture," *The Wolf and the Lamb, Popular Culture in France,* Stanford French and Italian Studies, III (1977).
———, *Society and Culture in Early Modern France* (Stanford: Stanford University Press, 1965).
Despois, Eugène André, *Le Théâtre français sous Louis XIV,* 4th ed. (Paris: Hachette, 1894).
Dictionnaire de Biographie française (Paris: Letouzey et Ané, 1933-).
Dinaux, A., "Les Masques arrachés," *Archives historiques du nord de la France,* nouvelle serie, V (1844), pp. 325-26.
Doutrepont, Georges, "Les Types populaires de la littérature française," *Académie royale de Belgique,* 2nd series, XXII (1926-28).
Duby, Georges, ed., *Histoire de la France* (Paris: Librarie Labrousse, 1970).
"Estrée, Paul d'," [Henri Quentin], *Le Théâtre sous la Terreur 1793-1794* (Paris: Emile-Paul frères, 1913).

Flandrin, Jean Louis, *Familles, parenté, maison, sexualité dans l'ancienne société* (Paris: Librairie Hachette, 1976).

Fouilleron, Joel, "Fabre d'Eglantine et les Chemins du Théâtre," *Revue d'histoire moderne et contemporaine,* XXI (1974), pp. 495-515.

Fromageot, P., "Un Fils de Louis XV, Auteur dramatique," *Le Carnet,* XII (1902 Avril-Juin), pp. 161-79.

Funck-Brentano, Frantz, *La Bastille des Comédiens, Le For l'Evêque* (Paris: Albert Fontemoing ed., 1903).

Gaiffe, F., Le Drame en France au XVIIIe siècle (Paris: Librairie Armand Colin, 1970, originally published 1910).

Genest, Emile, *L'Opéra-Comique connu et inconnu* (Paris: Librairie Fischbacher, 1925).

Goodwin, Albert, *The French Revolution,* revised ed. (New York: Harper and Row, 1965).

Gossman, Lionel, "Literary Education and Democracy," in Macksey, Richard, ed., *Velocities of Change, Critical Essays from MLN* (Baltimore and London: Johns Hopkins University Press, 1974).

______, "The Worlds of *La Nouvelle Héloise,*" *Studies on Voltaire and the Eighteenth Century,* XXXXI (1966), pp. 235-76.

Gottschalk, Louis and Lach, Donald, *Toward the French Revolution* (New York: Charles Scribner's Sons, 1973).

La Grande Encyclopédie (Paris: H. Lamirault et Cie., 1886-1902), 31 vols.

Greene, E.J.H., *Menander to Marivaux, The History of a Comic Structure* (Alberta, Canada: The University of Alberta Press, 1977).

Grenet, André and Jodry, Claude, *La littérature de sentiment au XVIIIe siècle* (Paris: Masson et Cie., 1971).

Hallays-Dabot, Victor, *Histoire de la censure théâtrale en France* (Paris: E. Dentu, 1862).

Hampson, Norman, *A Social History of the French Revolution* (Toronto: University of Toronto Press, 1970, 1974).

Hatin, Eugène, *Bibliographie historique et critique de la presse périodique française* (Paris: Firmin-Didot, 1866).

Hérissay, Jacques, *Le Monde des théâtres pendant la révolution* (Paris: Perrin, 1922).

Isherwood, Robert, "Entertainment in the Parisian Fairs in the Eighteenth Century," *Journal of Modern History,* 53 (1981), pp. 24-48.

Jacob, P.L., ed., *Bibliothèque dramatique de Monsieur de Soleinne* (Paris: Administration de l'Alliance des Arts, 1843-1844), 5 vols.

Joannidès, A., *La Comédie Française de 1680 à 1900. Dictionnaire général des pièces et des auteurs* (Paris: Plon-Nourrit et Cie., 1901).

Kaplow, Jeffry, *The Names of Kings: the Parisian Laboring Poor in the Eighteenth Century* (New York: Basic Books, 1972).

Lucan, Adolphe, *Traité de la législation et de la jurisprudence des théâtres* (Paris: A. Durand, 1853).

Lagrave, Henri, "La Comédie-Française de XVIIIe siècle ou les contradictions d'un privilège," *Revue d'Histoire du Théâtre,* 32 (1980), pp. 127-41.

______, *Le Théâtre et la public à Paris de 1715 à 1750* (Paris: C. Klincksieck, 1972).

Lanson, Gustave, *Histoire de la littérature française,* 12th ed. (Paris: Hachette, 1912).

La Place, Roselyne, "Des théâtres d'enfants au XVIIIe siècle," *Revue d'Histoire du Théâtre,* 32 (1980), pp. 21-31.

Lebègue, Raymond, *Le Théâtre comique en France de Pathelin à Mélite* (Paris: 1972).

Lecomte, Louis Henry, *Histoire des théâtres de Paris, 1402-1904* (Paris: H. Daragon, 1905).

______, *Histoire des théâtres de Paris, Les Variétés Amusantes* (Paris: H. Daragon, 1908).

Leconte, L., "Un pamphlétaire de la Révolution brabançonne," *Fédération archéologique et historique de Belgique,* Annales de Congrès 35e (1953), pp. 417-46.

Leveaux, Alphonse, "Mague de St. Aubin," *Bulletin de la Société historique de Compeigne,* II (1875), pp. 71-81.

Liéby, A., "La presse révolutionnaire et la censure théâtrale sous la Terreur," *Révolution française,* XLV (1903), pp. 306-53, 447-70, 502-29; XLVI (1904), pp. 13-28, 97-128.

Lough, John, *An Introduction to Eighteenth Century France* (New York: David McKay Co., 1960).

——, *Paris Theater Audiences in the Seventeenth and Eighteenth Centuries* (Oxford: The University Press, 1957).

——, *Writer and Public in France from the Middle Ages to the Present Day* (Oxford and New York: Clarendon Press, 1978).

Lunel, Ernest, *Le Théâtre et la Révolution* (Paris: H. Daragon, 1911).

Lyonnet, Henry, *Dictionnaire des comédiens français* (Geneva-Paris: Revue universelle internationale illustre, n.d.), 2 vols.

Mandrou, Robert, "Cultures populaires et savantes: Rapports et contacts," *The Wolf and the Lamb, Popular Culture in France,* Stanford French and Italian Studies, III (1977).

——, *De la culture populaire aux XVIIe et XVIIIe siècles, La Bibliothèque bleue de Troyes* (Paris: Stock, 1964).

——, *La France aux XVIIe et XVIIIe siècles* (Paris: Presses universitaires de France, 1967).

Manne, Edmond Denis de and Ménétrier, C., *Galerie historique des comédiens de la troupe de Nicolet* (Lyon: N. Scheuring, 1869).

Maugras, Gaston, *Les comédiens hors la loi* (Paris: Calmann Lévy, 1887).

Mazauric, Claude, "La Fête révolutionnaire manifestation de la politique jacobine, Rouen, 1793. An II," in Ehrard, Jean and Viallaneix, Paul, eds. *Les Fêtes de la Révolution Colloque de Clermont-Ferrand (June 1974)* (Paris: Societe des Etudes Robespierristes, 1977), pp. 181-90.

Méthivier, Hubert, *Le Siècle de Louis XV* (Paris: Presses universitaires de France, 1972).

Mic, Constantin, *La commedia dell-arte ou le théâtre des comédiens italiens des XVIe, XVIIe et XVIIIe siècles* (Paris: J. Schiffrin, 1927).

Michaud, Joseph François, ed., *Biographie universelle, ancienne et moderne* (Paris: Michaud frères, 1811-1862), 55 vols.

Moffat, Marguerite, *Rousseau et la querelle du théâtre au 18e siècle* (Paris: E. de Boccard, 1930).

Monselet, Charles, *Les Originaux du siècle dernier, Les Oubliés et les dédaignés* (Alençon: M. Lévy frères, 1857), 2 vols.

Moore, A.P., *The Genre Poissard and the French Stage of the Eighteenth Century* (New York: Publications of the Institute of French Studies, 1935).

Mornet, Daniel, *French Thought in the Eighteenth Century,* trans., Levin, L.M. (New York: Prentice-Hall, 1929).

Nicoll, Allardyce, *The World of Harlequin, a critical study of the commedia dell'arte* (Cambridge, England: Cambridge University Press, 1963).

Niklaus, Robert, "La Propogande philosophique au théâtre au siècle des lumières," *Studies on Voltaire and the Eighteenth Century,* XXVI (1963), pp. 1223-61.

Nouvelle Biographie Générale (Paris: Firmin Didot Frères, 1853-66), 46 vols.

Pitou, Alexis, "Les Origines du Mélodrame français à la fin du XVIIIe siècle," *Revue d'histoire littéraire de la France,* XVIII (1911), pp. 256-96.

Pougin, Arthur, *Dictionnaire historique et pittoresque du théâtre* (Paris: Librairie de Firmin-Didot, 1885).

——, *L'Opéra-Comique pendant la Révolution* (Paris: A. Savine, 1891).

Quérard, Joseph Marie, *La France littéraire, ou Dictionnaire bibliographique des savants, historiens et gens de lettres de la France pendant les XVIIIe et XIXe siècles* (Paris: Firmin Didot père et fils, 1827-1864), 12 vols.

Reynoard, Paul, "Les Comédiens pendant la Révolution," *Annales Révolutionnaires,* VIII (1916), pp. 626-50.

Rolland, Romain, *Le Théâtre du Peuple* (Paris: Librairie Hachette et Cie., 1913).
Rudé, George, *The Crowd in the French Revolution* (Oxford: Oxford University Press, 1959).
Salvatore, Paul J., *Favart's Unpublished Plays* (New York: Publications of the Institute of French Studies, Inc., 1935).
Soboul, Albert, *The French Revoution 1787-1799,* trans., Forrest, Alan and Jones, Colin (New York: Vintage Books, 1975; originally published Paris, 1962).
______, *The Sans-Culottes,* trans. Hall, Remy Inglis (New York: Anchor Books, 1972; originally published Paris, 1968).
Starobinsky, Jean, *Jean-Jacques Rousseau, la transparence et l'obstacle* (Saint-Armand/Cher, France: Gallimard, 1971).
Suther, Judith, "Harlequin on the Revolutionary Stage," *Washington State University. Research Studies,* 43 (1975), pp. 235-44.
Vivien, "Etudes Administratives, III. Les Théâtres," *Revue des deux mondes,* nouvelle serie, VI (1844).
Vovelle, Michel, *La Chute de la Monarchie* (Paris: Editions du Seuil, 1972).
______, *L'irrésistible ascension de Joseph Sec, bourgeois d'Aix, suivi de quelques clefs pour la lecture des naïfs* (Aix-en-province: Edisud, 1975).
Welschinger, Henri, *Le Théâtre de la Révolution, 1789-1799* (Paris: Charavay Frères, 1880).
Winter, Marian Hannah, *The Theatre of Marvels,* trans. (New York: Benjamin Blom, Inc., 1964; original ed., Paris: 1962).

Index